Intimate Practices

Literacy and Cultural Work in
U.S. Women's Clubs,
1880–1920

Anne Ruggles Gere

University of Illinois Press
Urbana and Chicago

Winner of the Illinois–National Women's Studies
Association Book Award

Library of Congress Cataloging-in-Publication Data
Gere, Anne Ruggles, 1944–
    Intimate practices : literacy and cultural work in U.S. women's clubs,
1880–1920 / Anne Ruggles Gere.
        p.   cm.
    Includes bibliographical references (p.) and index.
    ISBN 0-252-02301-3 (cloth : acid-free paper). — ISBN 0-252-06604-9
(pbk. : acid-free paper)
    1. Women—United States—Societies and clubs—History. 2. Women—
United States—Intellectual life—History. 3. Women—United States—Books
and reading—History. 4. Self-culture—United States—History.   I. Title.
HQ1904.G48   1997   96–25327
305.4'06073—dc20   CIP

For Mary Jane

Contents

Acknowledgments

❖═◑◐═❖

THIS book has preoccupied me for over a decade, and during that time I have incurred many debts of gratitude. Karen Blair, my colleague when we were both at the University of Washington, lent me her copy of Jennie June Cunningham Croly's *History of the Woman's Club Movement in America* when I first began to wonder about the literacy practices of women's clubs. Her pioneering work on clubwomen helped me think through my own project and convinced me of its value. At the University of Michigan, collaborations with Deborah Keller-Cohen, Bruce Mannheim, and Walter Mignolo gave me new perspectives on literacy. A faculty colloquium with Anne Herrmann and Abby Stewart and a reading group with Ruth Behar, Julie Ellison, Joanne Leonard, and Patricia Yaeger deepened my understanding of feminist theory. Lawrence Berlin offered continuing insights into the history of education, while Jonathan Freedman and Pamela Moss helped me clarify my thinking on many points. My students in the Joint Ph.D. Program in English and Education, particularly Margaret Marshall, Deborah Minter, Sarah Robbins, Laura Roop, Margaret Willard, and Morris Young, continually challenged me to think harder, to ask better questions, and to stop talking and start writing.

Conversations with members of the invisible college created by common research interests alerted me to many important ideas and sources of information. These colleagues include Martha Banta, Don Bialostosky, Wendy Bishop, Lynn Bloom, Lil Brannon, Lillian Bridwell-Bowles, Jean Ferguson Carr, Robert Connors, William Cook, Beth Daniell, Lisa Ede, Katheryn Flannery, Elizabeth Flynn, Alice Gillam, Cheryl Glenn, Joseph Harris, Gail Hawisher, Shirley Brice Heath, Carol Heller, Karen Hollis, Glynda Hull, Andrea Lunsford, Donald McQuade, Susan Miller, Carol Peterson, Linda Peterson, Mike Rose, Jacqueline Jones Royster, Cynthia Selfe, Louise Z. Smith, Nancy Sommers, John Trimbur, Martha Woodmansee, Driek Zirinsky, and the many members of the Women's History List Serve Group.

Travel funds from the National Endowment for the Humanities; two Rackham Research Partnership grants along with financial support from the Office of the Vice President for Research, the College of Literature, Science and the Arts, and the School of Education at the University of Michigan; and the Illinois–National Women's Studies Association Manuscript Prize provided some of the material support that made this work possible, but the more important support took human form. The staff at the University of Illinois Press, particularly Karen Hewitt, Terry Sears, and Jane Mohraz, attended helpfully and efficiently to all the details of transforming the manuscript into a book. The Harris Family and the Ruggles-Dow family sheltered and fed me while I worked at nearby libraries. With the example of her own fine scholarship on women's associations and her interest in my project, Martha Vicinus helped create a nurturing climate for my work. Mallory Hiatt, my administrative assistant, saw me through seven years of this project, and her departure was made tolerable by the arrival of Michelle Thomas, who carried on the tradition of alerting me to overdue books, helping with complicated printing tasks, and doing a thousand and one other things to keep me sane. Karen Ammon, Ronelle Laranang, Christine Paschild, Jennifer Richardson, and Argentina Rivera all saved me hours of combing the library for books and articles. Deborah Fox provided invaluable aid when my duties as an officer of the Conference on College Composition and Communication brought this book to a near standstill.

I had always known the importance of librarians to scholarly work, but this project gave me new appreciation for their skills. My thanks to the professional staffs at the Atlanta History Center, the Burton Collection of the Detroit Public Library, the Chautauqua Institution, the Colorado Historical Society, the Hamilton College Library, the Jane Addams Memorial Collection at the University of Illinois at Chicago, the Jewish Women's Resource Center of New York, the LDS Church Historical Department, the Library of Congress, the Lucas County Library of Toledo, the Moorland-Spingarn Collection at Howard University, the Northwest Collection of Suzallo Library at the University of Washington, the Mabel Smith Douglass Library of Rutgers University, the Rare Books and Manuscripts Division of the Boston Public Library, the Schlesinger Library, the Sophia Smith Collection, the W. H. Smith Library of the Indiana Historical Society, Special Collections at the University of Utah Library, Special Collections at the Chicago Public Library, the Western History Department of the Denver Public Library, the Women's History and Resource Center of the General Federation of Women's Clubs, the Woodruff Library of the Atlanta University Center, and the Utah Historical Society. The extraordinary helpfulness of librarians at the Bentley Historical Library, the Interlibrary Loan Office, and the Reference Department deepened my appreciation for the institutional home provided by the University of Michigan. Many of the materials I read remain in private collections, and I am grateful to the clubwomen who trusted me with their records. In particular, Olive Foltz, Helen Kaplan Heller, Dorothy Kaufman, Clairmarie Keenan, Luella Kirkwood, Maud Loyle, and Jane Moore opened important doors for me.

As ideas began to take written form, I benefited from opportunities to share drafts of various chapters with faculties at UCLA, Ohio State University, the University of Illinois, and Colgate University as well as the University of Michigan. Some of the material in this book appeared in different form in four other articles, and I am grateful for permission to use it here:

"Gendered Literacy in Black and White: Turn-of-the-Century African-American and European-American Club Women's Printed Texts," *Signs: Journal of Women in Culture and Society,* vol. 2, no. 13 (Spring 1996): 643–78 (with Sarah Robbins). © University of Chicago.

"Common Properties of Pleasure: Texts in Nineteenth-Century Women's Clubs," in *The Construction of Authorship: Textual Appropriation in Law and Literature,* ed. Martha Woodmansee and Peter Jaszi (Chapel Hill: Duke University Press, 1994), 383–400.

"Literacy and Difference in Nineteenth-Century Women's Clubs," in *Literacy: Interdisciplinary Conversations,* ed. Deborah Keller-Cohen (Cresskill, N.J.: Hampton Press, 1994), 249–66.

"For Profit and Pleasure: Collaboration in Nineteenth-Century Women's Literary Clubs," in *New Visions of Collaborative Writing,* ed. Janis Forman (Portsmouth, N.H.: Heinemann, 1991), 1–18 (with Laura Roop).

A number of generous colleagues took time from their own work to read and respond to mine. Michael Bérubé, Julie Ellison, Catherine Hobbs, Margaret Marshall, Walter Mignolo, Adela Pinch, Marlon Ross, and David Scoby all offered very helpful suggestions to various portions of the book. Karen Blair read the entire manuscript twice, and each time she sent me back to the computer with fresh ideas. Sarah Robbins, whose graduate school career coincided with the development of this project, became a colleague whose work continually intersects with my own, and I am especially grateful for her thoughtful readings and suggestions.

Sam Gere moved from elementary school to college while this book was taking shape, and he acquired considerable skill as a research assistant during these years. Keyboarding footnotes, carefully identifying archival materials, and duplicating many copies number among his contributions to this project. More significantly, he and Budge Gere signaled their respect for my work by providing time and space for it to flourish, even when I needed to change vacation plans to stop at another archive anywhere from Anchorage to Atlanta. Cindy Gere kept me writing with her recurring question: "When are you going to be done with that book, Mom?" At the eleventh hour Dorothy Chamberlain, the nonagenarian in our household, lent her proofreading skills. The dedication of this book acknowledges, with heartfelt appreciation, the supportive love of Mary Jane Ruggles, with whom I shared that early female society known as "Margaret and the girls."

Intimate Practices

Introduction

◆▷ The spirit of national unity has also been promoted. It is impossible to represent in statistics the value of the movement to the nation in this way, but no one who understands human nature will be disposed to underestimate that value. The sense of working for common ends, the frequent intercommunications, the better understanding of one another promoted by the biennials, by the visits of Federation officers and other club members, all work to this end. . . . The club movement with its "common interests and noble purposes" is accomplishing the work of unifying the women of the country far more quickly than a premeditated movement to that end could do it.

MARY WOOLLEY,
"The Woman's Club Woman," 1910

WRITING in 1910, Mary Woolley, president of Mount Holyoke College, offers an assessment of the women's club movement that had taken shape over the preceding three decades and would continue to flourish for another.[1] After enumerating six pages of tangible contributions to civic life and improvements in women themselves, Woolley turns to another category, "the spirit of national unity."[2] Acknowledging that contributions in this category cannot be measured "in statistics," such as the number of libraries established or the amount of sanitation legislation enacted, Woolley still insists on their value. She argues that they create a "common ground" connecting "California, Illinois and Boston," but they extend beyond the transcending of local boundaries to "other lines" as well. Although her terms remain largely inchoate, Woolley suggests a way of

1

thinking about the role of women's clubs in the United States at the turn of the century.

Like most commentators on the women's club movement, Woolley ignores the contributions of various classes, races, and religious groups by equating clubwomen with the predominantly white middle-class Protestant members of the General Federation of Women's Clubs, but her claims for the "value of the movement to the nation" depart from typical representations of women's clubs. Woolley acknowledges and values the intangible "other lines" of club work as well as its more obvious contributions to material changes and national unity. In this book I take up Woolley's point by probing the meanings of and the processes for accomplishing projects that cannot be represented in statistics. By so doing, I participate in the recent reevaluation of clubwomen's contributions to national life through the arts, education and social services.[3] But in extending my investigation to the less tangible projects clubwomen undertook at the turn of the century, I move the reevaluation project in a new direction. Specifically, I show how clubwomen enacted cultural work through their literacy practices.

Examining the cultural work of women's clubs poses special challenges because it calls on a past that can never be entirely recovered. Traces can be found, however, in the written records left by these organizations because they document the thinking, the circulation of ideas, and the textual labor that both underlay and responded to changes in national life. Such records show clubwomen making their own history and defining their own cultural identity. Papers written by members about the assimilation of immigrants, the status of women, the conditions of factory work, the importance of "race literature," or approaches to Emerson's essays; petitions drafted in support of a new library or the establishment of a tuberculosis ward; annual programs listing topics for discussion and suggestions for reading, along with club constitutions and bylaws; record books containing minutes of meetings and financial transactions; newspapers and magazines produced by clubwomen; memorial resolutions for deceased members; poems, plays, and humorous sketches that celebrate club achievements; club histories members wrote to mark anniversaries—all of these texts reconstruct, however partially, the ways clubwomen's literacies intersected with other cultural practices at the turn of the century.

Such reconstructions depend on material conditions, and until a few decades ago many clubwomen's texts were not available to researchers. In 1944 Mary Ritter Beard tried to establish a women's archive at Radcliffe College, arguing that "formal institutional education has robbed women particularly of their consciousness of their previous intellectual power as learning and the ability to express themselves."[4] In Beard's view, establishing an archive would foster consciousness of and appreciation for women's extracurricular learning in such sites as clubs, and clubwomen's texts numbered among the documents Beard sought to collect. Beard was, however, a woman before her time, and neither archives nor members were ready for these deposits until recent feminist work generated recognition of women's role in history. Although Beard's dream of one comprehensive women's archive has not been realized, significant collections of women's materials have been established or enhanced, with club records figuring prominently among accessions.[5] While some clubwomen have relinquished their carefully preserved materials to archives, others have resisted depositing them. Some of this resistance derives from a desire to protect treasured materials from scrutiny by a public that has a long record of representing women's clubs negatively. In other cases the resistance has emerged from a lack of appreciation for the value of materials that did not seem unusual. For some members club records remain cloaked in the invisibility of the ordinary.[6] While changes in archives have increased clubwomen's appreciation for their own materials and mitigated some of their concerns about the scrutiny of outsiders, many clubs still retain possession of their records.

Archives represent one form of memory, while public perceptions constitute another. The latter have stereotyped women's clubs as white middle-class groups, thereby erasing the varying class, racial, and ethnic/religious backgrounds represented in the club movement. This book counters such stereotypes by considering clubs formed by women from Mormon, Jewish, working-class, African American and white Protestant backgrounds.[7] Women representing a rich variety of social positions formed clubs in cities and towns across the country. Some groups affiliated with national federations, while others remained local. Although a few leaders, such as Mary Church Terrell, Julia Ward Howe, and Sadie American, achieved national prominence, the majority of clubwomen lived relatively commonplace lives in their individual communities. Yet members of both local and national groups shared the conviction that they were participating in an unprecedented social phenomenon of national significance, that in joining with other ordinary women they accomplished something extraordinary.

I affirm their view by asserting that women's clubs enacted important cultural work at a time when expanding national boundaries—nine states joined the Union between 1880 and 1920, adding over 800,000 square miles to the United States—were paralleled by major shifts in national definition, economic power, gender politics, cultural standards, and professional identity. As defined here, women's clubs include both large "departmental" clubs of several hundred members and groups of less than twenty-five. Regardless of their size, such organizations developed out of needs perceived by individual women; created their own leadership structures (as distinct from, say, church hierarchies); collected or raised their own funds and decided on their allocation (as opposed to responding to mandates from male leaders); and shaped their own agendas for study projects, sometimes in concert with and sometimes independent from philanthropic work. Accordingly, this definition does not include the Women's Convention of the Baptist Church or the League of Catholic Women, even though each carried out many philanthropic and study projects similar to those of women's clubs, because both remained under the direct control of male church leaders during the time period under consideration here. It does, however, include such groups as the Mormon Cleophan Club of Salt Lake City and the African-American Coterie Club of Denver, which functioned as autonomous study groups.[8]

Even as it insists on autonomy from church hierarchies, this definition recognizes that clubs were not exclusively secular. Representative statements from many clubwomen suggest their religious underpinnings. Sadie American, a founding member of the National Council of Jewish Women, explained, "As Jews, holding fast to one great faith, certain problems are forced upon us to be solved which present themselves to no one else—certain circumstances and conditions, certain privileges and duties, certain aptitudes and powers are ours, and therefore certain work lies before us, peculiarly our own, demanding our first attention."[9] In urging the founding of a national organization to make Jewish clubwomen more visible to their gentile peers, Sadie American recognized that this group would face issues resulting from its members' religious heritage, and the National Council of Jewish Women embraced education in Judaism as one of its central purposes. A history of the Naugatuck Study Club reports, "Because many members were also members of the Congregational Church which had opened the Parish House in 1888, there existed a close association with the Ladies' Aid Society. So close that in 1911 it was voted to purchase 6 dozen spoons and 6 dozen forks to present to the Aid Society."[10] This gift gave material form to the strong relationship between the Naugatuck Study Club and the church-controlled group. Although they established themselves as independent from religious control, clubwomen affirmed their connection to institutions that represented their religious heritage.

In addition to working cooperatively with church-sponsored groups, clubwomen often held their meetings in churches or synagogues, invited church leaders as speakers, and included texts by religious figures on their programs. The Mormon *Woman's Exponent* contained frequent discussions of theology, along with arguments in favor of woman suffrage and reports of study groups. The National Association of Colored Women included "church clubs, evangelistic work and religious work" among its nineteen departments, and it sponsored the National Training School for Women and Girls in concert with the Baptist Women's Convention. Such programmatic and institutional affiliations demonstrated and fostered the shared spiritual values that strengthened the bonds among members of individual clubs. Their common religious roots deepened friendships, and their traditions of studying the Bible, the Torah, or the Book of Mormon enhanced their reading and writing.

Within the intimate social spaces created by shared religious beliefs and common goals, club members carried out cultural work that aided a refashioning of the nation. By examining aspects of social reality, dramatizing conflicts, and proposing redefinitions of the social order, women's clubs shaped and were shaped by the way the nation thought about itself.[11] Although they enacted a variety of cultural practices, including pageants, banquets, and musical productions, clubwomen's most common and effective means of expressing and shaping their world appeared in their literacy practices. Through reading and writing, social practices embedded in the historical circumstances of turn-of-the-century America, clubwomen engaged with and helped transform perplexing issues of their time. Reading about and writing papers on woman suffrage, for example, put these women in dialogue with the larger culture, helping them understand and negotiate with conflicting ideologies of womanhood.[12] Through their literacy practices, clubwomen "processed" new concepts—of nationhood, economy, gender, culture, and professionalism—sometimes resisting and sometimes fostering them, but always contributing to their shape. Their numbers, along with the social and geographical distribution of clubs, lent effect to these shaping forces. Although estimates vary, it is reasonable to assume that well over two million women participated in the club movement at the turn of the century, and since most of these women interacted, as daughters, mothers, sisters, wives, or friends, with a circle of others, club influence extended to a good portion of the population.[13] Clubs took root in every state as well as in such territories as Oklahoma, Utah, and Arizona, and because they extended across ethnic, religious, class, and racial lines, they shaped and were shaped by a wide range of perspectives.

White middle-class clubwomen, for whom race was a prominent feature of self-identification—just as it was for women from other social backgrounds—devoted considerable energy to constructing and affirming their positions of privilege and power by using exclusionary tactics, both literally and figuratively.[14] Their General Federation of Women's Clubs refused admission to a qualified African American woman at its 1900 national convention and upheld this decision at subsequent meetings, despite northern members' impassioned pleadings against the color bar.[15] Although some Jewish women joined federation clubs, many white Protestant groups barred them, borrowing from the construction of Jews as nonwhite and the ready fund of anti-Semitism.[16] In addition to such acts of exclusion, these clubwomen affirmed their whiteness with discussion topics rooted in genteel high culture or benevolence projects designed to underscore the differences between white middle-class clubwomen and those they helped. Working-class white women excluded African Americans from their clubs and their workplaces, thereby gaining the compensation of feeling superior and somewhat privileged despite the difficult material conditions of their lives. African American clubwomen, aware that race excluded them from white women's clubs, asserted the need for race-oriented groups to deal with "those things which are of vital importance to us as women, but also the things that are of especial interest to us as *colored* women."[17] In creating the National Association of Colored Women, these clubwomen asserted their desire to affiliate with their white sisters and to assert their race-related interests. Although not numerous enough to form a national group, Native American women's clubs affirmed their own racial identity by claiming as a central purpose "preserving the traditions and customs for a true history of the Indian, who is not a vanishing race but a returning people of America."[18] Difference as well as similarity marked the groups clustered under the term *women's club,* creating a diverse and multifaceted social movement.

Despite their differences, clubwomen in all social locations controlled their own literacy practices, writing and reading as they chose, and the texts they produced and consumed outline the terms of their own representation. Nonmembers who found fault with clubs presented women's participation in the most negative way, frequently combining distortion with criticism. For example, when former President Grover Cleveland attacked clubwomen in a 1905 issue of the bestselling *Ladies' Home Journal* for disturbing "the even tenor of the ways of womanhood" and threatening "the integrity of our homes," he misrepresented both the name and the purposes of the General Federation of Women's Clubs.[19] Critics of African American women's clubs claimed that they led members to "neglect the precious interests of home and motherhood," and those who opposed the National Council of Jewish Women worried over "neglected children" and husbands left to fend for themselves.[20] Such statements by unsympathetic nonmembers contrast sharply with the accounts of improved domestic life in clubwomen's own texts.

Clubwomen enacted their textual autonomy in, among other things, thoughtful considerations of their self-designations. Records of the National League of Women Workers, for example, recount discussions about naming clubs. Aware that people looked down on those who worked, condescendingly terming them "the working girls," one group considered alternatives and then concluded, "Our organization is truly the child of the daughters of labor. Our fathers and mothers work; before them their fathers and mothers worked; and we, too, work. Let us call ourselves the 'Working Girls Society' and show New York that we are not ashamed of *work*."[21] In 1899 this organization of working women's clubs changed its name to the National League of Women Workers, explaining "the name of Women Workers as defining more exactly than the term 'Association of Working Girls' Clubs' their membership."[22] The insistence on highlighting *working* and substituting the more dignified *women* for the asexual and youthful *girls* shows the growing self-confidence and pride that shaped the self-definition of these club members.

African American clubwomen, who faced the deprecations born of racism, embraced their racial identity by naming their national federation the National Association of Colored Women and countered the indignities imposed by the white world by using such respectful titles as Mrs. or Miss in club records. Mormon clubwomen often used such religiously derived terms as *saint* or *sister* to refer to one another, and in their discussions of what given names to use they considered alternatives offered by Julia Ward Howe, Elizabeth Stuart Phelps Ward, Mrs. Henry Ward Beecher, Amelia E. Barr, and Ella Wheeler Wilcox on what name women should use and concluded "it is better for all purposes that a woman use her own name" rather than her husband's. Members of the National Council of Jewish Women spent considerable time debating whether to refer to one another by their own or their husbands' names.[23] Even the term *club* prompted considerable discussion, as Caroline Severance noted in her reminiscence of the founding of the New England Women's Club; for women (as opposed to men) to designate themselves as members of a club represented a considerable departure from tradition.[24] That clubwomen from all social backgrounds used *women* rather than *ladies* represented a political statement because *lady* had long indicated higher class position, and *women* echoed the term *new woman,* which connoted social change.[25] Club records contain many such discussions, demonstrating that members made thoughtful choices about the terms of their self-representation. These records constitute what Michael Shapiro terms a political act, a form of "representation" that does not simply "imitate reality" but constitutes a practice "through which things take on meaning and value."²⁶ By naming themselves and recording the conversations that decided these names, clubwomen wrote themselves into the larger society on their own terms, appropriating and redefining such words as *club* and *women* to describe themselves and their activities.

In addition to controlling the names by which they were called, clubwomen determined who would have access to their texts. A system of circulating texts among clubs—even before the formation of national organizations—enabled clubwomen to share their literacy practices with one another. A paper written by a clubwoman in Boston might be sent to and read aloud by a peer in Buffalo or Chicago. New clubs sought copies of constitutions and bylaws from established groups to use as models. With an eye to sending them to "sister clubs," most clubs produced a surplus of their annual programs or yearbooks. As Mary Woolley's account at the beginning of this introduction indicates, clubwomen visited one another, and these encounters also helped circulate texts. The 1893 World's Columbian Exposition in Chicago included a public exhibit of club yearbooks, study guides, outlines of methods, portraits of officers, and photographs of clubhouses. An observer noted that "many clubwomen from various parts of the country spent hours, even days, studying the materials, making penciled notes, and discussing club methods with each other."²⁷ These textual exchanges fostered, in the words of one clubwoman, "a stimulating interchange of courtesies and extending fellowship, as well as giving direct benefit by the dissemination of knowledge and the introduction of new elements into club life."²⁸ As this makes clear, the exchange of texts had both affective and practical implications. Embedded in networks of friendship among clubwomen, textual exchanges strengthened bonds among women separated by distance and/or time, adding an affective dimension to their literacy practices.

National organizations formalized and extended this textual circulation. The General Federation of Women's Clubs (founded in 1890), the National League of Women Workers (founded in 1885 as the Association of Working Girls' Clubs and reformulated and renamed in 1897), the National Council of Jewish Women (founded in 1893), and the National Association of Colored Women (founded in 1896) each established centralized offices that in part served as a clearinghouse for club texts. In addition, most national organizations established publications to which clubwomen across the country contributed. The *Woman's Era* (1894–97) and *National Association Notes* (begun in 1897) kept members of the National Association of Colored Women apprised of one another's work. The *Woman's Cycle* (1899), the *Home-Maker* (1890–93), the *New Cycle* (1893–96), the *Club Woman* (1897–1904), the *Federation Bulletin* (1905–13), and the *General Federation of Women's Clubs Magazine* (1913–present), usually known as simply the *General Federation Magazine,* served as national publications for the General Federation of Women's Clubs. *Far and Near* (1890–94) and the *Club Worker* (1899–1921) enabled members of the League of Women Workers to share one another's texts. The *Young Woman's Journal* (1899–1929) and the *Woman's Exponent* (1872–1914) circulated among Mormon clubwomen. Although never adopted as the official organ of the National Council of Jewish Women, the *American Jewess* (1895–99) informed sections in different cities about one another's work. Textual exchanges linked these national publications, so that editors of, say, the *Woman's Cycle* received copies of the *Woman's Exponent* and drew material from it.[29]

Clubwomen also used mainstream newspapers and magazines to circulate their texts. In 1906, for example, the *Federation Bulletin* was sent to "forty-seven newspapers having a combined circulation of nearly two million copies," and many of these newspapers established "club departments" in which excerpts from the *Federation Bulletin* were published.[30] The National Council of Jewish Women, which did not initiate the *Jewish Woman* until 1921, was particularly dependent on mainstream newspapers, and council members noted the importance of such attention in their own records.[31] Many local newspapers, particularly between 1894 and 1897, featured "women's editions" written entirely by clubwomen. Although they appeared as irregular and single editions of mainstream newspapers, these editions provided clubwomen with a means of bringing their concerns and accomplishments into public view. Unlike the traditional "women's page" or "club department" in regular issues, these editions, published under the direction of "amateur editresses," allowed women to produce an entire edition. Even though they attracted attention as much for their novelty as for their substance, these editions provided clubwomen another way to represent themselves in their own terms.[32] National organizations fostered other means of circulation, notably officers and speakers who carried texts and ideas from one club to another. For example, clubs belonging to the League of Women Workers could count on a visit from the secretary "at least once in two years, although isolated clubs, which do not come in touch with other clubs by means of the directors' or annual meetings, could expect more frequent visits."[33] Officers of all national groups visited local clubs, and annual conventions brought together members from individual clubs in each state and across the nation.

Such circulations of texts, which remained largely invisible to outsiders, gave clubwomen a sense of connection with one another. As one clubwoman put it, "*The Federation Bulletin* affords a medium of expression for this most hopeful 'sign of the times,' so aptly described by John Graham Brooks as the 'all-together feeling.' Its coming into the world means, to the federated organizations, an enlarged opportunity, greater power and broader development; to the individual members of these organizations, an added sense of social and civic unity and solidarity."[34] The "all-together feeling" this clubwoman articulated recurred among her various peers as they wrote and read one another's texts. The literacy practices that generated and sustained their national publications enabled clubwomen to see themselves as part of a larger whole, strengthening their perception of their own power to effect changes and increasing their feelings of connection to one another.

Circulating and consuming one another's texts resembles the "normally impersonal" reading Michael Warner attributes to the colonial American experience. Printed texts fostered a subculture in colonial America, Warner claims, wherein "the reader does not simply imagine him- or herself receiving a direct communication or hearing the voice of the author. He or she now also incorporates *into the meaning of the printed object* an awareness of the potentially limitless others who may also be reading. For that reason, it becomes possible to imagine oneself, in the act of reading, becoming part of an arena of the national people that cannot be realized except through such mediating imaginings."[35] Warner argues that the idea of print as normally impersonal emerged in this country in the late seventeenth and early eighteenth centuries when individuals, through reading, began to see themselves as participating in a national culture. I extend his argument to the culture clubwomen created because they, like residents of the earlier republic, used "normally impersonal" printed texts to see themselves as part of a national movement wherein an "all-together feeling" united clubwomen across time and distance, strengthening their emotional ties in the face of social censure and hostility.[36]

Clubwomen understood the complexity of their political position, and their texts often reflect a keen awareness of the criticisms continually leveled at them. One of the most frequent attacks emphasized the selfishness inherent in study or self-improvement. Since the ideology of womanhood dominant in the late nineteenth century counted selflessness a virtue, clubwomen began to conceal or minimize their own reading and writing projects in favor of emphasizing their service to the community as it became clear that self-improvement attracted negative attention. In the 1870s and 1880s such club leaders as Julia Ward Howe and Jennie Cunningham Croly had encouraged women to divert energy away from helping others and toward forming groups that propagated self-improvement through study. As clubs grew (and met with more criticism), however, these leaders and those of the next generation avoided describing themselves in these terms.[37] In particular, clubwomen became careful about how they portrayed their own literacy practices.

When she published a history of white women's clubs in 1898, Jennie Croly couched club literacy practices in a rhetoric of evolution. Croly, a founding member of the General Federation of Women's Clubs and New York's Sorosis, knew well the tenuous public sanction within which most women's clubs functioned. Both her local club, founded in 1868, and the General Federation, founded in 1890, had been lampooned in newspaper articles, magazine editorials, and cartoons. Although she had originally encouraged the self-improvement aspect of women's clubs, by 1898 Croly recognized the political importance of emphasizing clubs' contributions to social welfare. In the introduction to her book, she explains:

> It should be remembered in this connection that, down to the last quarter of the present century, there was little sympathy with organizations of women not expressly religious, charitable, or intended to promote charitable objects. "What is its object?" was the first question asked of any organization of women, and if it was not the making of garments, or the collection of funds for a church, or philanthropic purpose, it was considered unworthy of attention, or injurious doubts were thrown upon its motives.

Although Croly uses the past tense, her rhetorical stance indicates her recognition that public service continued to be a requirement for women's groups in 1898. Croly's awareness of the disparity between what clubwomen considered important and what the dominant (male) society expected of them also appears in her account of the first meeting of the New England Women's Club: "The women, for the most part, emphasized the intellectual and social side of the proposed work; the men the domestic, or what they called the 'practical' side. Mr. Weiss proposed the consideration of the vexed question of domestic service . . . and the others the establishing of some sort of school. The women mentioned these plans, yet looked deeper and recognized another and profounder need."[38] This "profounder" need, for substantive intellectual work in an intimate social context, did not disappear even when clubs developed service projects, but, as Croly shows, it often took on the protective coloring of community service.

Writing for an audience that included critics of women's clubs as well as clubwomen anxious to know more about their own traditions, Croly opens her history with an account of the work religious orders or sisterhoods did beginning in the fifth century. These women, according to Croly, "were inspired by love of well-doing," "at the sacrifice of every personal indulgence." She continues by narrating the "moral awakening" that accompanied the Enlightenment, and she embeds women's clubs in its continuing and ideal-shaped tradition. *Duty* is a key term for Croly, and she affirms that "the sense of duty is always strong in the woman." Accordingly, she describes the women's club movement as "a light-giving, and seed-sowing center of purely altruistic and democratic activity." As such, it eschews the "very narrow and self-absorbed mind that only sees in these openings opportunities for its own pleasure, or chances for its own advancement, on its own narrow and exclusive lines." Instead, it aims to help others because "if we miss this we miss the spirit, the illuminating light of the whole movement, and lose it in the mire of our own selfishness."[39] Having dismissed the charge of selfishness in women's clubs and established the public service motive for the movement, Croly proceeds to introduce clubs that constitute the General Federation. Her strategy of linking women's clubs with the tradition of religious sisterhoods lends credence to her description of them as "purely altruistic," so that by the time she arrives at her defense against "selfishness," little question about the purposes of women's clubs remains: They are to perform the kind of visible community service that will provide light and growth for others.[40] Croly was not, of course, the first to adopt evolutionary rhetoric in describing club work, but the prominence and comprehensiveness of her book gave this strategy new status, and many clubwomen followed her example, creating narratives of service that protected their own reading and writing. Appropriating the ideology of selfless womanhood, clubwomen constructed themselves as carrying out projects of public service, thus creating political cover for their self-improvement projects.[41]

Given the terms in which clubwomen represented themselves, this study acknowledges that their texts withhold as well as reveal. It also recognizes that study and service coexisted in various and complicated ways. Even when their work included many public projects, clubwomen often identified their literacy practices as the source of their capacity to carry out projects of social welfare. Edith Isaacs, in concluding an essay about the National Council of Jewish Women's philanthropic work, explains that the real purpose was not to relieve the ills of poverty but to understand its causes: "It is with the Ultima Thule in mind that the Council leaders lay fundamental stress upon the things of least interest to outsiders, the lecture and study circles, the religious schools, the conferences and entertainments, even the purely social functions which make for solidarity and for a fuller understanding of the vital American principle that 'in union there is strength.'"[42] Isaacs demonstrates a clear awareness of the difference between members, who emphasize literacy practices, and "outsiders," who credit only the tangible results of community service.

Kate Rotan, writing in the *Federation Bulletin,* argued that the women's club "is most useful when adhering most closely to its original intent of intellectual improvement. Upon that foundation other structures may be reared in a fraternal spirit, but concentration rather than division of interest is the rule of successful club endeavor."[43] The "concentration" important to Rotan depends on an integration of self-improvement and community service. During the flurry of war support that absorbed most clubwomen in 1918, True White observed, "One danger of the year just passed has been that clubs in their zeal for charitable work would give up their study program." After noting that clubs had found ways to combine study with their sewing and fund-raising projects, White continued, "We are all learning that we must keep heads as well as hands and hearts in the best possible condition for the many new duties the war is bringing."[44] The literacy practices Isaacs, Rotan, and White described were of central importance to club life, even though they were frequently integrated with other activities and screened from the view of outsiders.

Women's clubs were part of public life, but as intermediate institutions located between the family and the state, they also fostered intimacy among members. That is, clubs had political as well as personal dimensions, and literacy figured prominently in both. Although clubs occupied a subordinate political position, they offered strong and creative resistance to that subordination through literacy practices that cultivated the making of meaning in the company of others. At the same time that clubwomen used literacy to resist the limitations, distortions, and denigrations imposed on them, they used it to develop strong affective ties. Literacy is, as Roger Chartier has observed, at once a private, hidden practice and a manifestation of power, "power more effective than that of public office," and clubwomen used this power in their cultural work on behalf of the nation and themselves.[45] Assuming, along the lines Nancy Fraser suggests, that the public sphere is an ideological construct based on gender- and class-biased notions, I identify women's clubs as one of the *competing* publics at the turn of the century.[46] This move calls into question the category of "separate spheres" common in academic feminism, urging instead more complex interpenetrations of women's clubs and other social formations.[47] Looking at women's clubs as one element in a multifaceted public sphere makes it possible to see the cultural work that resulted from the interactions between these groups and other social institutions. This work, as Mary Woolley suggests, cannot be represented "in statistics," but it has palpable value. Probing and assessing that value requires careful consideration of what and how clubwomen read and wrote about various aspects of national life.

To elucidate the complex interpenetrations of women's clubs and other social formations, this book juxtaposes club texts with significant fin de siècle documents. Taking these documents as representing, albeit imperfectly, discourses circulating in American society at the turn of the century, it considers clubwomen's literacy practices in the light of them. By including clubs from a wide range of social localities rather than only one or two populations, it offers a broadly representative perspective on the women's club movement. This methodology recreates the discursive interactions that constituted clubwomen's cultural work at the turn of the century. Considering clubwomen's reading and writing alongside such documents as the 1917 Immigration Act, Josiah Strong's *Our Country,* Edward Bok's *Ladies' Home Journal,* "new woman" journalism, George Santayana's "Genteel Tradition," Thomas Higginson's "Men and Women," and Edward Beer's *Mauve Decade,* this book shows how meanings moved among these texts and those written and read by clubwomen. Through reading and writing about the issues raised in these documents, clubwomen enacted the cultural work of exploring and shaping several of the key issues preoccupying the nation at the turn of the century.

The chapters progress from the broadest dimensions of national life, beginning with the state and the economy and then moving to the increasingly specialized discourses of gender, culture, and professionalism. Chapter 1 examines the ideologies implicit in the 1917 Immigration Act in relation to those enacted in women's clubs by considering the situated literacy practices of each. In doing so, it points to inadequacies in constructions of literacy that overlook its affective dimensions and the circulations of power that surround it. This chapter also distinguishes between written and printed club texts as a means of exploring the meanings and authority clubwomen assigned to their self-representations; it challenges public-private dichotomies by describing women's clubs in terms of public culture; and it concludes by detailing the liking, love, and care that animated the literacy practices of clubwomen, lending their reading and writing transformative power. Small groups of women whose reading and writing shared gendered perspectives, reflected common religious traditions, emphasized social interactions, and employed conscious strategies of community-building developed an ideology of literacy best reckoned by the calculus of intimacy.

Dramatic increases in immigration, along with urbanization and industrialization, constituted powerful forces that impinged on clubwomen as well as the rest of the population at the turn of the century. Chapter 2 explores the ways clubwomen in all social locations delineated, (re)defined, embraced, and railed against these forces. In particular, it shows how Josiah Strong's doctrine of Anglo-Saxonism interacted with discourses born of clubwomen's social backgrounds as they explored and shaped cities, factories, and recent arrivals through their reading and writing. It asserts that clubwomen in their differing social positions reconfigured what Lauren Berlant calls the "national fantasy" as they looked toward an Americanization of their own making, one that reflected their particular religious, race, and class positions.[48]

The flowering of consumer culture at the turn of the century generated economic forces that preoccupied clubwomen in a number of ways. Chapter 3 considers how clubwomen both supported and resisted the emerging cash nexus and the advertising industry embodied in the *Ladies' Home Journal* under Edward Bok's editorship. It examines the discourses surrounding clubwomen's establishment of such public service institutions as libraries, employment agencies, parole offices, and treatment centers in terms of the competing social impetus toward generating profits and amassing capital. This chapter goes on to show how clubwomen's reading and writing about philanthropy introduced new themes to the nation's public policy discourses.

The social turmoil engendered by economic and political change was accompanied by changing perceptions of women. Beginning with the premise that womanhood—or manhood—is varied and continually changing rather than a fixed and static entity, chapter 4 considers the ways clubwomen interacted with the ideologies of womanhood at the turn of the century. Journalists' construct of the "new woman" provided one pole on the continuum of views on womanhood, while the home-centered mother provided another. Through their everyday literacy practices of taking minutes, writing essays, reading various texts, and printing their annual programs, clubwomen helped articulate and refashion "truths" about "woman."

Chapter 5 traces the progression, during the 1880–1920 period, from what Raymond Williams calls a culture of personal value to one of general intellectual method.[49] Arguing that this progression was not as smooth or coherent as Williams implies, this chapter shows how clubwomen helped expand the meaning of culture to include a wider spectrum of life. It asserts that clubs provided women sites for examining, managing, and resisting the terms of what George Santayana calls the genteel tradition; for producing and displaying cultural objects; and for fashioning a gender-based articulation of culture. In considering texts read and written by clubwomen in various social positions, it argues that the literacy practices surrounding these texts both disseminated and reconfigured meanings for culture.

Chapter 6 offers a revisionist account of the narratives of professionalism in English studies. Beginning with Thomas Higginson's expression of anxiety about women's control of literature, it describes women's clubs as the other against which professionalized English studies defined itself. Reconsidering the amateur-professional dichotomy, it argues that the agonistic relation between professors and the amateurs who enter lower-division English classes every semester can be ameliorated by reconsidering the model of English studies offered by fin de siècle clubwomen. It goes on to elaborate on contemporary accounts of professionalization by showing that the literacy practices of women's clubs embodied and enacted many of the conflicts and dilemmas that preoccupy today's considerations of the relationship between English departments and the society that supports them.

The final chapter asserts that the cultural work of women's clubs remains largely invisible because the last stage in any such cultural project is forgetting. The shifts in perspectives on Americanization, the modification of capitalism's consumer culture, the changed view of womanhood, the reconfigurations of culture, and the professionalizing of English studies—none of this cultural work would have had an effect if the processes of its achievement had not been erased from the national consciousness. Static and reductive images of clubwomen that distorted, trivialized, and even vilified them supplanted the memory of the archive, making it easy for the public to assume that the 1920s perspectives on nationhood, economics, gender, and culture had always been in place.

This volume bears the ideological weight of my own perspective, and, while I cannot reduce it, I can acknowledge it. My mother was a clubwoman, and I felt the presence of her club continually as I grew up in a small New Hampshire town. The force of this presence reemerged recently as my mother's death left me the legacy of her club scrapbooks and led her club friends to memorialize her with the gift of a book to the public library. My father, who carried a black lunch pail to work but read voraciously and played the violin in the community orchestra, taught me how easy and dangerous it is to underconceptualize those who fall into the category of working class. My children, both born to other mothers, give me direct experience with the world of racial politics and help me attend to representations of difference with sharpened attention. For twenty years I have worked in the areas of composition studies and English education, and this experience has instilled the pedagogue's insistence on understanding the processes as well as the products of literacy, along with the conviction, nourished by responding to thousands of student papers, that submerged texts, such as those produced and consumed by clubwomen, reward thoughtful reading.

1

Literacy and Intimacy

➤ I confess to having been more interested in the sight of the dear, familiar, new-old faces, than at first in the reading, and to have paid very little attention to the selection from Lubbock, read by Mrs. Root. About the usual portion of Emerson was read and comments were made over some knotty passages. It seemed to me that we as a club have benefitted by our association, in the matter of conversations—of being able to think aloud with less timidity and with more directness. Three or four of Browning's short poems were read by as many ladies— glimpses of another thought field. The intellectual food proffered by our gracious "bell ringer" has had often the effect to send me home ready to read and think like a philosopher.

ZELLIE EMERSON,
Minutes of the Friday Club of
Jackson, Michigan, 1889

➤ Whereas it has pleased the Heavenly Father to remove by sudden death our beloved President Lillias A. W. Hazewell, therefore resolve that by the death of Mrs. Hazewell we as a society have lost the guiding spirit by whose rare genius we were originally brought together and sustained til now. While we sincerely mourn her loss, we remember with gratitude her unselfish labor, her untiring zeal, and her noble consideration to the work of helping mothers and little children. Knowing that the influence of her bountiful life will live and continue to bless the world long after this society is forgotten, Resolved that we endeavor to carry on the work that she has begun by seeking in all things to follow her good example. Resolved that this testimonial be entered upon our record and that a copy be sent to son and husband and to the mourning mother and sisters praying that the loving God will comfort their stricken hearts.

Minutes of the Women in Council of
Roxbury, Massachusetts, 1889

⊷≋ That night a deep laid and mysterious conspiracy was completed which ended in something of a tempest, but loving friends tried and true held steadfast on their way and on Feb. 26 a large company assembled at Dr. E. R. Shipp's residence where an ovation was given Mrs. E. B. Wells as a surprise. It was in honor of the coming out of her sweet book of poems styled "Musings and Memories."

The crowning expression of our appreciation of her book was the presentation of our book to her. In this book each leaf reflected personally the love and good wishes of a friend, in original or selected prose or poetry, with somewhere on the leaf a quotation from her book and also adorned with beautiful hand painted flowers, expressing the feelings and tastes of the giver of the leaf. There are nearly one hundred leaves in the book, making an unique and costly memento of the birth of her brain-child and also of the seventieth year of her life.

ROMANIA BUNNELL PRATT,
"Utah Woman's Press Club: President's Farewell Address,"
Woman's Exponent, 1898

⊷≋ Judith Horton of Oklahoma (we call her the Fire Brand) who has charge of the Child's Labor Question for the National, has recently lost her husband. Mrs. Horton has the sympathy of the clubwomen of the national. Mrs. Horton has been a staunch supporter of the work of the national. She has been for the past two years a most devoted and untiring wife to her husband. Mr. Horton's name is known wherever the Y.M.C.A. is known. Somehow or other I feel that the Master gives no burden to us which he does not give strength equal to it.

National Association Notes, 1917

⊷≋ In the death of our beloved past president Miss Bella Goldman, we have all suffered a loss that is beyond the power of any words of mine to express. For many years she gave of her best to the club and to us

who were its members. To most fittingly express the deep love and affection which each one of us felt for Bella Goldman, your Board
thought best that this year's banquet be sacrificed and the money usually expended for this purpose or the sum of one hundred dollars be
donated to the United Jewish Charities as a memorial. In response to
this and other gifts the superintendent's room of the United Jewish
Charities will hereafter be known as the Bella Goldman Room and a
plate with a fitting memorial inscription will be placed therein.

Minutes of the Detroit Section of the National Council
of Jewish Women, 1914

↬ We feel we are a family and know one another well. There are no
cliques, no jealousy. We know one another's joys and sorrows. In a big
club we might not even know for whom a girl is in mourning. . . . We
carry out of the Good Will Club more than from any other organization
we belong to because we really love it so much. We hum and sing at
work because of what we get there.

A Good Will Member,
"The Small Club: Its Advantages,"
Club Worker, 1900

↬ Much has been written of the love between man and woman, but
not so much of the love of women for one another. When the latter is
fully recognized, there will be a new force in the world.

"How to Be Charitable without Money,"
Far and Near, 1891

↬ Youth is not a matter of years; it is an attitude of mind. To a degree
it depends upon one's interests and aims in life. But some are younger
than others in the faith, hope and confidences with which they meet
life's perplexities and troubles. Of such was Mrs. May Alden
Ward. . . . She was always present, sweet, calm, gentle and dignified. No
matter what the provocation, she was never swayed from the well
poised attitude which was so distinctive a feature of her character. To
have known and loved her and to have shared in her friendship will
always be a precious memory. . . . Her clear intellect, exquisite English,
sympathetic understanding, and keen sense of humor won for Mrs.
May Alden Ward the admiration and affection of those who shared

with her the priceless privilege of serving on Mrs. Decker's board. I
feel my life was the richer for having known and loved her.
                    MRS. PERCY V. [ANNA J. H.] PENNYBACKER,
                    "Mrs. May Alden Ward,"
            General Federation of Women's Clubs Magazine, 1918

↦⊜ The title of "club" had been chosen after considerable discussion
as being broad, significant and novel, and with the hope and the promise to the few objectors, that it would be redeemed from the objectionable features of many of the clubs of men. It was claimed to be an escape from the old special titles used for women's unions, in church and
other activities, while inclusive of all these within its membership, and
therefore significant of a new departure in fellowship and effort. It was
a "woman's club"—an unknown quantity heretofore and therefore
novel. The historian of the club in searching for the etymology of the
title found it defined in Anglo-Saxon and in German as "to embrace,"
"to adhere," which well covers the sincere cordial companionship and
the faithful adherence of the membership of women's clubs as since
developed.
                    CAROLINE SEYMOUR SEVERANCE,
                    1906

⊶⊜⊑⊷

IN the 1880s the U.S. Congress began imposing restrictions on immigration,
and literacy quickly emerged as one of the measures for assessing the "quality"
of those who sought to enter the country.[1] In 1917 the Sixty-fourth Congress
overrode President Wilson's veto to pass Public Act No. 301, commonly known
as an immigration bill. In addition to specifying a head tax of eight dollars for
every alien and prohibiting the admission of mentally retarded persons, pau-
pers, criminals, polygamists, prostitutes, and contract laborers, the bill excluded the following: "All aliens over sixteen years of age, physically capable of
reading, who can not read the English language, or some other language or
dialect, including Hebrew or Yiddish." While the bill exempted the wives,
mothers, grandmothers, and daughters as well as fathers or grandfathers over
age fifty-five of "admissible aliens," it stipulated:

for the purpose of ascertaining whether aliens can read the immigrant inspectors shall be furnished with slips of uniform size, prepared under the direction of the Secretary of Labor, each containing not less than thirty nor more than forty words in ordinary use, printed in plainly legible type in some one of the various languages or dialects of immigrants. Each alien may designate the particular language or dialect in which he desires the examination be made, and shall be required to read the words printed on the slip in such language or dialect.[2]

Although this was not the first bill to restrict immigration, it was the first to identify literacy as a characteristic of "admissible aliens."[3] From the 1890s onward, as the tide of immigration rose, Congress had struggled with legislation linking literacy and immigration. Each of the three presidents preceding Wilson had also vetoed a bill similar to the one passed in 1917. Between 1890 and 1917 the topic of literacy—often a lightning rod for social contests—occupied a prominent place in national discourse. Anxieties springing from the changing demographic, economic, political, and cultural landscape of the United States found expression in arguments about literacy. A wide variety of clubwomen participated in these contests over literacy, shaping, in the process, their own ideologies. Their participation took the form of discussing the issue and enacting practices that both questioned and supported the view of literacy reflected in the 1917 bill.

This chapter examines clubwomen's texts in relation to assumptions about literacy inscribed in the 1917 bill as a way of highlighting the innovative views of literacy that emerged from clubs' alternative public spheres. Clubwomen's ideologies of literacy developed from and reflected the values of their particular social locations. All of them, however, sought to create a version of what Benedict Anderson describes as an "imagined community." Nations are, according to Anderson, *imagined* communities because members cannot all know one another and must create mental constructs of fellow citizens. Literacy fosters an imagined community as multiple and widely distributed copies of the same text create the "possibility of a new form of imagined community" among readers who can envision themselves and many others consuming the same texts at the same time.[4] Clubwomen affirmed the imagined community of the United States when enormous changes and social dislocations threatened the construct of the nation. Their literacy practices enabled them to imagine themselves as participants in a widespread activity that connected them with multiple but invisible others. Through writing and reading, they established new and intimate relationships that extended across the open spaces of the expanding nation.

The exclusionist impulse of the 1917 bill drew force from its supporters' insistence that illiteracy was a barrier to democracy.[5] Although the United States had no equivalent of the English Education Act of 1871 that had unleashed a tide of fear and opposition in Britain by extending literacy to a wide portion of the population, a segment of the public opposed the 1890 Morrill Land Grant Act, which made college education accessible to more people, including women and blacks.[6] This mixture of on the one hand requiring literacy of potential citizens while on the other hand opposing the extension of sophisticated literacies to a wider portion of the population suggests the complicated and contested relationship between literacy and nation.

From their various social positions, clubwomen used their own reading and writing to explore the contested relationship of literacy and citizenship. African American clubwomen who contended with racist colonization societies that proposed sending them back to Africa figured literacy prominently in articulating their own "civilization" and right to citizenship. During the slave era, whites had exerted considerable energy in preventing slaves from learning to read or write.[7] In addition to the practical fear that literate slaves could escape more easily, this prohibition reflected whites' desire to differentiate themselves from the human beings they enslaved. This meant, as Michael Warner notes, that "black illiteracy was more than a negation of literacy for blacks; it was the condition of a positive character of written discourse for whites."[8] In beating or even killing slaves who tried to become literate, white slave owners demonstrated the strength of their commitment to preserving the "positive character of written discourse" for themselves. Accordingly, after emancipation African Americans made enormous financial sacrifices to establish schools, lobby for better education for their children, and train and support teachers in order to secure the power of literacy for members of their race. Although northern missionaries and philanthropists often receive credit for founding and maintaining schools for African Americans in the South, much of the capital and labor was, as Thomas Holt and others have shown, supplied by African Americans themselves.[9] Clubwomen called on literacy as they justified citizenship for members of their race. Victoria Earle Matthews, founder of the Woman's Loyal Union of Brooklyn, received accolades from her club friends for her 1894 plan to write "a series of text books, historical primers, for the youth of the race, which will trace the history of the African and show that he and his descendants have been prominently identified with every phase of this country's history including the landing of Columbus."[10] Literacy provided a means for Matthews and her peers to insert themselves into the history of a nation that tried to erase and demean them.

Jewish clubwomen, even when their families had lived in the United States for generations, faced anti-Semitic attempts to discredit their claims to citizenship. Sometimes they were classed with Jews who had recently immigrated, and sometimes they were deprecated on the basis of their religion. Charged with being "foreign" or somehow not fully American, these clubwomen emphasized literacy in their programs, forming study circles and encouraging the development of reading and writing. Mormon clubwomen, many of whom until 1896 were residents of territories rather than states, also faced religiously based discrimination, and displays of their literacy practices constituted one of their frequent responses.

Although white middle-class Protestant clubwomen did not have to contend with racist colonial societies or religious discrimination, they also explored the literacy-citizenship issue. Minutes of the Roxbury Women in Council in Massachusetts for November 26, 1907, report, "The speaker [Edward Livingston Underwood] emphasized the need of restricted immigration. An educational test was necessary so that a mass of densely ignorant people should not be thrust upon us. We need the immigrant, he said, for industrial work and it was our business to enlighten him when we got him here and not to leave him to the ward politician."[11] These minutes articulate a theme of the ongoing national debate between those who wanted to use literacy to control the "quality" of immigrants and those (usually in business) who wanted immigrants—ignorant or not—in the work force. In the same year, Congress established the Dillingham Commission to study the relationship between literacy and social deviancy among immigrants. As Congress struggled with the relationship between literacy and citizenship, women's clubs explored the issue for themselves.

By focusing only on reading, with no attention to writing, the 1917 bill adopted an asymmetrical perspective on literacy. Those who drafted and supported this bill conceptualized literacy only in its consuming mode. Reading, or the taking in of text, stands as the sole indication of literacy. While reading cannot be described as entirely passive—readers do, after all, actively construct texts in their heads—it provides only limited opportunity for individuals to create a new relationship with their culture. The introduction of writing changes the nature of reading, transforming it from a public performance to what François Furet and Jacques Ozouf describe as "a great silence, inside which the individual carves out a private space for himself." Reading, in their terms, implies "neither the autonomy of the individual, nor the obligation to exercise at least a modicum of intellectual freedom, nor again the beginnings of an inner break with the restraints of the community."[12] If one goal of the 1917 bill was to encourage conformity to the norms of the nation, limiting literacy to reading served that objective and reflected an ideology of literacy that encouraged compliance. In requiring that immigrants "read the words printed on the slip," framers of the 1917 bill and its supporters were attempting to retain control of immigrants and their literacy. Although immigrants could select the "language or dialect" in which the words would appear, they could exert no control over the text itself, and their futures rested on their ability to reproduce in oral form the words on the page. By conceptualizing literacy as exclusively reading, the 1917 bill emphasized social control and reenacted conceptualizations and pedagogies of literacy circulating in the national culture since colonial times.[13]

Clubwomen, in contrast, enacted a more symmetrical literacy, one that included writing as well as reading. Early in the development of their organizations, clubwomen realized that their efforts would be much more effective if members wrote as well as read. The records of the Saturday Morning Club reflect this. In 1874 President Marion Gray read a paper on club discussions in which she lamented the lack of focus, the poor preparation, and the small attendance on discussion days (the club listened to lectures by outsiders at alternate meetings). The club approved her proposal that six members take responsibility for leading discussions and prepare themselves a fortnight in advance. The report of the ensuing discussion includes this: "It was suggested that some might like to put their thoughts in writing on the subject under discussion which idea was favorably received, and the president expressed her willingness to read any short papers which might be sent her anonymously if the writer so chose."[14] The paper requirement was soon institutionalized in the Saturday Morning Club, and two categories of membership emerged, substitute and regular. To advance from substitute to regular, the member had to present two satisfactory papers to the club.

Although clubs did not necessarily attach writing to probationary status, most did require members to write papers. As one commentator put it, "A woman's club without a paper or papers taking up a definite line or thought or research is a very singular phenomenon."[15] The following synopsis typifies the writing requirement of many clubs: Topics for discussion were chosen by the club, or in larger clubs by the chair of the department in charge of a given month's program; presenters were selected to prepare papers on the subject; and at the meeting, as one club member recounted, "recitations are rendered which, with the discussion of the question, constitute the entertainment."[16] Frequently papers were assigned a year in advance, and authors were expected to conduct extensive research and produce a polished text. Clubwomen did not merely assign writing; they also provided assistance to developing writers. The Saturday Morning Club president's offer of help soon took the form of this line in the club yearbook: "Papers shall be read to the president (or to someone designated by her) at least a week before the discussion date."[17] Club minutes contain frequent references to members helping one another, sharing books, and providing critical responses to papers. Clubs also encouraged writing by providing instruction, sponsoring contests, and publishing members' work. The Mormon *Young Woman's Journal* encouraged readers with this: "Whenever there is one who has any literary talent, either dormant or to some degree developed . . . write and forward to us, so that their productions may appear from time to time in our magazine." Later the journal instituted an essay contest.[18] *Far and Near* regularly urged clubwomen to contribute articles on specified topics, such as "how can we best cultivate club feeling" or "the ideal club," and also mounted writing contests. In addition to receiving a prize (usually a book), the winner would have her text published.[19] Through these practices that encouraged a symmetry and synergy of active reading and ongoing writing development, clubwomen developed an ideology of literacy that emphasized participation rather than passive reception. Both its symmetry of reading and writing and its concern with the active development of skill marked this ideology as different from the one shaping the 1917 bill.

In trying to ascertain "whether aliens can read," the 1917 bill operated from a principle of inherency, seeing literacy as defining people. Opponents of the bill contested this principle, framing literacy in more social and political terms. President Wilson, who vetoed the bill, spoke for many when he claimed that "it seeks to all but close entirely the gates of asylum, which have always been open to those who could find nowhere else the right and opportunity of constitutional agitation for what they conceived to be the natural and inalienable rights of men, and it excludes those to whom the opportunities of elementary education have been denied without regard to their character, their purposes, or their natural capacity."[20]

Social workers, settlement directors, and others who worked directly with immigrants shared Wilson's view that literacy did not constitute an inherent quality. Lillian Wald, founding director of the Henry Street Settlement House, recounted the testimony of a Polish physician: "My father . . . came an illiterate to this country because the priest of his parish happened not to be interested in education, not because my father was indifferent. He has struggled all his life to give his children what he himself could never have, and has worshipped the country that gave us opportunity."[21] Wald's account lent strength to Wilson's concern about conceiving literacy as an identifying feature of people because it demonstrated how life's circumstances contributed to the development or lack of literacy. By framing literacy in social rather than individual terms, opponents of the 1917 bill acknowledged the power relationships surrounding literacy. Just as the local priest prevented the doctor's father from becoming literate, so the father's insistence that his children receive what he "could never have" enabled the doctor to acquire a position of relative prestige and power in the family's new nation. The circulations of power associated with literacy can remain invisible only when reading and writing are conceptualized as solitary processes that define persons. By focusing on literacy as an individual attribute, the framers of the 1917 bill avoided confrontation with its power dynamics.

Clubwomen embraced a much more political view of literacy, and those in marginalized positions emphasized how literacy related to power. Members of a working women's club in New York approached their mentor Grace Dodge with a question: "Don't you think that New Yorkers think working girls are stupid?" to which Dodge responded, "Yes, Bessie, I think as a whole they do." "We thought so," the girl replied. "Now we want to prove that working girls are not stupid and have a plan to represent to the girls tonight. . . . We propose to start a newspaper to be managed by girls and all the articles written by them."[22] As this exchange shows, these clubwomen saw literacy as a means of changing the way others perceived them, of demonstrating that they were not "stupid." Literacy conferred the power of self-fashioning on these women, and it also provided a means of changing the material conditions of their lives.

Like clubwomen in other social positions, working women wrote papers, but their topics focused on issues related to their everyday lives, such as "The Value of a Public School Education," "Why Women Earn Smaller Wages than Men," "What Is Domestic Science?" (domestic service was a field frequently urged on working women by middle-class women who saw it as a means of producing more and better domestic help), and "Women and Men as Employers." Such papers were published in the *Club Worker,* where they circulated to all the members of the National League of Women Workers, simultaneously displaying working women's capacities as writers and addressing issues central to the way they lived. Even the poetry published in this journal often focused on work, and issues included regular articles about the National Consumers' League, an organization that used women's buying power to pressure factory owners to improve working conditions.[23] Books these clubwomen read included *The Woman Who Spends, The Employment of Women in the Clothing Trade,* and *Women's Work and Wages.*[24]

Even when working women took positions similar to those held by women from other groups, their motivations reflected their class position. They opposed child labor not only for the obvious maternal reasons but also because children represented a competing labor force and tended to depress wages.

Focusing on the connection between illiteracy and child labor, working-class clubwomen wrote and read texts arguing that "the years of childhood be held sacred to the work of education, free from the burden of wage-earning," and they pointed to the positive correlation between states with high levels of manufacturing and low child literacy rates, thus framing issues of working conditions in terms consonant with their emotional and economic lives.[25] Similarly, these clubwomen used literacy to examine their living conditions by writing and reading articles that described the housing of the 292,000 working women in Massachusetts.[26] These working women developed an ideology of literacy that made direct connections between texts and action even as it countered the prevailing view that literacy fostered economic gain. Possessing the ability to read and write did not ensure reasonable wages for these clubwomen. Still, however, writing and reading about housing conditions, unequal wages, or child labor opened the way to changing these conditions. Furthermore, by deploying literacy to examine the conditions of their lives, working women knew they could make themselves more visible (and similar) to those in positions to help improve their housing and wages.

African American clubwomen also called on the transformative power of literacy. In keeping with what Janet Duitsman Cornelius has described as the "magico-religious" significance that African Americans often attached to reading and writing, transformation could take spiritual as well as material form.[27] A paper written by Florida Ridley for the Woman's Era Club, shows how clubwomen articulated the spiritual:

> Some people's measure of good is an entirely material one; they recognize little that cannot be seen or handled, and consider nothing an advantage that does not add to material prosperity. We are all too much under the control of material things, and too slow to recognize the power of thought. A woman's club may not build a home for the unfortunate, but if it opens the eyes and the hearts of its members to the condition of these unfortunates, if it considers ways in which their misfortune might be averted, if it extends its intelligence and influence over the conduct of those who have the institution under management, it is fulfilling its mission, and a noble one, too; and the woman who cannot see it is sadly in need of the enlightenment she could find in the club.[28]

This excerpt, later published in the *Woman's Era,* points to a transformation that extends beyond the material. The "thought" Ridley affirms flows directly from reading about the conditions of "unfortunates" and ways those conditions might be changed as well as writing to influence those who have the "institution under management." Her claim for the "power of thought" as opposed to that of "material things" shows that something of the spiritual dimension described by Janet Duitsman Cornelius found its way into the ideology of literacy African American clubwomen constructed. In insisting that transforming the desires of members by opening their "eyes and hearts" constitutes a noble mission for clubs, Ridley articulates an ideology of literacy that recognizes forms of change beyond the material.

Identifying these nonmaterial transformations does not imply that African American clubwomen failed to seek changes in the material circumstances of their lives. The Neighborhood Union, an Atlanta club organized for "the moral, economic and social advancement of Negroes," exemplifies the many ways clubwomen attempted to combat racism and improve the conditions of their own and others' lives. Concerned about the inadequate and overcrowded schools their children attended, these women issued a printed petition that introduced the authors as residents and taxpayers of Atlanta and then listed concerns (based on careful research) about sanitary conditions, the lack of a school in South Atlanta, inadequate provisions for "feeble-minded children," and double sessions. It concluded by asserting, "We earnestly trust that your honorable body will grant our petition, the ultimate aim of which is to reduce crime, and to make of our children good citizens." By printing this petition, the Neighborhood Union sought to give it authority. In addition to demonstrating their capacity to carry out research and mount a logical argument, club members aimed to transform racist descriptions of them as lacking in moral character. That teachers' salaries were raised and a school for African American children was established in South Atlanta suggests their strategy was effective.[29]

Jewish clubwomen also saw literacy as a means of transformation, although their efforts often focused on recent arrivals. Recognizing they might be categorized with immigrant Jews from eastern Europe, these clubwomen inscribed their concerns about "Jewish immigration and the duties it brings us." Their duties, as Birdie Pick of the Detroit Section of the National Council of Jewish Women put it, included going into immigrants' homes to "show them the clean healthful life" and fostering literacy by teaching them to read and write English. Pick encouraged member participation by explaining, "Classes in English are held at the Hannah Schloss Memorial Building every evening and on Sunday mornings, and the need of volunteer teachers is great."[30] Such appeals were repeated in sections throughout the country as Jewish clubwomen employed literacy to transform their immigrant sisters into people recognizable as and acceptable to Americans.

The transformative power of literacy was particularly apparent when club-women chose to represent themselves and their activities in print. Although they used it for slightly different purposes and in varying forms, clubwomen in all social locations used print to fashion themselves and their organizations. Printing their own national publications and other documents enabled club-women to assume some authority in a sphere dominated and controlled by men. Newspapers, magazines, and book publishing remained male-governed throughout the nineteenth century, and women who tried to succeed in the world of print encountered enormous difficulties. By underwriting their own publications and regulating their contents, clubwomen created an alternative to the male-controlled mass market in which women could only rarely present themselves in their own terms. The uncertainties as well as the misrepresenta-tions risked by depending on mainstream publications inspired most clubwom-en to develop their own systems for producing and distributing printed texts. Like national federations, most local clubs used print to display their activities.[31]

While printing national publications can be explained by print's capacity to reproduce identical and multiple texts for wide circulation, printing by local clubs requires more explanation. Among the documents printed by clubwom-en were yearbooks; official documents, such as constitutions and bylaws; cel-ebratory or memorial notices; club histories; and political statements, such as the Neighborhood Union's petition. Most of the information in these texts was common knowledge among club members or could have been conveyed by other means, such as handwritten notices or word of mouth.[32] Yearbooks typ-ically included a month-by-month outline of the club program, lists of offic-ers and members, and the club motto. Some clubs included constitutions and bylaws in the yearbook, while others printed them as separate documents. Whether these texts were printed separately or together, clubwomen relied on print to display the organization and nature of club work. By printing a year-long program detailing topics and presenters, clubwomen provided evidence of their capacity for sustained and structured work. These printed displays also as-sumed an authority derived from the technology of print that, by its distance from the hand, connoted what Michael Warner calls a "political condition of utterance," and in using it to present their work, clubwomen appropriated its political power.[33]

Clubwomen recognized and articulated the importance of printing their programs, as did this historian of the white middle-class Monday Club in Clin-ton, New York: "The first calendar was written in long hand in 1897. In the fol-lowing year it was typewritten. Since that time, for thirty-eight years without a break, the yearbook of the Monday Club has been printed every spring in the print shop of Mr. H. P. Osborne."[34] Printing official documents highlighted the systematic nature of club transactions. In a world where clubs were frequently dismissed as silly and unstructured, these texts offered a powerful counterstatement, and clubwomen gave high priority to printing them. Minutes of the Chautauqua Circle, an African American women's club founded in Atlanta in 1913, indicate that this group allocated funds for a yearbook within its first year of existence, discussed details of the printing during several meetings, and soon decided to send their yearbooks to a larger audience.[35] Printing celebratory and memorial notices and histories lent authority and authenticity to the past of this and many other clubs. Like programs and constitutions, these more personal texts illustrated club work, and clubwomen took pride in circulating them. Minutes of the African American Woman's Improvement Club of Indianapolis, for instance, include this: "The President asked for expressions from the members concerning the printing of a folder setting forth the history of the club . . . this folder to be sent out with all communications of the club as an advertisement of our work."[36] The juxtaposition of *printing* and *advertisement* shows that these women saw the printed version of their history as displaying their work to an audience beyond the membership, offering substantive evidence of their projects. Such texts provided an antidote to the half-truths and distortions circulating about most women's clubs. For African American clubwomen this was particularly urgent because most public statements about clubwomen assumed that all were white and middle-class and entirely ignored such groups as the Woman's Improvement Club.

This desire to represent themselves in print extended to all clubwomen but particularly to those—such as Jewish, working-class, Mormon, and African American women—rendered invisible by the stereotypical view of clubwomen as white middle-class Protestants. Rosa Sonneschein, a founding member of the St. Louis Pioneers Club in 1879, established the *American Jewess* in 1895 in an attempt to decrease anti-Semitism in the women's movement. She aimed to create a publication read by non-Jewish women that would reduce prejudice by developing common understandings among women. The *Woman's Exponent* included on its masthead "The Rights of the Women of Zion, and the Rights of Women of all Nations," indicating it prioritized advocating for Mormon women. Continual references in both the *Woman's Exponent* and the *Young Woman's Journal* to favorable notices sent from clubwomen in the East give credence to the *Exponent*'s claim of "doing missionary work in many respects" and demanding more support, "considering what it has done, and is doing all the time for the women of this Territory, and of the Church of Latter-day Saints throughout all the Stakes of Zion."[37] Print provided a means by which Jews, African Americans, and Mormons, like clubwomen from other social locations, could represent themselves in their own terms to a wider audience.

Working women were financially constrained in printing representations of their clubs, but they shared with their peers from other backgrounds a desire to appropriate print's authority. National publications, such as *Far and Near* and the *Club Worker,* provided a forum where local clubs and individual members could display their intellectual and philanthropic activities. In addition, some working women substituted their own labor for cash to produce printed texts. Clubs that trained women in the trades could call on the skills of their own compositors to present local club activities in print.[38]

Although white middle-class clubwomen received more public attention than other clubwomen did, they also struggled against damaging and inaccurate representations of their clubs and projects. Grover Cleveland's 1905 attack in the *Ladies' Home Journal* typified the negative and careless statements published about these clubwomen in the mainstream press. In addition to misnaming the General Federation of Women's Clubs, Cleveland betrayed his ignorance about club work by equating it with the suffrage movement, ignoring its philanthropic dimensions, and portraying clubs as women's retaliation against men.[39] The editors of the *Federation Bulletin* issued an immediate response, opening with these questions: "Has it really come to this? Are Julia Ward Howe and Mary A. Livermore to be lectured on the nature of home and motherhood, by Grover Cleveland?" The editors observed, "When a distinguished man undertakes to write about a subject of which he knows nothing, the more distinguished the man the more ridiculous his failure. There are thousands of men in this country who know the women's clubs thoroughly. . . . But if none of the men who really know the women's clubs are employed to write about them, the question arises as to why Mr. Cleveland is so employed." They pointed out other inaccuracies of Cleveland's article, including his claims that the General Federation did not concern itself with philanthropic or intellectual issues, asserting that he attacked "the one women's organization in this country which stands for the home in all its broadest meanings" and asking, "Is it necessary for us to say to anyone in America, except Mr. Cleveland, that we are not a political organization, that we are not a suffrage organization, and we are not a social organization?"[40]

The anger evident throughout this editorial fueled both the refutation of Cleveland's claims and the affirmation that clubwomen have the right to define themselves, to name the terms with which they will be described. To support their assertions, the editors of the *Federation Bulletin* looked to their previous accomplishments, highlighting their work in legislation on child labor, worker protection, the age of consent for girls, nature conservation, pure food, and citizenship. Casting these as philanthropic, they tried to avoid the accusation of being political. The force of Cleveland's attack evidently pushed clubwomen to look to authorities beyond themselves, and in the next issue of the *Bulletin* the editors reported having received many letters of support "from men who stand at the head of the great public movements with which their names are associated." They went on to recount remarks Edward Hale made on the occasion of Julia Ward Howe's eighty-sixth birthday, when he described women's clubs as having appeared "just at the time when they were most needed" and offering "moral power" in society. A column titled "Men's Views of Women's Clubs: A Symposium by Men Who Are Recognized Leaders in the Philanthropic and Reform Movements of America" included statements from a number of nationally prominent men. The geographical distribution and the range of positions represented by these men suggest widespread and authoritative support for clubwomen, which is reinforced with such statements as "I know of no body . . . representing so much of culture and influence . . . as the General Federation of Women's Clubs," "I have found these clubs of great value, especially in . . . the reform of the Civil Service," "Women's clubs . . . have championed every good law and secured the passage of nearly all the advanced legislation . . . for the protection of the home and the children," and "Women's clubs have taken a leading part in many of the most important reform movements in elementary education within the last twenty years."[41]

That clubwomen turned to men, instead of relying entirely on themselves for their rebuttal, can be read as an acknowledgment of their own powerlessness or as a regression to the tentativeness that led clubwomen to seek approval from ministers and rabbis as they founded their organizations. It can also be read as a recognition of the very real power men continued to wield over disfranchised women, a power echoed in the *Federation Bulletin* when it pointed out that the *Annals of the American Academy of Political and Social Science*'s issue on clubwomen reached "a class of men who influence public opinion in America to a very great degree—a class of men who are our best thinkers, philanthropists, and publicists."[42] In retaining control of the selection and arrangement of the men's statements, however, these clubwomen asserted their own authority. They also indicated that they would exert administrative control even over those who spoke on their behalf and that they reserved the right to represent themselves and their defenders in their own terms and to use their own forms of print.

Similarly, as club officers contracted with printers and oversaw their work, they inverted more traditional patterns of female labor directed by male management. Many clubs established, along with programming and nominating committees, printing committees to oversee the production of club documents and negotiate with local printers. Records of Boston's New England Women's Club, for instance, mention the printing committee beginning in 1880. As this excerpt from the 1900 minutes of the Naugatuck Study Club indicates, clubwomen did not hesitate to exert their managerial authority over the (male) printers they hired: "The corresponding secretary reported an interview with Mr. Perry regarding the prospectus not being satisfactory to the club, the work and the paper being inferior to that of previous years. Mr. Perry expressed regret and promised it right, which he accordingly did."[43] The combination of their economic power to purchase the services of printers and their collectively developed standards of quality led clubwomen to assume administrative roles often denied them in other spheres.

In addition to transforming themselves and their gendered roles, clubwomen used print to transform events. The 1899 meeting of the National Association of Colored Women (NACW) in Chicago aroused considerable controversy when Mary Church Terrell succeeded herself as president and supporters of Josephine Ruffin, the alternative candidate, criticized the "highhanded unparliamentary rulings of the presiding officer, and the unconstitutional elections."[44] In 1900 the NACW issued *Press Comments,* a printed brochure containing excerpts from newspaper editorials, accounts by observers at the convention, and a list of the NACW officers for 1899–1901. Excerpts from the *Chicago Daily News, Chicago Tribune,* and *Chicago Inter Ocean* all describe African American clubwomen as having "good sense and judgment," possessing "essential dignity, evident refinement of manner," and being "practical and helpful." A piece titled "Talks with Clubwomen" from the *Chicago Sunday Times Herald* recounts positive comments about the proceedings, giving special attention to Mary Church Terrell as "a woman who has had advantages" and who has "improved them." The list of officers, of course, begins with Mary Church Terrell as president.[45] (Re)printing these texts in a format that highlights positive statements about the NACW and ends with the list of officers served to strengthen Terrell's position in the organization by transforming the conflicts of the 1899 meeting into a favorable statement about the race. These accolades from the white press, which usually said nothing or only negative things about African American clubwomen, enhanced the stature of the NACW itself. At the same time, this collection of statements from the white press displays and explicitly comments on the surprise that greeted African American clubwomen's accomplishments, reminding its readers of the need to remain unified against the continuing assaults of racism. By reproducing them, these clubwomen signaled their awareness of and ability to use the power of literacy in print.

As the exemption of wives, mothers, grandmothers, and daughters from the literacy test makes clear, the 1917 immigration bill gendered reading and writing abilities as male. That women could not, in 1917, participate in national life by voting offered one justification for their exclusion, but the more complicated anxieties about women's literacy surely lay behind this gendering. During the nearly three decades of debate about the immigration bill, controversies about the education of women also raged. Proponents argued that society, domestic life in particular, would be improved by more highly educated women, while opponents claimed that women's education endangered families and the continuation of the species. These debates played out themes that had long surrounded women's literacy, a site where, as Kate Flint observes, "one may see a variety of cultural and sexual anxieties displayed."[46] From the colonial period onward, literacy had existed as a site of gender differentiation. Since writing was important for work outside the home, men tended to receive this training, while women learned reading only. Although an increasing number of women learned to write in later centuries, the gendered differences between consuming and producing texts remained, with women having less access to textual production.[47] Late nineteenth-century debates about women's literacy, then, were part of a longer tradition, but they took on particular force. The range of specialties of the participants in these debates provides one measure of the heightened cultural anxiety about women's literacy. People with expertise in medicine, theology, psychology, and education participated in the debate, and they expressed concerns about women's literacy causing infertility, a loss of religious conviction, nervous disorders, and the destruction of family life.[48] Prior to the turn of the century, most of this specialist discourse remained in professional journals with low circulation, but as anxieties grew, discussions about the deleterious effects of women's literacy began to appear in "publications with the potential to reach a wider readership."[49] Cultural anxieties about women's changing roles and sexual anxieties about women's fertility both fueled and supported these discussions, creating a relatively hostile climate for women's literacy development, one in which immigration legislation could comfortably exclude women from any measure of reading or writing.

Clubwomen resisted this gendered construction of literacy as they encouraged literacy in club activities. By assigning reading on specific topics, creating libraries, offering book reviews in their publications, requiring members to write papers as well as club histories, minutes, and a variety of other documents, women's clubs pushed members to become more insightful readers and better writers. Club records contain many testimonies of women who faced the literacy requirements with great trepidation. In particular, many women feared writing and delivering papers to their peers. Members of the Washington, D.C., Section of the National Council of Jewish Women, for example, reported that initially members felt that they could not study, "and as for essays, why they just couldn't think of writing one. But as in the case of all phantoms, nearer approach causes lesser fears."[50] Even as they expressed hesitations about writing, clubwomen testified that such requirements helped them improve their literacy skills. From 1867 through the early 1890s clubs often provided a substitute for college since relatively few women had access to higher education prior to 1890. As more women entered college, clubs served a postgraduate function, providing a place where women could continue the literacy practices begun in college classes. Working women, for whom college attendance remained largely impossible after as well as before 1890, looked to clubs for classes or courses that furthered their education.

The literacy clubwomen developed both resembled and differed from the gendered literacy that shaped the 1917 bill. While clubwomen embraced opportunities to acquire some aspects of (male) knowledge, the processes of their reading and writing took alternative forms. To some extent, these differences resulted from the contexts in which women's clubs met. Gathering in one another's homes, libraries, or club rooms that carried a domestic imprint, clubwomen assumed a less formal posture than that enacted in the classroom. Academic discipline of the body was supplanted by comfortable chairs, handwork such as sewing or knitting, and the consumption of food and drink. These accommodations to the body never appeared in the classroom, where students occupied hard seats in lined rows, with the figure of the instructor often towering over them on a dais, and where handwork and refreshments of all sorts were explicitly forbidden.

Clubwomen's literacy practices also took physical form in gesture and tableaux. The Delsarte "science" of attitude and gesture, adapted from the system of movement developed by François Delsarte and popularized by such Americans as Elise Wilbor and Anna Morgan, became enormously popular during the last decades of the nineteenth century, fueled by Charles Darwin's *Expression of Emotions,* which claimed that since humans shared common expressions, it was possible to understand the feelings of strangers by observing their body language.[51] Clubwomen in all social locations incorporated aspects of Delsarte into their literacy practices. Minutes of a Mormon club include evaluative comments about the "feeling rendition" and the "impressive" recitation of poems under discussion.[52] An

African American club reports on an "evening performance of texts by Longfellow."[53] Working women shared recommendations for texts to perform as well as suggestions about how to rehearse and plan productions.[54] White middle-class groups frequently held author parties, which required members to dress as and act like their favorite author. All of these performances depended on the physical arrangement of the body and the use of the voice, although tableaux required no speech at all. As Martha Banta has observed, the Delsarte system fit comfortably with late nineteenth-century views on "the classification of physical and spiritual types . . . enthusiasm for scientific methods of self-advancement . . . and appeals to women to free themselves from society's self-demeaning control over their bodies and dress."[55] The Delsarte system also provided a socially sanctioned rubric for the physicality of clubwomen's enactments of literacy.

Along with the individual gesticulation and the corporate "still" of the tableaux moment, clubwomen employed drama in literacy practices. Club anniversaries and national meetings, in particular, provided occasions for original compositions of plays, masques, and pageants. Mary Church Terrell, a founding member of the National Association of Colored Women, wrote a pageant based on the life of Phillis Wheatley in an attempt to give greater prominence to the literary achievements of a member of her own race. Abby Farwell Brown, a member of the white middle-class Saturday Morning Club, wrote "The Masque of the Green Trunk" to commemorate the fiftieth anniversary of the club. Working women produced a pageant detailing the history of women's labor for the 1914 convention of the League of Women Workers. Such performances demonstrate how clubwomen deployed the physicality of their literacy to historicize themselves and their organizations.

These performances also underscore the highly interactive nature of the literacy clubwomen enacted. In contrast to the 1917 bill's stipulation that a single individual demonstrate his reading ability to an immigration official, clubwomen enacted literacy as an explicitly *social* practice. Since many perspectives on literacy emphasize its asocial dimensions, it is worth pausing over this distinction. Even current advertisements conceptualize readers and writers as individuals who work alone, shutting out the distractions of conversation and interaction, as lines advertising "isolated cottage suitable for writer" on the real estate pages attest. Scholarly tradition, theoretical constructs of authorship, university reward structures, and the silence imposed in libraries all posit readers and writers in solitary terms. Most investigations into the ways people create visible texts have concentrated on the mentalities of single individuals, whether published author or student writer. Although recent work in composition studies acknowledges the social dimension of writing, the dominant models for research and pedagogy assume that student writers work alone, and institutional prohibitions against plagiarism reinforce this view. Theoretical constructs of readers in various traditions of literary theory posit a singular reader, whether "ideal," "phenomenological," or "psychoanalytic." Educational institutions reinforce these constructions of readers and writers, penalizing students who receive too much "help" from their peers, calling on faculty authors to delineate precisely their contributions to coauthored works (as if to divide them into two separately authored pieces), and creating any number of institutional barriers to collaboration.

The difficulty with these constructions of readers and writers is not their lack of veracity. Certainly literacy requires quiet moments when one escapes the commotion of conversations and other interactions to make meaning from a written text or to inscribe ideas on paper. The problem lies in their partiality; the story of reading and writing does not begin or end with solitary performers. We all learned to read and write from *someone,* in a socially interactive setting. That someone, an actual or constructed maternal figure, nurtured our early attempts, encouraging us to join the community of literacy by talking about reading and writing, showing us how she did these things. Although the maternal figure recedes, literacy's need for society endures. Empirical studies of adult reading show, as Elizabeth Long observes, that "social isolation depresses readership, and social involvement encourages it."[56] Similarly, as Linda Brodkey notes, "writing is a socially constituted act whose meaning and value to writer and readers depends on contingent social arrangements."[57] These observations point to the truth of Deborah Brandt's description of literacy as a craft "passed hand-to-hand and mouth-to-mouth" through human interactions. The interrelation of literacy and human interaction is manifested, as Brandt notes, in the fact that "the more an institution produces and depends upon written language, the more talk about written language plays a role in that institution."[58] Conversations at office watercoolers, courtroom testimony, committee deliberations, religious services, and classroom discussions all show how social interaction sustains literacy. Yet the solitary aspect of literacy remains dominant, frequently obscuring its social dimension.

The highly social nature of clubwomen's literacy may help account for its receiving only slight attention; because it does not fit the dominant model, it is harder to see. When Zellie Emerson, secretary of the Friday Club, writes, "I confess to having been more interested in the sight of the dear, familiar, new-old faces, than at first in the reading," the concern with texts slips to the background, while the social relationship is foregrounded. Several sentences later, Emerson asserts, "The intellectual food proffered by our gracious 'bell ringer' has had often the effect to send me home ready to read and think like a philosopher," thereby confirming how powerfully her social experience with texts affects her private reading, but that sentence is embedded in Emerson's reflections on the importance of the women's associations with one another and their conversations. Emerson's description of her experience typifies accounts given by clubwomen in all social locations. Literacy meant social interaction as well as private activity.[59]

Like medieval communities in which the scarcity of manuscripts necessitated oral reading, some clubs read aloud from the one available text. Scarcity of texts was not the only reason for oral reading, however. During World War I some clubwomen elected to read aloud "notable books of recent years" while "busy fingers fashioned comforts for our soldier boys." In other cases oral reading was a long-standing club tradition.[60] Most commonly pleasure rather than exigency led clubwomen to read aloud. Like Zellie Emerson, they *enjoyed* sharing a common text, pausing to raise questions and make comments about it. Texts read privately by clubwomen also fostered intimacy among members. Solitary reading provides, as Barbara Sicherman has observed, "space—physical, temporal and psychological"—and within this space women, at least momentarily free from gendered expectations and responsibilities, could indulge themselves in intense relationships with words.[61] The emotional engagement with a text, multiplied across many common readers, enhanced the feelings of connection and affection among members as they debated meanings, asked and answered questions, and drew analogies to their lives. Particularly in the 1890s reading literature came to be seen as an intensely emotional experience. Emily Dickinson's reception, as Willis Buckingham notes, highlighted extremely personalized relations between writer and reader.[62] Energy from this kind of reading seeped into club life, flooding it with intimacy.

Club writing also involved many forms of social interaction. Although clubwomen certainly wrote independently on some occasions, they participated in a variety of collaborative writing projects. Several members of Roxbury's Women in Council worked together to draft the Lillias Hazewell memorial resolution cited at the beginning of this chapter, and committees were often assigned to write club documents, such as revisions to the constitution, bylaws, or club histories. At its first meeting, the National Association of Colored Women charged committees with writing resolutions and letters.[63] The Chicago Fortnightly's "practice was to name a committee to write the memorial" for a recently deceased member.[64] Club papers, research-based explorations of topics that members spent as much as a year preparing, involved several kinds of collaboration. Members often shared their personal libraries as they gathered material for writing. As they completed drafts, they sought advice from other members, and some clubs actually mandated sharing, as the Saturday Morning Club did in requiring that paper presenters read their work to the president at least a week before the actual presentation. Response from members designated as "critics" often supplemented more general comments about papers.

Even writing club minutes could involve social interaction. Minutes taken by the secretary were read aloud at the next meeting, and these readings frequently became oral performances, sometimes evoking applause. Secretaries read and referred to earlier activities recorded by a peer. When the task of minute-taking moved from one member to another with each meeting, this collaboration became even more pronounced. One secretary, for example, mused about how to deal with the anxiety of influence: "Shall I allow myself to be carried away by the poetic fancies and melodious measure of a Carlton, or imitate the quaint humorous style of a Robb, steal the deep wisdom and philosophy of a Gibson, or, making *their* best my own, fuse the whole into one gigantic and glorious production, or thus cast suspicion on the originality of their matter and style, since mine must necessarily be the *epitome* of what is best in all?"[65] In her playful way, this secretary asserts that she does not work alone, even though the task of recording something in the "little book" falls to her this particular week. This acknowledgment of the interpersonal dimensions inherent in even the prosaic task of recording club minutes demonstrates the social nature of club writing.

In adapting literacy to their particular circumstances, participating actively—even physically—in reading and writing, extending literacy's gendered boundaries, and emphasizing social interactions with texts, clubwomen developed an ideology of literacy quite distinct from the individualistic, male-dominated, and static version inscribed in the 1917 bill. Most of the qualities embraced by clubwomen's ideology of literacy cluster under the term *intimacy*. Julie Innes defines as intimate an act that "draws its meaning and value from the agent's love, liking, or care" and involves "a choice on the agent's part about how to (or not to) embody her love."[66] Leaving aside the implications of sexuality, since intimacy may or may not involve this dimension, clubwomen's literacy practices embodied their love, liking, and care for one another. Viewed from the distance of another century, the exact nature of their relationships—whether, to use Judith Bennett's term, "lesbian-like," sisterly, or affectionately friendly—

remains unclear, and they were undoubtedly as various as relations among women are today. But the texts they so carefully preserved provide evidence that clubwomen formed strong and enduring attachments to one another.[67]

Clubwomen participated in, as Innes puts it, "the sharing of information about one's actions, beliefs, or emotions which one does not share with all, and which one has the right not to share with anyone," as they read and wrote about their lives. They exchanged information about their experiences as wives and mothers as well as their travels and other experiences outside the home; they shared their religious creeds along with their beliefs about higher education for women, suffrage, and a range of other issues; and they expressed their affection for one another. This intimacy shaped the institutional functionings of women's clubs. According to Innes, intimacy involves "considerations such as consent, fairness and mutuality."[68] The formalities of constitutions, bylaws, and parliamentary procedures (even in relatively small groups) provided a means for consent to be accorded or withheld. Club decisions emphasized benefits accruing to all, and club practices of reciprocity or text exchange extended mutuality from one club to another. Fairness guided most deliberations, and questions of unfairness appear so rarely in record books as to seem remarkable.

One force animating this intimacy derived from clubwomen's common religious heritages, since a majority of clubs were organized around denominational affiliations. Many clubs grew out of church/synagogue groups and sought, particularly in their early days, approval from religious leaders or those who set a high moral tone. Hannah Solomon cited a sermon by Dr. Emil Hirsch, "The Old and the New Woman," in which he argued for women's role in social service, as the impetus for organizing a Jewish Women's Congress, and Rabbi I. F. Leucht offered "wise counsel and encouragement" as the Jewish Woman's Council of New Orleans took shape.[69] Founding members of the white middle-class New England Women's Club invited ministers to its inaugural meeting, and a minister wrote the history of the Ladies' Literary Club of Ypsilanti.[70] Ministers or rabbis numbered among club speakers and visitors, their sermons provided topics of discussion, club meetings were frequently held in church/synagogue buildings, and clubs often opened and/or closed meetings with prayer. The National Association of Colored Women included among its departments the Department of Religious Work and urged members to participate in days of prayer.[71] Mormon clubs frequently received advice from church leaders, devoted many pages of the *Woman's Exponent* and the *Young Woman's Journal* to doctrinal issues, and included such phrases as "Mrs. Lucy Clark offered prayer" in their reports.[72] Even the National League of Women Workers, which specifically declared itself nonsectarian and brought together members from a variety of religious traditions, affirmed the spiritual dimension of club life: "In our club we find food for the three-fold part of us: the physical, the mental, and the spiritual; that is why we love our club so much."[73]

Except in working women's groups, common denominational ties constituted an important source of identity for many clubwomen. Writing in 1892, May Wright Sewall, a former president of the Indianapolis Woman's Club, extolled the "growing tolerance . . . in religious belief" fostered by women's clubs, but she was talking about relations between Methodists and Presbyterians: "I believe that the prevailing friendliness among all Protestant sects, the abatement of local strifes and jealousies,—which formerly separated communities into social sets, the barriers between which coincided with denominational lines,—is due in larger degree to women's clubs than to any other one influence. That the club may accomplish its perfect work in this direction, it is requisite that the Hebrew and the Romanist be brought into our club membership."[74] For the most part, "perfect work" did not emerge, and reaching across Protestant denominations constituted the extent of club ecumenism. Although a few Jewish women, such as Hannah Solomon, a member of the Chicago Woman's Club, joined white Protestant groups, the majority were excluded from such clubs or chose not to ally themselves with them, instead joining local sections of the National Council of Jewish Women. Similarly, Catholic women remained outside white middle-class groups, despite Sewall's pleas for the Romanist.[75] Both geography and popular antipathy toward the practice of polygamy forced Mormon women to form separate religiously based organizations.

Racism made it impossible for African American women to join most white women's clubs, and even though they represented religious traditions ranging from the evangelical Baptist to the more liturgically centered Episcopalian, they shared a common concern for the uplift—in both material and moral terms—of their people. These clubwomen constituted what Carla Peterson describes as a "loosely knit cultural group" in which class boundaries blurred and the lines between high and low remained unclear.[76] What remained clear, however, was the need for blacks to create race-exclusive clubs to address the special circumstances of their lives.

Working women prided themselves in affiliating with diverse individuals: "Most other organizations take their members from one section of the community, from one trade, or from one religious body, but our societies are subject to none of these limitations, and although we meet on a footing where our interests are identical, the lines of our lives are laid in very different places."[77] For these women common interests supplanted other ties, but the fact that working women's clubs did not survive World War I, while other groups did, suggests that ultimately something stronger than common interests—such as shared religious affiliation—was necessary to sustain club loyalties, particularly as unions masculinized labor.[78] Because investigations of women's clubs have focused on their contributions to secular life, the role of religion in both their origins and continuation has remained in the background, even though it is not unusual to trace religion's role in shaping other social formations.[79]

Texts written by and for clubwomen show how their common religion engendered intimacy among them. One text, among many, describes the Women in Council's reaction to the death of its founding president, Lillias Hazewell, in childbirth. Members of the council passed a resolution that began with "Whereas it has pleased the Heavenly Father to remove by sudden death our beloved President . . ." and continued by enumerating Hazewell's qualities of leadership, including unselfishness, zeal, and consideration, before proceeding to the resolution: "Resolved that we endeavor to carry on the work that she has begun by seeking in all things to follow her good example. Resolved that this testimonial be entered upon our record and that a copy be sent to son and husband and to the mourning mother and sisters praying that the loving God will comfort their stricken hearts." This intermingling of the language of their common liberal Protestantism and the language of loss adds intensity to this resolution, making it no surprise that members of the council transformed their grief and affection for Lillias Hazewell into action. Administered by the Memorial Committee, the Hazewell Memorial Trunk provided "tiny garments" and other necessities to babies of "poor unknown mother[s]" each year for the next three decades, recording its beneficence on a printed report that was carefully pasted into the club record book. Few club reports were printed, and in most years only the council's annual report and, sometimes, the report of the nominating committee joined the Memorial Committee report in the print shop. Even during World War I, when many club activities were curtailed, the Memorial Committee carried on "in loving memory of the founder" by providing, in 1919, six outfits and "three for France." Both the sustained enactment and the method of recording of this memorial testify to the strength of the council's commitment to its original resolution, a commitment strengthened by common religious beliefs as well as powerful bonds of affection.[80]

An article published in the *Woman's Exponent* under the title "For My Dear Friend, Camilla C. Cobb, on the Death of Her Darling Gracie" demonstrates how the shared beliefs of Mormon women shaped their prose. After several paragraphs of sympathy for the mother whose daughter's eyes have closed "to open no more in this life," the author urges the mother, "Let all the thoughts of your darlings be of the great happiness they now enjoy, in their heavenly home; how they anxiously await your coming, how they watch over you and love you more and more," reflecting their shared belief in the literal unification of families in the next life and their common reading of the Book of Mormon. After several more paragraphs offering comfort to the bereaved mother, the author closes with a poem full of reassurance that in the afterlife she will "weep no more."[81] In concluding with a poem, the discourse enacts some of the transcendence for which it argues. The shared beliefs of these clubwomen enabled them to address one another from the perspective of shared knowledge, just as clubwomen from other religious traditions did. They could, for example, make reference to their common leader Brigham Young, as did the author who wrote an introduction to Elmina Taylor, president of the Young Ladies' Mutual Improvement Association: "Brigham Young used to say that he was always delighted to find a child with plenty of temper, always adding that the mother's duty was to teach the child how to control that temper. Sister Taylor's life well exemplifies this principle. . . . she possesses a strong will, well controlled." The comparison of Taylor and Young, like the report that they open meetings with a prayer—and, for that matter, the gender politics of assigning temper control to mothers—emerges from their common religion.[82]

A piece that appeared in *National Association Notes* also deals with death, that of club leader Judith Horton's husband. After offering sympathy to Judith and detailing some of her contributions to club work, the author concludes, "Somehow or other I feel that the Master gives no burden to us which he does not give strength equal to it."[83] Reference to a "Master" who does not burden humans with more than they can bear echoes the intersections of belief and life experiences of African American women, for whom racism and poverty created many burdens. It also reminds readers of the Bible, their common text, which contains this idea. By offering sympathy to Judith Horton in these terms, the author summons the traditions she shares with Horton and the thousands of readers of the *Notes*. Records of individual sections of the National Council of Jewish Women resound with references to "Jewish Womanhood" and clubwomen's role in sustaining their religious heritage. The memorial resolution for Bella Goldman, with its stipulation that funds be given to United Jewish Charities and that the superintendent's room there be named for her, demonstrates how their common religious heritage strengthened the ties of affection among these clubwomen. These examples suggest how their shared religious traditions helped clubwomen from a variety of faiths instantiate their ideology of literacy. By using their common languages of belief, the names and terms that carried particular meanings associated with a shared theological discourse, and references to a higher power or an afterlife, clubwomen connected literacy with the affective power of their spiritual lives.

Clubwomen disclosed their religious beliefs and feelings for one another under the cloak of privacy. Privacy means, as Alan Westin puts it, "the claim of individuals, groups, or institutions to determine for themselves when, how and to what extent information about them is communicated to others." Seen in these terms, intimacy does not mean retreat from others. Rather, following the lines of Michael Cooke's description of African American literature, intimacy means engagement, "a recognition of the self in the world . . . an interaction of the self with the world."[84] For clubwomen this meant regulating (or attempting to regulate) the information about them and their activities that circulated to nonmembers. Clubs, in other words, provided spaces where women could exert some *control* over the terms of their representations. This use of privacy does not mean, as I will explain shortly, that women's clubs existed in what has been termed the "private sphere," a space separated from the public realm. Rather, privacy, as Westin describes it, connotes a right (to control), not a location. Record books contain frequent references to clubwomen insisting that their deliberations remain beyond the gaze of nonmembers. Members of the white middle-class Saturday Morning Club of Boston refused to allow any observers in their conversation sessions, the New England Women's Club stipulated that no reporters could be present when they discussed such sensitive issues as Josephine Ruffin's ejection from a convention of the General Federation of Women's Clubs, and members of the Friday Club simply stopped talking when the man of the house entered. African American clubwomen shared their white peers' emphasis on privacy. Mrs. Waldon, president of Denver's Taka Club, reportedly became enraged "when someone told her that some member of the club was talking club news to other than club members and she would find out who it was if it was the last thing she did."[85] Although they were never able to shape entirely the terms of their representation in the press, clubwomen did attempt to control the information about them that appeared in this forum. Clubwomen instituted national publications as one way to exert power over their own representation, to keep private that which they chose not to reveal, and to shape the information that did appear.

For the most part, clubwomen made public their efforts on behalf of social good. They tolerated outsiders' scrutiny of their projects to develop libraries and kindergartens, to improve sanitation and water supplies, and to aid the indigent and ill. However, they typically insisted on keeping their literacy practices private. Papers written for the club might rest in the club archive or circulate to a sister club on reciprocity day, but they would rarely be published in the local newspaper. Titles of books read and discussed by a given club received little public notice, and access to club minutes, financial records, scrapbooks, and yearbooks was carefully regulated. Many clubwomen resisted (and some still resist) giving their records to an archive because they feared losing control of the ways their materials might be used, and individual clubs often allowed only members to have access to club archives.[86] These controls made intimacy possible; by insisting on keeping information about themselves and their activities out of the public view, clubwomen created the spaces in which they could develop intimate relationships with one another.

In addition to exploring the spiritual dimensions of their lives, clubwomen inscribed their feelings for one another in their texts. Such phrases as "the cord that binds our hearts," "deep love and affection," "dear, familiar new-old faces," "our loved President," "feelings of love and sympathetic interest," and "richer for having known and loved her" punctuate club records.[87] Charlotte Perkins Gilman, a writer and frequent speaker at women's clubs at the turn of the century observed, "Clubwomen learn more than to improve the mind; they learn to love each other," thus pointing to the synergy between clubwomen's literacy practices and their intimate connections with one another. Gilman's statement is confirmed by clubwomen themselves as they write that they valued the relations they created with one another at least as much as the self-improvement and community projects they shared. One commentator described a club as "where hearts are fed, where wealth of brains for poverty atone . . . and soul finds touch with soul."[88] Arguing for a small (as opposed to a larger) club, a working woman explained, "We feel we are a family and know one another well. . . . We know one another's joys and sorrows."[89] Another characterized club relations as restoring the "natural human relations that the complicated social life of cities has destroyed."[90] As Paul Tournier has observed, sharing one's inner thoughts constitutes the highest gift of friendship, and clubs nourished such sharing.[91] Indeed, many clubs appear to have deliberately fostered feelings of intimacy among members.

Not only did the rhetoric of club minutes and publications reflect a language of intimacy, but also expressions of dissent and difficulty between members appear to have been deliberately downplayed. In reading hundreds of club records, I found only occasional accounts of disagreements among clubwomen. One of these involved members of the African American Woman's Improvement Club in a dispute about whether to erect one or two buildings on the hospital grounds (the hospital refused to serve colored people at that time) as part of its antituberculosis project: "Mrs. Brown [the president] stated that there are not enough funds for both cottages, but that the club can do as they please with the funds as she intended to give up the work, at which time she tendered her resignation which was read by the secretary Mrs. Hammond." The vice president, who then ran the meeting, temporized, saying that "there is a misunderstanding between the president and the members of the club and that if the President would state her grievance and explain her reasons for resigning, perhaps there might be an adjustment." After further discussion and conciliation, the account of the meeting concludes: "It was then moved by Mrs. Bryand and seconded by Mrs. Porter that the club take her resignation under consideration until next meeting."[92] Even when faced with the confrontational politics of a president's resignation, these clubwomen, like their peers in other women's clubs, chose to ameliorate the situation, and no further mention of Mrs. Brown's resignation appears in the minutes. Members of New York's white Sorosis Club engaged in similar attempts at peacemaking when faced with a conflict about a member's financial responsibility to the club. In eight pages of handwritten text, the minutes detail a special meeting of the Sorosis executive committee to consider "the charges formally preferred by Miss Swayze against Mrs. Almina H. Warner of Brooklyn."[93] Warner, the current treasurer had, according to Swayze, accused her of failing to pay her dues, and Swayze took offense. After testimony from Swayze and several witnesses, and after Swayze had stormed out of the meeting claiming that she intended to resign from the club, the executive committee wrote a conciliating letter to both parties. The strong feelings evident in these two cases and the general tendencies of human nature suggest that these could not have been isolated events. Clubwomen must have disliked and disagreed with one another, but these difficulties were, for the most part, not recorded in the minutes. Instead, clubwomen used literacy to transcend conflicts and reinforce commonalties so that they could stay emotionally connected to one another despite differences in ideas and beliefs.

In addition to excluding most conflicts from their inscriptions of club life, clubwomen adopted other strategies to foster intimacy among members and downplay differences. Julia Ward Howe, writing retrospectively about one of her own clubs, explained "the need of a more intimate and friendly association among the ladies." Accordingly, she informed the board of managers of the New England Women's Club, "Ladies, we must eat and drink something together or we shall never get acquainted with each other." Through sharing at the tea table clubwomen began to know and love one another, much as women in smaller clubs did.[94] Accounts of most club meetings contain references to sharing food, and often commentators pause to comment on the social value of this sharing. The 1911 annual report of the New York Section of the National Council of Jewish Women, for example, includes this: "Besides the Teas after our meetings, which continue to promote sociability, diffuse true Council spirit, and to be generally enjoyed, the New York Section had two social events during the last season."[95] While unremarkable in itself, this statement shows that clubwomen consciously fostered intimacy among members. Although the ritualized sharing of food made clubwomen vulnerable to outsiders' mockery, the sacramental aspects of breaking bread together served to strengthen the ties among members.[96] A number of clubs listed among their purposes the promotion of sisterhood, thus articulating the intentional nature of the warm friendships that developed among club members.

When clubs dealt with such controversial topics as woman suffrage, immigration, imperialism, and war, they often structured their discussions in the form of "debates" so that each side received a hearing without club members' having to take one side or the other. To further avoid controversy, most national associations did not take public stands on contested issues, even though individual members did. When clubs faced a question on which members disagreed, one strategy was to table the discussion. Frequently, the tabled issues never appeared again in the minute books. Clubwomen did not, however, avoid controversial topics when they clearly served the interests of the entire membership. African American clubwomen took a very active role in the antilynching campaign (which, of course, was controversial for other clubwomen); Mormon women worked to achieve Utah statehood and counter attacks on polygamy (a practice that attracted enough public hostility to be named as a disqualifier for immigration in the 1917 bill); working women cooperated with labor unions to achieve better working conditions (unions were viewed with considerable suspicion by other clubwomen); and the National Council of Jewish Women worked against anti-Semitism in all of its sections (other clubwomen often expressed anti-Jewish sentiments).

Clubwomen appropriated, both literally and figuratively, the intimacy of the mother-daughter relationship. Membership lists of many clubs show that daughters frequently joined their mother's clubs, often taking leadership roles.[97] Even where relationships among clubwomen were not literally maternal, the emotional ties among members emulated what Carroll Smith-Rosenberg has described as the "intense devotion and identification between mothers and daughters."[98] More common still, clubs employed maternal language to describe their activities. Mary Church Terrell, speaking at the fiftieth anniversary of the National Association of Colored Women, described the association as "the tiny baby which I and other women mothered on July 21st, 1896" who had developed into "a full grown woman fifty years old working diligently to promote the welfare of her race. . . . To begin with, she had two mothers. One of them was Mrs. Booker T. Washington, who lived in Tuskegee, Alabama, and was president of the Afro American Federation of Women's Clubs. The other was Mrs. Helen Cook, who lived in Washington and was president of the National Colored Woman's League which was organized in 1892."[99] The Denver Section of the National Council of Jewish Women reported its membership this way: "Certainly there are no daughters of which the mother may be more proud than of Denver. We number one hundred and twenty-five members."[100] White Protestant clubwomen emulated this use of the mother figure, describing as club "mothers" the colonial Bible study mentor Anne Hutchinson, the 1840s conversation leader Margaret Fuller Ossoli, and the woman's rights advocate Julia Ward Howe, among others.[101] Both Sorosis and the New England Women's Club claimed the designation "the mother of clubs" as they argued about which of them could be described as the first woman's club.[102] Members of established clubs like these frequently helped younger women establish "daughter" clubs.[103] Among the "daughters" spawned by women's clubs were college women's literary societies. Even though clubs often were described as the "colleges" of women (particularly those who reached college age before 1890) to whom higher education was largely unavailable, clubs provided an intimacy women found missing in their college classes, and many college women created campus clubs to compensate for this lack.[104] These widespread practices of portraying clubs in maternal terms, tracing the matrilineal sources of clubs, and seeking clublike experiences on college campuses fostered intimacy. Clubs, both locally and nationally, took on highly personal qualities. Not only did clubwomen enjoy intimate friendships with one another, but also they imbued their literacy practices with terms of intimacy.

Large clubs (with fifty or more members) typically created smaller "departments" that focused on such topics as literature, social welfare, or art and functioned much as small clubs did, meeting in intimate groups and sharing personal as well as intellectual concerns. While expressions of affection no doubt emerged spontaneously in texts created in small clubs, the language of intimacy that appeared in national publications of various club associations might have been more calculated. The *Woman's Era* and *National Association Notes* published announcements of clubwomen's marriages, travels, and family affairs so regularly that the column about the death of Judith Horton's husband would not have seemed unusual to readers accustomed to seeing public condolences for private grief.

Although *Far and Near* and the *Club Worker* published less about individual members (in part because these publications had fewer pages), both included considerable information about club activities, including descriptions such as the one from the Friendly Workers describing their rooms as "more a *home* than a class-room." A column in *Far and Near* asserted, "Much has been written of the love between man and woman, but not so much of the love of women for one another."[105] One way *Far and Near* and the *Club Worker* tried to foster "the love of women for one another" was through direct communication from and information about the incumbent executive secretary of the League of Women Workers. The travels of this individual, like the circulation of club texts, enabled clubwomen to share ideas and experiences.

When Romania Bunnell Pratt, the outgoing president of the Utah Woman's Press Club, recounted the high points of her term, the surprise celebration in honor of Emmeline B. Wells figured prominently. Pratt's account, first delivered as a club paper and subsequently published in the *Woman's Exponent* shows how Mormon clubwomen gave tangible form to their warm affection for one of their number *and* how they represented it to a wider audience. Emmeline Wells, who served as honorary president of the club, was credited with founding both the Press Club and the Reapers' Club, and edited the *Woman's Exponent* for much of its existence, functioned as a "mother of clubs" in the intermountain region. Like Julia Ward Howe, she worked tirelessly on behalf of women's rights throughout her long life and traveled extensively to meet with clubwomen in other parts of the country. The carefully planned party to celebrate both book and birthday demonstrates the affectionate appreciation in which members held Wells. By publishing a detailed account of the "love and good wishes" expressed in the "unique and costly memento" presented to Wells by her "loving friends," Pratt extended this rhetoric of intimacy to readers throughout the territories of Utah and Arizona and other parts of the West.[106]

The *General Federation of Women's Clubs Magazine* and its various predecessors also made such a regular practice of using intimate rhetoric to profile officers that an article describing the recently deceased May Alden Ward as "always present, sweet, calm, gentle and dignified" and claiming that "to have known and loved her and to have shared in her friendship will always be a precious memory" did not appear unusual. At the time this article was published, the magazine circulated to over one million women in nine thousand clubs, but the highly affectionate and personal memorial statement resembled the one written about her by her own Boston club. Significantly, the picture included with the written text shows Ward surrounded by five other clubwomen, and the physical proximity of their bodies and the extension of their hands in this photograph reinforce the emotional connections between the deceased and other clubwomen.[107]

Whether the rhetoric of intimacy in these national journals resulted from explicit editorial policies or simply represented a spontaneous overflow of the warm feelings engendered by the close associations of local club groups does not matter. The effect was the same in either event: By using the language of intimacy familiar to clubwomen in local settings, national publications helped create warm feelings of connection among large constituencies. Reading and writing for these publications helped individuals see themselves as part of an "invisible community" that extended across time and space, making them part of an "all-together" experience.

In addition to fostering a sense of connection among clubwomen, the intersection of literacy and intimacy led clubs to historicize themselves. The tradition of keeping minutes of meetings immediately established a past for all clubs, since members could look at the written record of what had transpired at meetings one or ten or thirty years ago. This practice was enacted with a conscious awareness of its historical import, as this note from a reluctant secretary indicates: "An intense regard for the future reputation of the members of this club brings this sacrifice from me. Who knows that this small and seemingly insignificant checkered book may not be resurrected in some future age, carefully read and examined."[108] *Far and Near,* the journal of the National League of Women Workers, voiced a similar sense of the historical value of its work: "We wonder if all of us appreciate the greatness of the movement of which each Working Girls' club is an integral part and that we as members are helping to make the history of the last half of the nineteenth century."[109]

Clubwomen also created their own archives, preserving copies of yearbooks and annual programs, clippings of newspaper articles, papers delivered by members, and a variety of other club documents. In 1910 the outgoing president of the California Federation recommended the establishment of a bureau of information to deal with the "accumulation of printed matter, yearbooks, programs and records of past years' work, in the nature of the archives of our organization."[110] Frequently such archives served as resources for club histories complied at a later date. The 1902 *History of the National Association of Colored Women* consists of documents produced by conventions held in Boston and Washington, D.C., in 1895 and 1896 respectively. In addition to minutes from the meetings, this history includes Josephine Ruffin's call for the 1895 meeting, convention programs, letters and resolutions produced by committees working at the conventions, officers' speeches, poems composed for each occasion, treasurers' reports, reports from member clubs, and a directory of member clubs and delegates from each. In collecting and printing these documents a half dozen years after the conventions, the National Association of Colored Women indicated the value it assigned to preserving its own records in a form that could be widely distributed and that carried more prestige than handwritten copies of the texts.

This impulse toward historicizing their own clubs existed in both national and local organizations. In 1907 the Utah Woman's Press Club recounted its history in the *Woman's Exponent,* and in 1911 Susan Gates published a history of other Mormon groups; the National Council of Jewish Women published a history in 1924; and the National League of Women Workers published its history in 1914. Jennie Cunningham Croly's 1898 *History of the Woman's Club Movement in America* dealt mainly with the General Federation of Women's Clubs, and a number of other histories of the federation succeeded it. Local clubs exhibited similar energy in developing their own histories. Club anniversaries provided opportunities to write and publish histories and to produce plays that recreated important club events or featured founding members' reminiscences. Clubwomen often showed foresight in thinking about their own history. After writing a brief history of the El Paso Woman's Club in 1909, President Fennell "recommended that an historian be appointed to write a history of the club from its birth. Mrs. Fennell also supplied most of the yearbooks of the early years, making it possible for the club to have a complete file of yearbooks."[111] Texts generated by such occasions became part of the club archive and provided material for the next anniversary, so that the history clubwomen created for themselves entered into a continually evolving narrative of the group's ability to sustain and perpetuate itself.

In the process of historicizing themselves, clubwomen called on the authority of print. These printed histories bound members, past, present and future, into a stream of anecdotes, personal reminiscences, and details of accomplishments that reminded them of the continuing legacies and responsibilities of the club. At the same time, club insignia, mottoes, photographs of members, variations in type face, careful attention to layout of text, and decorative designs all worked against the impersonality of print. Clubwomen thus constructed for themselves an alternative (personal and intimate) ideology of print that shaped their own representations.[112]

Another form of self-historicizing appeared in club resolutions and memorials to the deceased and the various other efforts to honor members after they died, such as when the Detroit Section of the National Council of Jewish Women established the Bella Goldman Room and Roxbury's Women in Council created the Hazewell Memorial Trunk. These texts and symbols can be read as trivial products of sentimentalism, but they can also be read in more radical terms as gestures toward immortalizing clubwomen. In a culture that encouraged and expected self-effacement from women, any attempts to honor and dignify women's nonmaternal achievements risked censure. Within clubs, however, women could, with both words and physical objects, immortalize their sisters.

Clubwomen focused on strategy as much as sentiment. Through linking their literacy practices with intimacy, they coped with the pervasive sexism (and racial and ethnic prejudice) that dogged their lives. As subordinate groups (often on more than one dimension), clubs in various social locations used intimacy strategically, creating the "supportive female networks" that Barbara Sicherman describes as enabling women to "overcome some of the confines of gender and class."[113] When they formed and met in clubs, women at the turn of century recognized that, as Hannah Solomon, founder of the National Council of Jewish Women, observed, "to join an organization of 'women'—not ladies—and one which bore the title 'club,' rather than 'society,' was in itself a radical step," and that their individual desires to participate in clubs frequently met with social censure. Clubwomen faced this censure strengthened by their affective connections with one another, living out the meaning that Caroline Severance, president of the General Federation of Women's Clubs, attributed to the word *club:* "to embrace," "to adhere."[114] The networks of intimacy they created through their literacy practices helped clubwomen deal with—and change—the disjunctures between societal expectations and their own desires for education, new roles, and entry into other areas of public life.

In contrast to the ideology of literacy embodied in the 1917 immigration bill, clubwomen developed ideologies of literacy that foregrounded intimate social interactions, symmetry between reading and writing, physicality, and gender equity. Rather than a force for exclusion, this alternative construction of literacy enabled what Anthony Giddens describes as a "wholesale democratizing of the interpersonal domain, in a manner fully compatible with democracy in the public sphere." When clubwomen inscribed ways of sharing leadership, negotiating the distribution of tasks, and finding equitable ways of dealing with their economic resources, they enacted an interpersonal democracy that supplied a model for practices in the larger community of the nation.[115] With these literacy practices clubwomen could address such larger social issues as Americanization, consumerism, constructions of womanhood, definitions of culture, and professionalism. In so doing, they engaged in cultural work that included examining social reality, dramatizing conflicts, and redefining the social order. Intimacy infused these continuing textual negotiations with special power because the warmly supportive environments of clubs gave members the capacity to imagine new possibilities for themselves, to change their desires.

Clubwomen at the turn of the century belonged to an alternative public. Prohibited from voting, attending many colleges, and assuming most professional roles because of their gender, they nevertheless insisted on probing the pressing issues of their time. Clubwomen constituted what Kathryn Kish Sklar has described as "women's public culture," a culture marked by essentialist views of women, a use of religious justification, and its difference from men's public culture.[116] This was especially true for clubwomen who occupied stigmatized racial, ethnic, or religious positions. Within their clubs, members undertook literacy practices that often included sharing critiques of the dominant culture. Creating what James Scott describes as "hidden transcripts," or "discourse that takes place 'offstage,' beyond direct observation by powerholders," clubwomen examined and criticized existing social formations.[117] Sustained and emboldened by their own languages, they often moved from critiquing to developing and implementing alternatives to the status quo.

That clubwomen carried out these projects in a context of intimacy did not diminish their public effect. As Nancy Fraser has observed, intimate personal life need not be excluded from legitimate public contestation.[118] Their common reading material—both that written by professional authors and selections by clubmembers—enabled clubwomen to share on both subjective and social levels. Reading and writing connected the consciousnesses of clubwomen, and within the spaces so created, women could articulate and explore new desires. Clubwomen wanted different things, depending on their social locations, but for all clubwomen literacy connected with social and political struggles to transform the goals and conditions of their lives. The ideology of literacy they adopted, in other words, included the belief that their own production and consumption of texts could change material circumstances, and they articulated their belief in their own capacity to effect transformations.[119] Linking literacy with intimacy and enacting practices that reflected their situated ideologies, clubwomen developed their own educational programs, social reform projects, and historical traditions. Careful reading of the texts clubwomen produced and consumed in enacting these programs provides insight, however partial, into some of the ways these (extra)ordinary women both fostered and resisted the cultural transformations of their age, how they produced and consumed discourses that enabled them to explore and change social formations.

2

Constructing and Contesting Americanization(s)

⟡⟶⟩⟨⟵⟡

⟶⟩ Fifty four members of the club and their friends listened to a paper by Mrs. Julia Ward Howe on Alien Races in America, the Club having prepared itself for the subject by agreeing to dress two dolls as ancient Greeks and send them West to a fair for which Mrs. Howe promised them. She said that old maxim America for Americans has made way for the new law of impartiality. We are not yet up to the idea of America. There is no chosen people; the Earth is the Lord's. We have difficulties with the question of immigration which our forefathers had not. Foreigners were few then; they are in hordes now. We must take into account the good points of these aliens and their bad ones. How are we to direct our moral capital to the place needed? There are many dangerous elements in the Italian immigrants, as an example, and we cannot afford to import crime. Yet there are noble Italians here, and the best is not preempted by birth, fortune or profession. At Chautauqua Mrs. Howe saw a promise of salvation for America in the cultivation of the good sense of the people. She thought the plan of the Chautauqua classes could be extended so as to reach a lower station of society than at present. College settlements are doing much now, Indian and Negro colleges are forming, the poor whites are assisted to read. But provision should be made for the political ignorance of the aliens here, investigations into the knowledge of voters—the restraining hand of discipline be laid on our upper classes and we should try to reach the best of the immigrants and as in all ways fulfill the unifying idea of the Pentecost where was neither Jew nor Greek, neither bond nor free but a new creature.

Minutes of the Saturday Morning Club of
Boston, 1891

⤳ To summarize briefly, the thoughts of this paper, woman's duty to her country as an individual is:

First, to develop the qualities of loyalty and fidelity in herself and then to develop them in her children.

Secondly, in all outside life, publicly and socially to be really loyal to America and its institutions. Especially in coming in contact with those who, though living under the protection of our government are alien, through ignorance or prejudice, to her interests.

Lastly, to recognize ourselves, in our clubs and associations, as actual parts of a movement which may even influence the history of the coming century.

Let us become more and more united, therefore, in working for one grand cause, and let us bring as many as we can to the recognition of this great new fellowship, so that when the prophesied social crisis comes, among us, at least, there shall be neither rich nor poor, wage-earner nor member of any leisure class, but we shall be all working women together to make the world's revolution a peaceful one.

EMILY MALBOURNE MORGAN,
"A Woman's Duty to Her Country,"
Far and Near, 1892

⤳ Politics has been from girlhood an interesting subject to me. . . . I read Daniel Webster's Speeches, the "Union Text Book" of our American Statesmen including the Constitution and Declaration of Independence, and many other works like John Stuart Mill "On Liberty" and the more I read, the more I felt the *positive necessity* of woman being not only a wife and mother in name, but *in very deed.* Intellectually strong, brave, wise, prudent, efficient and capable.

J. P. M. FARNSWORTH,
"Written for the U.W.P.C.R.C.W.S.A. Reception,"
Woman's Exponent, 1893

↔ None but fools seriously believe that the colored people of the United States can be colonized without their consent. Their deportation would bankrupt the government. . . . It is a physical and legal impossibility to deport the colored people. It is not impossible to keep out of the country the riffraff of other countries who owe no allegiance to man or God, who are opposed to any government that compels them to work for a living, and to observe and not encroach upon the rights of other men. The audacity of foreigners who flee their native land and seek refuge here, many of them criminals and traitors, who are here but a day before they join in the hue and cry against the native born citizens of this land is becoming intolerable. No government upon earth would permit it but the United States, and all the signs of the time point to a time not far off where self defense and self protection will force this government to protect its own people and to teach foreigners that this land is for Americans black or white and that other men are welcome and can come here only by behaving themselves and steering clear of plots and schemes against the people and the citizens who are here by right.

"The Difficulties of Colonization,"
Woman's Era, 1894

↔ The American Jews of to-day (and by these are not meant the oppressed Russian exiles who find a home here, but the descendants of the earlier settlers throughout the country) hold positions of influence and culture, commingle with the other citizens of the United States in all vital questions, and are in reality lost sight of as Jews, excepting in religious belief. They exert a healthful influence over immigrants from other countries, in which oppression has been the lot of their brethren, and although we occasionally hear of a wave of antisemitism in civilized countries, nevertheless persecutions cannot become general in our enlightened age, nor endure for any length of time.

PAULINE HANAUER ROSENBERG,
"Influence of the Discovery of America on the Jews,"
Papers of the Jewish Women's Congress, 1894

↔ Americanization and citizenship are two identical words to the majority of the American born citizens. Under conditions as they now exist, the two words are as far apart as the North and South pole. We

have only been interested in making a citizen of the immigrant in order that he may vote and do our menial labor, never realizing that 1000 unthinking votes bear just as much weight at the polls as do that number of votes of a thinking farmer or men in industries. It has taken a war like the terrible conflict that is now going on to make us seriously ask: Are all of our voting citizens Americanized?

GRACE RAYMOND HEBARD,
"Americanization of the Immigrant,"
General Federation of Women's Clubs Magazine, **1917**

~⊶≡◦≡⊷~

THE 1886 publication of Josiah Strong's *Our Country* galvanized white Protestant America. Selling over 175,000 copies between 1886 and 1916, Strong's book outlined the perils facing the nation where "many American citizens are not Americanized," and it delivered a message comparable in power to that of *Uncle Tom's Cabin.*[1] Published for the American Home Missionary Society, *Our Country* conflated evangelical Protestant religious fervor with the doctrine of Anglo-Saxonism, a belief that those who descended from certain northern European stock possessed the superior capacities of intellect, energy, and aggressiveness that qualified them to lead the nation and "exercise the commanding influence in the world's future."[2] Strong's voice was among the more forceful, but many others joined it as such events as the 1886 Haymarket riot, which suggested connections among urban problems, the presence of immigrants, and industrial strikes, underscored the urgency of addressing the perils *Our Country* identified. Clubwomen from various social locations joined the ensuing Americanization discourses—fostering, resisting, and modifying Strong's message—thereby helping to construct new meanings for the term *American.*

To the extent that clubwomen have been credited with participating in Americanization projects, they have been portrayed as white middle-class women paying "friendly Americanizing visits to immigrant homes" or mounting patriotic pageants or supporting the war effort by raising money, knitting or sewing, and providing entertainment and support services for soldiers.[3] Such characterizations of clubwomen's participation in Americanization overlook the wide range of clubwomen's social locations and the many ways their literacy practices both constructed and contested Americanization. The term *American-*

ization is sometimes used to describe projects carried out by the National Americanization Committee under the leadership of Frances Kellor between 1916 and 1920, but here it refers to the longer-term and more complicated projects that over a period of several decades attempted to (re)connect individuals with the abstract construct of the nation state. The dominant form of Americanization drew on Strong's book by taking a racist, exclusionary, and elitist perspective on citizenship, putting white Protestant Anglo-Saxon males at the top of the national hierarchy, and insisting that immigrants attempt to emulate that model. As Priscilla Wald has observed, this version of Americanization's efforts at assimilation "used the traditional American family as both metaphor and medium." Educational programs in schools and settlement houses encouraged simulation or replication of the American family through training, followed by a return to the ethnic community, where the gendered family structure could be reproduced.[4]

Clubwomen, for whom the traditional family structure loomed large, produced and consumed texts that explored the ideas surrounding Americanization. Taking pride in their contributions to the nation, some (mostly white middle-class women) advocated the dominant form without reservation. Testimony to the self-awareness with which they proceeded appears in a club president's claim that "the general federation [of women's clubs] will lift women out of the provincial limitations which induce sectionalism, into the national perceptions which secure patriotism."[5] Clubwomen from other backgrounds frequently resisted the (for them) unattainable model of Americanization, preferring to substitute another of their own making.

A wide variety of clubwomen participated in the Americanization project, varying their perspectives according to the social positions—shaped by class, race, religion, and, of course, gender—they occupied. In addition to reflecting its author's position, each text explored discourses within the culture, articulated problems facing the nation, and proposed solutions for these problems. To accomplish this, clubwomen interacted with the discourses and social formations of the larger culture through their literacy practices, creating what Benedict Anderson calls print communities in which they imagined alternatives to the status quo.[6] Through their circulation of texts, clubwomen occupying similar social positions, such as white working-class laborers, could, while remaining physically distant from one another—in Boston or New York or Pittsburgh—create communities in which together they imagined their own version of the United States.

The summary of Julia Ward Howe's speech to the Saturday Morning Club reflects Josiah Strong's Anglo-Saxonism, with its disdain for and fear of Italians and all others who did not trace their ancestors to the British Isles, a position embraced by the Americanization efforts of the white middle class.[7] By invoking Chautauqua, a program of (literacy) education rooted in the Methodist church, as the "means of salvation" and commending settlement houses, "Indian and Negro colleges," and literacy programs for "poor whites," this account simultaneously reinforces the importance of reading and writing to the assimilation of alien others and asserts the Anglo-Saxonist need to replace southern or eastern European heritages with white, middle-class, Protestant, and British-identified ones. In describing the club's preparation of dolls dressed as ancient Greeks, Howe suggests both the exoticism assigned to southern Europeans and the possibility of including "the best of the immigrants" in a reconceptualized America, particularly when they represent the classical traditions of Western society, as "noble Italians" do. The tension—exemplified in the inclusiveness of "There is no chosen people" and the restrictiveness of "we cannot afford to import crime"—between embracing and spurning immigrants permeates this account, suggesting the ambivalence with which these white middle-class clubwomen viewed the burgeoning immigration of the 1890s. While this tension between accepting and rejecting immigrants remains unresolved, the admonition that "we should try to reach the best" reinforces the idea of transforming or Americanizing them to emulate the Anglo-Saxon model.[8]

Clubwomen in other social locations resisted this race- and class-based model of Americanization and offered their own alternatives. "A Woman's Duty to Her Country," Emily Malbourne Morgan's paper quoted at the beginning of this chapter, represents one alternative. While Morgan urges loyalty to the nation, she evades Anglo-Saxon terms. Instead, she assumes that women from various backgrounds can be equally patriotic. The movement from the personal and domestic sphere—where the woman's role as mother who develops national loyalty "in her children" takes precedence—to the public sphere—where one encounters those who are "alien"—suggests a broad view of women's participation in nation-building, a perspective reinforced by Morgan's assertion that working women's clubs "may even influence the history of the coming century." In suggesting that working women—immigrant and native-born, Christian and Jewish—will play a role in the future of the nation, Morgan articulates a view of Americanization that differs from the one offered by Julia Ward Howe's dismissive comments about aliens and "poor whites," and she underlines this difference with her concluding statements about "working for one grand cause." Rather than the elitist Anglo-Saxon model, Morgan advocates an inclusive perspective that unites women across social classes and avoids social disruptions by looking to the common goal of a peaceful "world's revolution." Instead of the tension between inclusion and exclusion that characterizes Howe's account, Morgan emphasizes unity among diverse groups, insisting that one (privileged) group does not have the monopoly on loyalty to the nation.[9]

Still another perspective appears in the paper written by J. P. M. Farnsworth for a joint meeting of the Reapers' Club, the Utah Woman's Press Club, and the Woman Suffrage Association. In addition to making clear her position on woman suffrage, Farnsworth affirms the "American" heritage she shares with her audience as she describes her reading of "our American Statesmen" as well as the Constitution and the Declaration of Independence. Farnsworth's assertions seem innocuous enough until we consider the circumstances in which she wrote. In 1891 Utah still sought statehood. Mormons, who wished to practice their religion—including polygamy—without interference, preferred the relative autonomy of statehood over that of territory (which allowed federal intervention in local affairs), but the U.S. government balked at granting statehood to a region that countenanced polygamy.[10] Both women and men in the territory recognized the need to enhance the image of their religion if Utah were to achieve statehood. Josiah Strong's *Our Country* described Mormonism as one of the perils facing the nation. According to Strong, this "hideous caricature of the Christian religion," which sought to "hold the reins of the United States government," saw an opportunity for leadership in potential dissolution of the Union in the Civil War, and after the war it continued to extend its despotic power through its "systematic colonization."[11] In claiming the heritage of such figures as Daniel Webster and such documents as the Constitution and in blurring the terms of "our American statesmen," Farnsworth, as well as the clubwomen who heard or read her paper, resisted an Anglo-Saxonist Americanization that would exclude Mormons and insinuated the territory of Utah into the nation by inscribing themselves into its traditions.[12]

"The Difficulties of Colonization," which appeared in the *Woman's Era* and is quoted above, resists Josiah Strong's Anglo-Saxonism by urging that behavior and birthplace rather than race define Americans. Although the author shares Howe's concern about immigrants, her brave insistence that it is impossible to "deport the colored people" betrays the vulnerable race-constituted position she occupies, particularly in contrast to Howe's situation of established privilege. Howe might have been concerned about the kinds of people the tides of immigration washed up on the shores of the nation, but she and her peers faced no threat of deportation. The colonization movement, fostered by the American Colonization Society (founded in 1816) proposed to send African Americans to establish colonies in Africa. This movement, which remained active until

1909, exerted particular social force between 1873 and 1903, providing a forum for white racists who "touted colonization as the final alternative to either 'mongrelization' of whites or 'extermination' of blacks."[13] As the author of "The Difficulties of Colonization" makes clear, this project angered African Americans, who felt they had legitimate claims as "native born citizens" and who recognized the economic as well as "physical and legal impossibility" of deporting them. By establishing an opposition between the immigrant "riffraff . . . who owe no allegiance to man or God" and her own "native born" people who behave themselves and insisting that "this land is for Americans black or white," this author defines the nation in terms that include African Americans as "citizens who are here by right."[14]

Similarly, Pauline Hanauer Rosenberg's paper presented to the Jewish Women's Congress in 1893 argues that "American Jews" play an important part in "vital questions" that face the nation. In distinguishing between the "earlier settlers" and the more recently arrived "oppressed Russian exiles," Rosenberg echoes the author of "The Difficulties of Colonization" in proposing length of residence rather than race or religion as identifying an American. As an alternative to Strong's Anglo-Saxon model, Rosenberg suggests that (assimilated) Jews are especially well suited to "exert a healthful influence" over their immigrant brethren because they "commingle with the other citizens" and are "lost sight of as Jews, excepting in religious beliefs." In highlighting cultural features rather than religious beliefs, Rosenberg creates a division between the more recently arrived Russian Jews and those who have assumed "positions of influence" within the nation. Religion thus ceases to function as the identifying feature for citizens, and Jewish women who hold "positions of influence and culture" can transform newly arrived immigrants into fully Americanized individuals. Still, in mentioning the occasional "wave of antisemitism," Rosenberg acknowledges that the position of Jews, like that of African Americans, remains tenuous in the face of continuing prejudices that question their right to citizenship.[15]

In producing and consuming such texts, clubwomen participated in the creation of what Lauren Berlant calls a "national fantasy." "Fantasy," as Berlant explains, describes how "national culture becomes local—through the images, narratives, monuments and sites that circulate through personal/collective consciousness." Berlant describes as "National Symbolic" the tangled cluster of juridical, territorial, genetic, linguistic, experiential, and political spaces of the nation, and she argues that in addition to regulating citizens' lives through law, the National Symbolic aims to "link regulation to desire, harnessing affect to political life through the production of 'national fantasy.'"[16] Although Berlant focuses on literature as one means of producing this kind of national fantasy, I argue that the literacy practices carried out in the intimate settings of women's clubs constitute another. Reading and writing about their own versions of the United States provided clubwomen ways of exploring their affective connections with the nation. Monuments such as the "Blue" and "Gray" soldiers' graves that gave the Civil War local significance in Utah; images such as African colonization, a world revolution of workers, and anti-Semitism "in civilized countries" that connected personal fears with national movements; and narratives about college settlements and Chautauqua that offered the hope of transformation—all of these linked the regulated life of the nation with the emotional lives of individual clubwomen. Similarly, in their common reading and writing about the problems of urbanization, industrialization, and immigration—three of the "perils" Josiah Strong identified as most threatening—clubwomen developed personal and emotional connections with these national issues, always, of course, shaped by the perspectives of their particular social locations.

Between 1880 and 1920 the United States shifted from a predominantly rural nation in which three-quarters of the population lived on farms or in villages of less than four thousand to one in which more than 50 percent of the population lived in cities. For advocates of Americanization, the shift to an urban population posed a threat to the nation. Josiah Strong's *Our Country* described the city as a "menace to . . . civilization," a place where threats to the nation—immigration, Catholicism, secularism, intemperance, socialism, and excessive wealth—were "enhanced and . . . focalized."[17] Many of Strong's contemporaries echoed his views. While titillating readers with salacious accounts of prostitution, adultery, and "assignation houses," J. W. Buell's *Metropolitan Life Unveiled* described cities as filled with "abominations which curse humanity" and being "exceptionally full of iniquity."[18]

Although Mormon clubwomen, for whom urbanization remained largely irrelevant, paid little attention to these issues, other white middle-class women's clubs often reflected this negative view of urbanization in their texts. One illustration of how these clubwomen viewed urban areas appears in their discussions of library projects. The Nineteenth Century Club of Oak Park, Illinois, like many of its peers, maintained several traveling libraries to provide books to communities that had no ready access to reading materials, and an 1899 club report includes this: "Owing to the failure of the library commission bill in our recent legislature, the state of Illinois is without any system of library supervision and extension. Realizing the value of good reading matter in the mental and moral betterment of the city and the great good to be accomplished by taking the best from the outside world to the country people and in order to extend the influence of our club along educational and philanthropic lines, it seems advisable to inaugurate a system of traveling libraries."[19] The unnamed author of this report reinscribes Americanization's preference for the rural over the urban. In suggesting that city residents will receive "mental and moral betterment" from "good reading matter," this writer implies that residents of Chicago, unlike their rural counterparts, lack appropriate mental and moral qualities and must be improved by the "good" texts the Nineteenth Century Club provides. Fostering literacy to improve individual residents of the city will lead, in turn, to the "betterment of the city." Country residents, by contrast, apparently have no mental or moral deficiencies but will simply receive a generalized "great good" from reading "the best." While the mental and moral qualities of urban readers must be somehow transformed or changed, this report implies that country readers need only be improved. These clubwomen assign transformative power to reading, and by using such terms as *good* and *the best,* they imply that certain individuals (such as members of their Nineteenth Century Club) should regulate the literacy practices of others. At the same time, it demonstrates how some white middle-class clubwomen reinforced a bias against urbanization.

The editor of "The Book Table" column in the *Federation Bulletin,* the official publication of the General Federation of Women's Clubs, includes in her selections Wilbert Anderson's *Country Town* (1906), and she opens her review with the observation that country communities are in a "very bad way" because "following upon the rural revolution brought about by the introduction of machinery have come the depletion of population and social deterioration."[20] Positioned first among the half-dozen books reviewed in a journal with a circulation of several hundred thousand, *The Country Town* surely attracted a readership among clubwomen throughout the nation and might well have served as a source for clubwomen's papers that dealt with national problems.[21] Anderson's concern about urbanization and the resulting depopulation of the countryside echoes other commentators, but the inclusion of his book in a *Bulletin* review demonstrates that white middle-class clubwomen, in their reading as well as their writing, took the issue of urbanization—along with Americanization—as their own. They acquired this at some cost because, as Michael Kimmel has observed, hostile males portrayed the city as an embodiment of female attempts to domesticate the world.[22]

Such textual enactments conform to Michael Olneck's description of the

Americanization project itself, as "an effort to secure cultural and ideological hegemony through configuration of the symbolic order."[23] Those who stood to benefit most from it, such as white middle-class clubwomen, reinforced an Americanization that privileged their own race and class positions. The widely circulated *Federation Bulletin* provided one forum for this project. Articles in this journal frequently reflected an Americanization that enabled white middle-class clubwomen to claim for themselves the cultural power of its discourse. "The Real America," a column initiated by the *Bulletin* in 1905, offered a "monthly review of current and recent literature which is unusually significant in portraying American life," and it frequently raised alarms about "the rising tendencies in our recent life which are antagonistic to the existing order, and if unchecked would become subversive of them."[24]

Concern about possible changes in the status quo, the potential for corruption, and the moral and intellectual superiority of Anglo-Saxon ancestors reverberated in white middle-class clubs across the country. Records of the California Federation include a speech Mrs. George Law Smith wrote in 1904 that urged, "Let us not lose sight of the fact that we have a responsibility to see that true citizenship forms part of the curriculum of schools. We should unite in the cultivation of patriotism, whose only rival should be love of home."[25] In 1919 the General Federation of Women's Clubs adopted and subsequently published a resolution on Americanization that urged "the conservation, development and absorption of American ideals of national, civic, and social life, particularly among the foreign born," and it urged club Americanization workers to help develop a "higher conception of citizenship."[26] The General Federation also encouraged Americanization through pageantry, calling on the expert Hazel MacKaye to write for the national magazine.[27] In articulating the rhetoric and rituals by which Americans could be recognized, white middle-class clubwomen helped limit "the field of legitimate action and choice" for those—including African American, working-class, and non-Protestant clubwomen—they sought to transform.[28]

Although white middle-class clubwomen frequently tried to control the terms used to discuss urbanization, clubwomen from other social locations offered important challenges and resistance to their rhetoric. White working-class clubwomen (both Jewish and Christian), along with their Mormon and African American sisters, resisted definitions of urbanization that featured them as problems to be solved. African American clubwomen developed textual strategies for improving the quality of city life and announced the benefits cities provided for people of their race. Jewish clubwomen used similar means to reduce the "otherness" of their recently arrived sisters. Working women, to whom cities offered opportunities for employment, challenged the dominant discourse by undertaking self-improvement projects.

While African American clubwomen often addressed the effects of urbanization, they took a different approach, frequently employing literacy to document the degradations of racism. Members of the Neighborhood Union of Atlanta, for example, undertook a survey that had a written description of each household in a specified area. When the Neighborhood Union began its work in 1908, there were no social service agencies for African Americans in Atlanta, and members—armed with questionnaires about the number of children in the household, home ownership, and employment of adults—gathered information about their neighborhoods so that help could be provided as needed. Similarly, when the Neighborhood Union sought to redress problems of overcrowding and unsanitary conditions in segregated schools, they carried out a "careful inspection of the public schools for Negroes" by visiting each school and recording answers to questions about enrollment, teacher compensation, and supplies.[29] Lugenia Hope, a founding member of the Neighborhood Union and the wife of Atlanta University's president, had worked with Jane Addams at Hull-House before moving to Atlanta and corresponded with her thereafter. Hope avoided focusing on the evils of the city and instead concentrated on ways to alleviate specific difficulties imposed by urbanization.[30] In doing so, Hope reinscribed the dominant culture's construction of urbanization as an abstract problem into specific challenges individual city dwellers faced.

For many African American clubwomen, cities represented attractive sites of opportunity not available in the rural South, and a majority of African American women's clubs developed in urban centers.[31] In response to the Jim Crow legislation passed in southern states during the 1880s and 1890s and the employment opportunities offered by increased industrialization during the early decades of the twentieth century, half a million African Americans migrated from the rural South to cities in the North.[32] As this voluntary movement suggested, many African Americans saw cities in more positive terms than did advocates of Americanization who lamented urbanization. Accordingly, while club texts note such problems as those addressed by Atlanta's Neighborhood Union, they refrain from condemning cities and occasionally even praise urban centers, as this excerpt from the *Woman's Era* does: "Boston and Boston only will be 'home' to many of our best girls and boys who, on the completion of their schooling here, go out into various parts of the country carrying their gifts and graces to contribute towards the world good work." The author goes on to explain the "love of Boston and the intense desire of the cultivated colored people to spend as much time as possible therein" and asserts, "The agility shown by the Boston worker in southern fields in getting home when school closes is only equaled by that shown by the clerks and sales people in a big dry goods establishment in getting out when the gong sounds."[33]

Like her white peers, this black clubwoman acknowledges the growing urbanization of the nation, but she interprets it in much more positive terms. Instead of pointing to problems, she affirms the cultural and educational opportunities the city offers, contrasting the "Boston atmosphere" members of her race see as "home" with the "southern fields" from which, despite the employment opportunities, they wish to escape. The city provides the professional training by which members of her race become self-supporting, improve their own lives, and at the same time "contribute towards the world good work." By calling on the image of the "big dry goods establishment," an institution of city life, this author reinforces the urban base on which she founds her observations. In doing so, she calls the Anglo-Saxonist idealization of country life into question, transforms the city into a source of beneficent power, and resists an Americanization that portrays urbanization in entirely negative terms. In portraying the city as an entity that could be ameliorated or even controlled through literacy practices that negotiated new relationships or developed new possibilities, such as those carried out by Atlanta's Neighborhood Union, African American clubwomen offered an alternative to the dominant view of cities as inherently evil.[34]

The middle- and upper-class members of the National Council of Jewish Women adopted similar methods to exert influence over the urban spaces they inhabited. As Pauline Hanauer Rosenberg's paper suggests, acculturated Jewish women tried to distance themselves from the "oppressed Russian exiles" by pointing to their "positions of influence and culture" and by emphasizing their long history in the country. Members of the Detroit Section, for example, participated actively in planning and implementing the 250th anniversary of Jews in America, thereby reinforcing the long tradition of Jewish contributions to the nation.[35] Council members recognized that since most of the new Jewish immigrants crowded into cities where council sections were located, members needed to ameliorate the difficult living conditions under which their less affluent peers lived but at the same time maintain some distance from them. Clashes between wealthy women who offered a "healthful influence" and poor women destined to receive it created class conflicts in the Jewish community, and these class hostilities engendered resistance to the National Council's attempts to shape urban spaces.[36] Middle-class clubwomen prevailed, however, helping to transform recent immigrants into Americanized individuals.

Working women's clubs, which included both Jewish and gentile women, native-born and immigrant, expressed other reactions to urbanization. Drawn to cities by the prospect of employment, working women usually found themselves relegated to the "least skilled and lowest paid occupations."[37] The single women who dominated the female labor force at the turn of the century could rarely afford more than a tiny (shared) room in the city, and the unequal distribution of such municipal services as water, sewer systems, lights, garbage collection, and paved streets usually meant this room was located in an unsanitary and unsafe neighborhood.[38] Clubs provided spaces for women who wanted to enrich their lives by meeting with other women. For these women, club literacy practices ameliorated the challenges and constraints of urban life. In particular, reading and writing helped them demonstrate that they "need no longer be as dull as the materials with which they labor."[39] Not surprisingly, the city itself served as a frequent object of study as clubwomen read and wrote about "the laws of our city . . . especially those relating to factories and tenement houses."[40] Low wages and long working hours constituted major constraints for working women, and clubs addressed these directly. The National League of Women Workers created the Mutual Benefit Fund to provide working women insurance against sickness and unemployment and established the Alliance Employment Bureau to connect clubwomen with the world of work by locating jobs, providing training, and helping them find room and board. The work of these two club-sponsored agencies constituted part of the text of the National League's annual report each year. This written evidence of their success in developing institutions that protected them against some of urbanization's dangers enabled these clubwomen to construct alternative representations of urbanization and themselves.

Critics of urbanization emphasized women's vulnerability to corruption by the city, portraying them as unfortunates who would fall victim to seduction.[41] Far from accepting the classification of (potential) victim, these clubwomen represented themselves in terms of strength and value, as did the author who wrote this for the 1890 Convention of Working Women's Clubs: "It took the world a long time to learn that work is honorable, and every human being, man or woman, should be a worker. Let us not be ashamed of the work we are doing. What we can do depends on natural fitness, education and opportunities."[42] As this demonstrates, members of working women's clubs employed literacy to assert their own ability to negotiate successfully the challenges and constraints of urbanization. Faced with more affluent women who tended to cast them as victims unable to act on their own behalf, working women constructed their independence through their texts, asserting the integrity of their positions rather than focusing all their energies on trying to leave the working class.[43]

Although their perspectives differed, clubwomen contributed to an acceptance of urbanization as a feature of American life. Even as they pointed to the dangers and disadvantages of cities, white middle-class clubwomen acknowledged the increasing urbanization of the nation, inscribing in their texts this transformation of the national culture. Jewish, African American, and working-class clubwomen who portrayed cities in more positive terms frequently saw urban environments as sites for displaying their own abilities. Resisting racist attacks, African American clubwomen utilized literacy to improve the living conditions for the city dwellers of their race. Similarly, Jewish clubwomen who worked to improve the lives of immigrants in New York and other cities used reading and writing to make their newly arrived sisters more recognizable to the white Protestant middle class. Asserting their ability to transform the conditions of their own lives, working-class clubwomen helped show that cities could become more hospitable. In both their conforming and resisting discourses, clubwomen employed literacy to make individual connections with a nation that was becoming increasingly urban.

Industrialization, of course, contributed significantly to the negative qualities associated with cities. For Josiah Strong, the "age of machines" leads directly to socialism because it fosters the "development of classes" or "the widening of the breach between them." In Strong's view, industrialization creates a "class of capitalists and monopolists" who know little about their workers and often organize against them, spurring workers to do the same. Discontent, another incentive toward socialism provided by industrialization, comes with the monotony of factory work and the insecurity bred of changing technologies, according to Strong.[44] Just as they decried the negative effects of urbanization, advocates of the Anglo-Saxonist version of Americanization lamented the nation's growing industrialization.

Depending on their social locations, women's clubs responded in different ways to Americanization's negative portrayal of the "machine age," but consideration of industrialization shaped and was shaped by the reading and writing of all clubwomen. For women employed in factories, literacy practices focused on their working conditions. The Maud Gonne Club of Chicago, for example, was founded by a group of women facing a wage cut. Despite subtle negative pressures from middle-class club supporters, concerns about the union image, and discouraging responses from union men, some clubwomen joined unions, and even when they did not, they explored ways of organizing to improve their own working conditions.[45] They affirmed, as did the author of a speech at the 1890 Convention of the National League of Women Workers, that "a working-girl is doing other working-girls an injury when she consents to work for less than living wages."[46] This concern for fair wages and the welfare of all women workers pervaded the discourse of working women's clubs, contributing to the ease with which the nation, as Richard Hofstader notes, adapted to organized labor.[47] These clubwomen recognized that their life circumstances constrained their literacy practices: "Time is the difficulty with most of us, we cannot read much, and we must read what we need most, and we club members want *Far and Near* to fill that ideal to us—the paper we need most. What do we need? Everything. Yes, indeed, but what do we need most in our everyday, practical lives as working women and club members?"[48] Ever aware of the scarcity of time, these clubwomen affirmed the value of literacy in their lives and looked to their national publications to help them address the pressing and practical issues of their lives by making their reading more efficient.

Acknowledging industrialization's role in their lives led working women's clubs to explore unionization in their reading and writing. Clare De Graffenreid, writing in an 1893 issue of *Far and Near,* lists the advantages of trade unions for women as educational, humanizing, and economic. She recognizes the limitations of unions but asserts they can lead to "the shortening of hours and rise in wages," they can "fix the piece-work pay for men and women at the same rate," and they can equalize wages. De Graffenreid acknowledges that "the good results of trades-unions are not to be achieved by an offensive but by a defensive policy, not by leaps, by pursuing sudden or selfish impulses, nor by revolution. On the contrary, they are attained by slow and often painful education, by biding one's time, by obedience, and even submission, and never without loyalty to law."[49] De Graffenreid asserts working women's need for better wages and working conditions, but she inscribes these needs into a nationalizing discourse that does not condone hasty action or, especially, revolution. Rather, she affirms the higher authority of the nation, insisting on "loyalty to law" above all else. The writing and reading of this article provided a broader view of Americanization, one that acknowledged and addressed the needs of working women while still adhering to the constraints of U.S. law.

In addition to considering the benefits and liabilities of unionization, clubwomen explored, through their literacy practices, ways they might improve

Intimate Practices

their own circumstances in industry. In an 1894 article Leonora O'Reilly pointed to the need for working women to take responsibility for their own financial futures and for continuing efforts to organize workers. O'Reilly also
warned against "workers in one so-called 'skilled' or superior occupation looking with contempt or indifference as to the fate of a less skilled or poorly paid
occupation." She went on to assert that "the false pride, the shrinking into their
narrow customary sphere, and the fear of foolish strikes, which keep working
women from any kind of large industrial union may fairly be laid upon those
to whom working girls and women look for advice and example."[50] The middle-
class women who offered "advice and example" frequently pictured working
women as incapable of acting on their own behalf. Also, they often actively
discouraged union activity because their class allegiances lay with management.
In insisting that working women take responsibility for their own finances and
organizing and act less deferential, O'Reilly offers an alternative construction
of working women that affirms their abilities, rendering the advice and example
of middle-class sponsors irrelevant.

African Americans, who were much less likely than white middle-class clubwomen to employ domestic servants and who were less likely than white working women to obtain the factory jobs, produced and consumed fewer texts
about industrialization. White workers made concerted efforts to keep African
American women out of unions, and when blacks did obtain factory work, it
was heavy labor or janitorial tasks, not machine labor: "Poor as the wages and
working conditions in these [southern] mills were, white workers struck thir-
ty-one times between 1882 and 1900, not to organize unions, but to keep black
workers from being hired to work on machines."[51] Yet industrialization directly affected their lives, as evidenced by the ongoing debate between Booker T.
Washington and W. E. B. Du Bois about whether industrial training constituted appropriate education for people of their race.[52] Of course, the meaning
Washington assigned to industrial training had little to do with machines; instead it described preparation for nonintellectual work. Because Margaret Washington occupied a prominent position among clubwomen and her husband
wielded significant power in the white establishment, criticism of African Americans' role in industrialization remained muted, but many progressive clubwom-
en who fought lynching, separate train cars, and other insults to the race found
a much more sympathetic ally in Du Bois and probably shared his hesitations
about industrial training for African Americans.

One African American clubwoman inscribed these complicated attitudes toward Washington's version of industrialization in an account of the 1896 Atlanta

Exposition, the first international exposition to have a Negro building. Her report, which runs for several pages, enumerates the several African American institutions represented in the exhibit, distinguishing among their various educational programs: "The Tuskegee Normal and Industrial Institute is the center of attraction at the Negro building; in fact, nine-tenth of the visitors ask for it as soon as they enter the building. . . . The tailoring department furnishes clothes for some of the best people in the city." After describing the exhibit, she continues, "Howard University stands for higher education. The photographic exhibit of the buildings and grounds is very creditable. The statistical report, showing 1402 graduates in the different departments, speaks well for the school." This account acknowledges the attributes of Tuskegee's programs, but implicitly asserts that it does not, like Howard University, represent higher education. The training Tuskegee provided would equip graduates to serve others as tailors and servants. In noting that the Tuskegee exhibit occupies a central place in the Negro building, the author also acknowledges, without embracing, the assumption (prominent among whites) that this sort of training offered the best option for African Americans. She insists, however, on distinguishing between this (approved) training and the higher education represented by Howard University, which, by its statistical reports, indicates that African Americans can enter professional life. This author reenacts many aspects of the Washington–Du Bois debate in her comparison, and she acknowledges its effect on the controversy surrounding the Atlanta Exposition itself by noting that it "did not consist of the best work done by the race nor did it have the support of one-third of the influential people in the respective sections."[53] This quiet acknowledgment of divisions among African Americans illustrates the complicated positions clubwomen had to negotiate as they dealt with competing views of industrialization.

The severe lack of capital among African Americans exacerbated these difficulties. Tracing what happened to Joseph Lee underscores this point. In July of 1896 the *Woman's Era* noted that "Mr. Lee is not only the prosperous proprietor of one of the finest suburban hotels of Massachusetts, but has greatly added to his fame and fortune by his bread-mixer and bread comber. These machines which are not identical are his own inventions, and because of their practical value and adaptability are being called for by the leading hotels of the United States."[54] It then refers readers to an ad about Lee's hotel. The front page of the January 1897 issue carries an article about the failure of Lee's twenty-one-year-old business under the headline "A Public Calamity" and concludes, "In the restaurants conducted by Mr. Lee in several large fairs recently, it was a decided novelty to see the help mixed, colored and white waitresses, clerks, cooks, etc. The work that was being done by him was so valuable that we feel, to repeat, that his failure is a great public calamity."[55] The intensity of this lament suggests the paucity of African American businesses during this time and the importance the community attached to them. Through writing and reading articles such as these, African American clubwomen participated in the construction of an alternate definition of industrialization that extended beyond the boundaries of socioeconomic, political, and racial constraints to include people of their own race.[56]

For the more affluent white clubwomen, who frequently benefited directly from the capital generated by industrialization as well as from the products emanating from it, most considerations of industrialization centered on the working woman. Disgruntled about the difficulty of finding servants, middle-class clubwomen often embraced views similar to Strong's about the negative effects of the machine age, but they focused on the women who worked in factories, most frequently by making working women an object of club study. The Seattle Woman's Century Club (founded in 1891), for example, included in its first year of required papers Harriet Parkhurst's "Working Women and Their Wages."[57] Many clubs created "social economic" departments that regularly investigated working women. The appropriate education for working women was a popular topic for such groups. This excerpt from a department meeting typifies their position: "It is unusual to find this artistic line being used in work with this class of people, and I feel that we are making a great mistake in stressing the commonplace so much in our work among the working class. . . ." Although she urges that working women should receive more than narrow vocational training, this clubwoman reveals her clear (arrogant) sense that she and her peers know what is best for "this class of people," and her ultimate goal is, as she goes on to say, to transform them: "There are so many lessons in etiquette which may be brought out through this means and girls who were coarse and vulgar before, have developed into beautiful sweet girls through the influence of this woman and the interest in the higher and better things of life."[58] Ultimately, of course, this clubwoman and her peers sought to transform working women into "beautiful sweet girls" who fit the model of Anglo-Saxonism.

White middle-class clubwomen felt free to pronounce on working women's education and goals, but they were less comfortable about acknowledging their own complicity in creating the difficult and often dangerous conditions under which less affluent women labored, as this account from the minutes of the Friday Club demonstrates: "The startling and unpleasant statement was made, that the moral responsibility of untold suffering among the Jews rested with certain unsuspecting women, who had brought about hideous suffering for other women in buying ready made garments at bargain counters." Members debated the issue and concluded that there might be unsuspected good in the situation since "they are trained to good work, to give it and to understand that only good work will count, it is an education, and cruel as the system may seem, perhaps for them could be obtained in no other way, and the good that is in it may yet redeem the workers."[59] This convoluted attempt to exonerate clubwomen from any responsibility for the sufferings of workers by suggesting that the very poverty in which they labor "may yet redeem" them reflects middle-class clubwomen's complicated attitudes toward women workers. Uncomfortable with the idea that their own habits of consumption might contribute to the difficulties of others and yet unwilling to ignore working women entirely, they developed elaborate strategies for justifying their own comforts. Identifying the workers as "Jews" who might be redeemed suggests that an unspoken anti-Semitism might have helped the members of the Friday Club construct women workers as the "them" for whom a cruel system offered the only means of acquiring an education. Even though they squirmed to justify their own positions, the frequency with which white middle-class clubwomen studied working woman implies their continued fascination with them. In the larger culture middle-class women dressed like workers and took factory jobs to report on women laborers, some middle-class men found photographs of women dressed as workers particularly titillating, and fiction included portrayals of middle-class women who disguised themselves as working women.[60]

These complicated attitudes toward working women insinuated themselves into texts describing actual contact between the two groups of women, particularly as middle-class clubwomen tried to change the material conditions of working women's lives rather than simply study them. The minutes of the New England Women's Club (NEWC) record an early attempt by white middle-class clubwomen to aid "our working women" by opening "comfortable rooms or parlors to be used in the evening by those who have no comfortable homes to go to at the end of their day of work." Having claimed a panoptic view of the living conditions of working women and having decided their comfort level, the report goes on to describe the role of NEWC members: "It is proposed that ladies shall be at the parlors every evening to welcome the guests and make them feel comfortable and at home. The lady will take the charge of each evening, that is, will be responsible for the management in all ways, but will be assisted by a staff of five or six others." These ladies will provide "quiet and simple parlor games" along with books and music: "One lady will be the musician of each evening, that will be competent to play pleasant pieces on the piano or to accompany a song. It is hoped to have a good deal of music, and it is intended to close each evening with a good hymn." Having established the goals and activities, the report looks at the site: "The rooms are for the present at the Bureau of Charity in Chardon Street. The city kindly allowed us the use of them for the months of January and February to try our plan. Fears have been expressed that the name of the building will repel those whom we wish to welcome, but we think if they come once and see how bright and pleasant the rooms look they will not be troubled by the name." Sweeping aside working women's possible humiliation or objection to the Bureau of Charity, the report assures the audience of its motives and merits:

> The ladies who go to meet and welcome these girls, go in a friendly spirit and with no thought of patronizing them. It does not seem as if it would be difficult to establish kindly and simple relations with them so that they may feel that they have friends among the ladies to whom they may have recourse; if they need help or counsel. We think that the knowledge that such an association exists will prove a check upon any of their employers, who may be inclined to be insolent, overbearing or oppressive. There is one other good thing about our plan. It is not likely to be a costly experiment, and we shall not need to beg for it. $500 we are assured will cover all our expenses for a year, if we are not obliged to pay rent.[61]

This report presents many of the issues that plagued relations between working-class and middle-class white women's clubs. Despite its disclaimers, this record contains a good deal of condescension. On the most obvious level, the distinction between "the ladies" and the "working women," "guests," and "these girls" demonstrates both the distance from and discomfort with those the club proposes to help. The proposed activities of "simple parlor games," books, and music, concluded with a "good hymn," suggest Protestant middle-class ideas about what constitutes satisfactory entertainment. There is no indication that the "guests" have been consulted about what activities they might prefer. The use of the term *simple* in relation to both the games and the desired relationship between the two groups implies that these "guests" might not be capable of anything more complicated and suggests that the middle-class women did not want to enter into a more complex association with the lives and working conditions of those they sought to help. The attitudes expressed in this piece of writing confirm the reservations expressed by Harriet Hanson Robinson, a woman of working-class origins who joined the New England Women's Club. In her diary, Robinson complained about the class distinctions expressed by club members who "referred to servants as 'those people' and to working women as 'women of that sort.'"[62]

More substantively, this piece of writing demonstrates some of the fundamental confusion and naiveté of middle-class clubwomen who took on the task of helping their working-class peers. In suggesting that the guests might bring their "own work" to the rooms, the report blurs the central purpose of the room since the guests could not simultaneously play parlor games and complete their sewing. Unlike members of the New England Women's Club who typically sewed for aesthetic or benevolent purposes, working women sewed for money, and playing games instead of plying their needles could reduce their incomes. This conflation of the middle-class parlor and the working-class sewing room typifies the lack of understanding and concern for the economic situation of working women evident in the written records of many white middle-class clubs. Like the women of the Friday Club who appeared to believe that experiencing poverty could somehow "redeem" working women, the women writing this report demonstrate little understanding of the needs and motivations of women who worked to support themselves. Concluding with financial assurances to members demonstrates the committee's capacity for and concern with economic terms, but these abilities do not extend to serious consideration of the financial situation of working women.

Members of the New England Women's Club were not unique in their inability or unwillingness to confront the painful truths about working women's incomes. While many clubs talked about the difficulties working women faced, few framed these difficulties in actual dollars. An exception appears in the annual report of the Social Economic Department of the Nineteenth Century Club of Oak Park, which describes its project with a women's work room in Chicago: "Our Dept. contributed monthly . . . so that we sent in all $18.50. This money went directly to paying women for their sewing as material was produced from different institutions in the city. No woman was allowed to earn more than $1.50 a week, a small pittance indeed toward support of a family."[63] This recognition of the desperate economic conditions under which many women lived appears very rarely in club texts about helping working women. A similar lack of awareness appears in the NEWC report's comments about the "ladies" providing recourse for working women and serving as a check on employers who might be "insolent, overbearing or oppressive." Apparently the authors did not consider the fact that these employers might be members of the New England Women's Club, since a large proportion of working women during this period served as domestics and NEWC minutes, like those of clubs

Intimate Practices

across the country, are filled with complaints about the difficulty of finding good domestic help. Club records trace the ongoing conflict between middle-class clubwomen who countered industrialization's effect on their lives by seeking to help, and even train, others to fill domestic positions, and working women who in turn resisted these efforts in favor of the more autonomous jobs industry provided.[64]

Texts of middle-class clubwomen frequently portrayed working women as passive victims. Minutes of Roxbury's Women in Council report that Mary Boyle O'Reilly gave a talk titled "The Working Woman Who Fails": "She told of the unfortunates who fill the women's prisons, many of them driven there from being over-tired, over-strained morally, over-taxed physically. They are poorly paid for exhausting work and are insufficiently nourished. . . . A large proportion are led into wrong doing through ignorance or sheer desperation, and many are mentally defective."[65] This account of O'Reilly's speech illustrates the language of victimization that middle-class clubwomen frequently used in portraying their working-class peers. Significantly, there is little mention of their strength and independence. Women "are poorly paid," "are driven" to prison, and "are led" to wrong. Like the clubwomen who avoided the implications that their habits of "buying garments at bargain counters" contributed to the poverty of working women, the clubwomen who read and wrote this passage evaded—by deleting agents—any implications of responsibility for these conditions. To their credit, these clubwomen did not, at least, blame working women for their own difficulties and recognized, with their use of the passive voice, the larger social forces operating in urbanization and industrialization.

One attempt to ameliorate the differences between middle-class and working-class women took place in the Women's Educational and Industrial Union (WEIU), a cross-class union of women founded in Boston in 1877 to "increase fellowship among women in order to promote the best practical methods of securing their educational, industrial, and social advancement."[66] As the name implies, this group took industrialization as a given instead of resisting it, and its texts show considerable attention to the problems working women faced. The printed version of the president's address for 1892, for example, describes the WEIU as striking "at the root of many existing evils, by offering to every woman according to her needs, an opportunity for self-support, intellectual and practical advancement, and devoted service to others."[67] Speaking in 1913, the WEIU president noted the need for "vocational schools of many kinds" and "teachers combining culture with industrial intelligence and skill." Recognizing that few teachers were trained to "rightly direct this new industrial work in the educational institutions," she proposed that the WEIU help by "trying out methods of preparing such teachers and obtaining results for normal schools to follow."[68] As these texts indicate, WEIU members understood the complexities that came with industrialization and saw their organization as a body prepared to address some of these. Since the WEIU leadership remained largely white and middle class, however, it ultimately fell short of its goal of uniting women across class lines.

The relatively affluent members of the National Council of Jewish Women shared with other middle-class clubwomen the material benefits of industrialization and a generally condescending attitude toward working-class women, but their ethnic/religious heritage complicated their position. As one council member put it in a speech at the 1902 Triennial, "We, who are the cultured and refined, constitute the minority, but we shall be judged by the majority, the Russian Jews, by the children of the Ghetto."[69] This identification with their working-class peers led council members to take a more active role in trying to improve the material conditions of working-class women. In keeping with their ambivalent attitudes toward women working outside the home, council members created such alternatives as thrift shops where home-produced goods could be sold, but they also attempted to improve working conditions in factories. Annie Nathan Meyer, an active council member, founded the National Consumers' League and worked for legislation that would protect the "girls of today [who] are the mothers of the future," thus advocating a view of (potential) motherhood synonymous with that promoted by advocates of Americanization who emphasized the gendered family structure. The National Council of Jewish Women supported the National Consumers' League in its attempt to introduce safety, sanitation, and more humane conditions in factories. Even these efforts, however, often reflected the class-based distances between the two groups of women. Council women who sought to reduce the length of the working week failed to consider the effects of fewer hours of labor on the workers' pay envelope, as one of the working women made clear: "The sooner that society women understand that they must keep their hands off the working woman, the sooner the working woman will be better off."[70] For working women, class identity took precedence over the Jewishness inscribed on them by council members.

Tensions emerged from conflicting views of industrialization held by clubwomen from various social locations. In portraying working women as passive victims in need of help from reformers, white middle-class women, both Christian and Jewish, cast themselves as possessing power and agency, and they proposed using these assets to transform working women into a closer approximation of middle-class femininity. Not surprisingly, working women responded with representations of their own, affirming the importance and value of their work and resisting attempts to transform them. Because their lives were the most directly affected by the ways industrialization changed the nature of labor, working women focused on the implications of time-directed labor and factory conditions. Similarly, African American clubwomen, who identified themselves with people excluded from much of industrialization, constructed their own meanings for the machine age and resisted the (white imposed) limitations on training and work appropriate for members of their race. Although clubwomen in all social locations addressed the forces of industrialization, not all of them shared Americanization's negative construction of it.

Immigration, another of the forces with which Americanization contended, also engendered a wide variety of responses from clubwomen, depending on their social positions. From 1890 to 1910 immigration doubled, with the largest influx of newcomers occurring between 1901 and 1910. The national origins of immigrants also shifted, as immigration from northern Europe declined and arrivals from southern and eastern Europe increased. Public discourse about the number and type of immigrants reflected considerable anxiety. People associated immigrants with increased crime, called attention to their increased numbers, and highlighted their differences from earlier arrivals by pointing to their "alien" qualities.[71] Josiah Strong's *Our Country* claimed that the United States had "suffered a peaceful invasion by an army more than four times as vast as the estimated number of Goths and Vandals that swept over Southern Europe and overwhelmed Rome." Strong described the typical immigrant as "a European peasant, whose horizon has been narrow, whose moral and religious training has been meager or false, and whose ideas of life are low," and he cited statistics on the criminality of this population.[72] The trope of invasion portrayed immigrants as intending harm, and Strong exploited this idea with descriptions that conflated (peasant) class status and immorality. Other publications echoed Strong's negative description of immigrants.[73]

In contrasting immigrants arriving at the turn of the century with earlier arrivals and constructing them as invaders and criminals, these discourses employed what Etienne Balibar calls racism without race, creating distance between groups by developing myths about them.[74] Quantifying immigrants according to their country of origin and "alien" features attached the weight of numbers to this strategy, and in keeping with a cultural shift toward greater quantification, such as reports and actuarial tables, statistical reports on immigration began appearing in popular magazines. The U.S. Department of Labor exhibit at the 1915 Panama-Pacific Exposition in San Francisco featured an electrical diagram of immigration between 1820 and 1914, including, as the historian Robert W. Rydell reports, the "race of alien arrivals, occupations of those admitted, causes of exclusion; and arrests and deportations by classes . . . [making it] clear that the composition of the white ethnic population of the United States was changing . . . for the worse."[75] The reference to the "race of alien arrivals" demonstrates how racism without race functioned. Although they subsequently "became white," turn-of-the-century immigrants from Ireland as well as southern and eastern Europe were frequently constructed as "nonwhite" by Americans of native-born or northern European stock who adhered to the orthodoxy of Anglo-Saxonism. Immigrant Jews of this period were also constructed as nonwhite.[76] This use of race enabled Anglo-Saxonists to summon the power of both nationalism and racism to heighten anxieties about immigration and create support for their version of Americanization.

Josiah Strong, who credited the Anglo-Saxon with impressing on humanity the two great ideas of "civil liberty" and "a pure spiritual Christianity," described him as "divinely commissioned to be, in a peculiar sense, his brother's keeper," thus encouraging the transformation of immigrants into people who conformed to an Anglo-Saxon model.[77] This characterization of Anglo-Saxons as the superior race destined to dominate the nation reverberated in the prose of influential commentators in the twentieth century. Many immigrants, despite conflicting loyalties to their national/ethnic/religious group, actively supported efforts to transform them and tried (with varying degrees of success) to "become white." Motivated by what David Roediger has described as the "status and privileges conferred by race" that compensated for "alienating and exploitative class relationships," these immigrants worked, voted, and struggled their way into whiteness.[78] Similarly, although with less success, some African Americans endeavored to become "black Yankees" or "Anglo Africans" by seeking education and adhering to the values of Anglo-Saxonism.[79]

As the report of Julia Ward Howe's 1891 speech to the Saturday Morning Club indicates, white middle-class clubwomen participated in these discourses, often constructing immigrants as alien, expressing concern about their political ignorance, and reinforcing the racism of Americanization. Howe's use of "dangerous elements" and "lower station of society" portrays the world in hierarchical terms, with Anglo-Saxons positioned at the top ready to aid "the best of the immigrants" who might emulate white middle-class norms, while keeping "the restraining hand of discipline" on the majority who manifested "political ignorance." In addition to taking an elitist and racist view of immigrants, such clubwomen made immigration an object of study. The Ladies' Literary Club of Salt Lake City, for example, included "America, the Melting Pot" among its topics in 1918.[80] Members of the Nineteenth Century Club of Oak Park wrote and produced what they described as an Americanization play, "The Sword of Tomorrow," featuring events in the lives of recent Russian Jewish and German Polish immigrants.[81]

While such topics reinforced the relationship between these clubwomen and the nation, it was a relationship complicated by the fact that they were not, strictly speaking, citizens. Citizenship, as Ernest Gellner has observed, requires mutual recognition, as when persons "recognize certain mutual rights and duties to each other in virtue of their shared membership."[82] Constraints that barred women from voting, most women from receiving a college education, and women from owning property made it impossible to describe them as having the same rights and duties as their male counterparts. However, by focusing on a shared American tradition, these clubwomen asserted their claim to the nation and the hegemonic discourse of Americanization. Programs of white middle-class clubs frequently included year-long studies of American history or literature, and members found ways to insert themselves into the American traditions they studied by including female historical figures, women writers, and issues of concern to women.[83] By constructing, through the texts they produced and consumed, an American tradition that included women's experiences and perceptions, these clubwomen extended the discourse of Americanization—a discourse heretofore largely limited to white Anglo-Saxon males—to include people like themselves.

Most white middle-class clubwomen paid considerable attention to Great Britain, spending a year or more on British history and/or literature, thereby fostering the neocolonialism of Anglo-Saxonism that revered all things British.[84] In immersing themselves in reading and writing about British topics for a year or more, clubwomen across the country reaffirmed the importance of the U.S. connection with Great Britain and the Anglo-Saxon peoples. The underside of this emphasis on Great Britain appeared in its reinforcement of the racism of Americanization. When members of the Ypsilanti (Michigan) Ladies' Literary Club responded to a call for current events on February 5, 1896, one reported that a colored woman had been admitted to the Chicago Woman's Club. Although there is no comment on this event, its inclusion in the minutes suggests its import to the members of the Literary Club. The history of the North Carolina Federation of Women's Clubs opened with a statement about clubs developing women "into proper mates for educated manhood" to produce "higher types" because "individual security has yielded to the call for race progress, and in that progress woman is a large factor."[85] In some cases the clubwomen's racism took a more obvious form, as this excerpt from the minutes of the Friday Club of Jackson, Michigan, indicates: "Mrs. Webster read a very amusing Negro dialect poem entitled 'Washington's Birthday.'"[86] Minutes of the Monday Club of Clinton, New York, report, "Mrs. Lathrop then read us, with inimitable dialect, some stories of the colored people which were greeted with hearty laughter."[87] The *General Federation of Women's Clubs Magazine* published an article describing the African American mother of a World War I soldier speaking "in that old high musical voice, only a few generations removed from the deep gutturals of the jungle."[88] Whether affirming their whiteness through reading and discussing texts produced in Great Britain or distinguishing themselves from African Americans by writing and listening to accounts that emphasized differences in speech patterns, white middle-class clubwomen participated in and to a large extent reinforced the racist dimensions of Americanization.

As the selection titled "The Difficulties of Colonization" quoted at the beginning of this chapter shows, African American clubwomen took a different view of immigration—and of Americanization—than their white counterparts did. Rather than an America characterized by the racial/ethnic purity advocated in the doctrine of Anglo-Saxonism, the writer seeks one free of "criminals and traitors" who have fled their home countries. Howe's expression of the impulse to replicate oneself is absent here. Instead, the author of "Difficulties" asserts the right of the native-born (black or white) to "teach" immigrants standards of conduct, such as avoiding crimes against other citizens. In doing so, this author offers an alternative description of what it means to be an American. What one does rather than what one is becomes a defining characteristic. In defining citizens as those who are "behaving themselves," this author anticipates what Evelyn Higginbotham has called the politics of respectability.[89] Through careful monitoring of manners and morals to emulate those of the white middle class, African Americans claimed respectability for themselves. Given the sexual exploitation they had suffered during and after the slave era, moral purity loomed especially large in this political stance.[90] Although such behavior could be read as servile emulation of a superior group, I share Higginbotham's view that it represented an assertion of "the will and agency" of African American women to "define themselves outside the parameters of prevailing racist discourses."[91] By asserting their own "respectability" in writing, African American clubwomen inscribed proof of their own (and their race's) uplift from the degradations of slavery and created an alternative to the Anglo-Saxonist language of Americanization that described them as inherently inferior.

The National Conference of Colored Women (NCCW), which met in Boston in 1895, enacted the politics of respectability by asserting colored women's virtue. Such speakers as Agnes Jones Adams of Baltimore, who delivered an address titled "Social Purity" in which she affirmed the righteousness and high moral standards of women of her race and attested that they had a "uniform record for patriotism" even though they had been treated with "ingratitude through a callous ignoring of the common justice" due them, insisted on the contributions of her people to the nation. Like the author of "The Difficulties of Colonization," Adams discounts the Anglo-Saxonist view of racial purity and actively resists whiteness as a criterion for being American. Instead, employing the politics of respectability, she upholds the standard of "social purity" and calls on the discourse of patriotism to claim the importance of extending the "honor" of "justice, culture and civilization" to women of her race.[92]

Rather than allow the deprecations generated by neocolonialism and Anglo-Saxonism to incapacitate them, African American clubwomen used the new veneration of things British for their own purposes. In particular, building on a tradition of British antislavery support that dated from the 1830s, they sought support for their work from sympathetic residents of England. Mary Church Terrell, a prominent clubwoman who published widely on many subjects in U.S. presses, resorted to British presses for her essays on race.[93] London's Anti-Lynching Committee, established in 1894, distributed information on lynching in the United States and gave "expression to public opinion in condemnation of such outrages."[94] Ida B. Wells, whose campaign against lynching occupied a central place in the work of the National Association of Colored Women, published in London her 1892 *U.S. Atrocities,* in which she detailed the increase in lynchings from 1882 to 1891. Claiming that the U.S. press contained "unreliable and doctored reports of lynchings," Wells urged support for Afro-American papers because they are "the only ones which will print the truth," and she provided compelling evidence of the diminishing civil rights of African Americans.[95] Catherine Impey, who organized the British antilynching campaign, published *Anti-Caste,* a newspaper in which she frequently provided "space for black writers to 'present their case.'"[96] When the National Conference of Colored Women convened in response to Josephine Ruffin's 1895 call, it charged a committee with writing a letter to Catherine Impey. This letter, which expressed sympathy to Impey on the illness of her mother, also described the

NCCW as "assembled in Boston in the interest of the race and in the cause of oppressed womanhood," thus establishing a clear link between African American clubwomen and the British antilynching movement.[97]

African American clubwomen also appropriated Anglo-Saxonist traditions for their own purposes. Among the papers of Mary Church Terrell, the first president of the National Association of Colored Women, is her explanation for writing the *Phyllis Wheatley Pageant-Play,* which was performed during the early part of the twentieth century in high schools attended by African Americans.

> I also wanted to present George Washington to our youth in such a light that they would feel they had good and sufficient reasons for revering him as the Father of our common country as well as the young people of other racial groups. I wanted to show our children that even though George Washington was a slave holder, in accordance with the deplorable custom of his time, nevertheless he was broadminded, generous-hearted and just enough to make written acknowledgment of the talent of an African girl and to pay homage to her, while she was still being held as a slave.
>
> We must teach our children that we are citizens of this country and as such, whenever the opportunity is afforded, we must take part in every national movement in which other groups join.

In explaining her intention to portray George Washington as a "broadminded and generous-hearted" man who was willing to "pay homage" to a slave, Terrell takes the position that young people of her race can find positive qualities in white leaders and perhaps even identify with them. The insistence that "our children" see themselves as citizens and participate in national movements is matched by an insistence on recognition of and respect for African Americans. Terrell also observes the problem of many historical pageants that portray blacks with "imperfect English, with . . . mirth-provoking antics used to make the audience laugh," indicating her knowledge of the mockery evident in the laughter of white women's clubs and her refusal to accept it. She notes that although colored children learn a great deal about the achievements of whites, "they know comparatively little about the creditable things which their African forebears have done."[98] By portraying George Washington, that most "American" of white males, as respectful of an African American poet, Terrell not only highlights the accomplishments of a member of her race but also demonstrates that the history of African Americans—as opposed to more recently arrived immigrants—is the history of the United States and that these longtime residents merit respect.

While white clubwomen reinforced an American tradition that emphasized Anglo-Saxonist texts, their African American peers extended that tradition to include texts underscoring the talents and accomplishments of their race. Minutes of meetings describe programs on Amanda Smith, the Evangelist; Alexander Crummell; Elizah McCoy; W. E. B. Du Bois; Sojourner Truth; Negro preachers; the Negro voice; Negro inventions; the Negro vote; and race history. A number of clubs sang the Negro National Anthem regularly, and club debates included such topics as "Resolved that the responsibility for the political condition of the Negro rests upon the women of the race."[99] Frederick Douglass, who died in 1895, was memorialized at the Atlanta Congress of Colored Women's Clubs with essays and poems by clubwomen from around the country. Fannie Barrier Williams gave a talk titled "The Small Virtues of a Great Man," Frances Harper delivered an address on Douglass, and Margaret Tate read an ode.[100] The April 1895 issue of the *Woman's Era* included a photograph and a page-long memorial poem by H. Cordelia Ray, and the record books of other African American women's clubs contain entries about honoring the memory of Frederick Douglass and contributing funds to preserve his Washington, D.C., home as a memorial.[101] These clubwomen thus created a monument of the sort Berlant describes as making national culture local, but their version of national culture permitted the legacy of Frederick Douglass to circulate through the personal and collective consciousness of African Americans and others throughout the nation.

These programs and activities developed out of a conscious sense of their importance. The minutes of Atlanta's Chautauqua Circle include a list of "timely suggestions for Circle improvement" that included "paying attention to Negro authors."[102] Faced with the pressures of increased immigration and heightened racism, African American clubwomen countered with a broader vision of the United States. In addition to employing the politics of respectability in their texts to define "American" on the basis of behavior rather than color, they created an alternative discourse of Americanization in which they could recognize themselves. Reading the fiction, poetry, and essays of African Americans and writing papers about the accomplishments of members of their race in such areas as politics, music, literature, religion, publishing, industry, and science enhanced their understanding of and appreciation for the work of their own people. By perusing a black-owned newspaper such as the *Crisis,* writing about African American ministers and voting rights, and memorializing such leaders as Frederick Douglass, these clubwomen gave voice to their own aspirations and affirmed their national identification. Empowered with the authority of a knowledge they created for themselves through their own reading and writing, they developed an alternative to the dominant culture's view of the United States.

In similar fashion, the National Council of Jewish Women included on their programs reading and writing that reinforced their particular version of the United States by focusing on topics that emphasized the relationship between Jews and the nation. Study groups occupied a central place in each local section of the National Council and gave considerable attention to the Bible and Jewish history as a means of helping members preserve their common heritage. Jewish women's clubs founded before the National Council took shape also followed this pattern, as this statement from a member of the Pioneers, a Jewish women's club founded in 1879, shows: "Perhaps no year in the history of the Pioneers has been more gratifying and advantageous than the one just brought to a close. The path that we elected to follow was the course of Jewish history. . . . No course of study could have stirred the ethical consciousness of the club more deeply than the tragic, yet divinely glorious history of the Jews."[103] Records of the New York Section of the National Council report such topics as "The Jewish Woman in America" to commemorate the 250th anniversary of the arrival of Jews in the United States. Celebrating this anniversary emphasizes the continuity of Jewish contributions to the nation, while at the same time retaining a distinctive identity.

Struggling to demonstrate acculturation without becoming so assimilated that they lost their Jewish identity posed a continuing challenge for National Council members. Like their Christian peers, they considered such gender-focused issues as "The New Aspect of the Higher Education of Women," but they also sought to underscore their particular heritage with such topics as "The Jewish Woman in the Home," "The Jewish Woman's Club among Clubs," "Yiddish Poets," "Great Women of Israel," and "Jewish Dramatists." Even in their memorials for deceased members, Jewish clubwomen underscored their religious heritage, while affirming their common club life. The death of Ida Ginsburg, the founding president of the Woman's Club of Temple Beth El, which became the Detroit Section of the National Council, prompted a statement that identified her as "a mother in Israel" and went on to commend her "love for Judaism. . . . Religion, pure and simple, she loved with all her heart and soul.

And that love it lay with her to communicate for the only reason of her sincerity and her perfect faith."[104] Although Ginsberg's friends valued her many contributions to club life, her firm faith in Judaism marked her for special approval.

As Pauline Rosenberg's speech at the Jewish Women's Congress indicates, middle-class Jewish clubwomen, recognizing that the most recently arrived Jews could reflect negatively on their people as a whole, took responsibility for exerting a "healthful influence" on recently arrived Jewish immigrants. Unlike other immigrant populations, Jews included many women in their numbers, so the National Council of Jewish Women focused on their immigrant sisters, trying to prevent them from becoming a burden to the general community. For women arriving at Ellis Island, the National Council provided a woman to meet them to "help and warn them before it is too late" so that new immigrants would not be lured into prostitution.[105] The records of the Brooklyn Section contain this explanation: "The Immigrant Aid Service was started by Brooklyn and New York as well as by other Sections under the aegis of our National Organization. In 1903 our Federal government asked NCJW [National Council of Jewish Women] to combat the white slave trade market which had sprung up in connection with so many single women and girls who came to our shores during great immigration waves. Through a NCJW official immigration station on Ellis Island these newcomers were put into the care of Council Sections."[106] Through a very efficient system of meeting each ship, checking passenger lists, ascertaining the legitimacy of family connections claimed, and maintaining contact with recent arrivals, National Council members minimized the white slave trade and helped acculturate their immigrant sisters. Perhaps the best testimony to the success of this effort appears in an article by President Anna Pennybacker of the General Federation of Women's Clubs as she urges her constituents to offer more aid to immigrants: "We may well imitate the Jewish race in this regard; no Jewish woman lands in Ellis Island without some Jewish sister keeping in touch with her until she is delivered into the hands of her friends."[107] Like clubwomen who used texts to shape their urban environment, National Council members rationalized the masses of immigrants through writing. Annual section reports contained detailed lists of the origins, skills, educational levels, and family affiliations of those aided during the previous year. This systematic rendering of the data generated by their work inscribed a narrative (in Berlant's sense) that could circulate among National Council members, reminding them of their local roles in the national culture.

Jewish clubwomen faced a more complicated task than other white middle-class women did because they tried to help immigrants become acculturated while avoiding the complete assimilation that would threaten their religious heritage. This "profoundly ambivalent" view of cultural adaptation led clubwomen to inscribe tensions between fostering acculturation and avoiding total assimilation.[108] As a member of the Denver Section observed, "While we bring to them [immigrants] Americanism, we may at the same time be inspired with some of the spiritual passion which glows in the breasts of these ardent Jews, who are, after all, the rock which is the foundation of the house of Israel."[109] As this woman indicates, the transactions between native-born and immigrant Jews moved in both directions: the new arrivals strengthened the religious commitment of the native-born Jews, thereby complicating their acculturation projects.

Working women's groups included both immigrants and the native-born, and differences between the two created tensions. Some native-born women workers saw immigrants as competitors for scarce jobs and supported more restrictive immigration laws. A "World Events" column in *Far and Near* for 1893 asserts that "immigration has now assumed an ominous phase" for workers and that "legislative restriction is the only solution."[110] This restrictive view of Americanization distinguished between native-born and immigrant in terms of patriotism, asserting that the more recently arrived would hold the nation less dear. Since many immigrants, including Irish, Italians, and Jews, were cast as "nonwhite," they often took an active part in projects designed to enhance their "American" qualities, particularly when the projects focused on changing their "nonwhite" status. Fluency in English represented one means of becoming more "white," and some working-class clubwomen participated in English classes in settlement houses and evening schools. *Far and Near* regularly published such articles as "Learning to Write English," "Some Common Errors in English," and "A Talk about Letter-Writing," which urged clubwomen to read and write regularly to improve their skills, warned them against such utterances as "He don't know nothing about it" and "Them is my two sisters," and rehearsed conventions of format and punctuation for writing.[111] Recognizing the complications of shedding an immigrant identity, *Far and Near* also provided instruction on personal conduct, clothing, and relations with men. "Aunt Jane's Talk with Juniors," a regular column in the paper, advised readers on a variety of subjects, including avoiding patent medicines, wearing suitable clothing for work, refusing to enter the home of a stranger, and dealing with men in the workplace. A regular fashion column offered advice on the latest styles and ways to make inexpensive clothing, and articles with such titles as "Putting the Best Foot Forward" urged against dressing ostentatiously.[112] The white (middle-class) norms urged by articles like these in *Far and Near* reminded immigrant women of the many requirements for achieving a "white" identity and simultaneously provided native-born workers with strategies for transcending their class position.

Regardless of whether they sought to become more "white," working-class clubwomen united behind an insistence on both personal and institutional autonomy. Faced with projects designed to transform them into "sweet beautiful girls" who conformed to the Anglo-Saxon model, they affirmed their identity as workers in the texts they wrote and read, underscoring the value of their labor and thereby resisting the middle-class model of leisured women. When confronted with affluent women who presumed to teach them about how to conduct their lives, they could respond in spirited fashion: "You are better dressed, have more learning and more money than we have. But these things give you no more right to come down here and tell us what we shall wear, and how we shall spend our money, than we have to go uptown and tell you how you shall spend your money and what you shall put on."[113] Constructing their own version of the United States, they also insisted on workers' value to the country: "A healthy, hardy, industrious and ambitious people—in that alone lies a nation's permanent strength and wealth," adding that *people* does not mean "solely the men of a nation" but includes "women in equal measure."[114] In producing and consuming such texts, members of working women's clubs inscribed a broader definition of American that included themselves and their work.

Similarly, these women asserted the autonomy of their clubs, even though most working women's clubs owed their origins to more affluent clubwomen. Grace Dodge, for example, founded the New York Working Girls' Society in 1885 to provide a place where working women could "have a good, useful time in the evening." The wealthy daughter of a New York City merchant and philanthropist, Dodge provided material support for this organization but continued to misread (and misrepresent) the goals of its members. In Dodge's view these working women were "not desirous for man's work or place, but remaining where circumstances have placed them." The clubwomen themselves, however, focused on improving their own working conditions and wages, and, as Kessler-Harris puts it, "slowly Dodge lost control over the content of discussions and in time she withdrew."[115]

As their more affluent sponsors moved to the background, working women took charge of their clubs and, with the founding of the National League of Women Workers in 1897, established principles of self-government and self-support. Acknowledging that "in the earlier days the democratic form of the club constitution was often a shell and the power was actually wielded by those of greater preparation who were in the clubs solely for an altruistic purpose," these clubwomen instituted changes that made clubs dependent on "the exercise of common sense and judgment by each individual for the common good," offering as a rationale the belief that "club training comes quite as much from the contact of one girl upon another, under organizational conditions, as upon the influence of the leaders or workers."[116] By revising the bylaws, clubs made policy changes that put workers in leadership positions and raised the dues so that they could become financially independent.[117] The principle of self-support, particularly in cities with prohibitive rents for meeting rooms, proved difficult to uphold. Even though they collected regular dues and conducted fund-raising projects, some clubs found it impossible to function without some external support. Acknowledging that they had to learn "when to accept and how to make a return other than monetary for values received," these clubwomen described subsidies for meeting rooms in nation-building terms: "recognizing that the strength of a nation lies in the health and ideals of its youth, it is possible for the community to make, not a gift, but an investment, in whatever will give opportunity for health and ideality to the coming generation."[118] By connecting the well-being of the nation with the health of their clubs, working women took control of the terms of their own representation, insisted on their own autonomy, and inserted themselves into an enlarged vision of the United States.

With nonsectarianism, the third principle of the National League of Women Workers, the literacy practices of these clubwomen further expanded on what it meant to be an American. Arguing that nonsectarian did not mean "non-religious" but allowed for "the application of the spiritual standard to the common problem of living," they consciously included women of all religious groups.[119] This inclusiveness offered a happy alternative for Jewish working women who struggled with discrimination within and beyond their religious community. Sexism in their community frequently denied them education or the opportunity to advance, and a dominant culture that advertised positions for "Christian American young women" made it difficult for them to find work. As one Jewish woman explained to an interviewer, Jews often had to deny their heritage to get a job: "I said I was a Unitarian. . . . To get a job. I have to work. . . . It's no use signing you are a Jew. Even Jews don't take you. The agent said, 'You'd better not put down you're a Jew. I can't get you work.'"[120] In flouting the Anglo-Saxon Protestant code by including Jewish women as well as Catholics of various ethnic groups in their organizations, working women's clubs inscribed novel connections between the nation and some of its newest residents.

Speaking at the Berkeley Lyceum in 1905, Jane Addams observed, "The way to learn about conditions isn't to go to work in a factory for a few months and then write a book, but to have genuine sympathy and continued relations with those who work day after day, year after year, to do our part to help them express themselves and make articulate their desires."[121] Jane Addams and her peers at settlement houses across the country did a great deal to improve the lives of working women, but, finally, working women helped themselves in their clubs. These clubs provided a space where clubwomen could, while adhering to their principles of self-government, self-support, and nonsectarianism, become more "white" and construct their own representations. Here, through their literacy practices they learned to "express themselves and make articulate their desires" to be identified as workers, to be recognized as self-sufficient, and to become part of America on their own terms.

Clubwomen in all social locations, then, constructed versions of the nation as they interacted with the forces of urbanization, industrialization, and immigration at the turn of the century. By insisting on representing their own racial, gendered, ethnic, and class experiences as "American," clubwomen eschewed what Lauren Berlant calls "Utopian America." In Berlant's terms, utopian America creates a "national fantasy" of "collectively held affect" that requires participants to shed "local identities" and enter a new political order, "which has a mystical relation to everyday history."[122] In the "historical United States," or the nation, by contrast, everyday life occupies a central place, and citizens are not required to cast off their local identities. Grace Hebard articulated a version of this distinction in a 1917 article published in the *General Federation of Women's Clubs Magazine*. Hebard differentiated between Americanization and citizenship, arguing that Americanization involved more complicated processes than simply satisfying requirements for naturalization. Hebard lamented the "few questions" required for citizenship and urged her audience to participate in Americanizing immigrants, helping them understand the principles of government and the meaning of liberty. Hebard anticipates Berlant's categories of "utopian America and the historical United States" as she asserts the inadequacy of simply satisfying requirements for citizenship and urges clubwomen to embrace an Americanizing project that seeks to imbue immigrants with the "national fantasy" of "collectively held affect." It will not be sufficient, Hebard argues, for immigrants to conform to the laws of the nation; they must enter the utopia of the national fantasy. Writing at the end of the thirty-year reign of Josiah Strong's *Our Country,* Hebard echoes his assertion of "facts" about the nation—particularly the number of recent immigrants and their "ignorance and poverty"—and his insistence on an Anglo-Saxon "utopia."[123]

Hebard fails to recognize that clubwomen, even the relatively homogeneous white middle-class readers of the General Federation's magazine, did not wholly embrace the utopia of national fantasy. They insisted, in various ways, on retaining the local identities inscribed by their literacy practices, and in response to the dominant constructions of Americanization, they proposed alternative utopias. To be sure, white middle-class clubwomen were more likely than any other group of clubwomen to identify with the national fantasy, as Julia Ward Howe's speech to the Saturday Morning Club demonstrates. In holding up the "idea of America," in which all "aliens" will "fulfill the unifying idea," Howe articulates a version of the utopia of national fantasy, but she also acknowledges the local and everyday life of "Indian and Negro colleges" as well as the "noble Italians" distinguished by their individual "birth, fortune or profession."[124] Similarly, even as these clubwomen sought to transform immigrants and working women into "sweet beautiful girls," the texts they produced and consumed show their confrontations with the poverty, limited opportunities, and exploitation that marked the everyday lives of working women. Furthermore, with programs on women writers, women and history, and a variety of women's issues, they contested the gendered representation of traditional narratives, thereby resisting the male dominance of national fantasy, and insisted on a fantasy that included people with everyday lives similar to their own.

Working women's clubs also embraced many aspects of the national fantasy. In particular, those who sought to become more "white" by shedding their identity as immigrants, invested much in the utopian promise of America. Learning English, struggling to obtain the cultural capital of book learning, and distancing themselves from African Americans, these clubwomen attempted to transcend their local existences in favor of the "boundless identity" of utopian America. At same time, these women retained a clear focus on their everyday lives as they fought for reasonable wages and improved working conditions. Their club texts reflected an emphasis on self-government and self-support, along with their insistence on autonomy from their more affluent supporters. In defining themselves as workers and insisting on the value of their labor, they pointed to the possibility of multiple identities, as opposed to the all-encompassing identity of utopian America. Even though the national fantasy explicitly excluded them in many ways, African American and Jewish clubwomen adhered to many of its terms. As they espoused the politics of respectability and proved their ability to adhere to white middle-class norms, African American clubwomen asserted their claim to utopian America. They declared their right, on the basis of birth and behavior, to take precedence over recent immigrants, and they based their declaration on the "boundless identity" (rather than a racialized one) of utopian America. Similarly, Mormon clubwomen resisted constructions of the nation that stigmatized their religion or denied them the full participation of statehood. At the same time, these women proposed alternatives to the utopian perspective. Berlant observes that "laws produce commentary on what constitutes national identity in the dominant cultural discussion." In advocating changes in laws that discriminated against them and in improving the lot of those with whom they could be identified, these women gave priority to their everyday lives over the more abstract principles of an American utopia, resisting what Berlant calls "the interarticulation . . . between the United States and America, the nation and utopia."[125] African American clubwomen also called the national fantasy into question as they searched for solutions to problems of urban life and reflected on industrialization as it was defined for or by members of their race. As they appropriated such Anglo-Saxon figures as George Washington, highlighted the accomplishments of members of their race, affirmed their patriotism, and spoke out against the prejudices that always stalked them, they called further attention to the need for a more inclusive American identity.

Operating from their various social locations, clubwomen carried out, through their literacy practices, cultural work that both resisted and fostered constructs of the nation that emerged from demographic and economic shifts. By producing, circulating, and consuming texts, they developed affective connections with the utopia of America. The very existence of their own clubs enabled them to consider new political confederations outside the utopian construct, and they used these confederations to question as well as support the nation. In textual terms they opened the possibility of looking beyond the national fantasy toward an Americanization of their own making, one that included greater respect for diversity and an appreciation for the contributions of *all* citizens.

3

Valuing and Devaluing Dollars

✦〜◉⇌〜✦

❧ Thousands of colored women subscribe for the *Ladies' Home Journal;* hundreds of colored women are active workers in getting subscribers; and yet its editor tells Mrs. Mossell that he can not accept contributions to the columns of his paper from women known to be colored for fear of antagonizing his southern white subscribers. Think of this, you colored women whose dollars and efforts are going that this man may live in princely style; think of your money going to support in luxury the writers of that paper, while you hesitate to give ten cents toward the encouragement of writers of your own race! O, the pity of it!

JOSEPHINE RUFFIN,

"Editorial," *Woman's Era,* 1895

❧ The committee believes that only by doing for other groups of women, who here and there are making isolated attempts at self-culture, what older clubs did for our own in its weakness, can this club pay the debt it owes to such clubs. It would, moreover, seem that the same effort which has been spent in intermittent letter writing would result in vastly more benefit to all concerned if it could be systematized. The committee therefore recommends that an agreement be entered into among the best known clubs, to exchange programs and new plans of work at the beginning of each club year. . . . Also it recommends an exchange of copies of constitutions and similar documents whenever the same are revised. Further that programs of special meetings, entertainment, and the like be sent from each club to the others whenever such meetings occur. This will enable clubs to mark one another's growth, and will be suggestive of better methods to all.

Minutes of the Indianapolis
Woman's Club, 1882

~≡ Miss Kate Field of New York was introduced to the meeting as interested in organizing a similar club in that city and wishing to know of plans and purposes. A statement of the general principles and purposes of the Club was made and conversation ensued. Miss Field expressed sympathy with our movement and took a copy of the constitution; it was also proposed that the two clubs be affiliated.

Minutes of the New England
Women's Club, 1868

~≡ Would it not be possible for each club to give five or ten minutes at every business meeting to consider what is to be put on the monthly statement? By means of these reports, help will be given not only to the clubs in our own League, but to club life all over the country, for, as the League becomes better known as a bureau of information for club work, we shall have more and more inquiries. At the present time the morning's mail often brings half a dozen. Will you help the League meet these inquiries?

"The League,"
Club Worker, 1899

~≡ The Utah Woman's Press Club met at the office of the *Woman's Exponent,* Wednesday evening, June 3rd, 1896, president E. B. Wells in the chair. Opened with prayer by Mrs. C. C. R. Wells. Minutes of previous meeting read and with two exceptions approved. The exceptions were that Miss Barton president of the Red Cross society be mentioned by her full name Clara Barton. Also that Mrs. Brown who wrote the club the interesting letter from Washington, D.C. be mentioned by her full name Isabella Cameron Brown. A visitor to the club for the evening was Miss Sybil Stewart. . . . Phoebe C. Young read an interesting paper on "The Armenians," which will be published.

"U.W.P.C.,"
Woman's Exponent, 1896

↝≡ Mrs. Rottenheim, feeling that we should signalize the possession of our new home by some specific act for the good of others, outside of our regular work, moved that Mrs. Ascher be appointed a committee of one to represent the NY Section in the distribution of stamps, to be sold for the relief of Jewish War Sufferers.

Minutes of the New York Section of the
National Council of Jewish Women, 1915

↝≡ Working for others develops club feeling. When a committee goes out with flowers to sick friends, when a member goes with a Christmas stocking or an invitation to a tree for poor children, when a hospital ward is visited by a group—all in the name of the club, the feeling grows that it is good to be a club girl and thus doing for others makes the privilege of doing for themselves more appreciated.

"Thoughts from Club Members,"
Far and Near, 1891

↝≡ Mrs. Bakeman also read a communication from Professor W. E. B. Du Bois asking for information relative to charitable and other institutions maintained for the race. Her answer to Professor Du Bois's communication was also represented and read.

Minutes of the Detroit
Study Club, 1909

↝≡ Woman's fitness for the work of charity is emphasized throughout the old Hebrew writings. According to their idea the perfect woman must possess energy, strength of purpose and active zeal in ministering to the poor at her door, giving them her time, her trouble, her loving sympathy. She *may* open her mouth to wisdom, but her tongue *must* know the law of kindness. As the needle to the pole, so should a true woman's heart turn to deeds of charity. If man's proper study is man, woman's proper study is charity. This is the work that lies nearest her, and should be dearest to her.

CARRIE SHEVELSON BENJAMIN,
"Woman's Place in Charitable Work—What It Is
and What It Should Be,"
Papers of the Jewish Women's Congress, 1894

Intimate Practices

⇢⇨ The woman's club movement has also an economic value. The modern woman is capable and restless and requires a field for her energies; she would enter into the competitive struggle for existence far more than she does at present, when necessity is usually the spur which forces her into the labor market, did not these altruistic organizations furnish her with occupation.

DORA TWEED,
"Woman in Club Life,"
Papers of the Woman's Club of Olympia, Washington, 1896

⇢⇨⇦⇠

IN 1883 the Curtis Publishing Company issued the *Ladies' Home Journal*. Like *Godey's Lady's Book* before it, this new publication addressed a female audience, offering, under the initial editorship of Louisa Knapp Curtis, a variety of selections designed to interest women. Unlike *Godey's,* the *Journal* gave a prominent place to advertising, both graphically and rhetorically. Particularly under Edward Bok, who was editor from 1889 to 1919, it played an important part in the growing consumer culture, affirming and guiding women in their new social roles as consumers. As capital-intensive production flourished, purchasing power increased, and material goods helped standardize tastes, consumption, long the term to describe a fatal disease, became the constitutive social act, and "wise buying" entered the list of criteria by which a woman's domestic skill could be measured.[1]

The *Journal* aided this process by making advertisements more prominent and by advising women on their consuming. Creating what William Leach calls a "commercial aesthetic of desire and longing," a set of enticements constructed to induce people to purchase—or in some cases steal—the commodities that spewed forth from factories, advertisements fostered buying, and the *Journal* provided a means of circulating ads.[2] Reading these sensually appealing enticements served to connect individual women to the circuit of production and consumption.[3] Advertisements had been included in such magazines as *Godey's,* but they had been concentrated at the back of the magazines so they would not intrude directly on the texts of articles. Printed in relatively small type with few pictures and little attention to graphic detail, advertisements published before 1880 were relatively obscure. In contrast, the advertisements in the *Jour-*

nal employed eye-catching photographs and graphic details accompanied by memorable terms and phrases. To further emphasize their importance, the advertising pages were cut when magazines arrived, while article pages remained uncut. Readers could thus immediately gaze at the commodities the advertisers offered, but they had to use a knife before they could read the written texts. The sheer number of advertisements also increased, occupying more than 60 percent of the *Journal* by 1920.[4] Edward Bok also instituted editorial practices designed to change the *processes* of reading. Beginning in 1896, he instituted a layout practice called "ad-stripping" or "tailing," which divided articles and ran them into columns in the back pages next to advertisements so that readers would be more likely to see the ads.

In addition to making his readers more aware of advertisements, Bok tried to increase their confidence in these enticements. The *Journal* reassured its readers that it would help them with their (new) task of evaluating manufactured commodities. Emphasizing practical suggestions for domestic efficiency rather than the powers of moral influence *Godey's* encouraged, the *Journal* portrayed buying as a way of belonging, both to the "family" of the magazine and to the larger culture.[5] To establish the *Journal* as protecting its readers from "swindlers" and other disreputable advertisers, Bok inaugurated a campaign against misleading patent medicine and offered to reimburse readers who felt cheated by an advertiser. These strategies simultaneously increased the *Journal*'s circulation and fostered the growth of consumer culture. By 1886 it had a circulation of 400,000 (compared with *Godey's* earlier circulation of 150,000), in 1911 it established the first marketing research department in the magazine industry, and it remained a best-seller through the early decades of the twentieth century.

At the same time that design features, layout, and editorial policies lent new prominence and credibility to advertisements, the content of the *Journal* reflected the values of consumer culture (while retaining enough of the familiar to reassure readers). Practical advice on dressmaking, flower arrangement, and housecleaning replaced discussions of morality and culture that had appeared in *Godey's,* and women were encouraged to serve as "their husband's aide-de-camp rather than his moral inspiration." In Bok's view, the way to encourage women's appreciation of beauty was "not to print an essay by Ruskin but to tell them how many packages of flower-seeds you can buy for fifteen cents, and print a diagram of how to plant them." This emphasis on utility shaped the reader-writer relationship. Instead of encouraging the "gentle reader" to think about complicated issues meriting more than one interpretation, writers for such new magazines as the *Journal* presented uncomplicated "facts" designed to improve readers' lives. Critics of this shift charged that it sacrificed "the active yet gentlemanly [*sic*] exchange between reader and author," turned "modern readers into mere paragraph skimmers," and "no longer adhered to the liberal arts spirit," but control of the new popular magazines remained in the hands of editors like Edward Bok, who injected them with practical energy.[6]

Despite its claims about informing women, the *Journal* ultimately encouraged passivity in consumers because, as Christopher Wilson observes, "the reader was inclined to rely upon her 'friend' and adviser, the *Journal,* to do the real scrutinizing," so she could feel she was discharging her duties as a consumer responsibly, without needing to examine products and advertisements closely herself. Just as new presentations of advertisements encouraged passive consumerism even while it seemed to create more informed purchasers, so the "realistic" and efficient voices of magazine writers constructed readers who passively consumed texts much as they did other commodities. Bok's policy of advising women about their domestic tasks built on the tradition established by eighteenth-century British periodicals that constructed private life through textual representations. As Kathryn Shevelow has shown, just when British women of the eighteenth century became visible as readers and writers, literary representations of women adopted an increasingly restrictive model of femininity.[7] Although circumstances in late nineteenth-century America differed from those Shevelow describes, periodicals such as the *Journal* followed a related pattern in simultaneously empowering women by highlighting their roles as consumers and restricting them by encouraging them to consume passively through relying on the advice of others. The *Journal* granted women authority in their domestic consumption roles and at the same time carefully regulated that role. Its discourse inscribed an ideology for women's domestic lives and constructed the home as a site of consumption, with women (guided by the *Journal's* advice) directing its purchasing.

Clubwomen both supported and resisted the consumer culture represented by the *Ladies' Home Journal* so that, despite Bok's careful strategies, the design of the commodity known as the *Journal* did not entirely determine its cultural role. Using what Daniel Miller calls consumption after purchase, clubwomen frequently transformed the *Journal* into forms quite different from what Bok intended.[8] Mormon clubwomen, for example, drew on a *Journal* article as a point of departure for a discussion of whether they should use their own or their husbands' names. Rather than accept a *Journal* ideology for their lives, they embarked on a process designed to develop their own meanings. The working women's Improvement Club of New York did tableaux of both the cover and advertisements from the *Journal*'s 1896 Christmas issue. The secretary of the Improvement Club recommended that other clubs try this activity, warning, "In giving such tableaux, however, the point would be lost unless the advertisements were those appearing in the periodicals at the time."[9] Even as the secretary acknowledges the currency and circulation of the advertisements, she devalues them by recommending their transformation into dramatic material for a club performance. In doing so, she and the other members refashioned the intended function of the *Journal*, recasting it as a script in which they became the subjects rather than the objects of the discourse. Instead of an item to be purchased and consumed through solitary reading, the magazine became a means of strengthening clubwomen's relationships with one another by producing their tableaux, a purpose they affirmed by recommending it to others.

This use of the *Ladies' Home Journal* by working-class clubwomen points to another dimension of its consumption. Although Bok constructed a white middle-class audience in his production of the *Journal*, women from all social groups purchased the magazine and reconstructed it. Like working women, many African American clubwomen also read the *Journal*, even though Bok deliberately excluded any representation of them from its pages. Josephine Ruffin expressed her views about this in a *Woman's Era* article quoted at the beginning of this chapter. In reminding her readers that their hard-won "dollars and efforts" help support the "princely style" in which Bok lived and the "luxury" his writers enjoyed, Ruffin frames her comments in consumerist terms. The women who purchase the *Journal* are, according to Ruffin, contributing to the production of a racism that promises equalization through consumption but insists that all models for this consumption remain white.[10] As Ruffin shows, Bok could exclude all representations of African Americans, refuse to publish the work of the highly educated journalist Gertrude Mossell, and still attract African American readers with the (false) promise of equality.[11] By framing the *Journal* in these terms, Ruffin uses it to advance her own cause of urging support for the *Woman's Era*, which, in contrast, offers "encouragement of writers of your own race." By looking past the consumer product itself to some of the forces and decisions that guide its production, Ruffin suggests another way of consuming the *Journal*, by transforming it into an artifact against which African American women can unite by supporting the *Woman's Era*.

Consumer culture also shaped books during this period, even though their physical appearance did not change very much. Throughout much of the nineteenth century, books represented cultured refinement, good taste, and even spiritual qualities. By the turn of the century, books took on additional meanings as commodities to be bought and sold in the marketplace. A white middle-class clubwomen underscores this in her satirical description of books' being bought according to their "decorative value" and "cubic contents," and she concludes, "Now that I see them there in brave array of gold and green and crimson, I am inclined to think that every anticipation has been met by this shrewd house furnisher."[12] Not surprisingly, advertising began to feature books alongside clothing, soap, and new appliances. Publishers, who had long relied entirely on reviews and catalog listings to make their books known, began to invest heavily in advertising for their products during the last two decades of the nineteenth century. In 1900 publishers spent more than $5 million to merchandise their products, and in the next two decades they instituted campaigns focused on "the revival of reading" and "home libraries" to encourage further consumption of books. They also paid much more attention to the aesthetics of book jackets and covers and enhanced their physical appeal. In response newspapers instituted book departments so that they could attract publishers' advertising.[13] The increased advertising of books heightened their status as commodities, especially as manufacturers began to produce an increasing amount of paraphernalia to accompany books. In addition to portraits of authors and bookmarks, the turn-of-the-century marketplace began to offer bookplates, book covers, porcelain representations of characters from novels, and a variety of other commodities. The 1894 George Du Maurier novel *Trilby* generated Trilby hats, jewelry, dinner plates, chocolates, sausages, and ice cream, prompting an African American clubwoman to comment in the *Woman's Era:* "Here in Boston we have had Trilby indeed. Not only have we had the play, the original drawings for that most famous book, and every article of wearing apparel designated as 'Trilby,' but an enterprising baker advertises Trilby pies."[14] All these artifacts, along with the increased advertising of books, demonstrate how consumer culture insinuated itself into literacy practices as the link between printed texts and dollars became more prominent. With comments such as the one on *Trilby,* clubwomen inscribed resistance to these insinuations.

Indeed, resistance to consumer culture, along with emulations of it, appeared regularly in women's clubs. Years before such organizations as the National League of Women Workers, the National Council of Jewish Women, the National Association of Colored Women, and the General Federation of Women's Clubs took shape, individual clubs created textual alliances with one another. They sought, as the Indianapolis Woman's Club put it, to minimize "isolated attempts at self-culture" by establishing procedures to "exchange programs and new plans of work at the beginning of each year" and by sharing "copies of constitutions and similar documents" as they explored the new and often difficult terrain of club life. Recognizing the insufficiency of models men's clubs offered, women sought innovative ways of organizing themselves and looked for help from "older clubs." By 1882 the Indianapolis Woman's Club had already shared its work with many other clubs, developing cross-group solidarity to face a society that often portrayed clubs as a threat to homes and created obstacles for women who joined them. Reading one another's programs of study, official club documents, club members' papers, and newspapers published by the clubs helped clubwomen feel, as Jennie Croly once put it, "a little less alone in the world."[15] As is evident in the request from the editor quoted at the beginning of this chapter, working-class clubs circulated their texts just as other groups did, and in the process they contributed to "club life all over the country" as well as within their own league. The editor of the *Club Worker* captured the sentiments of many when she wrote, "It is a help and inspiration to keep in touch with work similar to ours by means of these exchanges."[16] Distance posed no obstacle in sharing texts; members of the Pacaha Club in Helena, Arkansas, for example, reported adopting "a charter modeled after the Ladies' Library Association of Kalamazoo, Michigan." Mormon clubwomen in Utah corresponded, as shown by the minutes quoted at the beginning of this chapter, with peers in Washington, D.C., and through reading about such women as Clara Barton and publishing papers about Armenia, they participated in textual circulations that extended far beyond the intermountain region.[17] Such exchanges implied, as the Indianapolis Woman's Club indicates, both receiving and giving. Clubwomen turned to "older clubs" for help, but they also recognized the need to "pay the debt" to other clubs, leading clubwomen from all social positions to produce—often using the major portion of their budgets—printed representations of themselves and their work.

Clubwomen's travel and relocation certainly aided the transmission of club materials. Frances Harper, who spoke frequently to African American groups, undoubtedly carried ideas from one club to another; Rosa Sonneschein, who founded the Pioneer Club in St. Louis before moving to Chicago, surely brought club materials along with her furniture; Ellis Shipp, who took her degree at the University of Michigan and participated in an Ann Arbor club while there, probably transported club papers back to Utah along with her new medical supplies. For the great majority of clubwomen, however, letters and the sending and receiving of club documents constituted the chief means of exchange. A club in Madison, Wisconsin, would write a group in Columbus, Ohio, to ask for a copy of its yearbook, offering one of its own in exchange, and neighboring clubs held a joint meeting, often called reciprocity day. Although they followed different procedures and responded to varying priorities, clubs representing various race, class, and religious groups joined in this circulation of texts. Beginning as early as 1868, when Kate Field of the nascent Sorosis Club "took a copy of the constitution" of the New England Women's Club back to New York, and extending into the early decades of the twentieth century as clubwomen continued to organize both within and outside national affiliates, clubs shared their writing with one another.[18]

The creation of centralized publications helped formalize the circulation of texts. Like the group in Indianapolis, other clubs recognized the value of "systematized" sharing, and, even in the absence of a national organization or without direct affiliation with one, publications emerged to facilitate exchanges. One of Josephine Ruffin's first acts as president of a Boston woman's club was to establish the *Woman's Era,* in which African American clubwomen could share texts with one another. Both the *Young Woman's Journal* and *Woman's Exponent* enabled Mormon clubwomen to participate in textual exchanges that embraced their religious sphere but also extended beyond it. Although associated with the Relief Society and a reporter of its activities, the *Exponent* remained an independent woman-directed enterprise supported by subscriptions. Similarly, the *Journal*'s close affiliation with the Young Ladies' Mutual Improvement Association did not, particularly under Susa Gates's editorship, preclude its including a wide range of club matters. Both the *Exponent* and the *Journal* published frequent references to the activities of General Federation clubwomen in other parts of the country (presumably drawn from General Federation publications) as well as mention of being cited or "kindly spoken of" in General Federation journals.[19] The *American Jewess,* although never adopted as an official publication of the National Council of Jewish Women, aided communication among various sections during the early years of the council. When national organizations emerged, they created mechanisms to facilitate exchanges. The National Council of Jewish Women appointed the Committee on Reciprocity at its first triennial meeting to facilitate closer cooperation with other women's organizations in America and Europe. Member clubs of the General Federation of Women's Clubs created reciprocity committees and extolled their benefits: "With an exchange of speakers near home and an exchange of papers for clubs that are far apart, club will come in touch with club, State with State, and the more we give the more we shall have." The General Federation itself established the Bureau of Information to serve clubs across the nation. The National League of Women Workers numbered textual exchanges among its priorities, asking members to share texts regularly so that the national office could serve as a "bureau of information" for clubs within and beyond the league.[20]

Textual exchanges also occurred in ritualized meetings among clubs that gathered to share oral presentations of selected papers, as the minutes of the Ypsilanti Ladies' Literacy Club illustrate: "The President suggested that we notice particularly the papers as they are read at each meeting that we may be ready to decide by vote of the Club which papers shall be set aside for Reciprocity Day."[21] Reciprocity meetings usually included luncheons and socializing, but reading papers was the main activity. In some instances, textual exchanges facilitated by clubs took on the function of university extension programs, which later replaced them.[22] The process of exchange transformed these texts into gifts, creating what Igor Kopytoff calls a "never-ending chain of gifts and obligations."[23] These gifts served both mystical and functional ends. In practical terms, clubwomen gave and received valuable information that ensured the smooth functioning of their clubs, but in creating these (invisible) systems of circulation for their texts, they also developed a means of transcending their local circumstances and communicating with a larger whole through the affective ties created by gifts.[24] Unlike the exact exchanges associated with capitalism's construct of debt, where the recipient of a commodity returns to its seller a specified amount of money, the "debt" incurred by clubwomen could be paid only by circulating their texts to still another group. Lewis Hyde describes gratitude as what we suffer "between the time a gift comes to us and the time we pass it along." A gift, unlike a commodity, contains transformative powers that work on people, and "passing the gift along is the act of gratitude that finishes the labor."[25] In sending their texts to others, then, clubwomen completed the gift exchange that began when they received texts from others.

By producing their own texts and developing, through gift exchanges, systems of distribution outside the marketplace, clubwomen resisted the capitalistic incursion on writing as well as the construction of themselves as passive recipients of texts. But clubwomen were also implicated in capitalism and were supporters of it. Printing did, after all, cost money, and it often represented the largest single item in club budgets.[26] The willingness of clubwomen to make economic sacrifices to print club documents underlines the importance they attached to representing themselves in print and sharing these representations with others, since one of the functions of yearbooks (in addition to informing members of the content of coming meetings) was to display their projects and activities to others. An entry in the minutes of the African American Chautauqua Circle demonstrates this: "The committee on yearbooks reported that the books cost $5. The committee was asked to find the cost of 50 more books. A motion was carried that the secretary send a yearbook to the honorary members of the circle."[27] Honorary members of the Chautauqua Circle included prominent women who were members of other clubs, both local and national. Such increases in volume often exceeded club budgets for printing, and minutes contain references to special assessments to cover the extra costs. Clubwomen apparently valued textual exchanges highly enough to make financial sacrifices for them, and the display of club activities was thereby extended.

Within the cash nexus of printing, clubwomen negotiated special rates from printers, as the records of Atlanta's Chautauqua Circle show: "Mrs. Johnson stated for the program committee that as a personal favor the printer would make 50 books for $3 using black letters on the back. It was voted that the committee have the work done. To pay for [printing] these books it was voted that $2.25 be drawn from the treasury and that the ladies be assessed five cents each to make up the difference." Records of Atlanta's Neighborhood Union report that "the kindness of Rev. E. R. Carter, D.D." enabled them to publish its *Charter* for $25.[28] Mormon clubwomen, who often faced shortages of cash and who expressed a strong feminist spirit, made a proud claim in 1893 that the *Woman's Exponent* was one of only three papers west of the Mississippi "edited and published entirely by women," including women typesetters. Similarly, working women could not always afford to pay to print their own texts, but they shared the same interest in making others aware of their work. Accordingly, such groups as the New Century Guild of Working Women of Philadelphia undertook the task themselves as part of their program to train women in the trades: "All the type-setting for our own papers is now done by our compositors." The editors of the New Century Guild's *Working Woman's Journal* observed they had originally seen this publication as "a convenience to our own guild members" but soon realized it served to "interest outsiders also in our aims and doings."[29] Other working women who did not have the facilities to do their own printing sent reports of their work to *Far and Near* or the *Club Worker* for the "Club Notes" column. In like manner, working women who could not afford a yearbook submitted their annual programs to the national journal for printing. These various strategies show how clubwomen in different social positions called on and simultaneously resisted the cash nexus of printing. Lacking the capital to purchase their own duplicating equipment but wanting to represent themselves and their projects—rather than passively receive the representations of others—in the authoritative form of print, they negotiated arrangements that supplemented dollars with personal affiliations or their own labor to produce texts they circulated through their own systems of distribution.

Whether they actually did the printing themselves or directed someone else to do it, clubwomen took an active part in the production of texts for which they were also primary consumers, thereby subverting the separation of production and consumption that accompanied capitalism at the turn of the century.[30] In contrast to merchants who deliberately separated consumers from scenes of production that often contained painful reminders of the human costs attached to generating commodities, clubwomen moved directly from the print shop to the meeting site, thus uniting the production and consumption of their texts. Appointing a committee to develop the material to be printed, engaging in negotiations with printers, discussing how costs of production might be covered, arranging design features, and negotiating the list of recipients—these activities occupied many clubwomen. Clubwomen who lacked direct control over the printed representations of their work also expressed their views, as did the working women who complained about the "size and form" of the *Club Worker,* arguing that it should be "a much larger sheet . . . [and] that the paper should be of a grade not so easily torn and rumpled while passing though the mails."[31] Middle-class white women often paid considerable attention to the aesthetic details of their publications, thus projecting onto their texts the sense of taste and style they conveyed in home decoration. Using artistic features and layout designs to capitalize on the technical capabilities of print, these women simultaneously distanced themselves from the uniformity and mechanized quality of print and deployed its authority.[32]

Unlike such editors as Edward Bok, clubwomen did not aim to make large profits from their printed representations of themselves and their work. By conceiving of their texts as part of an elaborate system of gift exchange rather than as commodities for generating profits, clubwomen evaded the distanced and impersonal transfers of capitalism, substituting for them the emotional (even erotic) connections implied by gift giving. Clubs circulated their texts for a number of reasons—to share their ideas and activities with others, to display their accomplishments, to represent themselves in their own terms—but underlying all of these was a strong sense of affection for and affinity with other clubwomen. They shared their texts because they liked and cared for one another as individuals and as groups motivated by common goals and gratitude. Similar to the intensive bonding anthropologists describe accompanying gift exchanges, the circulation of texts created and sustained affective alliances among clubwomen.[33] Because the emotional ties among clubwomen invested their texts with an erotic valence, they operated outside capitalism's mandate of scarcity.[34] Instead of arranging the production and distribution of their texts according to a profit motive, clubwomen operated from the mandate of desire. If they wished to enlarge the number of yearbooks produced, as members of the Chautauqua Circle did, they simply allocated more money to the project instead of taking recourse in the principle of scarcity, which would have dictated that they reduce the number of items printed.

This is not to say that clubwomen did not worry about raising funds to support their publications. The *Club Worker* regularly ran contests to see which club or individual could generate the greatest number of subscriptions, and the *Young Woman's Journal* urged readers to help enlarge the subscription list so that the *Journal* could become both a "literary and financial success," admonishing subscribers not to lend their copies because it would "injure the circulation of the *Journal*."[35] Many clubwomen's publications emulated the capitalist world by including advertising. In 1902, for example, the *Club Worker* expanded its production run by negotiating with the publisher: "Mr. Hewitt agrees to publish from 1500 to 3000 copies of *The Club Worker* 10 months in the year free of charge to the League, taking his compensation from the advertisements. All advertisements are subject to the League's approval, and may be rejected if found in any way objectionable or unsuited to the character of the magazine."[36] Subsequently readers were encouraged to "cooperate with the advertising department" by reading and responding to the offers made by advertisers because "it is largely through them that *The Club Worker* has been so much improved." Assuring club members that advertisers were "interested in the growth of your movement and admire your courage and independence," the editor urged readers to "watch what they offer in our pages."[37] Clubwomen in other social locations took a similarly ambivalent stance on advertising.[38] They acquiesced to its economic power by including and calling attention to it in their publications, but they also attempted to resist and control it by regulating its content. Unlike Edward Bok, who conceived of advertisements as a means of generating profits, clubwomen saw them as a way to support their textual exchanges.

In seeing texts as gifts rather than as commodities, clubwomen contended with the ideology of authorship that had taken shape during the nineteenth century. After the Civil War, writing became an increasingly professionalized activity, adapting, as Susan Coultrap-McQuin observes, "some of the trappings of modern businesses, among them market orientation and competitiveness, emphasis on skills rather than inspiration, accommodation to editors' and publishers' wishes, and 'masculine' aggressiveness."[39] Just as the processes of magazine reading changed as a result of advertising, so the meaning and experience of authorship shifted as consumer culture led authors to see writing as a way of making a living. Public discussion of this shift appears in a *Ladies' Home Journal* piece that asserts that "money undoubtedly regulates the literature of today" and that "authors are recognizing the commercial tendency of the times."[40] The individualism and entrepreneurship implied by this approach to writing stands in contrast to women's clubs' view of texts. Individual women might work on a paper for a year since topics were often assigned far in advance to allow time for adequate research, but their efforts were on behalf of the club, not for personal gain. They labored with words to inform and delight club members rather than to join the "modern business" of authorship. Once presented, the paper no longer remained the possession of the writer, as this instruction by the Seattle Woman's Century Club demonstrates: "Papers read before the club will become the property of the club, and a fair copy on sermon paper must be filed with the Corresponding Secretary."[41] This club, like others across the country, assumed that members produced texts for the club rather than for themselves, and it privileged the rights of the club over those of the individual.

Clubs not only claimed ownership but also frequently made decisions about the disposition of texts written by members, as this item from the minutes of the Ladies' Literary Club of Ypsilanti indicates: "It was moved and supported that Mrs. Dickinson's paper on the telegraph be printed in the local papers."[42] Although Mrs. Dickinson is acknowledged as the author of the paper, custody and control of its future publication remain the province of the club. Even clubwomen who functioned as conventional authors outside the club acceded to these norms. Edna Dow Cheney, Louisa May Alcott's biographer, and Julia Ward Howe, a widely published essayist and poet, produced many texts for the New England Women's Club that remained the property of that club. Some clubwomen left their texts unsigned, and this, as Linda Kauffman has noted, also subverts the ideology of authorship.[43] In producing and circulating texts without the mark of ownership, clubwomen signaled their preference for an ideology of communal ownership of texts. National publications reflected the same resistance to individual ownership of texts, as the *Federation Bulletin* showed by explaining how it sent advance copies to state and individual club journals so that they could print news simultaneously, "without giving credit to us, since we treat it all as General Federation property."[44] This undercutting of capitalistic concern with private ownership of texts recurred in clubs across the country as groups made decisions about which papers should be repeated for reciprocity day, published in newspapers, or preserved in club archives.[45] Far from seeing their texts as commodities to be sold for monetary gain, clubwomen invested their writing with communal power, highlighting its capacity to strengthen affective connections among themselves.

Another dimension of this textual circulation extended across time as clubwomen preserved their writing for future generations. The Saturday Morning Club, for example, maintained a club archive known as the Green Trunk, and a proposal to place a club member's paper in the Green Trunk constituted a very high compliment to its author. Through this process of selecting and preserving individual members' writing, the club historicized itself, establishing its own traditions and sense of the past and thereby enhancing its importance and value. The significance attached to the club archive and its contents is manifested in a play composed for the fiftieth anniversary of the Saturday Morning Club. Titled *The Masque of the Green Trunk,* the play casts the trunk as the central figure in which the wisdom of the club resides.

Preserving texts in their own archives gave clubwomen both material and models for historicizing themselves and their projects. Most groups approached the creation of their own pasts quite self-consciously, even when they resisted the labor of writing, as some members of the Friday Club did: "We have also to record an unwilling spirit among some of our members to place their autographs between the covers of the little checkered book, which is expected will pass down the history of this club, even into the next centennial."[46] This gentle rebuke justifies itself in terms of the historical value of the "little checkered book" in which club members, however unwillingly, recorded minutes. An editorial in the *Woman's Exponent* asserted, "It is well for the sisters to realize that they are making history all the time, as the days and months and years roll on," underscoring the self-consciousness with which Mormon clubwomen inscribed their own history.[47] Clubwomen often historicized their organizations with texts, usually written by one or more members, in commemoration of a club anniversary. For middle-class white women this often took the form of a book.

Typical of these is Katherine Barrett Parsons's *History of Fifty Years: The Ladies' Literary Club of Salt Lake City, Utah, 1877–1927.* Printed by Arrow Press and underwritten by the membership, this book places the Literary Club in the context of the national club movement by detailing the founding of the Ladies' Educational Society in 1833, Minerva in 1859, and Sorosis in 1868. The book goes on to describe the various sections of the club, the creative literary work of its members, distinguished visitors, federation, the World's Fair Book the club produced for the Columbian Exposition in Chicago in 1893, the construction of the first clubhouse and their celebrations when they occupied it, and the twenty-fifth anniversary of the club. This account of the club, emphasizing its connection to the national women's club movement, its associations with prominent individuals, and its achievements, resembles histories written by clubwomen across the country. Instead of writing for economic gain or individual aggrandizement, women like Katherine Parsons wrote to create a past for their clubs. Their texts, like club papers stored in the Green Trunk, functioned as gifts to the organization, offering appreciation for the friendship and support the membership provided.

Because of the expenses associated with printing, working women often submitted club histories to the *Club Worker* for printing and distributing. The Myrtle Club's account, written on its twentieth anniversary, typifies these in describing its origins, purposes, and activities. After explaining the members' early interest in (and subsequent disillusionment with) the Knights of Labor, this history traces the club's establishment of a sick benefit fund, a library, a savings program, and various classes. The account concludes, "Unlike its members, the Myrtle Club does not seem to grow old, even the late fire rejuvenated it. For a number of years past we have been able to keep the same membership, about one hundred. We can safely say we do not lose members because they do not like the club, but because they are more useful in some other line of work, often inspired by the spirit of Myrtle Club."[48] In claiming a generative capacity as well as stability and longevity, the Myrtle Club displays itself to readers as possessing a history and tradition worth preserving and emulating.

Similarly, individuals wrote histories of national federations of women's clubs. Jennie Croly's 1898 *History of the Woman's Club Movement in America* focuses on the General Federation of Women's Clubs, tracing the emergence of several large clubs, including her own Sorosis, and documenting the work of state federations and individual clubs within those federations. In her preface, Croly asserts the need for this history as "the natural character of the woman's club development, as the outgrowth of national conditions, and the cumulative evidence of the woman's ideals and strongest tendencies," and she signs herself "The Historian," thus emphasizing her role in this development rather than her personal identity.[49] Although Susa Young Gates's *History of the Young Ladies' Mutual Improvement Association of the Church of Jesus Christ of Latter-day Saints from November 1869 to June 1910,* published in 1911, focused on a church-controlled women's group, it included many descriptions of study groups and devoted an entire chapter to the *Young Woman's Journal,* tracing its financial and editorial challenges in reaching a circulation of 15,000. Underscoring the noncapitalistic functioning of the *Young Woman's Journal,* Gates explains that it makes improvements as fast as finances warrant: "This Plan is chosen rather than that of storing up money in the bank." Having reaffirmed members' lack of profit motive in publishing, this history closes with an affirmation of clubwomen who have been "mutually helped, blessed and mutually improved," thus reinforcing the affective connections among them.[50]

In 1902 the National Association of Colored Women published *A History of the Club Movement among the Colored Women of the United States of America,* detailing important events of national conventions held during the 1890s and reproducing papers delivered on these occasions. These texts, plus photographs of prominent leaders and buildings where meetings were held, a list of officers and delegates, and budgets, speak for the organization. No individual is listed as author; rather, the National Association itself occupies the author position. Similarly, although Jean Hamilton, secretary of the National League of Women Workers, probably wrote much of the organization's 1914 *History,* no individual is listed as author of the monograph. Like an article published earlier in the *Club Worker,* the *History* details the mission of National League of Women Workers, explains its evolution from working girls' clubs to a federation, notes dates of important events, and describes special member services, such as annuity insurance. The National Council of Jewish Women is the author of a history that covers 1893 to 1938, and the elements of development, important persons, and events resemble those of other histories. All of these organizations, then, supplanted the dominant ideology of individual authorship with one that gave precedence to the group.

Women who wrote club papers or composed histories did so because of their affection for and loyalty to the group. In many instances they made explicit statements of gratitude to the club, sometimes extending their thanks across generations, to clubwomen they never knew personally. Carolyn Poplett, author of *The Gentle Force,* a history of the Nineteenth Century Club, expresses her appreciation to the early members of the club "who not only dared to belong to a club but also cared more about empowering others than themselves. One cannot appreciate enough their foresight and excellence in planning, their courage and drive to reform, and their concerns for democracy, philanthropy, and service—all of which coexisted with learning, friendship, civility, and fun."[51] The generosity of spirit that Poplett admires in others and that she herself exemplifies in producing a text for her club stands in sharp contrast to the ideology of authorship that emphasizes individual ownership of and profit from texts. At the same time that she expresses gratitude for the gifts of courage, reform, and service she has received from women long dead, Poplett offers her own text as a gift to future generations, thus continuing the circulation of gifts in her club.

Club archives and histories point to another dimension of clubwomen's textual exchanges. Members avoided the problem of spinning out of control in constantly giving and receiving because they kept their archival and historical writings while giving other texts away. Members of the Saturday Morning Club might share their yearbooks and printed constitutions with other clubwomen, but the bound book containing a calligraphic account of the club's performance of *Antigone* remained forever in the Green Trunk, along with handwritten minutes. This can be understood in terms of what Annette Weiner calls "inalienable possessions," possessions a group keeps out of circulation, even in the face of pressure to exchange them, because "their historicities retain for the future, memories . . . of the past," because they reveal "social identity," and because they represent an "exclusive and cumulative identity with a particular series of owners through time."[52] For all clubwomen, certain texts became inalienable possessions because they connected the club with its own distinctive past, helped members understand club identity, and created continuity among club members across several generations. These inalienable club possessions affirmed differences among clubs, helping individual groups construct distinctive social identities while allying themselves with larger networks and federations. In preserving the inalienable property of their unpublished texts, clubwomen asserted their right to privacy, their right to control the products of their own literacy practices, their "right to be let alone."[53]

Clubwomen "earned" their right to privacy through another set of exchanges with the larger community. Known variously as benevolence, charity, and social welfare projects, these exchanges helped justify clubs to potential critics.[54] While the transactions between clubwomen and the society surrounding them did not foster the intimacy generated by exchanges among equals, the philanthropic work of women's clubs sometimes drew on motives of gratitude. Underlining the debt owed to working women in a paper delivered at the Massachusetts Federation of Women's Clubs and later published in the *Federation Bulletin,* Jean Hamilton reminded her middle-class audience that our "burdens of the last two generations have largely been lifted from our shoulders by the factory girl, the shop girl. She is now doing a large part of what our grandmothers once did; we are in consequence able to have free days like this to meet together. Do we not owe her some definite consideration of her life and duties and problems?"[55] If Hamilton's assertions led members of the Massachusetts Federation to projects on behalf of working women, their gratitude was no doubt laced with guilt about the negative effect their own habits of consumption had on working women. Feelings other than gratitude motivated most clubwomen's benevolence, but no gift is, as Marcel Mauss has observed, disinterested, and clubwomen had good reasons for working in behalf of others. Clubwomen exchanged their gifts of money, time, and talent for recognition, social control, and autonomy or the right to be left alone.[56] With the exception of purchasing clubhouses or renting meeting spaces, the majority of clubwomen's capital outlays contributed to some aspect of social welfare. Even clubs that did not define themselves as philanthropic usually gave away any large sums they accrued, or they carried out a few small charitable projects. Like clubs that defined themselves as explicitly philanthropic, they provided an alternative to the capitalistic profit motive. Instead of accruing capital, they sought to disperse it. The texts clubwomen read and wrote demonstrate the multiple, complicated, and compelling forces that operated in these gift exchanges.

From colonial times but particularly during the first three-quarters of the nineteenth century, women engaged in projects of benevolence. Much of their work remained invisible, but it created and maintained valued social institutions.[57] Often actively encouraged by male ministers or community leaders, women raised money for a variety of religious and secular charities. The ideology of women's moral superiority enabled women to engage in these activities without calling attention to their economic and political significance. Because they were seen as acting out the female's essential goodness, women who raised money to pay for the construction of church buildings were not wielding economic power but simply supporting men's projects.[58] Indeed legal restrictions often limited women's power over the funds they generated. In a society where an earlier generation had awarded husbands prizes for their wives' needlework, it was not surprising that women were prohibited from forming corporations or owning property.[59] Still, as Lori Ginzberg observes about the period 1825–85, "Extremely talented and ambitious women spent decades operating the 'machinery' of a movement, sitting on committees, writing, printing and mailing reports and leaflets, organizing speakers, carrying on huge correspondences, and otherwise performing tasks that were 'invisible' only if one chose not to look."[60] By focusing on women's virtue rather than their power, the ideology of female benevolence "chose not to look" at the full implications of women's charitable projects. This ideology found expression in a rhetoric that emphasized women's special qualities of heightened moral sensibilities, superior virtue informed by spirituality, and a self-effacing pleasure in serving the needs of others both within and beyond the home.

Clubwomen resisted the rhetoric of female benevolence by inscribing their own accounts of procuring and dispensing money. Record books show them discussing fund-raising strategies and deciding how to allocate the money they raised. Members of the Nineteenth Century Club, for example, recorded many conversations about what kind of support, if any, to give the West Side Workroom, a charity where women in need of work were paid a small fee for sewing.[61] Records of the Phillis Wheatley Club of New Orleans include discussions of the mission of its Philanthropy Committee and the conclusion that it should focus on prisons, where members would give "sympathy, advice and reading matter to the inmates."[62] In writing about their charity projects, clubwomen reflect their complicated negotiations with the ideology of female benevolence and their own goals of recognition, social control, and the right to independent action. Even the statement of purpose, or "object," of various clubs contains traces of these negotiations. The Woman's Club of El Paso, for example, asserted, "The object of this club shall be to form an organized center for the intellectual culture of its members, and to assist in the betterment of physical, intellectual, and moral conditions in the community."[63] Part of the "intellectual culture" of this and other clubs across the country included the independent action of self-improvement through reading and writing, but by claiming a role in "the betterment" of the community, these clubwomen sought recognition for their attempts at social control through good works. The rhetoric of female benevolence offered protective coloring behind which clubwomen could explore alternative models of philanthropy and refashion themselves in opposition to the stereotypical Lady Bountiful.

In 1915 the Chicago Woman's Club printed and distributed a text titled *Statement of the Civic Achievements of the Chicago Woman's Club Prepared at the Request of the Building Committee by the President of the Club*. Covering the period from 1876 to 1915, this publication was to inform both the membership and a wider audience of the many contributions the club had made in nearly forty years of service to the city. In other words, it aimed to garner appropriate recognition for the club's benevolence. Another goal, suggested by the fact that the request was made by the building committee—which had just completed a capital funds campaign to finance the construction of a clubhouse—was to "justify" the club's decision to invest heavily in its own desires and to create a textual structure (to match the physical one of the clubhouse) that historicized the organization.[64] By drawing attention to the club's significant contributions to others, these clubwomen—particularly those on the building committee—hoped to win the right to be left alone, not to be charged publicly with selfishness for building a clubhouse. Members of the New York Section of the National Council of Jewish Women had a similar impulse to balance the "selfish" act of constructing a clubhouse with an altruistic one, as the quotation at the beginning of this chapter shows.[65]

Helen W. Coaley, author of the Chicago Woman's Club report, uses the rhetoric of female benevolence in describing members as "volunteer workers" and asserting their belief that "there is a finer gift than money that women can make to society; that the highest service is not merely in relieving the condition of the poor and ignorant, but rather in creating an intelligent and aroused public sentiment concerning the underlying conditions which create ignorance and poverty and in altering those conditions." In identifying women as uniquely qualified to relieve conditions and arouse public sentiment about their causes, Coaley points to women's superior virtue as well as their capacity to use their "influence" to change the feelings—and potentially—actions of others. These themes of female virtue and influence dominated the rhetoric of female benevolence. By beginning the text in this way, Coaley establishes herself as an adherent to the tradition. Coaley goes on, however, to point out that the Chicago Woman's Club spent $13,000 to establish an employment center, which placed nearly two thousand women and demonstrated clubwomen's ability to lift woman's philanthropy "out of the realm of 'futile emotionalism' into a real constructive force" that would be emulated by the City Welfare Department, which "plans to establish a Municipal Center along similar lines."[66]

By citing the specific amount spent and the impact of the club's work on both public opinion and public policy, Coaley departs from the ideology of female benevolence. The rhetoric of that ideology obscured economics and rarely mentioned dollar amounts. Coaley not only makes the exact terms of the club's contribution clear but also identifies it as setting precedents in the public sphere. Instead of acting at the direction of a (male-dominated) institution, the Chicago Woman's Club has followed the mandate of its own 1881 annual report in giving priority to such issues as "the diffusion of physiological and hygienic knowledge among women" and has established its own institutions. The ideology of female benevolence vanishes with this description of clubwomen undertaking independent public action. Having introduced this alternative rhetoric, Coaley retreats in the next paragraph to the more familiar terrain of women who with "unselfish motive" have "made themselves felt in all kinds of constructive work," and she portrays the club as "one of the preventive, constructive agencies of the city." Throughout the text, Coaley continues to juxtapose the rhetoric of female benevolence with language about clubwomen who take initiative on a variety of public issues. She enumerates the founding of the Probation Office, the Juvenile Protection Agency, the Industrial School for Girls, the State Board of Charities, the Public School Art Society, the Outdoor Art League, the School Children's Aid Society, the Legal Aid Society, neighborhood marketing clubs, story hours, traveling libraries, kindergartens, night school, sanitation, and lunches for school children. She also lists amounts totaling more than $455,000 that the club has contributed to the welfare of Chicago. Having made this rhetorical departure, Coaley returns to less threatening language as she concludes by describing clubwomen as having "devotion and self-sacrificing energy," both terms prominent in the rhetoric of female benevolence, and by reaffirming clubwomen's "fine philanthropic intuitions" and their efforts toward that "harmony of things that will bring mankind tranquillity and inner happiness."[67]

Coaley frames her description of club work in the rhetoric of female benevolence, but the projects she details and the way she portrays them deviate significantly from that rhetoric. Coaley asserts the Chicago club's right to public recognition as an important agency in the city, she details the social control the club has exerted in both institutional and personal terms, and she justifies the club's autonomy, its right to be left alone to build a clubhouse without public censure. The cumulative effect of forty years of raising funds, establishing socially valuable institutions, and contributing to the welfare of others—especially when quantified—merit significant recognition for the club. Although she does not name it explicitly, Coaley's account also shows how clubwomen exerted social control through benevolence because they frequently assumed managerial or supervisory roles in the institutions they created. Identifying suitable positions for unemployed women, deciding what pieces of art should be displayed in schools or what literature should be included in traveling libraries or story hours, determining how delinquent youth should be treated, and shaping the kind of legal protections available to those who could not afford to purchase their own—in all of these administrative actions clubwomen exerted social control. Even though the dominant society rarely accorded women executive privileges, clubs provided them opportunities to take on managerial roles. Finally, of course, Coaley's report defines the club as an independent entity, with structures of funding and organization comparable to those of business enterprises. In this assertion lies an implicit hope for autonomy, as well as the right to be left alone.

To be sure, the Chicago Woman's Club occupied an unusually prominent position and commanded more resources than most clubs did, but it differed from other white middle-class groups only in degree, not kind. The types of activities Coaley describes appear in the record books of clubs throughout the country, and these accounts reflect similar tensions between traditional female benevolence and more self-assertive forms of philanthropy. In addition to displaying altruism, record books show clubwomen seeking—and receiving—recognition, social control, and autonomy in giving gifts.

One form of social control popular among white middle-class clubwomen was to construct and maintain class boundaries. Even though the goods and services provided by clubwomen improved the circumstances of the poor, they served as reminders and reinforcers of the differences between these benevolent women and those they sought to help. Each time a clubwoman visited the home of an impoverished working-class family, she reminded herself and those she visited of the distance that divided them, and whenever a clubwoman provided clothing, food, books, or jobs for the less affluent, she—and they—recognized that she did not require similar help. The highly personalized forms of philanthropy clubwomen practiced (as opposed to the distance paid professionals maintained) reinforced this social control. Records of the Nineteenth Century Club, for example, include discussion of an art exhibit composed of pieces community residents owned. Clubwomen who called on workers to solicit pieces for the exhibit saw this as a "means of getting into most of the homes" and doing a bit of "Americanization," by which they meant attempting to make immigrants conform to their middle-class values.[68]

Thrift figured prominently among these values, and middle-class clubwomen instituted stamp savings programs among school children "of the smallest means" and urged the importance of banking even small amounts of money.[69] The emergence of installment-plan buying led white middle-class women to investigate and ultimately condemn in writing this method for "persons with small means to realize their wants and to satisfy their needs in advance of the money to pay for them." They argued it opened the "temptation to extravagance" for those who could not afford it. While urging the limitation of a "convenience [that] has always been available to the well-to-do" can be seen as an attempt to resist consumer culture, it stands more powerfully as an attempt at social control.[70] The philanthropic goals of white middle-class clubwomen did not include extending the privileges they enjoyed to less affluent groups.

Even though they had access to more resources than did many of their peers, white middle-class women did not have a monopoly on philanthropy. All clubwomen sought recognition, social control, and autonomy by contributing to charitable projects. Given their limited resources, working-class clubwomen avoided defining their benevolence in specific dollar amounts. As a representative of the Century Club observed, "It is not so much the amount that is given, but the spirit in which it is given." A clubwoman writing for *Far and Near* went so far as to observe that it was possible to be charitable without money simply by loving other women.[71] Nearly all working women's clubs undertook and wrote about seasonal projects, such as providing Christmas gifts for poor families, or working with specific populations, such as hospitalized children. They often carried out these projects at the cost of their own pleasure, as indicated in this note: "Instead of our usual program of informal dancing on our social evening, [we] gathered to paste pictures on a linen screen to be given to one of our hospitals which has a children's ward."[72] Seeking recognition occasionally led to competition among clubs: "They sometimes engaged in "good-natured rivalry . . . in the matter of generosity."[73] This rivalry, like the accounts of gift giving, demonstrates the desire for recognition that accompanied working women's benevolence.

For working women, social control focused more on shaping their own activities than on regulating the lives of others. The Century Club, like many of its peers, institutionalized its benevolence with its Philanthropy Committee, which looked after ill members as well as needy others. In so rationalizing their activities, these clubwomen demonstrated their capacity for control as well as their autonomy. Both self-support and self-government figured among the principles of the League of Women Workers, and their philanthropy reflected these goals. Like more affluent clubwomen, members of working women's groups provided aid to "poor children" and "hospital ward[s]," as indicated by the quotation at the beginning of the chapter, but they also visited their own "sick friends" and did "for themselves," in keeping with league principles.[74] Initiating their own benevolence projects was one way working women could resist middle-class efforts to turn them into objects of charity. Like all clubwomen, workers explored the meaning of their actions in their texts. The rhetoric of female benevolence figured less prominently in their discourses because their social positions dictated other priorities. Rather than assume a moral superiority that led them to impose their worldview on others, working women sought to aid peers and demonstrate their own capacities for self-support and self-governance through their benevolence.

African American clubwomen devoted considerable energy to charity in their own communities. Recognizing that the ideology of female benevolence excluded them and knowing that the poorest members of their community reflected on the status of their group as a whole, they often approached benevolence from a public relations standpoint, seeking to help those who might create negative images of their race. Like their peers, these clubwomen welcomed and often sought recognition for their good works. A major disagreement erupted in the Woman's Improvement Club of Indianapolis over a question of recognition when a newspaper published an account of the club's summer camp for tuberculosis patients. The minutes include this: "Mrs. Porter expressed her opinion of the unfairness of the advertisement of a few members contributing to the support and success of the camp, when all have taken an interest in the camp and have at some time contributed to its success."[75] Although this can be read as an individual's desire for publicity, the ensuing discussion suggests that members sought recognition for the club as a whole; they wanted their organization to receive public recognition for establishing a valued social institution, one designed to exert control over a disease that threatened their people.

Their version of social control focused on racial uplift. True to their motto of "Lifting as We Climb," these clubwomen took responsibility for their less affluent sisters. Black women from poor areas attracted more media attention than middle-class African American women did, and, as the clubwoman Addie Dickerson declared, "until we shall have helped this class, until we have raised them to our standard, there is danger of our being dragged to their level in the public eye by our enemies. . . . If we can save and help this class we are saved and helped ourselves to all eternity." The "standard" to which clubwomen like Dickerson sought to raise their poorer sisters embodied middle-class values. Not all African American clubs were middle-class groups, however, and like their white peers, working-class black clubwomen engaged in philanthropic projects.[76] Even as they displayed the politics of respectability to exert control over others, however, they acknowledged the racist power of the "enemies" who demeaned them.

Recognizing the enormous needs of their people led the National Association of Colored Women to take on a wide range of projects designed to improve the lives of African Americans. In 1896, shortly after its founding, the National Association of Colored Women asserted, "To attack the chain gang system of the South, the separate car law, to do rescue work in the alleys and slums of our great cities, and for the plantation woman and child, the founding of homes for our indigent, and to show greater interest in the fallen and wayward. These are some of the things clubs in the association are pledged to consider this year."[77] This sense of responsibility for the whole community is underlined by a narrative commonly used to explain the founding of Atlanta's Neighborhood Union. Several variations of this story appear in the Neighborhood Union's records, but one reads, "There was a woman in this neighborhood who sat on her front porch a great part of the day—she would neither speak to passersby nor associate with her neighbors. This woman was missing from the porch one day, and upon inquiry, she was found ill unto death, and in a few hours she died. She left three children to be cared for—here was a Community problem that called for united action."[78] In identifying this as a community problem rather than that of the asocial woman herself, this narrative points to the failure and responsibility of the community. That the community had failed this woman was evident in her solitary death, and this failure engendered responsibility, not just for seeing to the children but also for addressing the forces that created such isolated lives. Lugenia Hope, the founding president, explained the Neighbor-hood Union as "a community, not simply a group of houses of many families, but these families knowing one another, assisting and even loving one another."[79] The White Rose Mission established by Victoria Earle Matthews in New York represented similar cross-class affiliation. Matthews, who had been born a slave in Georgia, "readily identified with the plight of her southern black sisters mi-grating to the north" and founded the White Rose Mission to protect them from exploitative employers.[80] Working-class African American clubwomen also took responsibility for uplifting the race. The Kansas City Women's League report-ed that at its second meeting it collected "money from the members to assist in sending an invalid boy to his home in the South," even though these work-ing-class women themselves needed funds for classes in industrial skills.[81]

Jewish clubwomen spent considerable time helping poor immigrant Jews, particularly by meeting boats at Ellis Island. Newcomers who arrived in this country posed a potential threat to the acceptance of Jews in U.S. society. If their immigrant sisters could not be acculturated, their "strange ways" might reflect badly on the more acculturated clubwomen, especially if the recent ar-rivals appeared to pose an economic burden. Among the many inscriptions of clubwomen's work with immigrant Jewish women, one frequently recurs in the records of the National Council of Jewish Women, and it appears to function much as the founding narrative of Atlanta's Neighborhood Union does. Accord-ing to this account, "A disheveled peasant girl descending the gangplank to greet her betrothed, who had sent for her after twelve long years of waiting and sav-ing, found that her foreign appearance was so shocking to the Americanized man that he was ready to send her back to Europe. Sympathetic Council wom-en took charge of the sobbing, hysterical immigrant, bathed and groomed her, dressed her in American store clothes, and presented the changed girl to her grateful sweetheart."[82] As this story shows, the National Council of Jewish Women sought recognition by displaying its ability to transform immigrants into "Americanized" individuals. They exerted social control that changed "for-eign appearance" into something acceptable in American eyes, and the reference to "American store clothes" indicates their awareness of capitalism's role in acculturation.

In addition to embracing consumer culture, members of the National Coun-cil of Jewish Women emphasized a more "scientific" type of benevolence called preventive philanthropy. As Henriette Frank wrote, "In undertaking such prac-tical work it is not the purpose of the club to become a charity organization, but rather a discoverer of the best methods of advancing humanitarian princi-ples, and of helping individuals and organizations to become self-sustaining."[83]

While looking for the "best methods," council members sought a bit of science's glitter for themselves. Jewish clubwomen avoided social censure for appropriating social science methods because they could point to a religious justification for their benevolence. As Carrie Shevelson Benjamin observed when she addressed the Jewish Women's Congress in 1893, "the work of charity is emphasized throughout the old Hebrew writings" and "woman's proper study is charity." Since immigrant neighborhoods received frequent "friendly visits" from Christian missionaries, National Council members instituted their own program of home visitation, thereby exerting social control by increasing newcomers' isolation from one another.[84] The benefits of the National Council's philanthropy did not flow in only one direction, as Rose Brenner explained: "Just as Council has enabled the immigrant Jewess to become an intelligible and intelligent part of her American Community, so it has given to our native American Jewesses the opportunity to translate their precious Jewish heritage into terms of American service."[85] This written testimony to the powerful connections between benevolence and the strengthening of Jewish heritage demonstrates another circulation of the gifts of philanthropy. Those who positioned themselves as offering benevolence found that they received religious renewal at the same time.

Mormon women, like their Jewish peers, integrated philanthropic and religious aims, focusing many of their charitable enterprises on members of their own spiritual community. Unlike their Jewish counterparts, Mormon women linked philanthropy with missionary work, seeking to convert as well as help the poor. American Indians were among their most frequent targets, and reports frequently refer to the difficulties of traveling through their territory.[86] Most philanthropic work of the Mormon women was carried out by the Relief Society, a body Mormon women created in 1842. Although the Relief Society is now under the control of the male hierarchy of the church, it demonstrated considerable financial and political autonomy at the turn of the century.[87] The *Woman's Exponent,* published between 1872 and 1914, provided particularly convincing statements of the Relief Society's independent status. Along with news about suffrage and women's various endeavors, this publication contained, in its words, an "almost complete history of woman's work in Utah and matters pertaining thereto."[88] Mormon clubwomen (membership in clubs and the Relief Society overlapped) who carried out philanthropic projects sought a complicated form of recognition. On one hand they sought acceptance from eastern white middle-class groups with whom they shared texts, attended national congresses and meetings, and worked on projects of mutual interest. On the other hand they wanted to be commended as faithful Mormon wives and mothers who offered no challenge to the church patriarchy. The difficult negotiations between these two are inscribed in a *Woman's Exponent* editorial about the continuing ignorance and prejudice they encountered: "There are still, however, many among the people of the outside world who think Mormon women have no method by which they express their true feelings, and are ignorant on all the great questions of the day upon which other women are so well informed. It would be amusing, if it were not such a serious matter, to hear how women of the world speak of Mormon women."[89] Remaining true to their religious heritage engendered, as these women recognized, stereotypical and negative portrayals of them and their literacy practices.

Instead of distancing themselves from Mormon doctrine or practices, these women made explicit connections between religion and philanthropy. This description of the Relief Society's meetings indicates how members saw their own work: "The meetings were opened and closed with prayer, and systematic order was observed throughout. In each meeting reports were given by those whose duty it was to visit from house to house and inquire into the circumstances of the sick and destitute—donations were received and those subjects discussed which appertain to women's duties, influence and responsibilities."[90] Emphasizing the order of the meetings, the systematized procedures of carrying out charitable work, and the efficient handling of money shows that these women, like their peers in other groups, wished to exert social control by demonstrating their own capacity for rational and systematic philanthropy. At the same time, they embedded their scientific philanthropy in the context of their faith and ideology of womanhood by including prayer and a discussion of women's "duties, influence and responsibilities."

Despite their differences, clubwomen had a common gender-based approach to philanthropy. Occasionally a wealthy member would make a personal gift, but the great majority of clubwomen's philanthropic efforts depended on fundraising activities rather than personal solicitation.[91] Unlike men, whose philanthropy more frequently centered on individual contributions, clubwomen held oyster dinners, bazaars, dances, plays, musical productions, and a variety of other activities designed to generate funds. Given the continuing need to devise new fund-raising strategies, clubs actively sought one another's suggestions, as this request in the *Club Worker* indicates: "Could not those of our clubs whose fairs have proved successful send a short account telling of the different tables and booths, the articles sold, the amount raised, and any features particularly new or attractive."[92] This gendered approach to philanthropy resulted from and underlined the fact that women remained largely outside the centers of economic power as men and the means of production moved out of the household and, as Suzanne Lebsock puts it, "women were left at home, unproductive and earning nothing."[93]

Clubwomen did, however, have access to intellectual power through their literacy practices. In addition to writing about their fund-raising efforts and reading accounts of other successful projects, they educated themselves about philanthropy. Members wrote papers on such topics as "Women in Philanthropy" and "Clubwomen's Responsibilities." A paper presented at the Woman's Club of Olympia, Washington, in 1896 traced the philanthropic work of Hannah Moore, citing her as "a woman who exercised such an immense influence amongst the poor and rich."[94] The bibliography of the Social Economic Department of the Nineteenth Century Club for the 1899–1900 club year included such titles as *Problems of the Unemployed; Labor Movement; Children of the Poor; Eight Chapters on the History of Work and Wages;* and *American Charities.* Articles by Florence Kelley, Maud Nathan, and Jane Addams describing their own work and making suggestions to clubwomen appeared in the *Federation Bulletin,* along with reviews of such books as *Out of Work: A Study of Employment Agencies* and *Education of the Wage-Earners.* Reading texts like these gave intellectual substance to clubwomen's various charitable projects. Through such literacy practices, clubwomen represented and affirmed the systematic and serious nature of their philanthropy.[95]

In addition to helping the poor, clubwomen shared in creating institutions that enhanced public life. Free public libraries, social service agencies, educational programs, and health care facilities emerged with the help of clubwomen. In 1933, 75 percent of the public libraries in this country owed their origins to women's clubs. The growth of public libraries from slightly over 3,500 with 12 million volumes in 1876 to over 8,000 libraries with 40 million volumes in 1899 coincided with the growth of women's clubs.[96] Clubwomen's literacy practices played a direct role in this development since women charged with writing club papers quickly discovered the inadequacy of their personal book collections, borrowed from friends, and gradually evolved the practice of creating collections of books. In developing library collections, clubwomen frequently employed strategies that required no cash, such as the book social. A used book served as the price of admission to bazaars that featured homemade food, crafts, and games, thus enacting a gendered philanthropy that avoided the cash nexus. The traveling libraries established by many clubs to take books to isolated or poor neighborhoods served as precursors of bookmobiles. In 1904, for example, the General Federation of Women's Clubs claimed 4,655 traveling libraries, containing a total of 340,961 volumes.[97] Mormon clubwomen joined the Salt Lake Ladies' Literary Club in developing a traveling library in Utah.[98] Histories of individual clubs and state federations nearly always documented libraries created and maintained by clubwomen.[99] Jewish clubwomen in Denver found few library books dealing with the history of their people, so they approached the librarian, who reportedly "said that whatever money we raised for this corner they would double . . . we [now] have over two hundred books. . . . we also got the privilege of sending this library to any other women's clubs in the state who are studying Jewish history."[100]

Working women also contributed to the establishment and maintenance of libraries, as testimony from the Norwalk Library Club, composed of "young, self-supporting women, several trades and professions being represented," indicates. Founded for "those interested in reading good literature and those interested in arousing a wider appreciation of the necessities of the free libraries of the town," the Library Club determined its mission: "As the libraries are supported by taxation, a propaganda to convince unwilling taxpayers of the usefulness of good literature freely distributed was felt might be of use."[101] Mormon clubwomen established local libraries too, claiming proudly that these were "censored wisely and rigorously."[102]

Making the transition from transient and relatively invisible collections to established community institutions required clubwomen to negotiate with men who controlled the financial resources necessary for library buildings. Since women could not hold office in most municipalities, financial support for libraries often came at the price of losing control of the collections clubwomen had created.[103] Yet traces of clubwomen's originating role remain in public libraries' domestic ambiance and their distance from the profit motive. Clubwomen created libraries to circulate "gifts" of books and looked to an inexact exchange (in the form of contributions and tax support) rather than a capitalist-inspired system of exact payment and debt.

Other social formations instituted by women's clubs similarly challenged the profit motive by offering service to poor women and children, delinquent boys, students, and the unemployed in the form of family aid programs, probation offices, educational programs, and employment agencies. The Women's Educational and Industrial Union (WEIU) initiated a number of programs to aid women. The Handwork Department, for example, offered women the opportunity to sell their products in centrally located shops by paying a small commission. The Domestic Reform League served as an employment agency for women workers. None of these was conceived as profit-making. Indeed, in a report to the Massachusetts Federation, the WEIU explained why the industrial departments could not pay their own expenses and "how the yearly differences between receipts and expenditures is met."[104] Mormon clubwomen established exchanges where needy women could sell their handicrafts on consignment. The Working Girls' Employment Bureau was organized to "meet the needs of working women seeking employment and to offer fair employers an avenue through which they might secure reliable workers."[105] African American clubwomen in Indianapolis established an agency that helped more than 150 women find work in canning factories.[106] Even as they undertook such efforts to give women access to the dollars required to participate in consumer culture, clubwomen resisted capitalism by providing their services at little or no cost.

In their efforts to avoid becoming objects of charity, working-class clubwomen established instructional programs for themselves. Charging small fees—usually less than twenty cents—they encouraged members to expand their minds and vocational skills with courses in millinery, fancy work, basketry, dressmaking, and collar making. Clubwomen studied the effects of such classes by quantifying their popularity and exploring, in writing, shifting trends in interest.[107] Working women's clubs established summer instructional programs because that was when women workers ("always the first to be laid off") could attend. The New York Association's Summer School for Working Women opened in 1900 and, in an eight-week course meeting five days a week, taught women how to maintain and use sewing machines. Each worker paid $.50 for the course, and the club absorbed the additional $8.50 per person cost. Philadelphia's Association of Women Workers opened its trade class in the summer of 1906, offering classes in dressmaking and millinery, and fifteen of the forty-five students found positions in the fall.[108] Writing and reading about these successful projects of self-help strengthened working women's confidence in their own abilities.

In response to the exigencies of racism African American clubwomen frequently developed institutions to parallel those from which members of their race were barred. The Woman's Improvement Club in Indianapolis, for example, established Oak Hill, a summer camp for tuberculosis patients not permitted to enter the whites-only sanatorium. With an annual budget of less than eighty dollars, they provided food, medical care, and living facilities for patients. Club minutes contain accounts of fund-raising plans, negotiations with other agencies in Indianapolis, and discussions about representing this work to the public.[109] Since educational opportunities were particularly limited for African American women, clubwomen lent considerable support to schools and colleges for women of their race. Mary McLeod Bethune started an elementary school that developed into Bethune Cookman College. Lucy Laney intended her Haines Normal and Industrial School to be for women only, but ultimately it served both men and women because of the great need for educational opportunities for all people of her race. Nannie Burroughs founded the National Training School for Women and Girls. Bethune, Laney, and Burroughs all received considerable support from African American clubwomen in establishing and maintaining these institutions. The *Woman's Era* included a highly positive description of the Haines Industrial School, describing Laney as "one of the most energetic women of the race" and crediting her with many friends "who contribute largely to the support of her school."[110] Records of the Woman's Era Club mention raising a scholarship for Atlanta University, and the *Woman's Era* included a full-page description of graduation exercises at Hampton Institute, including a list of all the women graduates, and a full column letter from Emma J. Wilson requesting support for the Lowry Institute and Industrial School.

Jewish clubwomen also established a variety of educational institutions, including a kindergarten in Philadelphia and a summer sewing school in Chicago, where in 1894 fifty girls aged ten to fourteen were taught to sew and then employed to sew clothes for the poor. They were paid twenty-five cents daily for a five-day work week during the summer months. They were also given a two-week vacation in the country. As one analyst noted, "Henrietta Szold's Baltimore evening classes in English, American History, bookkeeping, and dressmaking established the model for evening schools."[111] Even though they valued the recognition and social approval that came with establishing social service institutions, members of the National Council of Jewish Women carefully screened potentially controversial projects from public view:

> We have been criticized frequently during the past year for not talking enough—an unusual accusation for a women's organization—for not advertising more generally the work of the Lakeview Home [for unwed mothers]. It is a just criticism. It is true that for some years, while the work was in its experimental state, it was deemed inadvisable to mention it broadcast. Remember this was before the days when sex problems, the social evil, and white slavery made parlor conversation, and when the Jewish community objected to having its daughter spoken of as not virtuous. . . . To-day conditions have been changed.[112]

In addition to establishing a new and much-needed institution, these clubwomen helped transform public views regarding women's sexuality. Although the statement that "conditions have been changed" does not specify who effected the change, these clubwomen clearly played a part.

In helping create new institutions, clubwomen also (re)defined work. Working-class members reconfigured wage work to include women and used the dollars they earned to enter consumer society.[113] While capitalism operated within a system of wage work, rendering invisible labor that did not receive remuneration, clubwomen defined it in the less profit-oriented terms that shaped such (feminized) professions as librarian and social worker. In 1910 over 78 percent of library workers in the United States were women; as Dee Garrison notes, "only teaching surpassed librarianship as the most feminized 'profession.'"[114] Like teaching, this profession paid low wages, and since libraries, like schools, were perceived as domestic spaces where "library hostesses" could reign, it appeared an appropriate profession for women.[115] The low pay and consequent low status of library work, according to Garrison, "did much to shape the inferior and precarious status of the public library" as a cultural resource, but this marginality also allowed libraries to establish "a more flexible, less coercive attitude toward its user."[116] In helping create the profession of librarian, clubwomen provided a means for women to enter the economic sphere (albeit as poorly paid members). Similarly, clubwomen helped establish the field of social work, another low-paying field that women entered in significant numbers. Social work emerged as it became clear that "friendly visits" by clubwomen did not achieve the desired community cohesiveness. The magnitude of social problems also dictated that a more comprehensive system be developed. By substituting expertise for class affiliation, the emerging profession of social work attempted to establish a new basis for the relationship between the helper and the helped. As Robyn Muncy has shown, the female professionalism that created the field of social work valued the capacity to "pull groups together, to heal the divisions between the educated and uneducated, between professionals and potential clients, between elite and mass."[117] This model of professionalism not only drew on the practices of women's clubs but also depended on these groups for enactment. When the Consumers' League or the National Child Labor Committee sought to address the rights of children, it called on thousands of volunteer clubwomen to conduct surveys, lobby legislators, and write reports.[118] This reciprocal relationship between clubwomen and public service agencies reflected female professionalism's emphasis on uniting professionals and laypeople in common efforts at the same time that it added to the women's wage-earning opportunities and increased their access to administrative roles.[119] The process of (re)defining work in club texts helped create categories of employment that enabled women to enter consumer culture with their own dollars.

Even as they interacted with and supported capitalism, clubwomen also resisted it. Some clubwomen wrote or read explicit statements against the materialism that emerged with consumer culture. "Modern Society," a paper Julia Ward Howe read for the New England Women's Club, argues forcefully against the power of money: "To me the worship of wealth means, in the present, the crowning of low merit with undeserved honor—the setting of successful villainy above unsuccessful virtue."[120] This distinction between wealth and quality echoes in records of the Mormon Reapers' Club, wherein clubwomen describe themselves as "priestesses at the altar of the home, often consecrated to plain living but also to high thinking, where the noblest ideals are cherished and where money is *not King*."[121] Implicit in this statement is an awareness of the conflict between respectability and the culture of consumption that would undermine an identity created by self-management and proper etiquette. Some clubwomen affirmed the identity of respectability, observing, as did Dora Tweed, who delivered a paper to the Woman's Club of Olympia, Washington, maintaining that clubs served an economic function by keeping a woman out of the labor force, which she would enter much more readily without "these altruistic organizations [to] furnish her with occupation." Clubwomen also resisted some of the commodities produced by consumer culture. Records of the African American Chautauqua Circle, which had a long-standing practice of singing the Negro National Anthem at meetings, report that on one occasion "we were enjoyably entertained by the Victrola," but members rejected this commodified form of music and in future meetings returned to "live music by members or those related to members."[122] Perhaps the most powerful form of resistance to commodified entertainment came in the pageants clubwomen mounted across the country. These alternatives to commercial entertainment provided, as Karen Blair has noted, "a cooperative art," in which the merging of music, dance, drama, and art engaged large numbers of amateurs.[123] The working women's national convention pageant detailing the history of women's work, the Mormon Mother's Day pageants, Mary Church Terrell's Phillis Wheatley pageant, the Minneapolis pageant for the Jewish War Relief Fund, and the peace pageant sponsored by the Woman's Club of Sioux City, Iowa, suggest the range of topics addressed and the ways clubwomen adapted the pageant format to fit their particular circumstances.[124]

Clubwomen employed their literacy practices to limit the human suffering associated with producing consumer goods. Maud Nathan, chair of the Committee on Industry of Women and Children, a department of the General Federation of Women's Clubs, served as founding president of the National Consumers' League. Established in 1889, this league promoted better conditions for retail and factory work. Members of the National Consumers' League identified employers who treated their employees well and encouraged women to buy from them. According to the Consumers' League, a "fair house" adhered to its standards regarding wages, working hours, physical conditions, and employment of children. The Consumers' League published a list of such stores and identified with a white label clothing produced in a "fair house" factory. Focusing on white undergarments because these were produced almost entirely by women and children, the Consumers' League originally gave its label to garments from sixteen factories, and by 1914 that number increased to fifty-seven. Because of Nathan's affiliation with both the General Federation of Women's Clubs and the National Council of Jewish Women, white middle-class clubwomen read and wrote about the work of the Consumers' League. The California Federation's report of the 1902 convention of the General Federation asserted, "The most lasting influence was left upon the convention by the Committee on Industrial Problems. Jane Addams, Jean Hamilton, and Mrs. Frederic Nathan spoke convincingly on the employment of women and children and upon educating the purchaser."[125] As Nathan put it, the Consumers' League moved beyond mere sentiment into adjusting the relations between employer and employee "through the power of the third factor, the consumer."[126] Articles in publications of the General Federation of Women's Clubs continued to remind clubwomen that "women who spend are in a great measure responsible for some of the existing abuses and evil conditions surrounding the women who work."[127]

Although middle-class white women took the lead in supporting the National Consumers' League, the National League of Women Workers quickly joined the cause because so many of its members stood to benefit from its work. Articles about the Consumers' League appeared regularly in *Far and Near* and the *Club Worker*. Most of this writing informed working women of the progress of the Consumers' League. In 1901, for example, an article reported, "Forty-one manufacturers of muslin underwear and corsets have signed a contract with the League, agreeing to observe the following conditions: 1) Children under sixteen years of age are not employed; 2) Overtime is not worked; 3) Garments are made wholly in the factory and are not given out to be made up in homes; 4) The factory law is observed in all its conditions," and women were encouraged to purchase clothing from these manufacturers.[128] In 1902 the *Club Worker* expanded and reported that "the National Consumers' League has been offered and has accepted two and one-half pages of space, for which they alone are responsible each month, and because of which they distribute 600 copies among their members." This statement inscribes the need for mutually beneficial exchanges between the Consumers' League and working clubwomen. Texts published in the *Club Worker* continued to inform members of the Consumers' League's successes in improving the conditions under which women worked. By 1914 Florence Kelley could write about the Consumers' League in historical terms, noting, "Many good provisions of the child labor laws and the laws for a shorter working day, to which we are all so accustomed that we rarely think of them, had not yet come into existence when the Consumers' League was started."[129] In such texts, working women displayed and found demonstrations of their ability to change the terms under which they participated in consumer society.

In concentrating its efforts on the needle trade, the Consumers' League acknowledged the complicated relationship between women and sewing. By the turn of the century, clothing, formerly produced by women in their homes, had become big business.[130] Women's clothing constituted the major portion of this industry, and women made up most of its work force. While shifting the production of clothing from home to factory increased some women's leisure time, it also raised the price of clothing beyond the means of less affluent women. The women who worked in factories producing women's clothing often could not afford to purchase what they made, nor could the department store clerks who sold this clothing to more affluent customers. For these—indeed for all—women, clothing represented, as Carolyn Steedman has detailed, a necessity for entering the social world.[131] Complicated and prescriptive standards of fashion at the turn of the century required women to learn and display intricate codes through what they wore. The story of the immigrant fiancée outfitted by the National Council of Jewish Women in *store* clothes illustrates the extent to which the consumption of clothing contributed to Americanization.[132]

Clothing also served as an important class marker among clubwomen.[133] In describing a working woman whose club leadership challenged that of a middle-class benefactor, Lillian Betts uses a glance at her clothes to dismiss the worker: "She was dressed in what at the time was called lacquera, a warm shade of tan—silk, trimmed with bead trimming; a lace collar and a most remarkable hat completed the kind of a costume that always is discouraging to a true club worker."[134] Betts, who allies herself with "the true club worker," uses a description of clothing to discredit the working-class leader. Portraying the woman as garishly overdressed and lacking taste, Betts conflates the other's class status with her unworthiness for leadership. While clothing could reveal class position, it also concealed, as Bessie Van Vorst and Marie Van Vorst demonstrated by simply changing their clothes to "become" factory workers.[135] The importance attached to clothing appears in the energy exerted by white middle-class clubwomen who attempted to control the spending of working women on clothes. One of the most common criticisms of working women (the majority of whom were poor and needed to work for economic survival) was that they simply worked to earn dollars for clothes.[136] Misrepresenting working women's motivations gave middle-class women an additional avenue to social control. Working women, especially those in immigrant families, resisted these attempts at control and used clothing to escape the constraints of traditional family culture. Images provided on movie screens offered models that evaded the prohibitions of both family and middle-class clubwomen.[137] While clothing did not constitute identity, it contributed substantially to women's experiences in the social world at the turn of the century.

For working clubwomen, dollars posed an obstacle to the clothing required for appearance in public, so with a combination of needlework and literacy they developed alternatives. Factory work provided access to sewing skills as well as information about fabrics and fashion. This background, combined with the texts provided in club publications, offered clubwomen an alternative to dollars as a means of obtaining clothing. Articles appeared regularly in *Far and Near* and the *Club Worker* offering advice on seasonal styles, instructions for sewing everything from underwear to dresses, and economies directed to readers who had few dollars: "Pamela wishes to say that she finds ready-made *laced* boots wear better than *buttoned* boots. The tightness about the ankle makes them keep in shape longer, and then the skirt does not wear them on the instep, or wears only the lacing and tongue."[138] The Mormon *Young Woman's Journal* also published regular articles on fashion and sewing, advising women, for example, to use a flat iron ("Nothing gives a home-made frock such as professional air as hard pressing.") and describing spring fabrics ("Korah moires [a new fabric somewhat resembling sateen], challies, India silks and embroidered batistes").[139] *National Association Notes* urged thrift, pointing out the value of "purchasing a dollar's worth of lace, combining it with other materials, producing a garment that if purchased, might mean eight or ten dollars."[140] Just as written texts enabled needlework that produced clothing, so needlework edged into the written language of these clubwomen. Elizabeth Arens, in advising new clubwomen, wrote, "In making a dress, we all know that if we have been careful about cutting out, laying the pattern on straight, basting carefully and fitting accurately, *then,* the trimming and finishing will be comparatively easy work—and so it is with a club."[141]

This convergence of literacy and sewing reflected the long-standing and highly contested ideology attached to women's needlework. From colonial times onward needlework was advocated as an alternative to literacy for women, even though women regularly transgressed by writing. Attempts to regulate women's literacy portrayed embroidery as preferable to reading, since novels could corrupt the female mind. Images of doing needlework in preference to reading or writing persisted throughout the nineteenth century. Rozsika Parker asserts, "Domestic arts were equated with virtue because they ensured that women remain at home and refrain from book learning. Ignorance was equated with innocence; domesticity was a defense against promiscuity. By the late 19th century, embroidery was to become synonymous with chastity."[142] This impulse to control women's sexuality by regulating their reading helps explain why women's clubs, which gave primacy to literacy practices, attracted so much negative attention and why many middle-class clubwomen, for whom needlework did not represent a means of obtaining clothing, felt ambivalent about using their needles. The records of many clubs recount discussions about whether women should be permitted to do needlework during club meetings.

While these women worried that needlework undercut the authority of their literacy practices, they also recognized the symbolic and actual value of needlework. Male hostility toward clubs could be minimized by describing them as sewing circles, even if women read or wrote as part of club work. Denver's African American Carnation Club, for example, included "doing needlework to beautify homes" in its statement of purpose.[143] Needlework also served club benevolence in practical ways. A good portion of the fund-raising carried out by clubwomen depended on bazaars or fairs that sold women's needlework. In addition, baby's clothing, hand-knitted socks and mittens, and other items emerging from clubwomen's needles could be given to the poor. Printed reports of the Hazewell Memorial Trunk Committee included thanks to members for their "very great help in sewing."[144] In making gifts of their needlework, middle-class white clubwomen enacted an ideology that credited them with superior taste as well as moral superiority. As Parker puts it, "When a middle- or upper-class woman embroidered, it was her 'taste' which shed a moral, spiritual light," and in giving the products of their needle craft to those perceived as less fortunate, these clubwomen could extend the range of their moral influence.[145] Given their limited dollars, many middle-class clubwomen embraced needlework as an alternative means of exerting social control over the less affluent.

Consumer culture exerted its influence on clubwomen, but they in turn contributed to its shape. Advertisers, recognizing that many women identified with clubs, incorporated the term *club* into their enticements. Even patent medicine ads found ways to include clubwomen: "The coming woman—who goes to the club while her husband tends the baby—as well as the good old-fashioned woman who looks after the home, will both at times get run down in health. They will be troubled with loss of appetite, headaches, sleeplessness, fainting, and dizzy spells. The most wonderful remedy for these women is Electric Bitters."[146] In contrasting the clubwoman who leaves her husband tending the baby with the "good old-fashioned woman who looks after the home," this ad supports traditional gender roles, but in including the "coming woman" as a potential consumer, it also brings clubwomen into the discourse of consumer culture. Advertisements for the Sorosis Shoe (echoing New York's Sorosis Club) appeared in magazines. An advertisement for the Old Colony Trust Company Bank's Ladies' Writing Room used language very similar to that used by the New England Women's Club to describe club rooms. The ad includes this: "The writing room is in charge of an attendant who will render any assistance to depositors that may be desired and will gladly look after any parcels which may be left with her during the day."[147] The New England Women's Club record book includes a discussion of providing a centrally located room where members could rest and leave packages.[148] Magazine publishers used the term *club* to encourage women to purchase several subscriptions at a group rate. *Godey's Lady's Book,* for example, offered "club" rates for up to a dozen copies of the magazine and later offered "special clubbing" with such magazines as *Harper's, Atlantic Monthly,* and *Peterson's Magazine.*[149] When Harry Scherman established the Book-of-the-Month Club in 1926, his use of *club* to describe a system of distributing books to purchasers echoed the sense of community reinforced by women's clubs.[150]

The activities of women's clubs also provided material for consumer culture. *Harper's* published sample programs, encouraging readers to use them as models in their own clubs.[151] Despite editor Edward Bok's opposition to women's clubs, particularly to those emphasizing self-culture, the *Ladies' Home Journal* featured columns on such topics as establishing a girls' literary club, "with the aim of mutual improvement and profit" in developing "the young writers of the future"; setting up reading clubs in the country; presiding over a woman's club without trying to "rule the opinions of the meeting"; and organizing a literary club that "talks, reads and writes."[152] As women's clubs became more prominent, Bok included a regular "department conducted under the auspices of the General Federation of Women's Clubs," written by officers in the General Federation. Although this column reinforced the view that only white middle-class women participated in clubs, it provided clubwomen access to the *Journal*'s wide audience and offered another instance of clubwomen's interactions with capitalism.[153]

Publishers and enterprising authors produced books that offered programs of study, sample constitutions, and rules of order for women interested in starting clubs. Typical of these, Caroline French Benton's *Complete Club Book for Women* offered over twenty possible programs, with outlines of topics, discussions of approaches, and suggestions for readings. Benton, whose earlier publications included *The Woman's Club and Programs: Or First Aid to Clubwomen,* also provided instructions for making a yearbook and a survey of study topics.[154] Such books imitated the material clubwomen published in their national journals, thus introducing as commodities texts that clubwomen circulated freely among themselves. These imitations and the emergence of *club* in the language of advertising show how the literacy practices of women's clubs helped shape the discourses and practices of consumerism.

Using a variety of strategies and approaches, clubwomen from all circumstances contested and collaborated with the consumer culture represented by the *Ladies' Home Journal.* The libraries, social service agencies, educational programs, and health care facilities clubwomen developed were shaped by capitalism as they took institutional form within the national culture, but they retained traces of their club origins. Guided by principles of gift exchange developed in their literacy practices and enacted in their circulation of texts and acts of benevolence, clubwomen offered a tangible critique of consumer culture by constructing social formations that introduced alternatives to the profit motive, but even in their philanthropy clubwomen relied on exchanges of dollars. The new forms of (women's) work that emerged with club-developed institutions did not give first priority to accumulating capital, even though they did provide entry to the realm of dollars. One reading of these new social formations posits that they made a virtue of necessity, since clubwomen often lacked money of their own and therefore needed to operate in "cashless" systems. Another interpretation dismisses these formations as artifacts of the long-standing separation of women from the uncertainties of the marketplace.[155] Although each of these explanations has merit, neither takes into account clubwomen's own textual constructions. Composing and circulating club documents, reading and writing about philanthropic projects, clubwomen gave voice to the various and unequal effects of consumer culture on women's lives, proposed alternative social formations, and fashioned their own ideology of benevolence.

4

Fashioning American Womanhood(s)

᪢᪢᪢

᪢ . . . the world has need of all the spiritual aid that woman can give for the social advancement and moral development of the human race. . . . If the fifteenth century discovered America to the Old World, the nineteenth is discovering woman to herself. . . . Through weary, wasting years men have destroyed, dashed in pieces, and overthrown, but to-day we stand on the threshold of woman's era, and woman's work is grandly constructive. . . . it is the women of a country who help to mold its character, and to influence if not determine its destiny; and in the political future of our nation woman will not have done what she could if she does not endeavor to have our republic stand foremost among the nations of the earth.

FRANCES HARPER,
"Woman's Political Future,"
The World's Congress of Representative Women, 1894

᪢ The adjective "new" has been applied to women with startling frequency of late. Almost every printed page bears evidence of her ubiquity as well as "newness" of the average contributor. What the new woman has done, is doing, or will do is so persistently set forth that one is led to think that a new order of the "genus homo" has been discovered; yet a little study and research shows that the discovery is, after all, only the finding of eyes to see and ears to hear, on the part of the discoverer, and not a very new order of women.

Does the new woman manifest, with voice and pen, an interest in questions of national importance? Did not Miriam, the prophetess, the sister of Moses, do the same. . . . Does the new woman compose songs of praise and thanksgiving? Is not her prototype found in Hannah, the Mother of Samuel. . . . Does the new woman ask for more just property rights? So did the daughters of Zelophehad. . . . Is the new woman suspected of a desire to wear the judicial ermine? Did not Deborah judge Israel for forty years. . . . Does the new woman advocate dress reform, and prepare garments similar to those worn by men. . . . It is but a brief period in the life of a race since the garments worn by men and women were indistinguishable.

ELLA R. BARTLETT,
"The New Woman,"
American Jewess, 1894

The new woman we shall consider, though, is not a new woman any more than the sun that shone today is a new sun. . . . The alarmist who with upturned eyes and an ominous shake of the head fears that woman is becoming too independent has cause for his fears. She has only just begun to try her strength to the utmost. . . . she will seek the knowledge necessary for her advancement, and, better still, she will train her daughters into that much feared independence and greater expansion of spirit; but best of all, she will train her sons that their love for the human race lies not in the hindering, but in the helping of woman's progress.

ELSIE ADA FAUST,
"The New Woman,"
Woman's Exponent, 1896

We, members of the Woman's Era Club, feeling that an expression of opinion upon the Hawaiian question is especially fitting from us as colored women and Americans, do hereby Resolve: lst, that we heartily commend the moral courage and independence exhibited in the attitude of the President of the United States upon this question. 2nd, That irrespective of party affiliation we condemn those journals which, blinded by prejudice and political feeling have sought to brand as unpatriotic the position of those who place truth and justice above national gain and power. 3rd, We also condemn those American citizens, who, having found in Hawaii wealth, health and homes, and who having grown greedy with all these have sought to obtain the country itself, now seek to excuse their rapacity by traducing the queen and the people who made possible this prosperity.

"Club Gossip,"
Woman's Era, 1894

⟶ Never before in the history of the world was the condition of woman as a responsible, independent personality so eagerly questioned as to-day. Women, driven out of the domestic sphere into the wild struggle of competition in the market against man (reducing man's wages in every case) is, however a modern phenomenon . . . there are only twenty-nine occupations out of 250, in which women do not struggle for an existence in these United States. . . . working women and girls are mistaken in the reverence they have for what is conventional and respectable. They try to carry into the workshop the sweet domestic virtues which have no place in the fierce competitive "war of business" and which become the strongest chains that bind them. . . . But above all, fear of getting into strikes, of incurring the displeasure of employers . . . for being thought creators of trouble, keeps thousands who know what might be done by organization from attempting it.

LEONORA O'REILLY,
"Some Mistakes of Working Women,"
Far and Near, 1894

⟶ Women, today are beginning to realize this and to see clearly that only by intelligence can they attain again to their lost position. The nations of the world have discovered that women must be educated, and they have placed the means within her reach. It has been said often and over, that woman's brains could not grasp and retain knowledge as man's could; well that policy has exploded, and today she stands by his side, and equal in literature, science, and art.

She has studied and mastered all the higher professions, she has done as good missionary work as man ever did, she has traveled with her husband and alone, as an explorer to the remotest regions of discovery.

M. A. V. GREENHALGH,
"Woman's Progress,"
Young Woman's Journal, 1891

⤙⟹ The appeal of Mrs. Washington to the clubs of the country to circulate protests against the Separate Car System, refers to a matter of
vital importance to every colored woman of the country. There is no
one among us, no matter what her culture or refinement, but who may
become the victim of this iniquitous custom, and the experience of
Mrs. Thomas Fox, who was put off in the woods at night, is an example
of what may befall any one of us, or of our daughters, if called to the
South. Mrs. Washington's movement is one of practical moment, and
there is no other to which our women should bend their energies with
more devotion and energy.

"Editorial,"
Woman's Era, 1896

⤙⟹ The National Association has been an education and an inspiration
to the women who have joined it. It has increased their confidence in
their ability to do things for themselves. Thus they have been encouraged to undertake what they would otherwise never have dared to attempt.

Intelligently and conscientiously the members of the National Association have been studying the questions which affect their race most
deeply and directly, hoping to find some just and reasonable solutions
to the vexatious problems which confront them. Against lynching, the
convict lease system, the contract labor system, Jim Crow Car Laws, unjust discriminations in the field of labor and trade and all other barbar-
ities and abuses which degrade and dishearten them, the members of
the National Association intend to agitate in the future as they have
done in the past with such force of logic and intensity of soul that
those who handicap and harass the race will either be converted to
principles of justice or be ashamed openly to violate them

MARY CHURCH TERRELL,
"What the National Association Has Meant
to Colored Women," no date

⤙⟹⟸⤚

FRANCES HARPER'S ringing declaration that the world, and the United States in particular, stood on "the threshold of woman's era" roused little

debate when it echoed among the enthusiastic crowd at the World's Congress of Representative Women in 1893. Held as part of the World's Columbian Exposition in Chicago, the congress, which was organized by and included many clubwomen, provided African American speakers a rare opportunity to address a largely white audience.[1] Muting race in favor of gender, Harper proclaimed women's capacities for "spiritual aid," "grandly constructive" work, and character molding. Contrasting this essentialist view of women with that of the greedy and lustful men who "have destroyed, dashed in pieces, and overthrown," Harper asserted that any hope for the United States to "stand foremost among the nations of the earth" rested with women. Appropriating Josiah Strong's statement that "our country" should "command the world's future," she reconfigured his male Anglo-Saxonist vision to rely on women of all races.[2]

While Harper's largely sympathetic audience raised no objection to her proclamation of the woman's era, many outside the Women's Building actively struggled with its implications of a redefined social order. Prior to the Civil War, women had little opportunity for anything except domesticity, but the dislocations of the conflict provided some opportunities for women to assume new roles. The postwar expansion of railroads enabled women to travel more freely, and improvements in printing technology and the distribution of books and newspapers gave them greater access to information about the world outside their homes. For more affluent women who could afford new appliances, technology also reduced the time and effort required for cleaning, laundering, and cooking. As women began to move into some areas of public life, a set of social movements complicated these (potentially liberating) technological changes, however. The emergence of specialized training and professionalization for such fields as medicine, law, and the professorate served, as Gerda Lerner has noted, "to institutionalize the exclusion of women."[3] The doctrine of separate spheres that had emerged at the beginning of the nineteenth century took on new force when, as Nancy Cott put it, secular and religious energies "reconnected woman's 'separate' sphere with the well-being of society."[4] Tensions between those who shared and those who disputed Frances Harper's claim that the nation stood "on the threshold of woman's era" grew during the 1880s and by 1893 had generated a public debate in which clubwomen played an important part.

Examining the ways clubwomen participated in this debate offers a perspective on the processes by which different ideologies of womanhood developed, changed, combined, and contested. These ideologies, often hidden behind normative gender roles, emerged from the dynamic and contradictory views of

womanhood circulating at the turn of the century. Recognizing that womanhood is a changing, historically situated entity rather than a set of fixed and
naturally occurring traits opens the way to exploring how institutions, ideas,
and daily practices at the turn of the century created "truths" about womanhood. Women who functioned in the public culture—spaces where power is
elaborated and made authoritative—of clubs produced and consumed many
texts on the subject of womanhood, showing how concrete individuals interacted with these "truths," accepting, resisting, and modifying them to fashion
new ideologies of womanhood.

Such institutions as the federal government, the church, medicine, and the
popular media constructed ideologies of womanhood that emphasized motherhood, moral purity, and mental limitations. In 1902 President Theodore
Roosevelt raised the specter of "race suicide" for the "native American family,"
the "upper class people who already tend to have too few children," branding
those who "refuse to have children sufficient in number to mean that the race
goes forward and not back" as "criminal."[5] As the refrain of "race suicide" reverberated across the land, nineteen states passed legislation supporting a
"mother's pension," and motherhood became institutionalized in what Eric
Hobsbawn and Terrence Ranger might call an "invented tradition."[6] In 1914
President Woodrow Wilson proclaimed the second Sunday in May as Mother's
Day, setting it aside for "displaying the American Flag and as a public expression of our love and reverence for the mothers of our country."[7] As the juxtaposition of flag and mother suggests, this celebration of motherhood was designed to reinforce the connection between maternity and national well-being,
and the force of "invented tradition" strengthened that connection. In his proclamation Wilson formalized and helped ritualize (two processes necessary to
Hobsbawn and Ranger's definition of invented tradition) a custom that had already emerged in many localities. Invented traditions appear most frequently,
according to Hobsbawn and Ranger, when "a rapid transformation of society
weakens or destroys the social patterns," and institutionalizing Mother's Day exemplifies one response to the changing position of women at the turn of the
century.[8] In connecting mothers with the flag (and the nation it symbolizes),
Wilson and the Congress that passed the Mother's Day resolution employed the
ancient materials of mother-honoring traditions for the novel purpose of
strengthening the nation. They also articulated, in the language of symbolic
practice, an ideology of motherhood that undercut the new woman by publicly
celebrating the importance of the private domestic relationship to the nation.

This governmental attempt to regulate domesticity marked the private as subordinate to the public, and religious institutions affirmed women's inferior status. In the Christian view women were inferior beings, and a stable society required their submission to men. The "Pastoral Letter" of the General Association of Massachusetts Preachers stated that the proper "duties and influence of women are clearly stated in the New Testament [and are] unobtrusive and private. . . . The power of woman is her dependence, flowing from the consciousness of that weakness which God has given for her protection, and which keeps her in those departments of life that form the character of individuals, and of the nation."⁹ The oxymoron of power through dependence captures the essence of the Christian view of women. Jews, whose liturgy for men included a prayer of thanks for not creating them as women, took a similar position, and even such issues as seating arrangements in the synagogue (when women objected to being relegated to the gallery) led to claims that women threatened Judaism.¹⁰ Mormon theology likewise emphasized the subordinate position of women, and the practice of polygamy reinforced this view. These themes of inferiority, centrality in the religious nurture of children, and responsibility for forming the character of the nation helped create the social category of "woman."

The growing professionalization of medicine also contributed to the ideology of womanhood. As women began to seek higher education, medical discourses warned that both mental and physical damage would result. In 1873 Edward Clarke, a professor of gynecology at Harvard, mounted one of the most influential and widely imitated arguments against women's education. He claimed that women who sought university educations risked a "future secure from neuralgia, uterine disease, hysteria, and other derangements of the nervous system," as well as their fertility, since "the system never does two things well at the same time. . . . Nature has reserved the catamenial week for the process of ovulation and for the development and perfection of the reproductive system. Previously to the age of eighteen or twenty, opportunity must be periodically allowed for the accomplishment of this task."¹¹ Clarke and those who echoed him had an economic interest in keeping women out of universities, particularly out of medical education, since gynecologists and obstetricians were usually the first to face competition from women doctors.¹² Regardless of their motivation, discourses such as Clarke's helped construct the "truth" about woman's fragile physique, predisposition to mental instability, and tenuous fertility at the turn of the century.

The ideas generated by governmental, religious, and medical institutions circulated through the popular media in such statements as these: "They [new women] are less apt than girls used to be to look around for a man. They are much more apt than girls were to look for a wage-paying employment"; "She wants to get the comforts and concessions due to feebleness at the same time as she demands the lion's share of power due to superior force alone."[13] Deprecations of women's minds, mockery of their purposes, ominous statements about their fertility, and criticisms of their methods sometimes took on ridiculous proportions. One commentator, for example, described urbanization and the depopulation of the countryside as "largely a woman movement," claiming it occurred because women pined for "neighbors, for domestic help, for pretty clothes, for schools, music, art, and the things tasted when the magazines came in."[14] Even (or perhaps especially) in their excesses, these commentaries produced descriptions of who women were and what they could—given their bodies—do.

Between 1890 and 1920 many writers devoted considerable energy to defining, criticizing, and poking fun at the "new woman," a journalistic encapsulation of changes in women's views and expectations.[15] This figure, whose chief attributes were self-reliance, independence, and a desire to experience the world for herself, created a surplus of meaning and a comic icon for the period.[16] "Indeed," wrote Margaret Deland in 1910, "one can hardly say 'The New Woman' with any hope of being taken seriously."[17] On a more serious level, however, the "new woman" provided an ideological site for the struggle to (re)define gender, class, and race at the turn of the century. Although popular discourse constructed the new woman as white, middle class, and college educated, women from other social locations also encountered resistance when they tried to achieve a measure of independence. Wage-earning women, for example, suffered continuing scrutiny by the federal government, private agencies, and journalists who issued a constant stream of prose between 1883 and 1914 about female workers. Information collected about working mothers included, as Alice Kessler-Harris observes, "where they lived, what they ate, how long they worked, their education, church attendance, number of children, recreation, clothing, and so on."[18] Even though the great majority of working women were single, studies carried out by the government and private agencies reinforced perceptions that wage work jeopardized mothers and therefore the nation.[19] Labor unions, particularly the American Federation of Labor, continued to reject women; only 1.5 percent of women in industry belonged to a union in 1910.[20] Jewish women confronted similar criticism from men, who accused the new woman of threatening motherhood and Judaism. Although Mormon women in Utah were granted the vote before women in most other parts of the country and were encouraged to seek higher education, Mormon women were warned away from the figure of the new woman with reminders of their responsibility for supporting the Mormon religion. Indeed, some observers suspect that liberties granted Mormon women in the 1890s represented part of Utah's long battle for statehood rather than actual belief in the equality of women.[21] Some African Americans defined racial progress by the percentage of mothers who avoided emulating the new woman by remaining at home to care for their children.[22]

The term *new woman* came to have many meanings, and some critical commentators conflated it with the figure of the clubwoman. Groups of women meeting in spaces screened from the male gaze aroused suspicions and hostilities, particularly at a time when "truths" about womanhood were unusually dynamic. As Martha Banta has shown, debates about the new woman permeated visual images as well as verbal ones.[23] Edward Bok, editor of the *Ladies' Home Journal,* regularly condemned women's clubs, accusing them of "stumbling" and "messing about with mediocre political, cultural, and literary pursuits."[24] African American clubwomen, like their peers in other social groups, received considerable criticism for their participation in clubs, including warnings that club life was injurious to women's digestion. Clubwomen, like the new woman herself, provided convenient figures on which to hang the numerous and complicated anxieties engendered by the contradictions and dynamic changes surrounding "womanhood."

Clubwomen were not passive observers of the processes by which institutions, ideas, and practices shaped the ideology of womanhood. Rather, they participated actively, through their literacy practices, in shifting the terms of their own representation. For one thing, they sought to (re)define "the new woman." Ella Bartlett began her discussion of the "new woman" in the *American Jewess* by attributing the "newness" to authors of newspaper and magazine articles rather than to the women themselves and asserting there was "not a very new order of women." Recognizing the power of religious arguments for her audience, Bartlett looked to the Bible to justify the "new woman" who, like Miriam, took an interest in "questions of national importance"; like the daughters of Zelophehad, claimed "property rights"; and like Deborah, wore the "judicial ermine." Bartlett even defended dress reform by arguing that throughout much of history "the garments worn by men and women were indistinguishable." In drawing on biblical texts to support the activities of women who wanted to be politically active, write for publication, own property, and retain guardianship of their children, Bartlett pointed to (sacred) historical precedents. She simultaneously appropriated much of the discursive power of the scriptures—commonly used to underscore women's inferiority to men—to justify women's roles in public life. In addition to providing biblical support for women's activities, Bartlett addressed the question of motherhood directly, assuring her readers that women would continue to marry their equals in "moral worth, dignity of character, high aims, and noble purposes" and concluding that "homes will be established and children adorn them, and the world of humanity be purer, and sweeter, and richer, because of the coming of the new woman."[25] Straddling the space between the fertility expected of women and the political and economic power usually denied them, Bartlett helped to modify the ideology of Jewish womanhood.

Bartlett's assurances about motherhood had strategic importance since the mother-figure was most frequently offered in opposition to the new woman. In this construction, the new woman resisted domestic life and motherhood (often enabled by the birth control movement that emerged under Margaret Sanger's leadership), thereby threatening social welfare, while the mother embraced home and children to create a new generation of healthy and productive citizens. Even for the "surplus women" who could not, because of demographic shifts, expect to marry and bear children, the personality of a mother was recommended because such women could "devote themselves to the sick and the suffering" and delight "households not their own."[26] In portraying new women as mothers, Bartlett dissolved and disempowered the dichotomy between the two.

Elsie Ada Faust, a Mormon clubwoman, emulated Bartlett's strategy of calling the "newness" of the new woman into question and reassuring her readers that motherhood would not be a casualty of women trying their "strength to the utmost" or seeking "knowledge necessary to [their] advancement." Like Bartlett, Faust negotiated the complex relationship between religious doctrine and women's roles by reaffirming the new woman's adherence to "God's immutable laws" and looking to the traditions established by the "Pioneer Mothers," who "pursued their way toward the setting sun here in this fair state to seek peace and room for their greater needs." Faust goes a step further by suggesting that the new woman would rear her children differently, encouraging "independence and greater expansion of spirit" in her daughters and "the helping of woman's progress" in her sons. In the process Faust reconfigures the new woman to make her at once familiar and strange: familiar because she follows traditional patterns and practices, and strange because she introduces new goals for motherhood. Indeed, motherhood, instead of affirming the past, encourages innovation and change as daughters and sons receive new training. As the statement of purpose for the Reapers' Club shows, Mormon clubwomen carefully negotiated the balance between asserting new roles for women and affirming traditional responsibilities: "The object of this club is social and intellectual development. Its design is to cultivate the heart as well as the brain which will form a good mental equilibrium and fit woman not only to shine as a greater light around her own hearthstone, but to be a more efficient custodian of home interests in the wider domain of the world."[27] Although this statement asserts women's role in the "wider domain of the world," it reaffirms the importance of her position "around her own hearthstone."

Mormon theology, with its emphasis on women's fertility, gave a central place to motherhood, which was reflected in the literary selections included in the *Young Woman's Journal*. During its early decades the *Young Woman's Journal* devoted the largest proportion of its pages to the Literary Department, which featured poetry, prose, and fiction written by Mormon authors. The table of contents for each volume included such titles as "On the Birth of an Infant," "My Baby Boy," "Kiss Your Children," "Baby Boy," "It's a Boy," "My Babes at Rest," "Mother's Butter," "The Child," "Mother's Smile," "The Vision of Motherhood," "My Mother's Song," and "Lines Lovingly Inscribed to Joy" (a deceased child) that venerated motherhood. In addition, some of the longer selections of romantic fiction that were serialized across multiple issues traced the outlines of courtship and polygamous marriage, concluding with mothers and babies rather than with a young couple heading into life together. Clubwomen's literacy practices thus provided continuing reminders of the importance of motherhood.[28] At the same time, Mormon women possessed many attributes of the new woman. As the excerpt from "Woman's Progress" at the beginning of this chapter suggests, advocates argued that education offered Mormon women their "lost position," and clubwomen in the intermountain region joined their peers from other groups in insisting on woman's capacity to equal man in "literature, science, and the arts." When Utah became a state in 1896, its women already had the vote. Polygamy meant that women lived in households where men were frequently absent, which "simplified their household chores, allowing them to participate in a broader range of activities than their eastern sisters," and they often depended on themselves for "financial support and physical labor."[29] Mormon women often traveled long distances alone, particularly to meet with such groups as the National Congress of Women. Minutes of the Salt Lake Mutual, for example, report that Mrs. Dougal gave an account of her trip to Washington for a woman suffrage meeting. Describing many of the women she met as "liberal," Dougal explained that she had exchanged ideas and "found they were dissatisfied with their religion, desiring something that touches the soul. She hoped many would be brought to a knowledge of the truth of the gospel."[30] For Mrs. Dougal "liberal" carries a double meaning. On the one hand it refers to women's access to the voting booth; on the other it describes persons willing to listen to the Mormon perspective. Even within the secular context of a group working for woman suffrage, Mrs. Dougal proselytized women she perceived as "dissatisfied with their religion." While she participated in activities that challenged a more conservative ideology of womanhood, Mrs. Dougal carried out the (paternalistic) mission of her religion.

White middle-class Protestant clubwomen focused a considerable portion of their literacy practices on the notion of the new woman. Aria Macdonald's 1896 paper "The New Woman and the New Man" described dress reform, current events, and needed changes in men for members of the Woman's Club in Olympia, Washington, and asserted, "I want all clubwomen to love this bright, beautiful new woman."[31] In her opening address to the 1910 convention of the General Federation of Women's Clubs, Mrs. Philip Moore, the retiring president, echoed Frances Harper by proclaiming, "There is a 'new woman,' the product of evolution, the result of social and commercial changes—she would be ashamed not to know something of the administration of the city, the state, the nation. She prizes good citizenship so highly that she trains her children to value citizenship as the highest gift of manhood and womanhood."[32] Identifying herself by her husband's name added further power to Moore's claims for the newly evolved woman as one who valued tradition, even as she learned about public administration. Like her peers in other locations and like Aria Macdonald nearly two decades earlier, Moore demonstrates an interest in (re)defining the term *new woman* into a more socially acceptable concept by linking it to motherhood. The long-standing ideology of womanhood as influencing others (such as husbands, brothers, or sons) conducting world's affairs could be incorporated into the emerging ideology of a politically active and aware woman who trains her children in good citizenship.

In addition to exploring the term *new woman* itself, clubwomen probed the meanings implied by the term as they wrote and read about women participating in new forms of public life. Even though few clubs took a stand on woman suffrage, it was a frequent topic of discussion in meetings. The African American Chautauqua Circle, for example, includes this in its minutes for October of 1913: "Our attention was then given to the discussion of the following subject: 'Should women have the right to vote?' Mrs. Bullock opened for the affirmative and was followed by Mrs. Johnson for the negative. It was shown by the argument that both ladies had given much forethought and study of the subject. Each argued according to her own conviction which made it the more earnest. The discussion was lively and was entered into by most of the ladies. All regretted that the time was not longer."[33] In both form and substance, this report typifies many from clubs in various social locations. As Mary Church Terrell observed, "It required a great deal of courage for a woman publicly to acknowledge before an audience that she believed in suffrage for her sex when she knew what the majority did not."[34] Clubs provided a setting where less brave women could discuss suffrage. By examining the controversial subject in a debate, members could consider it without putting their relational commitments at risk. Since the debate required no decision, women on both sides of the issue could express opinions without alienating dear friends. Because it focused on the preparation and study of both debaters instead of detailing their arguments, the report of the Chautauqua Circle avoided the difficulty of appearing to favor one position over another. Furthermore, concluding with a lament about the time constraints of the meeting that "all" shared, this account affirmed that harmony among members transcended individual opinions about suffrage.[35]

In addition to exploring the suffrage question, clubwomen read and wrote regularly about women's roles. White middle-class groups examined such topics as "woman's rights," "recent developments of women's work in politics," "the education and training of our girls," "women in civics and philanthropy," "women in professions," "women in the commercial world," "unusual lines of work for women," and "women in politics."[36] In her 1891 address at the inaugural meeting of the Woman's Club of Temple Beth El (which became the Detroit Section of the National Council of Jewish Women), President Ida Ginsburg began by observing, "Fifty years ago such a gathering of women representing so many callings and vocations of life would have been looked upon as a strange body of feminine creatures, hardly women, for to be employed in labor usually performed by men was not considered womanly." Subsequent speakers reinforced Ginsburg's self-consciousness about woman's changing role. J. Heller affirmed that "woman performs duties abroad in the world and in the home"; Rose Wolenburg claimed that women could do anything requiring "skillful hands" and "quick brains" and that her feminine qualities "shine like radiant stars in the business horizon"; and Rose Barlow described woman's role as a school teacher. These women, like their peers in other sections, used club papers to explore new roles for women.[37]

Working women also read and wrote a good deal about the nature of womanhood. A regular column titled "About Women" contained such items as "The first woman lawyer has just been admitted to practice in Arizona" and "In Kentucky a bill has passed the Legislature providing that a husband may inherit only one-half of his wife's personal estate instead of the whole as now." An article titled "Women in Business" pointed to the difficulties faced by persons who were "bread-winners and also home-makers." Another column reminded readers of the "widening of women's work" and encouraged them to consider training as "attendants for convalescents."[38] With these and the many similar articles, working women inscribed their interest in fashioning an ideology of womanhood that affirmed wage work.

In a paper given at an 1894 convention of working women, Leonora O'Reilly began by asserting, "Never before in the history of the world was the condition of woman as a responsible, independent personality so eagerly questioned as to-day." The attributes of "responsible" and "independent" evoke the image of the new woman, but O'Reilly goes on, "Woman, driven out of the domestic sphere into the wild struggle of competition in the market against man (reducing man's wages in every case), is, however, a modern phenomenon," thereby suggesting that necessity rather than choice pushes women into the public sphere of work.[39] This portrayal of women who must enter the work force because of financial exigency shifts the "truth" about working women. O'Reilly continues this modification by describing a study of women's wages, showing their inadequacy and arguing for unionization as a solution. The new woman, as portrayed by O'Reilly, will abandon "what is conventional and respectable" in favor of joining unions and, if necessary, strikes. O'Reilly's argument in favor of organizing "Boards of Correlation in the different trades" points to the tension working women experienced in straddling the line between club life and labor unions. While they sought the benefits—including higher wages and better working conditions—of organized labor, they feared the social censure associated with unions. In arguing against "conventional and respectable" responses, O'Reilly directly challenges the dominant construct of middle-class womanhood, and she privileges independence over respectability.

During succeeding years working women increasingly asserted the integrity of their own constructions of womanhood, particularly when faced with white middle-class clubwomen who treated them as objects of study. By 1914 they could write such statements as "Clubs joining the League are brought in touch, both through correspondence and the interchange of visits, with many workers who have interests and experiences in common. This enables them not only to profit by the experiences of others, but to contribute their share toward the success of the whole movement."[40] The women representing themselves here insist on the value of their own experiences and resist others' representations of them, including the middle-class impulse to describe them as "girls" rather than "women" to signal the temporary and asexual nature of their status as workers.

In 1905 the *Federation Bulletin* introduced a new column "The Real America" to review the "unusually significant in portraying American life, and especially that which vitally concerns American womanhood." Its explanation of purpose included this: "It is time the real American woman had more to say in her own defense. She is slandered at home almost as grossly as she is abroad. . . . We have been content with too feeble and with too apologetic a demeanor. . . . It is the purpose of this department to have something to say each month on the real American woman, and perhaps once in a while something about her professional traducers."[41] The women who wrote and read this column saw their literacy practices shape a new way of thinking—and talking—about American women. Embedding considerations of womanhood within a larger discussion of American life, these clubwomen created a direct link between national and gender concerns. The explicit link between motherhood and nation embodied in the institution of Mother's Day provided clubwomen the basis for creating an alternative construct by refashioning the ideology of motherhood. The dominant ideology, expressed in what Eva Cherniavsky has described as the "discourse of sentimentalism," assigned no agency to mothers.[42] Clubwomen, in contrast, created a more active image. Under such titles as "Motherhood of State," "Better Films for Children," and "The Problems of Maternity," the *General Federation of Women's Clubs Magazine* offered advice on "infant conservation" for new mothers, suggestions for dealing with popular culture, and information on childbearing.[43] Beginning in 1916, the spring issue focused on the Baby Week, sponsored by the General Federation of Women's Clubs. Scheduled in early May (around Mother's Day), this week-long observance challenged each community to study what it could do to protect its children. Instead of positing infant and maternal mortality as inevitable, this initiative portrayed these horrors as partly under human control. The processes of writing and reading articles about parenting and childbirth helped transform the ideology of motherhood from one centered on idolized and passive beings into one that featured active participants working to change the conditions under which they and their children lived. This ideology took concrete form as the clubwomen lobbied for and achieved the establishment of the Children's Bureau in the Department of Labor, thus providing tangible evidence of the impact of clubwomen's literacy practices on the body politic.

As they challenged the dominant construct of motherhood, clubwomen worked to create alternative roles for women. Weary of continuing resistance to their emergence in public life, these clubwomen recognized that the "mere circulation of news and announcements" did not address their foes, and they offered "some attention to defense and explanation of [their] real motives" in such publications as the *Federation Bulletin,* which was "read as an organ of opinion by men as well as by women."[44] More than once the *Bulletin* carried responses to "the stock arguments and thread-bare iterations about the failure of the American family and the American wife and the American home" published elsewhere.[45] Writing in 1907, Annette Meakin observed that Ibsen's *Doll's House* has "shown the world that motherhood, even though it be woman's most sacred duty, can never more be looked upon as her final destiny."[46] *A Doll's House* appeared on many programs, and discussions of it allowed clubwomen to consider alternatives to motherhood. A particularly interesting interaction with this text appears in the 1890 minutes of the Friday Club of Jackson, Michigan. After reporting the reading of the preface and an elaborate discussion of how members would take parts in the play, the secretary predicts their abilities to portray a drama none of the members has yet read: "Who can better portray the fond mother's affection or that conjugal love which risks all for the sake of her husband—into what meshes of duplicity it will carry her we have yet to learn—it will doubtless be the old story."[47] *A Doll's House* does not, of course, tell the old story but introduces a new one that calls maternal and conjugal love into question. Significantly, the minutes remain completely silent on the actual reading of and response to the play, but, following Susan Harris's line of thinking about the subversive readings often represented by silences, we can speculate that members of the Friday Club deliberately chose not to write about their encounter with *A Doll's House.*[48]

The record book of the Roxbury Women in Council in Massachusetts shows how another white woman's club negotiated conflicting ideologies of motherhood. Minutes for the year 1914–15 include this summary of a speech by Leslie Sprague of Chicago: "The problems generated by the women's movement will only be solved when the home is fitted into its place in the economic world. About 7 million women have followed the industries taken out of the home and are working under conditions not made by them which in many cases unfit them for their great function in life, motherhood. This slaughter of potential life is solely the result of man's indifference."[49] Taken by itself, this inscription of women's employment as a problem to be solved and the implication that working outside the home decreased women's fertility might suggest that the

Women in Council shared Sprague's view, but Agnes Repplier, the next month's speaker, personified the conditions Sprague decried. Repplier, who frequently gave public speeches, wrote essays for popular magazines, traveled alone, and took part in the suffrage movement, countered the ideology of motherhood in her daily life. In her speech Repplier devoted considerable time to literature for children, arguing that "books for children should be few and good and that nothing was so sure to shrivel the child mind as the insignificant stories which are flooding the book stalls at present" and asserting that (educated) mothers should regulate their children's literacy.[50] By positioning the woman as arbiter of taste in the home, Repplier supports a more traditional ideology of womanhood, but at the same time she affirms a less conventional version both by her own presence and her claims for women's power to control literacy.

A different message sounded when Judge Robert Grant gave a lecture titled "Feminism in Fiction and Real Life," arguing that it brought, along with greater opportunities for women, "an increasing disrespect for the sanctity of marriage."[51] Nothing in Grant's address suggested that women should assume active and independent roles outside their homes. Another perspective was articulated a few months later when Frances Curtis, a member of the School Committee, talked to the club about her work and "gave many convincing reasons why every intelligent woman should consider voting for the School Board not only a duty but a privilege."[52] By occupying a position on a publicly elected body and urging that women vote, Curtis represented the new woman who argued for woman's suffrage and the right to hold office. Yet by focusing on the School Committee (where women's maternal powers had already been sanctioned), Curtis softened the effect of her position. This array of topics and perspectives typifies the way many white middle-class clubwomen explored the ideology of womanhood in their regular meetings. Without jeopardizing their affiliations with one another, they considered a variety of perspectives on controversial issues. Even if they took no direct action on behalf of women, clubwomen's reading and writing helped change social perceptions and fashion "truths" about motherhood.

Although the dominant ideology of motherhood focused on white middle-class women, variations of it were used against and by other clubwomen. Working women, most of whom were unmarried, confronted concerns about the effects of wage work on their potential motherhood.[53] Unions argued against women members by invoking the ideology of motherhood, claiming that "if women labor in factories and similar institutions they bring forth weak children who are not educated to become strong and good citizens."[54] Even if the figure of the new woman rarely included factory workers, an ideology of womanhood that emphasized motherhood could be mobilized against them. Given their marital status, working-class clubwomen did little reading or writing about motherhood, and that silence speaks eloquently to their views on an ideology that attempted to define them.

African Americans, like their working-class peers, were largely excluded from the dominant ideal of motherhood, but, as Eva Cherniavsky has observed, the "existence of 'conditional' African-American mothers on the discursive margins of white middle-class culture tends to expose the equally contingent status of a supposedly original white motherhood."[55] In addition to shaping discourses about white motherhood, these clubwomen fashioned their own ideology, one that emphasized racial uplift. They followed Fannie Barrier Williams's injunction to "become civic mothers of the race" to "cultivate among the people a fine sensitiveness as to the rights and wrongs, the proprieties and improprieties that enter into—nay regulate the social status of the race."[56]

Reshaping the ideology of motherhood dovetailed with clubwomen's campaign for world peace. As early as 1874 Julia Ward Howe, a founding member of the New England Women's Club in Boston, had proposed June 2 as Mother's Day, on which "the topic of Peace should be earnestly presented."[57] While Howe's mother-peace connection resembles President Wilson's mother-flag idea, her concern with promoting peace reflects a very different emphasis from that of a president who proclaimed Mother's Day shortly before leading the United States into World War I. Howe continued the campaign for peace through much of her long life, frequently weaving it into her club work. Her paper for the 1904 Peace Congress was reprinted in the *Federation Bulletin*. In this paper Howe draws on the ideal of motherhood, arguing that women, because they give life "by great suffering" and maintain it by "cares and fatigues scarcely less severe," possess a "special interest and duty" in the promotion of peace.[58] Howe's position as a leader in the General Federation strengthened its stance on peace. In 1898 Ellen Henrotin, then president of the General Federation wrote a (widely reprinted) letter to President Wilson in which she called on the ideology of motherhood to support her plea: "On us war will fall heaviest, for we must give our sons, and during and after the war, must help to repair the ravages and losses and mitigate the sufferings which such a terrible event must inevitably bring in its train."[59] The 1912 convention of the General Federation included two "significant addresses on Peace," one by Baroness Bertha Von Suttner of the Austrian Peace Society, who cited the American peace movement as a model for her own nation, and another by Frances Squire Potter, who noted that the world had seen many declarations of war and stated, "The time has come when the world is ready for a new Declaration of Independence, one that shall put an end to war—a declaration so creative, so cosmic, so star-high and mountain deep, that the bugles and the gaudy pageantry of war shall shrivel to nothingness in its presence."[60]

The national associations of other clubwomen matched the General Federation's enthusiasm for peace. Hannah Solomon signed a peace petition on behalf of the National Council of Jewish Women in 1898, urging President William McKinley to avoid war with Spain; in 1908 the National Council established the Committee on Peace and Arbitration, with the goal of promoting world peace; and in 1920 it endorsed a resolution in favor of establishing the League of Nations to "safeguard peace."[61] Even as late as 1914 working women supported peace rather than war. An article in the *Club Worker* argued the merits of democracy over war and pointed to clubs as sites that call attention to "the constant need to be democratic" and encourage "race-tolerance," thereby providing an alternative to war. Another article urged mothers to teach their children that "lasting peace . . . cannot be secured by armed forces" and described the women's peace movement as "the rebirth of humanity".[62] Mary Church Terrell, a member of the Women's Peace Party as well as president of the National Association of Colored Women, joined her peers in urging alternatives to violence in resolving international disagreements.[63]

In addition to the proclamations national groups and leaders offered, individual club members wrote papers, read and discussed publications, and furthered the cause of peace by reconfiguring the ideology of motherhood. Mormon clubwomen regularly read and wrote about their concern for peace. As one commentator put it, "The Latter Day Saints above all people should be on the side of peace." Many individual groups adopted peace resolutions with such language as "Whereas there has been an appeal made to the women of Utah to participate in the Czar's International Peace Measure. . . . We the women of Castle Dale . . . heartily endorse this measure. . . . we do not endorse the present procedures of settling difficulties among the nations, because it destroys life, it causes sorrow and distress and leaves widows and fatherless children who mourn the loss of those who are slain."[64] Even though these clubwomen looked to their religion to justify their position on peace, it was their experience as mothers (of fatherless children) that gave energy to their claims.

With the onset of World War I clubwomen struggled with conflicting loyalties. Desiring to demonstrate their patriotism and loyalty to the nation, they sacrificed their own pleasures, provided goods and services, and aided conservation efforts. Printed yearbooks, annual banquets, and elaborate program presentations were among the casualties of war as clubwomen from all social groups volunteered in Red Cross workrooms, collected tin cans, and purchased war bonds. Club records also inscribed overtly patriotic acts, such as saluting the flag, singing patriotic songs, and listening to speeches by leaders of the war effort.[65] At the same time, some clubwomen found subtle ways to support the peace movement while remaining loyal to the nation. That women felt obliged to support the war despite their earlier peace work has sometimes been explained as the price of suffrage. Recognizing that any future support for their right to vote depended on showing themselves to be loyal citizens, clubwomen knew that they had to demonstrate support for the nation in a time of crisis.[66] Still, clubwomen often managed quiet expressions of their opposition to warfare, as did members of the North Carolina Federation, who described each clubwoman as "doing her duty as a home soldier, conserving food, practicing thrift, and hoping for peace."[67] This inscription of a hope for peace rather than victory demonstrates the deftness with which clubwomen resisted the aggression and imperialism that underlay war. While carrying out war-support activities and avoiding any reproachable behavior, clubwomen like these expressed their continued commitment to peace.

Clubwomen also used the war effort to further their own ideologies of womanhood. In reporting that a New York club had set up rooms where members made surgical dressings, the *Club Worker* added, "The particularly practical and appealing feature of this work is that a free employment bureau for women is being run in connection with it, and that, while without a position, many working women, who would otherwise have no source of income, find temporary work which gives them not only a very modest wage, but the inspiration of helping in a great emergency."[68] Along with showing how working women demonstrated national loyalty through service, this carefully crafted sentence uses the occasion of war work to further the idea of women as workers—in need of steady and well-paying employment.

African American clubwomen joined their white peers in supporting the war effort, often seizing this as an opportunity to prove themselves "just as good Americans," by adhering to the "same standards of conduct and quality of helpfulness in war work."[69] In a report on her experiences in a hostess house at Camp Upton, Lugenia Hope, president of Atlanta's Neighborhood Union, wrote, "This war has found Negroes ready to enter any door which has opened to them whether in industrial pursuits or ameliorative service," and she described her work in supplying houses with "colored women of culture and sympathy, so that hostess house #3 at Camp Upton has become a democratic place of assembly where all races and creeds meet." Even as she affirmed the value of this work, Hope acknowledged the discrimination that threatened the daily lives of her people—at a time when African American men were routinely lynched, and women of the race remained vulnerable to rape and sexual abuse by whites. She recounts the enthusiasm a group of colored soldiers expressed about "getting the Kaiser" and then observes, "But even in their high spirits there was a pathetic touch when one of them said, 'we want not only to make the *world* safe to live in but our *own* country too.'"[70] Writing about African Americans' patriotic support of the U.S. role in the world, Hope uses the occasion to help her readers recognize (this report circulated among whites as well as members of her own race) the need to address internal problems (of racism) as well as international ones.

The series of international expositions or world fairs held in the United States between 1876 and 1904 offered occasions for all clubwomen to demonstrate and reflect on their own capacities for active citizenship. The 1893 World's Columbian Exposition in Chicago, in particular, provided an occasion for clubwomen to undertake significant administrative work. The U.S. Congress charged the Board of Lady Managers with creating "the channel of communication through which all women or organizations of women may be brought into relation with the Exposition and through which all applications for space for the use of women or their exhibits in the buildings shall be made." Even though they tagged it with a trivializing title, in establishing the board, the World's Columbian Commission and the U.S. Congress departed from a long tradition of excluding women from public life.[71] As Rebecca Felton wrote, "It is the first time in the history of the Republic that the female sex has been recognized as competent to attend to any sort of public business for the national Government. It is the very first recognition of woman's services as a citizen and a tax-payer by Congress."[72] Bertha Palmer of the Chicago Woman's Club was named chair of the board, and she and her colleagues, who understood fully the implications of their task, wanted to prove themselves worthy of this recognition. They raised funds to design and construct the Woman's Building, established a network of communication with (club)women throughout the country, and continually negotiated with the male organizers, who tried to limit representations of women's contributions.[73] They also enacted racist policies.

Racism was, as Robert Rydell has demonstrated, central to the view of humanity the exposition offered. The Chicago Fair, which attracted more than twenty-seven million people, "making it the greatest tourist attraction in American history," excluded any reference to the accomplishments of African Americans, but it displayed a village of Dahomeyans on the Midway.[74] The ethnographic "displays" of Africans, American Indians, and Pacific Islanders, with their "huts of bark and straw," demonstrated a "chain of human progress along racial lines": Anglo-Saxons stood at the top, and various groups of "savages" were arranged below.[75] African American clubwomen, not surprisingly, strongly condemned the racist ethnographic displays and sought representation in the Woman's Building. As the Board of Lady Managers was taking shape, African American clubwomen requested, "in the interest of the colored women of this country," that a member of their race be appointed to the executive committee.[76] The board, as Virginia Darney explains, either "didn't understand blacks' requests for representation or were concerned abut the implications of equal black representation in exhibits and on the board."[77] Whatever the reason, no colored women were placed on the board. Subsequently African American clubwomen developed a petition they hoped to present to Congress, but Bertha Palmer managed to prevent it from reaching that forum.[78] Ida B. Wells, in collaboration with Frederick Douglass, wrote a broadside, "The Reason Why the Colored American Is Not in the World's Columbian Exposition," and distributed it to fairgoers.

Even though they did not ultimately prevail in their quest to include African Americans in the Women's Building of the Columbian Exposition, the black clubwomen who read and wrote about this issue used it to clarify and solidify their positions. In stating their objections to white clubwomen, members of Congress, and the general public, they did achieve something. Palmer, in response to pressures exerted by African American clubwomen, wrote to state boards requesting that they include women of color. Even though both Palmer and her opponents recognized this as a relatively empty gesture, it at least acknowledged the African American arguments being presented. That Gertrude Mossell, writing a year after the Columbian Exposition, included an entire chapter titled "Our Afro-American Representatives at the World's Fair" in her book *The Work of the Afro-American Woman* suggests clubwomen of her race accomplished important cultural work for the nation. Since the Chicago Exposition attracted visitors from many different countries, this work extended beyond national boundaries. Indeed, Ida B. Wells wrote her broadside to "distribute to foreign visitors," thereby taking a role in molding the perception of the United States among residents of other parts of the world. She and others of her race saw the Chicago Exposition as an opportunity to "give evidence to the world of the capacity of the race . . . what it has accomplished since Emancipation."[79]

Other African American clubwomen also resisted an all-white representation of women's contributions. In the New York State Building, where an exhibit called "Evidences of the Advancements of the Colored Women of the United

States" was housed, Joan Imogen Howard's report asserted that African Americans "feel themselves American as truly as do those who proudly trace their ancestry back to the Pilgrim Fathers, the Puritans of England, the broad, liberal-spirited Hollanders, the cultivated and refined French Huguenots; and as an element in the progress of this boundless home, we trust, the worthiest representatives of all nations there is implanted in the minds of the best of this struggling people a determination to rise to a common level with the majority."[80] In their newspaper accounts, letters, petitions, statements, and reports, African American clubwomen recognized and countered a race-based definition of American womanhood with one founded on their own achievements.

Jewish women worked alongside their white gentile peers in organizing the Chicago Exposition. Hannah Solomon and her sister had joined the Chicago Woman's Club in 1877, and acculturated Jewish women became members of clubs in many cities.[81] Latent anti-Semitism and a desire to foster the cultural development of their own people led these women to form Jewish organizations also. In 1891 the group that later became the Detroit Section of the National Council of Jewish Women met for the express purpose of elevating "the mental, moral, and social status of young Jewish women."[82] As this indicates, Jewish clubwomen wished to fashion an ideology of womanhood that included their religious heritage. Not surprisingly, then, Hannah Solomon welcomed the General Federation's invitation to organize a Jewish Women's Congress as part of the Women's Congress at the Chicago Exposition. Joined by Sadie American and other prominent Jewish women, Solomon organized participants for the national congress. The difficulties inherent in establishing communication with Jewish women in widely scattered locations convinced Solomon of the need to create a national network of Jewish women, and the National Council of Jewish Women emerged, with Solomon as president and American as secretary. Although they shared Christian women's interest in equal rights and social service, Jewish clubwomen created organizations suited to women of their own religion. For them, the ideology of womanhood included religious dimensions, even though organizing for public action put Jewish clubwomen at odds with the more traditional ideology of domestic Jewish womanhood. Rebekah Kohut's absence from the Chicago Congress (at her rabbi husband's request) and having her paper read by another woman manifested the tensions that clubwomen experienced. Kohut's paper, which connected women's public mission to the home, Judaism, and the Jewish community, articulated an integration of private and public life that Kohut herself was unable (in 1893, at least) to experience.

A monthly column titled "At the World's Fair," along with other articles in *Far and Near,* indicates that working women knew about and discussed the Chicago Exposition. Readers of the column received detailed directions about the logistics of visiting it economically, including suggestions for clothing (down to the number of changes of underwear) and instructions for personal hygiene and diet in Chicago. Other articles offered lively descriptions of sights and events at the exposition, apparently assuming that readers would not be able to see it for themselves. One column, for example, described the ethnographic displays, beginning, "chief in interest come the Dahomeyans, of whom so little is generally known, showing a grade of civilization bordering on savagery and a race of people likely to soon become extinct." Both the slightly patronizing assumption that readers would be unlikely to know much about Dahomeyans and the general description contained in this account position working women readers as not a real part of the exposition audience. In contrast, another column offered detailed suggestions for packing clothing, locating housing, and enjoying exhibits so that readers could "make the most of it." The final column in the series focused specifically on women's place in the exposition and praised their "executive ability, philanthropic enterprise and wide cognizance and appreciation of the great and growing necessities for helpful work" with others.[83]

The mixture of rhetorical stances—ranging from condescending to supportive to flattering— in these columns mirrors the complicated and conflicted attitudes with which working women struggled as they constructed their own ideology of womanhood. The middle-class patrons who often helped to found clubs assumed that working women shared their appreciation for a womanhood based on middle-class values. Working women themselves frequently had in mind a different womanhood, one that prized the independence of wage work (and of traveling alone to Chicago). This conflicted ideology found expression in the representation of working women at the Chicago Exposition. The New York Association of Working Girls' Societies, for example, produced a bulletin prefaced by this statement:

> At the request of the Board of Lady Managers of the Columbian Exposition, the following pages were prepared to serve as an Exhibit, to be placed in the Hall of Organizations, in the Woman's Building. The printed matter was engrossed on parchment, and the original photographs as well as certificates, were pasted in their proper place. The sheets were then framed and hung on a large standard, so that they formed movable screens. At the request of many Club members this pamphlet has been

prepared, and it is hoped that it may serve as an added impulse in arousing enthusiasm about our societies.[84]

No doubt the presence of Grace Dodge, along with other wealthy and socially prominent patrons on the board of directors, eased this group's way into the Woman's Building. Indeed, such names as Dodge, Henderson, Alexander, and Draper—all bearing an Anglo-Saxon echo—are the only ones that appear in the bulletin. Working women themselves do not appear by name since the bulletin lists only names of clubs and a description of club activities. Working women's clubs as they were "engrossed on parchment" and displayed in the Women's Building did not, then, permit working women to recognize themselves or allow others to see them because they remained hidden behind the descriptions of activities, the constitution, and club procedures inscribed by the more affluent women who served on the board. Bertha Palmer's speech on opening day of the exposition likewise evoked working women—lamenting their "frightful struggle" against sexist employers, who "disparage [their] work and obtain [their] services for a nominal price, thus profiting largely by the helplessness of their victim"—but provided no opportunity for them to represent themselves in their own terms.[85] Writing and reading club publications, such as the column encouraging independent travel to Chicago, provided working women opportunities to resist victim portrayals and affirm their own agency.

Like their peers in other social locations, Mormon clubwomen saw the Chicago Exposition as an opportunity to extend the range of their participation in public life. They prepared materials for exhibit, in both the Women's Building and the Utah Building. Although isolated geographically, they saw themselves as participating with women of "the whole civilized world," and through reading accounts in the *Woman's Exponent,* they kept abreast of how women in other parts of the country were preparing for the exposition. As one writer put it, the fair provided Mormon women "an opportunity of displaying taste, ingenuity, harmony, and skill."[86] These words suggest the ideology of womanhood these clubwomen aimed to fashion. Displaying (good) taste identified them as adhering to standards of culture dominant in other parts of the country. The availability of "very little ready cash," as well as a shortage of some goods, called for ingenuity. Harmony suggested the spiritual dimension that figured prominently in their religious lives, and skill included abilities developed through diligence and practice. Taken together, these qualities offer a sketch of the ideology of womanhood Mormon clubwomen wanted to convey to the larger world at the Chicago Exposition. All clubwomen saw the Chicago Exposition as an opportunity to enhance their sense of themselves as world citizens. In addition to traveling alone to such meetings as this one, clubwomen began journeying across the Atlantic to attend international congresses and conferences or simply to be tourists.[87]

Clubwomen read and wrote about foreign countries as travel became more affordable and commodified in the increasingly materialistic culture.[88] Minutes and records from all social groups indicate an increased interest in national and international events. White middle-class groups developed year-long programs on such nations as Germany, Russia, China, France, England, and India.[89] African American clubwomen monitored the imperialist designs of the United States. Members of the Woman's Era Club, for example, composed a resolution on the controversy surrounding the annexation of Hawaii, calling into question the deposition of Queen Liliuokalani and the economic goals of American sugar planters in Hawaii who wanted to be able to compete with U.S. planters without tariff barriers. In describing their opposition as "especially fitting from us as colored women and Americans," these clubwomen introduce race into the debate as they take the side of Queen Liliuokalani, another woman of color. By defining themselves as both "colored women and Americans," they also anticipate the "double consciousness" W. E. B. Du Bois described as characteristic for African Americans.[90] Unlike Du Bois, who sees this double consciousness as creating schizophrenia, they identify it as a source of authority for their opposition to annexation as they speak for "truth and justice" and against "national gain and power." Not surprisingly, their "world" gave more prominence to such nations as Haiti and South Africa than to the European countries on which their white peers concentrated. Jewish clubwomen likewise inscribed concerns about world events that reflected their own social locations, as this statement from a National Council of Jewish Women report shows: "Let us also hope that in the twentieth century the serious questions of theater hats and balloon sleeves may have been satisfactorily solved, and our statesmen can give proper attention to international treaties, and that they will negotiate only with nations treating subjects with some regard for the dictates of humanity."[91] With the specter of anti-Semitism always lurking in the background, these clubwomen prized humane treatment for all.

Working women's perspectives on world events reflected their life circumstances. *Far and Near*'s "World's Events" column featured such topics as the level of unemployment in England, the convention of the American Federation of Labor, and unionization.[92] For these clubwomen, "the world" included conditions and concerns associated with wage work. Similarly, "The World as Seen through a Woman's Eyes," a column published in the Mormon *Young Woman's Journal,* featured a discussion of professions open to women, the death of Mrs. John Booth in London, Princess Victoria's engagement to a German prince, and a description of Annie Besant as "the most eloquent woman in all England."[93] Writing and reading about notable women from other countries enabled these Mormon clubwomen to construct for themselves an ideology of womanhood that positioned them as world citizens despite their geographical isolation.

As they read and wrote about national and world events, clubwomen became more critical observers. Specifically, they began to raise questions about the increasingly imperialistic stance of the United States toward other nations of the world.[94] Questions about the role of business interests in U.S. foreign policy emerged as clubwomen began to scrutinize and condemn economically driven policy decisions. The 1906 records of New York's Sorosis report a paper that challenged the members by saying, "Let us show the Chinese that one nation at least is disposed to treat them fairly. Let us live some of the Christianity we profess, and show that to the United States the Gospel of Christ is not merely a gospel of grab. Other nations will follow if we do."[95] In addition to showing the anti-imperialist viewpoint of clubwomen, this author blends the "we" of those who abhor the "gospel of grab" with the "we" of the U.S. government, thereby positioning her readers/listeners as people able to assert leadership in world events.

Although all clubwomen faced challenges to their dignity and goals, African American clubwomen at the turn of the century confronted special challenges posed by racism. White clubwomen were among those who wrote and read myths about the futility of "attempts to transform the Negro by education," the lighter "weight of the Negro brain [as compared with that of] the average Caucasian," and the Negro as "fond of gay color, frantic over noise, and in touch with a bustling city."[96] As they attempted to counter such negative stereotypes and create new images for members of their race, African American clubwomen shaped and were shaped by the ideology of motherhood. The National Association of Colored Women included in its goals this statement: "Believing that the vital interests of our country hang largely upon the influence which mothers exert upon children; be it hereby resolved that we emphasize this fact, that the mothers are mainly responsible for the atmosphere which pervades the home, and it behooves them to aim assiduously to equip themselves for the emergencies encumbered upon the honored position of wife and mother, to the end that the children may be taught . . . love of God, fellow man, and country."[97] Claiming the nation-mother relationship to justify, much as white women did, the need to move outside the confines of the home and into clubs, this statement suggests a common ideology of motherhood. But race, as Mary Washington explained, added another dimension. Speaking to clubwomen in Colorado, Washington asserted, "I speak to you tonight as a woman and as a mother. There is a great burden on the mother of the race and rightly too."[98] Although they recognized and claimed the commonalities of motherhood they shared with white clubwomen, African Americans realized that their (stigmatized) racial status created unique "emergencies," including the need to be, as Gloria Wade-Gayles put it, "suffocatingly protective and domineering" to raise children who could become "whole and self-actualizing persons" in a society that degraded and devalued them. The success of such parenting is evident in Stephanie Shaw's examination of the lives of black professional women reared between 1880 and 1930.[99] Even though the ideology of motherhood might be used to justify their activities, they could not count on it to confer the same "honored position" white women enjoyed. The "mother of the race" assumed an extra burden.

Mary Church Terrell, the founder of the National Association of Colored Women, explained the nature of this extra burden:

> Contrast, if you will the feelings of hope and joy which thrill the heart
> of the white mother with those which stir the soul of her colored sister.
> Put yourselves for one minute in her place (you could not endure the
> strain longer) and imagine, if you can, how you would feel if similarly
> situated—As a mother of the oppressed race clasps to her bosom the
> babe which she loves as fondly as you do yours, her heart cannot thrill
> with joyful anticipations of the future. For before her child she sees the
> thorny path of prejudice and proscription which his little feet must tread.

Terrell draws on the common experience of motherhood to show racism's distorting power and to implore her largely white audience to "give [colored children] the opportunities which you desire for your own."[100] This move to implicate her white peers at the same time she identifies with them demonstrates how African American clubwomen could adapt the ideology of motherhood in efforts to transform the circumstances of their own lives.

Emboldened by an ideology of motherhood that required them to take up the extra burden of their race, African American clubwomen fashioned womanhood to address their special needs. Instead of merely attempting to influence others to act on their behalf, as might be dictated by a more passive concept of "woman," these women undertook direct action to improve the circumstances of members of their race. Heeding Ida B. Wells's 1891 claim that "nothing is more definitely settled than that he [the Afro-American] must act for

himself. . . . 'The gods help those who help themselves,'" they assumed activist roles.[101] Josephine Ruffin, who convened the first national meeting that drew
a hundred clubwomen from ten states to Boston in 1895, echoed Wells's insistence on agency for African American womanhood:

> While our growth intellectually and financially is opening many ways to
> us, yet that same growth is bringing us into relations not before contem-
> plated by the other race, which consequently is resenting the intrusion.
> In many respects our situation grows worse instead of better. So long as
> this is the case, so long as we all suffer together, just so long must we all
> work together to bring about a different state of affairs. . . . How use-
> less to be continually hoping that others are going to do more for us than
> we will do for ourselves.[102]

Ruffin's statement reflects her awareness that African Americans' claims to formerly all-white education and economic power aroused as much animosity as
admiration. Whites' active resistance to blacks' demonstration of "growth intellectually and financially" supported Ruffin's claim that instead of looking to
others for help, members of her race needed to "do for" themselves. At the Boston meeting, lynching occupied a central position on the program, and those
in attendance passed a resolution "commending the Republican Party for placing
in its platform a criticism of lynching" and dispatched a letter to sympathetic
British reformers.[103] Although white women and black men also aided the antilynching effort, these clubwomen led the way, predating the National Association for the Advancement of Colored People (founded in 1909) and claiming
a place in the history of reform.

Sometimes African American clubwomen's activism took the form of incit-
ing others to action. In 1918 Bertha Wilson, an African American, gave a talk
titled "The Problems of the Colored Race" at a meeting of the white Women
in Council of Roxbury. Although she appropriated the term *problem* that was
common among white clubwomen, Wilson took a different tack. Wilson framed
problems from the African American perspective, pointing to the hardships her
people suffered and arguing for social justice, especially in the light of their
service in World War I.[104] The effectiveness of Wilson's speaking on her own
behalf appears in club minutes two months later, when the Women in Council passed this resolution:

> Whereas our hearts are stirred by each recurrence of cruelty practiced
> on the Negro in this country, the spirit of whose institutions would se-

cure for all without regard to race or color, a right to life, liberty and the pursuit of happiness, And whereas our courts of justice exist to give all, black or white, who transgress the laws, a fair trial and adequate sentence, Be it resolved that we, Women in Council of Roxbury, Massachusetts, in annual meeting assembled, record our earnest protests at unjust discrimination against the black man, and inhuman treatment at the hands of his fellows, and that we plead in his behalf for a just and humane consideration of his rights throughout the land, Be it further resolved that we bespeak for the Negro, together with wide educational advantages, the opening of industrial opportunities commensurate with his ability and training. Be it resolved that a copy of this Resolution be preserved in our records and copy forwarded to the State Federation of Woman's Clubs.[105]

This insistence on social justice as well as education and employment opportunities for African Americans clearly resulted from Wilson's visit, demonstrating that African Americans acting on their own behalf could summon responses from white clubwomen.

In their dealings with white peers, African American clubwomen often operated within what Darlene Clark Hine has called a "culture of dissemblance," hiding some aspects of their lives while displaying others to receive assistance and support. The costs of this dissemblance were often reckoned in their own (private) texts, as an account from clubwoman Alice Dunbar-Nelson's diary demonstrates.[106] Dunbar-Nelson, herself an active member and national officer in the National Association of Colored Women, describes a day that begins with a trip to the pawnshop to "raise money" for "a half ton of coal" and "to pay the water rent. It was to have been shut off on the 31st." That evening she speaks at a white woman's club in Philadelphia, "a palatial place," and the account continues: "Very stimulating gathering and I 'speak fine' for an hour. Then much discussion. Coffee and cakes. About a hundred out. Very fine affair. Home by 12:40 to find Bobbo there on his way to Salisbury. We have whisky sours. A relief from the nervous tension of the night."[107] In addition to the usual anxieties that go with public speaking, Dunbar-Nelson points to the tensions she and other African American women experienced as they traveled between the pawnshop and the "palatial" homes of their white peers to vindicate themselves and their race. These cross-cultural journeys grew out of African American clubwomen's need to define themselves as simultaneously activist and refined.

Asserting their refinement in the face of continuing attacks on their virtue posed special problems for African American clubwomen because of the racist attacks regularly leveled at them. Writing in 1904, Eleanor Tayleur, for example, described the African American woman as "the Frankenstein product of civilization, a being created out of conditions of sectional hate and revenge, and set in motion by wild experimentalists who knew not what they did." Tayleur saw her as a person of "tropical temperament" who "loves madly and passionately" and is possessed of "a fierce passion of maternity that seems to be purely animal" but for whom "infanticide" is "appallingly common." Tayleur accounted for "the decadence of the Negro women" by explaining that "she no longer has the uplift of close personal association with white women." The African American woman seeking education receives scorn in Tayleur's article as "a girl" who goes to school "session after session for eight to ten years, without achieving anything more than the ability to read and write like a child in the second grade" and who develops an "insatiable ambition to be a school-teacher," which would be futile unless "the Government subsidizes every kinky-headed little coon and farms him out among the several million Negro girls in the South who are looking forward to the glorious career of being schoolma'ams." Tayleur further describes African American women as possessing "a settled determination not to work" and aspiring to insult white women with "childlike brutality"; characterizes African American families as ones in which "the marriage relationship as white people understand it does not exist"; and explains all this as the result of "a childish race, suddenly freed from slavery," mistaking "liberty for license." The indignities imposed by such discourses were paralleled by the experiences of women who found themselves relegated to certain cars on trains or, as the anonymous author of the *Woman's Era* editorial explained, "put off in the woods at night." As this author makes clear, the attributes of education and careful manners offered no real protection against the indignities of racism. No African American woman, regardless of "her culture or refinement," was exempt from the separate car system since race rather than gender determined the way (white) others saw her.[108]

White clubwomen actually saw very little of their African American peers. The segregation imposed by Jim Crow laws, race-determined living and working patterns, and the distortions of such racist prose as Eleanor Tayleur's all combined to exacerbate (willed) ignorance about the experiences of African American clubwomen. This limited contact enabled white clubwomen to develop and nurture highly distorted images of their black counterparts. As one African American clubwomen noted, "The more ignorant the Southern whites are of us the more vehement they are in their denunciations of us. They boast that they have little intercourse with us . . . but still they know us thoroughly."[109] Although she refers to the South, ignorance about African Americans extended to all parts of the country. To the extent that African Americans received any attention in white women's programs, they appeared in the form of a "problem" or, at least, an issue to be studied.

Although white women's clubs always exoticized African Americans, they took special interest in this "problem" as immigration decreased during and after World War I. Federal and private agencies discovered that between 1915 and 1920 more African Americans than ever before moved from one area of the country to another and concentrated in urban areas. The U.S. Department of Labor, the National Urban League, the U.S. Census Bureau, local city clubs, and the Association for the Study of Negro Life and History, among others, investigated the internal migrations of African Americans, concluding that "the migration of southern Negroes to northern cities has . . . raised many serious economic and social problems" in such areas as "housing, health, crime, education, politics, and race contacts."[110] Even when such studies acknowledged the constraints under which African Americans lived, they still portrayed them as responsible for the "problem." White clubwomen quickly picked up the theme. "The Negro" appears under the headings "Problems in Sociology" and "The Race Question in the United States" in the 1915–16 program book of the Monday Club of Clinton, New York, and yearbooks from many other clubs designated African Americans similarly.[111] Working women, who saw African Americans as competitors for scarce jobs, rarely considered the "Negro problem," but they objectified them in minstrel shows, perpetuating what Robert Toll describes as "the negative stereotypes of Negroes that endured in American popular thought long after the minstrel show had disappeared."[112] This objectification, accompanied by an ignorance about African Americans' substantial accomplishments, often enabled white clubwomen, both middle- and working-class, to resist any alternative ideology of womanhood that African Americans developed.

African American clubwomen in turn resisted ideologies of womanhood that failed to incorporate their racial identity. One illustration of this resistance appears in accounts of Josephine Ruffin's experience at the 1900 Milwaukee convention of the General Federation of Women's Clubs. Denied entrance as a delegate from the Woman's Era Club (which the General Federation had admitted to membership without realizing it was composed of African American women) and refusing, on principle, to enter as a delegate of the Massachusetts Women's Press Club, Ruffin took the position of an African American acting on behalf of her people, refusing to accept the racist compromise of acting as a (light-skinned) individual rather than as the president of her club.

Texts produced by the New England Women's Club in response to the Ruffin incident demonstrate how clubwomen wrestled with an ideology of womanhood that included African Americans. Minutes for the January 14, 1901, meeting begin by noting that reporters would be "excluded from the afternoon's session" and go on to describe the report of Anna West, "former chairman of State Correspondence of the National Federation of Women's Clubs." West "stated facts in regard to the admittance or rather non-admittance of the Woman's Era Club of Boston to the National Federation," explaining that Ruffin would have been received "as an individual," but the board objected to having a "club of colored ladies join the Federation." West explains Georgia's "amendment to the effect that only clubs of white women shall be admitted to the National Federation," and the account continues:

> Mrs. Ruffin was said to have conducted herself in a most becoming and dignified manner and the ladies of Milwaukee and visitors showed her much attention and respect.
>
> The representation of New England Clubs have been charged by some of the at-home members of not showing proper courage by settling the question at once, but Mrs. West said that if such members were able to consider everything concerned they would see that the ladies were more courageous in keeping silence.
>
> They were charged, by representatives at the Biennial, of having brought Mrs. Ruffin to Milwaukee for the very purpose of raising the color question, but the Eastern ladies showed in every way that it was wholly unintentional.

The report concludes with a discussion about whether the New England Women's Club should withdraw from the General Federation. The group decides it can serve the cause of African Americans better by remaining within the national organization, where it can provide "aid" to southern clubs because "northern clubs are more advanced in club work."[113] The paragraph about Ruffin's behavior in Milwaukee points to the unwillingness of even these liberal clubwomen to see their African American peers as fully capable. Since no comment about the dignity and manner of others who attended the convention appears anywhere in this account, the noting of Ruffin's behavior suggests it was seen as unusual enough to be worthy of note.

The accusations against the New England Women's Club demonstrate that few at the national convention expected an African American woman to raise "the color question" herself, without the aid or instigation of white clubwomen. The New England Women's Club members' own doubts about the capabilities of African American clubwomen to act on their own behalf are manifest in a resolution they subsequently passed and forwarded to the General Federation, the state federation, and "every federated club in Massachusetts": "Whereas the action of the General Federation of Women's Clubs in Milwaukee in failing to endorse the admission of a colored women's club—the Woman's Era Club of Boston—has thus presented a national problem to the Women's Clubs of the United States; therefore Resolved, that we, the New England Women's Club of Boston, hereby express our belief in the wisdom as well as justice of admitting women's clubs to fellowship and giving them equal opportunities, regardless of race, creed, or politics."[114] Even in its efforts to improve the situation of the Woman's Era Club, the New England Women's Club inscribes its resistance to the idea that African American women could help themselves. The wide circulation of this text did not cause the General Federation to admit clubs "regardless of race," but club texts from many parts of the country reveal internal strife around the issue.[115]

Although members of the New England Women's Club might not have recognized it, African American clubwomen had the capacity to confront and reject the "truths" about womanhood imposed by racism. When the Chicago Woman's Club rejected Fannie Barrier Williams, a very prominent clubwoman who had spoken at the Chicago Exposition in 1893, for membership, the *Woman's Era* titled a column "The Chicago Woman's Club Reject Mrs. Williams" and detailed Williams's many contributions to the women's clubs in Illinois, noting that "although [she was] well equipped to help on the work the woman's clubs are formed to do, the modicum of Negro blood in her veins outweighed her eminent fitness, and club principle made a weak surrender to personal prejudice, and her name was rejected," thus making clear the error of the "narrow-minded" Chicago women. The column continued by portraying Williams as a "philosophical and brave" woman who would soon be able to "recall with amused contempt the hysterical antics of her former associates in work, in their efforts to prevent the club giving legitimate recognition to the helpful work she had long been doing as an individual."[116] In refusing to portray Williams as a victim and insisting on her civic and moral superiority over those who rejected her, this column reaffirms the self-advocacy of African Americans, even in the face of painful indignities.

This capacity grew out of strategies developed by clubwomen who recognized the need to do for themselves what no (white) others would do. In a paper delivered at the first national conference of African American clubwomen in 1895, Josephine Ruffin noted the importance of meeting to discuss women's concerns, "but also the things that are of especial interest to us as *colored* women," including the education of their children, "what *we* can do in the moral education of the race with which we are identified," and how to make the most of their "limited opportunities," and she declared a common purpose was "to elevate and dignify colored American womanhood."[117] With this statement Ruffin inscribed a clear principle to which clubwomen of her race adhered: they would undertake unassisted action to improve the material conditions of their (and their peers') lives and to claim their own dignity.

Such action included publicizing African American accomplishments for white audiences. Indeed the constitution of the Woman's Loyal Union of Brooklyn contained a clause providing "for the dissemination of race literature." Described as the "object" of the club, this clause called for "the diffusion of accurate and extensive information relative to the civil and social status of the Afro-American (i.e.) that they may be led to an intelligent assertion of their rights, and to a determination to unite in the employment of every lawful and judicious means to secure and to retain the unmolested exercise of the same."[118] Clubwomen throughout the country took seriously the mandate to inform those "who need enlightenment on the present position of the Afro-American," allocating funds to print and circulate their programs, seeking representation in the white press, and accepting invitations to address or meet with their white peers. Despite these efforts, white clubwomen remained largely unaware of the accomplishments of their African American peers.

A more promising strategy for claiming their own dignity led African American clubwomen to circulate among themselves information about what women of their race had accomplished. Both the *Woman's Era* and its successor, the *National Association Notes,* regularly carried feature articles on outstanding clubwomen—including the musician Blanche Washington, the ice merchant Georgianna Whitsel, and the antilynching advocate Ida B. Wells—without neglecting more ordinary ones. In a review of Gertrude Mossell's *Work of the Afro-American Woman,* Medora Gould, editor of the "Literature Notes" column, observes, "It is a pleasure to note that Mrs. Mossell has not omitted to mention that great army of women workers, the home-makers, whom it would be impossible to call by name, but to whom as a race we owe far more for our advancement and improvement than we do to a few teachers and scribblers here and there."[119] These national publications also quantified clubwomen's accomplishments, publishing statistics on individual club work, such as "42 public meetings,

20,280 pages of literature distributed . . . 500 garments made, 5 colored children placed in good homes . . . 420 orders given for food and coal for the needy . . . have raised and expended $403.85 this year."[120] This report and many others like it provided textual confirmation of the fact that African American clubwomen had worked to improve the conditions of those around them.

Such repeated inscriptions of their accomplishments enabled African American clubwomen to recognize their own capacities and make them visible to others. In her paper "What the National Association Has Meant to Colored Women," Mary Church Terrell underscores the ways club life has increased clubwomen's "confidence in their ability to do things for themselves" by helping them "study the questions which affect their race most deeply and directly."[121] Terrell's retrospective view, strengthened by an enumeration of the many racist policies clubwomen addressed, articulates the ideology of womanhood that African American clubwomen helped shape. Many factors, of course, contributed to this transformation, but reading and writing about the accomplishments of members of their race, about the necessity for social justice as well as educational and employment opportunities, and about "the questions which affect their race most deeply and directly" contributed significantly. Through exploring, in their literacy practices, their own condition and ways to ameliorate it, African American clubwomen constructed for themselves an alternative ideology of womanhood and helped others begin to recognize them in terms of it.

African American, Jewish, Mormon, white middle-class, and working-class clubwomen all participated, through their reading and writing, in reshaping ideologies of American womanhood. Living at a time when what we now call essentialism led them to believe that women could effect large and positive changes in society, they approached their projects with an earnest self-consciousness. Ellen Carol DuBois claims that the Progressive Era saw a paradigmatic change in the definition of womanhood from "mother" to "worker," as the bonds of family gave way to the wage relationship, and that people developed new perspectives on how they "understood the relationships that made up their society."[122] My own investigation suggests that while the fin de siècle period did lead to new understandings of social relationships, "paradigmatic change" may not capture the nuanced and complex self-fashioning clubwomen enacted in their literacy practices. Still, DuBois's assertion of a paradigmatic shift offers a sturdy reminder that the ideology of womanhood did not remain unchanged between 1890 and 1920. The "woman's era" proclaimed by Frances Harper brought many new "truths" about womanhood into currency. Women in public activity, whether administering an exposition or speaking from a podium; doing wage work in factories, retail outlets, and offices; offering commentary on—and even objection to—U.S. foreign policy; undertaking independent travel and changes in the dress code; gaining the right to own property and, eventually, to vote— all of these activities reflected the changing ideologies surrounding women. Through their reading and writing, clubwomen in all social locations participated in these refashionings of womanhood.

At the same time, clubwomen shaped womanhood(s) to fit the needs of their specific racial, religious, or class positions. Working women resisted middle-class narratives for their lives; African Americans insisted on their own agency and its centrality to racial uplift; Jewish and Mormon clubwomen constructed womanhoods that included religious dimensions; and white middle-class women drew on the ideology of motherhood to support the peace movement and secure changes in public policy. Many forces and institutions have been credited with helping effect changes in the views of womanhood, and women's clubs should be among them. By exploring, both in national publications and in the intimate settings of local meetings, women's lives and everyday experiences, clubwomen altered the ways they and those they knew thought about the natures and capacities of women. With the texts they read and wrote, clubwomen created countercurrents that rippled against the tide of nineteenth-century constructions of womanhood. Exploring and elaborating on their dreams and desires through their literacy practices, they fashioned new American womanhood(s).

5

(Re)Calibrating Culture

◆━◯◯━◆

◆═◎ The object of this club is social and intellectual development. Its design is to cultivate the heart as well as the brain which will form a good mental equilibrium and fit woman not only to shine as a greater light around her own hearthstone, but to be a more efficient custodian of home interests in the wider domain of the world.

Constitution of the Reapers' Club of
Salt Lake City, 1896

◆═◎ The object of this club shall be to form an organized center for the intellectual culture of its members, and to assist in the betterment of physical, intellectual and moral conditions in the community.

Constitution of the Woman's Club of
El Paso, Texas, 1894

◆═◎ The Pioneers, alive to the intellectual stimuli that have caused Chautauquas, University extension courses and self-culture clubs to spring into life and prosper, has gradually undergone a change that we believe to be an advance. When in 1886 Mrs. Adolph Koth came into the chair, alternate meetings were set aside as class afternoons. The programs for such occasions were arranged to satisfy a manifestly increasing desire for systematic information.

LAURA D. JACOBSON,
"The Pioneers,"
American Jewess, 1895

⁓ The object of the Woman's League as outlined in the Articles of Incorporation is the education and improvement of colored women and the promotion of their interests.

Constitution of the Washington Colored
Woman's League, 1894

⁓ This is a literary club; that is, we are united for the purpose of cultivating literature.

Constitution of the Literary Union
of New York, 1891

⁓ I recall one winter evening long ago when the Italian women did not come, but sent their husbands instead. . . . It was not easy for the club to entertain a roomful of heavy Italians; but they had refreshments which everyone could understand. . . . And the evening went happily. At the close one of the women of the club said to me: "I am ashamed of the way I used to talk about Dagoes. I used to say that we must move off the street because there were so many Dagoes coming in. But they are just like other people, only you have to take more pains to find them out."

That was the result of cultivation, if we take the definition that it is extended experience. It is exactly the thing we send our children to Europe for, the result we hope for when we read books about all kinds of people—to get over the differences raised by barriers and traditions, that really we may be fair-minded and may know people as they really are.

JANE ADDAMS,
"The Hull House Woman's Club,"
Club Worker, 1901

⁓ Vocational schools of many kinds are needed in Massachusetts and elsewhere. . . . New types of teachers combining culture with industrial intelligence and skill in either trade or home making are needed in these schools. The normal schools are not yet ready to meet this call, for they are without experience in the conduct of business shops or in the requirements of commercial fields. It is difficult at present to obtain teachers or supervisors who can rightly direct this new industrial work in the educational institutions that are being opened throughout the country. The Women's Educational and Industrial Union can now give national service by trying out methods of preparing such teachers and obtaining results for normal schools to follow.

"Survey by the President,"
Papers of the Women's Educational and
Industrial Union, 1914

⚹⚞⚟ We have in Judaism and the Jewish life all of divine comfort and consolation—yet we pass it by and seek in Ethical Culture and its kindred cults an answer to our prayers. Ethical Culture is neither more nor less than the expression of the wide humanitarianism of the Mosaic creed as the ethics of all religions are the outcome of their faiths. It is the kite that flies heavenward and the tail but lends grace to the ascent.

"The Revival of Judaism,"
Papers of the New York Section of the
National Council of Jewish Women, 1893

⚹⚞⚟ Women who have daughters capable of culture can do nothing better for womankind as well as for the daughters than to give them the advantage of a college training, or an education that will have an equivalent value in the quality of·their intelligence. The mental discipline and culture that are the most important furnishings of a university education will save us from many humiliating mistakes in our public lives, and will tend to lessen the small jealousies, petty envies and the general unkindness of woman for womankind.

FANNIE BARRIER WILLIAMS,
"Illinois,"
Woman's Era, 1895

⚹⚞⚟ Colonel T. W. Higginson has recently written an article for one of the New York papers, in which he has affirmed that New York is the literary center of our country. This declaration has created much comment, principally among the Bostonians, who are looking to their laurels. Leaving the bitterness of this discussion to those who it most concerns, it is but just to state that the time seems to have arrived when no city or locality can claim a monopoly of literary taste or acquirement. In these days of rapid transit and universal travel, it is almost impossible to get beyond the culture and advanced thought of our civilization.

"The World as Seen through a Woman's Eyes,"
Young Woman's Journal, 1890

⤙═⊙ In these clubs a woman of deep learning and broad education meets with the woman whose opportunities for education have been limited, and who is now struggling for more information and a wider intellectual outlook. Both these women are gainers by their contact in the Literary Club, for they will both gain true culture the ideal club spirit is adhered to. One gains culture of heart in learning to understand the longings and the needs of her less educated sister, and in giving out of her wealth of intellectual attainment, she enriches her own soul.

MARY POPPENHEIM,
"Is the Club a Place for Serious Study or for
General Culture?" *Federation Bulletin,* 1906

⤙═⊙═⊙═⤙

IN a lecture delivered at Stanford University in 1911, George Santayana used the term *genteel tradition* to describe a concept of culture he attacked as "slightly becalmed," reflecting a diluted Calvinism and a romantic transcendentalism that made the United States a "young country with an old mentality." Contrasting the cultural with the practical side of the American mind, he adopted an architectural metaphor: "a neat reproduction of the colonial mansion—with some modern comforts introduced surreptitiously—stands beside the skyscraper. The American Will inhabits the skyscraper; the American Intellect inhabits the colonial mansion. The one is the sphere of the American man; the other, at least predominantly, of the American woman. The one is all aggressive enterprise; the other is all genteel tradition." After castigating the genteel tradition's culture for its outdated preoccupations, Santayana offered as an alternative the pragmatism of William James. Affirming James for thinking and feeling that "represented the true America," Santayana offered a Jamesian view of culture that highlighted "the relativity of morals, the strength of time, the fertility of matter, the variety, the unspeakable variety of possible life."[1]

Santayana's delineation of the genteel tradition versus a relativistic culture represents in microcosm a struggle over meaning that simmered between 1880 and 1920 and began to boil during the final decade of this period.[2] The fin de siècle pressures of materialism, spiritual doubts, changing demography, and shifting class structures raised questions about the nature of cultural experiences, the people who should have these experiences, and the relationship between culture and consumerism. The emergence of the terms *highbrow culture* (first used in the 1880s to describe aesthetic superiority) and *lowbrow culture* (initially coined in the 1890s to designate a lack of refinement)—both borrowed from phrenology—demonstrates how conflicts about culture generated a new language to describe it.[3] The use of terms that owed their origins to features inscribed on the human face represented attempts to locate culture in fixed and hierarchical categories. What Santayana called the genteel tradition drew on the mid-nineteenth-century tradition of evangelical Protestantism as well as the belief that the enhanced sensibilities derived from exposure to fine music, art, and literature would lead to general social improvement, decreased materialism, and increased spiritualism. Drawing on the doctrine of perfectionism or complete holiness, the genteel tradition urged self-improvement or "self-culture" because, in this view, as T. J. Jackson Lears put it, "social problems were entirely soluble through individual moral betterment."[4]

This merging of moral and aesthetic forces generated an idealistic view of culture that operated out of clearly established norms, took the improvement of humanity as its central task, and imposed narrow boundaries on what could be included in its realm. Directed, as John Tomsich explains, by "a group of men who represented older values threatened by the rise of the city, who were Protestant in religion and English or North European in ancestry," adherents to the genteel tradition controlled such quality magazines as *Harper's Monthly, Century, Atlantic Monthly,* and *North American Review,* along with "the major publishing firms, the major Eastern universities, the most influential social clubs, and the American Academy of Arts and Letters."[5] Standing in for theology and emphasizing manners, propriety, and tradition, the genteel tradition sought to regulate public behavior by fostering integrity and self-control and, coincidentally, to provide a means for middle- and upper-class people to distinguish themselves from the masses, both immigrant and native-born. It took as its goal, in the words of Charles Eliot Norton, "the development of the breadth, serenity, and solidity of mind, and . . . the attainment of that complete self-possession which finds expression in character."[6] Chafing against the narrowness and constraints of this view of culture, Santayana offered, by way of James, an alternative that privileged relativism, variety, and energy over hierarchy, standards, and constraints.

Although Raymond Williams describes the movement from "a personal assertion of value" to "a general intellectual method" or "emphasis on 'a whole way of life'" as "continuous" and coherent, the contest outlined by Santayana suggests a more complicated relationship between the two views of culture, and some present-day theorists reinforce that view.[7] Christopher Herbert, for example, takes exception to Williams's image of "unproblematic outgrowth," arguing that "the old assertion of value and the modern intellectual method are in large measure sharply antagonistic modes."[8] Broadening the terms of culture from those encapsulated in the genteel tradition to those that incorporated a more discontinuous and relativistic perspective involved considerable cultural work.

This chapter argues that clubwomen helped create a broader view of culture. Unlike higher education, the publishing industry, public lectures, and theaters or concert halls, which have been previously identified as arenas where the terms of culture were discussed and displayed, women's clubs have only recently been recognized for their contributions to the continually shifting definitions of culture.[9] Women's clubs were sites of both cultural production and calibration at the turn of the century, and given the variety of social groups they represented, they undertook a wide range of projects. Some called on the genteel tradition to preserve their class positions, while contending with its gendered constraints. Others saw acquisition of genteel culture as a vehicle for upward mobility but simultaneously sought to extend its range to include more their own "way of life." Through their processes of deliberating about and constructing annual programs of study; reading, discussing, and writing about books; composing their own poems and papers; establishing or raising funds for museums, symphonies, and scholarships for artists; founding libraries and monitoring the reading of others; and writing or producing their own plays and pageants, clubwomen participated directly in (re)defining and disseminating culture.

Just as Santayana distinguished between the "American man," whom he associates with the skyscraper, aggressive enterprise, and the American Will, and "the American woman," whom he equates with the colonial mansion, the American Intellect, and the (denigrated) genteel tradition, fin de siècle discussions of culture frequently involved gender. "The feminizing of culture" became an expression of warning as commentators simultaneously marveled at and exhorted against women's emergence. Writing in 1912, the Stanford professor Earl

Barnes wondered, "But who, fifty years ago, could have imagined that to-day women would be steadily monopolizing learning, teaching, literature, the fine arts, music, the church, and the theater? And yet that is the condition at which we have arrived. We may scoff at the way women are doing the work, and reject the product, but that does not alter the fact that step by step women are taking over the field of liberal culture."[10] Identifying the danger in this takeover, Barnes asserts women are interested in "the concrete, human, personal, conserving and emotional aspects of life," while men have a capacity for "the abstract, material, impersonal, creative and rational aspects." He goes on to proclaim, "If women were all to forget how to read overnight, there is little doubt that the newspapers would find it advantageous to print more statesmanlike editorials and more general and abstract news."[11]

Barnes's portrayal of women as "monopolizing" high culture and lacking the capacity for abstract thought typifies misogynist discourses of the period that expressed anxieties about the status of culture. In suggesting that a female readership caused newspapers to print less "statesmanlike" editorials, he echoes the continuing anxieties surrounding the woman reader, but he shifts the locus of harm from the woman herself to the larger society. The example of the newspapers points to another dimension of gendered discussions of culture. Mass culture became identified as feminine and inferior. As Andreas Huyssen observes, "The political, psychological, and aesthetic discourse around the turn of the century consistently and obsessively genders mass culture and the masses as feminine, while high culture, whether traditional or modern, remains the privileged realm of male activities." Most of the institutions of high culture did, indeed, remain the province of men, and, as Huyssen notes, "the universalizing ascription of femininity to mass culture always depended on the very real exclusion of women from high culture and its institutions."[12] Even though they had no power to shape cultural institutions, women were blamed for any perceived decline. Richard Butsch describes the specific instance of the theater, where women were actively recruited during the mid-nineteenth century to lend legitimacy: "Before women predominated, their presence was considered to have a 'civilizing' influence on male [theater] audiences. . . . But once women had become the primary audience for theater, commentators turned on them and blamed them for the perceived decline of American drama between the 1890s and the 1920s."[13] This pattern of recruiting and then blaming or rejecting women who participated in the genteel tradition recurred in other fields, such as literature, and the negative power attributed to women suggests the degree of angst their participation in culture evoked.

Because women's clubs and gendered discourse about culture emerged simultaneously, clubwomen both appropriated and were assigned cultural designations. Groups from every social location gave prominence to "culture" in their self-representations. Indeed, faced with the need to choose a single word to describe the terms in which a majority of women's clubs described themselves, one could do much worse than *culture*. This term encompassed the wide variety of self-improvement projects by which clubwomen justified themselves and sought to transform their own status. Sometimes, as in the case of the white middle-class members of the El Paso Woman's Club, the word *culture* appeared in the statement of purpose; sometimes, as exemplified by the statements written by the Mormon Reapers's Club, the Jewish Pioneers Club, the Colored Woman's League, and the working-class Literary Union, culture was glossed with such terms as *social and intellectual development, systematic information, education and improvement,* and *cultivating literature.* These statements of purpose quoted at the beginning of this chapter suggest the complicated constraints and negotiations that marked clubwomen's relationships with culture.

Even though they used the same word, they configured it to fit their own meanings. In naming social as well as intellectual development, the Mormon Reapers' Club claimed a purpose that extended beyond the narrow terms of the genteel tradition to include projects that had direct effects on people's lives. At the same time, "to cultivate the heart as well as the brain" echoes the moral and intellectual precepts of the genteel tradition. The "intellectual culture" of the El Paso group, in combination with the "betterment" of community conditions, also implies a view of culture that extends to a "whole way of life." Addressing members' interest in "self-culture" with "systematic study," the Jewish Pioneers Club of St. Louis sought to ally itself with the genteel tradition of the Chautauqua by means of focused effort. *Self-culture* had come to mean, as Mary Kupiec Cayton describes it, "the *process* whereby moral character might be maintained" and "collective standards of morality and acceptable behavior" defined, so the Pioneers sought to extend this aspect of the genteel tradition to include Jewish women.[14] By juxtaposing "education" and "improvement," the Colored Woman's League echoed the genteel tradition's emphasis on self-regulated behavior, but the "promotion of their interests" focused on the particular concerns of nonwhite women. The working-class Literary Union's aim of "cultivating literature" contended with the class-based definition of genteel culture by asserting working women's desire to participate in culture.[15] Each of these clubs, like thousands of others across the country, described their purposes in terms that modified, expanded, or redirected the meanings attached to *culture*. Regardless of the particular meanings for culture in their constitutions and bylaws, clubwomen in all social locations appropriated its authoritative language for their self-definitions.

Like the local clubs, the national organizations of women's clubs also claimed culture as central. The General Federation of Women's Clubs described its member clubs as providing "such a means of discipline and culture to the mind and heart that woman has found herself in a veritable new world."[16] The National Council of Jewish Women defined itself as interested in religion, philanthropy, and education, and it named the study of "the history, literature, and customs of the Jews" as one of its central purposes. In addition to its stated intent of studying culture as refracted through the Jewish experience, the National Council pledged to "secure the interest and aid of influential persons in arousing the general sentiment against religious persecutions, wherever, whenever, and against whomever shown, and in finding means to prevent such persecutions," thus pointing to what Sadie American described as the "certain problems . . . forced upon us to be solved which present themselves to no one else," creating work that is "peculiarly our own."[17] In like manner, the National League of Women Workers described itself as wanting to further "the social, educational and industrial interests of all working women by any means in its power." While working women shared with other clubwomen a desire for culture, their wages and working conditions dictated that furthering their industrial interests remain their foremost goal. Josephine Ruffin, who convened the first national meeting of representatives of colored women's clubs, observed that the organization provided women much-needed opportunities for "mingling freely with people of culture and learning."[18] Like Jewish, Mormon, and working women, African American clubwomen embraced a particular form of culture, just as they pursued, in the words of Fanny Barrier Williams, "a kind of club work . . . original, peculiarly suitable to our peculiar needs."[19] Since they could not mingle "freely with people of culture" outside their own race, the National Association of Colored Women provided a space in which clubwomen could pursue culture while attending to the special needs of their people. These particularized definitions of culture show how the affinities by which clubwomen grouped themselves locally extended to the national level and helped shape their meanings for the term.

Outsiders' descriptions, like clubwomen's self-representations, identified culture as central to club work, but such descriptions cut two ways. For those who viewed women's clubs in positive terms, culture functioned as a term of approbation. Editors of the *Kansas City Messenger* wrote in praise of the *Woman's*

Era: "The editors are ladies of culture and refinement, worthy representatives of their race. The *Era* should meet with great success among our people."[20] Equating culture with refinement and declaring women who acquire it as "worthy" indicate that culture enhances women's status. Similarly, Jewish women were described by gentiles as "passionate consumers of culture," a designation that affirmed their activities and rendered them less "other" to non-Jews.[21] Conversely, those who had less sympathetic views of women's clubs or who lacked direct knowledge of their activities frequently used *culture* as a term of disapproval. Aided by clubwomen's reluctance to expose their texts to the scrutiny of outsiders, those who wished to find fault with women meeting in groups used the term *culture* to dismiss whatever they took to be club activities. A male critic wrote that "mothers and grandmothers have joined the younger women in the pursuit of culture. They have formed clubs—study clubs, current event clubs, camera clubs, art clubs, literary clubs, civic clubs." After pointing out clubwomen's participation in university extension lectures, the University of Chicago correspondence courses, chautauquas, and foreign travel, he asserts, "Liberal culture has come into the possession of women; they have carried it by storm and have compelled capitulation."[22] Edward Bok, editor of the *Ladies' Home Journal,* asserted that the self-culture of women's clubs, which he described as "unintelligent," had done "incalculable harm" by fostering "what is jocularly known as "woman's club knowledge' but what is actually an undigested, superficial knowledge that is worse than no knowledge at all."[23] Nearly all such criticism posited women's clubs as white middle-class groups focusing on programs defined by the genteel tradition, but the literacy practices of clubwomen in all social locations reveal a much more complicated and contested approach to culture.

Part of the hostility directed toward clubwomen emerged from a desire to regulate women's experiences with culture. Since the genteel tradition cast women as the uncontrolled mass, holding onto the sorts of worn-out standards Santayana decried, clubwomen were viewed as needing direction to prevent them from absorbing dangerous or harmful ideas and to aid them in developing taste. This feature, more than any other, was central to the view of culture fostered by the genteel tradition, and it encompassed knowledge of *what* cultural artifacts to absorb and *how* to approach them. Critics of clubwomen and of women's more general participation in culture sought to control both the amount and type of women's activities. Since white middle-class women were so frequently taken as the model for clubwomen by those who criticized or lamented women's takeover of culture, they were the most frequent targets of programs designed to regulate women's cultural experiences. Jewish, African American, working-class, and Mormon clubwomen were largely ignored. Mass market publications, such as the *Ladies' Home Journal,* and such groups as the American Library Association participated in attempts to regulate women's experience with culture by recommending certain texts and activities. One list of books recommended for clubwomen begins by asserting that it contains some twenty-one hundred books worthy to be read or studied by girls and women. "Men and women who know have chosen the books," it proclaimed, implying that clubwomen did not number among the knowing. This introduction went on to assure readers that it would enable them to choose a book "intelligently," something of "great importance in an age when books, good bad, and indifferent, abound and super abound."[24] With its implication that intelligent choices about reading should be made *for* rather than *by* clubwomen and its warning about the danger of bad books, this text attempts to regulate clubwomen's reading by asserting the cultural authority of "those who know."

Although some clubwomen adhered to and even promoted a version of culture that affirmed the genteel tradition, they also resisted that tradition. In their public statements and their daily practices, clubwomen women appropriated its terms for their own purposes. Clubwomen from all social groups pushed culture toward a more relativistic definition by calling into question the central terms and precepts of the genteel tradition. Instead of allowing the genteel tradition's version of culture to shape their perceptions, many clubwomen constructed their own meanings. Deploying their literacy practices, these women—defined by gender, race, ethnicity, class, and religious affiliation—extended the genteel tradition's boundaries and questioned its assumptions. Clubwomen, like the art consumers David Halle described, demonstrated resistance and creativity as they consumed the precepts of the genteel tradition and adapted them to new purposes.[25] These processes of reshaping and reformulating led to new constructions of culture.

A good illustration of this reformulation appears in Jane Addams's 1901 speech to a conference of working women's clubs. In this text, subsequently published in the *Club Worker,* Addams describes an activity of the Hull House Woman's Club that brought together persons of Irish American and Italian background, repeating a comment from an Irish American: "I am ashamed of the way I used to talk about Dagoes. I used to say that we must move off the street because there were so many Dagoes coming in. But they are just like other people, only you have to take more pains to find them out." Addams explains, "That was the result of cultivation, if we take the definition that it is extended experience. It is exactly the thing we send our children to Europe for, the result we hope for when we read books about all kinds of people—to get over the differences raised by barriers and traditions, that really we may be fair-minded and may know people as they really are."[26] Addams, a privileged daughter of the white upper class and steeped in the genteel tradition, defines culture as "extended experience." Acknowledging her own background, she nods toward international travel and the reading of literature as vehicles for achieving the desired cultivation. But she goes beyond traditional ideas about high culture to affirm the experience of the Irish American woman who comes to understand that Italians are "just like other people." With this move Addams positions culture in a realm that remains accessible to all rather than to only the elite enfranchised by the genteel tradition. She underscores this expanded view by equating *tradition,* a word held in high esteem by genteel culture, with *barriers,* as something to be transcended rather than adhered to or preserved. Transgressing the class boundaries of the genteel tradition, Addams suggests an alternative that emphasizes mutual respect and appreciation for differences as it fosters knowledge of "people as they really are."[27] This insistence on equating intercultural encounters with reading literature assigns social value to areas of human experience completely outside the genteel tradition, and it challenges the dominant view of high culture.

The working-class clubwomen who heard or read this text did not occupy Addams's privileged position for challenging the genteel tradition, but they echoed its sentiments in their own textual negotiations with a definition of culture that excluded their life experiences. Addams, who in 1901 enjoyed international acclaim and wielded considerable influence, offered an authoritative text to support a view of culture that working women had been developing for the last decade as they were devising new ways of seeing value in their own experiences. The first biographical sketch appearing in *Far and Near* gave an account of Lucy Larcom's life. Larcom, author of *A New England Girlhood,* a chronicle of her experiences in the Lowell, Massachusetts, mills between 1835 and 1845, offered a model of a working woman's quest for self-education. Larcom details how she and her peers formed a reading group, the Improvement Circle, and published a magazine of their writings. The biographical sketch includes such Larcom quotations as "I could be a student wherever I was and whatever else I had to be or do, and I would!" Although she never made much money in her later career as a writer, Larcom declared, "Sympathy and recognition are worth a great deal; the power to touch human beings inwardly and nobly is worth far more." These statements of determination to pursue education in spite of limited time and resources and of a willing acceptance of modest means addressed the fact that working women did not have many hours to participate in self-culture because they worked so much of the day. This 1890 article marked the process by which working women claimed the genteel tradition for themselves. Although she did not occupy a position comparable to that of Addams, Larcom lent a certain authority to claims for a culture that extended beyond "book knowledge alone" to include "the world of human beings." This attempt to incorporate life experiences as well as reading literature under the rubric of culture anticipated Addams's move a decade later, and the statement at the end of the Larcom sketch reinforces this point: "The meaning of life is education; not through book knowledge alone, sometimes entirely without it. Education is growth, the development of our best possibilities from within outward; and it cannot be carried on as it should be except in school, just such a school as we all find ourselves in—the world of human beings by whom we are surrounded."[28]

Here education stands in for culture and her phrase "development of our best possibilities" suggests the doctrine of perfectionism central to the genteel tradition, but Larcom moves beyond this realm to define school as "the world of human beings," providing another precursor of Addams's declarations about learning from life experiences. For working-class clubwomen, whose formal education was necessarily limited and whose access to books was frequently restricted, this definition offered a culture in which they could participate, one that extended beyond books of the genteel tradition to include their own human interactions. Making culture accessible to working women who, as the editor notes, faced "circumstances which had made it necessary for them to begin early to win their daily bread,"[29] challenged the class-based genteel tradition, and similar challenges sounded throughout the decade.

In an 1891 article Harriet Robinson, a working woman who found the New England Women's Club snobbish and established her own club, reflected on her experience in the Lowell mills. Like Larcom, Robinson did not remain a mill worker and achieved some note as a writer. Her class allegiances, however, remained with workers, and she named as "the first woman's club" the Improvement Circle formed by mill workers in Lawrence, Massachusetts, in 1836. Robinson offered a model of someone who acquired culture despite her worker status, and she explains how working women accomplish this: "Their labor was monotonous and done almost mechanically, but their thoughts were free, and they had ample time to digest what they had learned or think over what they had read. . . . Many of the articles in prose and verse that were printed in the

Lowell Offering were thought out amid the hum of the wheels, while the skill-ful fingers and well-trained eyes of the writers tended the loom or the frame."[30] As Robinson portrays the body of the working woman, it can be separated from the mind, and although the fingers and eyes may remain fixed on the machines, thoughts can be free to pursue culture. The cognitive discipline necessary to individual improvement can, in Robinson's view, be accomplished regardless of—or even because of—material circumstances. The division between the mechanical labor required of the body and the freedom of the mind to move among ideas and texts portrays the mental exertion of culture as transcending the class-bound body of the worker.

In recommending home culture clubs, defined as "a small circle of persons who meet once a week at the home of one of the members," an 1893 article in *Far and Near* designates culture as "some pleasant and *profitable* pursuit." This broad meaning for culture is matched by an equally generous description of how "self-culture" can be achieved in such groups: "Some clubs take up a course of study; others simply read. Each member is encouraged, also, to read out of meetings as much as possible," but since the clubs are designed for those "who are too busy, too tired, or perhaps too inexperienced to read or study with advantage by themselves," such reading is not expected.[31] By failing to specify the sort of study that might fit under the designation "pleasant and profitable," the writer invites clubwomen to determine the meaning of culture for them-selves, and by acknowledging the conditions of their lives and adjusting club expectations accordingly, she suggests a version of culture in which they can realistically participate. Similarly, in a paper on self-culture given at the conven-tion of the Connecticut Association, the author asserts, "I cannot take up the question of what we shall read and study. The field of knowledge is too vast for any one to lay down rules about how it is to be entered. My advice is to take any subject in which you are interested, get a book on it, and begin to read it. Having once entered upon a subject it will open out more and more before you, and each book will lead naturally to another."[32] Far from insisting on "the best" according to a standard established by the genteel tradition, this author encourages clubwomen to create their own routes into culture, trusting that they will develop a broader understanding of the world from their own read-ing and will simultaneously transform culture into something more relativistic and contiguous with a whole way of life.

Lack of time figured prominently among the constraints working women faced. In an 1891 *Far and Near* article, Lucy Warner, a member of the Help Each Other Club, asserts that members of her club would welcome an "opportunity to obtain a higher education and greater culture" but that they have little "time and opportunity." Despite this, writes Warner, "there are many working girls who are spending every leisure moment in study, not because they think others will respect them more, but because such study is to them a delight."[33] Edith Howes of the Shawmut Avenue Club asserted, "We have so little time for reading that it becomes doubly important that we shall not waste that little. We were told of those who gave five, ten, fifteen minutes each day to some good book till they had completed it."[34] Another author urged clubwomen to "examine [their] present use of [their] time." She continued, "How to diminish this waste [of time] is the problem before us."[35] This theme is echoed by another writer: "It is really marvelous what an amount of steady, excellent reading can be accomplished by the half hour a day reading which one would never think it possible to do by any other means. The habit and taste is also formed for good literature."[36] Culture, in the form of good taste, thus becomes linked with time. Borrowing the language of the factory floor that encourages workers to not waste time, picturing reading as controlled by the clock, and emphasizing efficiency in consuming texts, these selections represented culture in working women's own language.

Just as they supplemented representations of culture with terms of efficiency, so working-class clubwomen sought to separate it from unattainable (to them) wealth. In an article objecting to the "newspaper notoriety" inflicted on working women's clubs, the author notes, "The consequence in many cases has been that picturesque and entirely untrue articles have appeared, drawing contrasts which no club member sees between luxury, wealth, and culture, and hardship, poverty and degradation, causing such offense that new members withdraw and old ones lose heart."[37] Clearly grounded in the perspective of the working woman who *must* see culture as attainable to those without great wealth, the offense and discouragement described by this author results when culture is once again portrayed as beyond the reach of all except the wealthy. In resisting the conflation of wealth and culture, working women insisted on making culture their own. By reminding readers of working women's material limitations and their enormous desire to attain culture, these writers alert their working-class peers to the value and accessibility of culture. Juxtaposing their time constraints with their highly motivated and intensely purposeful attempts to acquire culture, these clubwomen simultaneously acknowledge and dismiss the circumstances that stand between them and participation in a form of the genteel tradition. Echoing the claim that factory workers can control their minds if not their bodies, they refuse to allow their cultural choices to be determined by their lack of time. A similar resistance appears in discussions of the difficulties of obtaining books.

An article written by a member of the Literary Circle of the Walworth Club details how one group addressed the problem of "how to supply each member with a copy of the same book." As the author explains, "The leader loaned her own books, borrowed others of her friends and secured the rest from the Mechanic Library and the New York Free Circulating Library, receiving from the last the greatest aid. The Bond Street, Ottendorfer, Jackson Square and Muhlenberg Branches would loan us two or three copies at a time of the same book, with the understanding that we could keep them a month." This detailed explanation continues by reporting that clubwomen purchased "cheap editions" for "from fifteen to twenty-five cents a copy," "as a beginning toward forming a library of their own."[38] The composition and publication of this information about the complicated strategies clubwomen employed to ensure that they could read a common text serve as a reminder of the economic limitations under which working women carried out their cultural projects. Yet this account does not dwell on the difficulties but focuses on the solutions devised, and the closing line about forming a club library points toward a more comprehensive resolution. In writing and reading accounts like these, working women resisted definitions that positioned them as helpless victims of their circumstances. Instead, they represented themselves as agents acting on their own behalf to acquire the materials they needed for their pursuit of culture.

This sense of agency often extended into offering plans for others to emulate, as the Girls Enterprise Club of New Haven did:

> We have a "Reading Club" the members of which pledge themselves to read one hour and a half a week for three months. The reading must consist of standard literature, and each member must keep a list of the books she reads, which is to be presented at the end of the three months to a committee, who are appointed as judges. If the books read meet the approval of the committee, each girl is presented with a book as a prize, the use of which is given to the Club Library. On the fly leaf of each "prize book" is a short inscription, stating that the book was won for the Club Library by such and such a girl.[39]

The term *standard literature* and the disciplined approach to listing books read echo the canonical texts and careful self-regulation associated with the genteel tradition. As such, this plan displays working women's capacity for systemati-

cally directing their own self-improvement. At the same time, the plan addresses the particular circumstances of these clubwomen. By insisting that books
must meet "the approval of the committee," the plan assigns questions of ap-
propriateness or taste to members themselves, which affirms the agency of
these clubwomen. Similarly, the mechanism of giving prizes to the club library
addresses the shortage of books and shows clubwomen as able to claim culture
for themselves, even if they do not have the material resources of their more
affluent peers.

By the time Jane Addams offered her 1901 definition of culture as "extended
experience" and insisted on its accessibility to more than just wealthy white
Protestants, then, working women had already developed terms and strategies
for negotiating with the genteel tradition. Acknowledging the constraints of
limited time and books, they compensated with time-management skills and ingenuity learned in the factory. Positing the mechanized and routine nature of
their work as an advantage, they outlined a mind-body division that enabled
them, mentally at least, to transcend class boundaries. Inscribing and reading
such self-representations and approaches, working women's clubs translated the
self-control and proprieties of the genteel tradition into their own language and
opened the way for a less class-based view of culture. As Paul DiMaggio has
shown, the high culture of the genteel tradition was not just a form of ritual
classification but took shape in institutions, such as museums and symphonies,
that required the capital of the upper classes. Such "organizational mediation"
created an enduring connection between upper classes and the genteel tradition.[40] Working women's clubs challenged this connection from one direction,
and the Women's Educational and Industrial Union (WEIU) did so from
another.

Construing itself as "an institution wherein the needs of *all classes* of women
would be met, one held together by the bonds of a love whose effects would
be shown in mutual service and healthy co-operative activities," the WEIU opposed the "dreadful apartness caused by class feeling." In addition to transcending class boundaries, these clubwomen extended the definition of culture beyond the boundaries of the genteel tradition. According to the president's 1914
address, the WEIU combined "culture with industrial intelligence and skill" to
create a new model of education, one these clubwomen were prepared to share
with normal schools and other teacher-training institutions.[41] As the WEIU constructed them, vocational schools did not concern themselves exclusively with
work-related education. Rather, they combined culture with practical education, insisting that the learning associated with the genteel tradition not remain

the exclusive property of one social class. The 1885 WEIU report, for example, listed courses in "French, German, Music, Penmanship, Embroidery, [and] Millinery" and announced the establishment of "an Art and Literature Coterie" and a reading room, "supplied with standard books and periodicals." Taken by themselves, these can be read as attempts by middle-class women to impose their own version of culture on working women, but the juxtaposition of millinery (a very common source of female employment during this period) with such subjects as French and embroidery signals a recognition that female "accomplishments" alone would not constitute an adequate education. In addition to these courses, the report noted that the WEIU maintained a "registry of suitable boarding places," sold "on commission the handiwork of women," and investigated "employers [who] wrongfully withhold wages from their employees."[42] Inscribing concern with material issues, such as lodging places, sources of income, and fair treatment by employers, alongside a recital of courses and materials that partially represent the genteel tradition, this report challenges the hierarchical boundaries of gentility and insists on a more comprehensive view of culture.

Many Jewish clubwomen enjoyed a socioeconomic status similar to that of their Christian white middle-class peers, but they, too, pushed against the strictures of the Protestant-centered genteel tradition. In particular, their definition of culture made their own traditions central. Even as the Pioneers allied themselves with "self-culture clubs," these clubwomen turned their "systematic study" to their own tradition. As one clubwoman claimed, "Its [Jewish history] ramifications are as many as the nations themselves. It crosses all other roads; it merges into them; it emerges from them. The traveler upon it treads the blackest shadow and the whitest sunlight; he is lead from the most tearful vale to the heaven encircled mountain tops; he drinks of the bitter water of the well of sorrow; he eats of the heaven-sent manna of truth."[43] By taking such a capacious view of her own heritage, the clubwoman who wrote this and the many who read it affirmed a definition of culture that included Jews and their history.

Insisting on the value of their own versions of culture, Jewish clubwomen wrote explicitly against definitions that would exclude them. An 1896 paper published in the *American Jewess* opposed culture that would cause "an individual or set of individuals to move in a charmed circle," one that "would necessarily single out a class of men and women distinct from others, and give them a right to presuppose their importance and worth." Recognizing the powerful alliance between Protestantism and the genteel tradition, the author acknowledges that "culture and religion are one line with two opposite poles" and, in keeping with this view of culture, asserts that "the social value of culture equals the moral one." Then she pushes the boundary of the genteel tradition in another direction: "The world may look back to Greece for the beginning of art-culture, but it must turn its head still further back to trace the beginning of spiritual culture; for that it must turn to Jerusalem."[44] Adapting the religious dimension of the genteel tradition to her own purposes, this author uses it to insist on a meaning of culture that includes her own Jewish tradition as well as the Christian one more commonly claimed.

Although they asserted the importance of their own traditions, Jewish women remained ever mindful of the specter of anti-Semitism, and many of these clubwomen kept their cultural interests to themselves, as Rosa Sonneschein, founding editor of the *American Jewess,* learned when lack of funding forced her to stop publishing. In the final issue she wrote:

> We thought that so-called "enlightened" Jews would support litera-
> ture, but we were mistaken. Most of them are ashamed to have their
> neighbors and letter carriers know that they are interested in Jewish af-
> fairs. We have often admired the pluck and candor of the "barbaric Rus-
> sian" Jew, who spreads his Yiddish paper before him on the street car, in
> the ferryboat, or in the park. . . . It is a travesty on culture that interest
> in Jewish affairs and Jewish literature should be found only in the brain
> of the "uncouth" Ghetto Jew, while the minds of our "cultivated" and
> "emancipated" Jews should be bent on getting as far away from Jewish
> affairs as possible.[45]

To be fair, Sonneschein's disagreements with the National Council of Jewish Women contributed to the demise of her journal as much as clubwomen's desire to avoid calling public attention to their Jewish heritage did. Sonneschein often expressed public criticism of the National Council's decisions, and its leaders expressed their resentment by withholding support for her publication.

Nonetheless, Sonneschein's statement illustrates a view of culture many Jewish clubwomen promoted. The "literature" of the first sentence becomes "Jewish literature" by the fourth, and the "travesty on culture" extends to both Jewish affairs and literature, suggesting that more than belletristic texts fall under the category of culture. The obvious tensions between more acculturated German Jews and the "barbaric" Jews from eastern Europe illustrate the complications inherent in this broader view of culture. Although Jewish women wanted to affirm their religious heritage, they also prized the genteel tradition's designation of "cultivated" because it distinguished them from their immigrant sisters.

Nonetheless, Jewish clubwomen maintained an inclusive definition of culture that embraced their own tradition. The study groups that emerged as part of the National Council of Jewish Women assigned a similarly broad meaning to culture by creating spaces where women learned about history, politics, economics, and new techniques of social work. Members of the Philadelphia Section, for example, met twice monthly to "read papers, ask questions and discuss the Bible, Jewish history and topics of contemporary interest."[46] In 1903, setting the agenda for the coming year's work, members of the Detroit Section lamented the lack of attention to "topics distinctively Jewish" and asserted, "Our race has made characteristic and supreme contributions to the progress of civilization, and it is for us, as true Jewesses, to maintain these historic traditions."[47] Using the same methods that General Federation clubs did—preparing papers, reading texts in common, and discussing what they read and heard—National Council clubwomen constructed a meaning for culture that retained some of the prestigious features of the genteel tradition but contested the idealized and totalizing features of that tradition by extending culture to include the history and literature, both religious and secular, that enabled them to know their own heritage more fully.

The degree to which National Council members knew and honored their own traditions further complicated their view of culture, and they explored these tangled issues in their reading and writing. "The Revival of Judaism," a paper given at the New York Section in 1893, delineated the conflicted perspective on culture that many National Council members held: "We have in Judaism and the Jewish life all of divine comfort and consolation—yet we pass it by and seek in Ethical Culture and its kindred cults an answer to our prayers." The ethical culture this clubwoman decried represented secularization, a separation from religion, while issues of faith, in her view, belonged at the center of National Council life. This author, like many of her peers, saw the National Council as a vehicle for strengthening Jewish traditions by (re)informing women about sacred texts and rituals and stanching the losses of "our brightest intellects to Ethical Culture and to Unitarianism."[48] When the National Council first took shape, its leaders, such as Hannah Solomon, gained a sense of purpose upon learning that "hundreds proclaim indifference and confess absolute ignorance of Jewish history and literature."[49] National Council founders undertook to encourage religious observances in the home, since women were charged with transmitting Jewish identity, and sought a definition of culture that included religion.

Ada Chapman, a speaker at the founding meeting exhorted members, "Let our sanctuary be our homes, and let us beautify them with the undoubted, holy influence of our beloved faith."Yet National Council members wanted to prove themselves "worthy of acceptance into the world of women's clubs" and recognized that too great a religious emphasis would compromise that acceptance.[50] Accordingly, they struggled for a middle course that affirmed their faith without making it dominant. The National Council's 1896 debate about Sunday Sabbath observances typified this effort. Katherine DeSola, who sought National Council affirmation of the traditional Sabbath argued, "If we are an organization of Jewish Women, then we must do what Jewish Women do, and therefore must keep our Sabbath on Saturday and not on Sunday." Meanwhile, Henriette Frank, one of those who wanted to keep religious controversy out of the National Council, delivered a paper titled "Our Opportunities," in which she claimed, "Not the choice of the calendar day, but the manner of its observance makes of it a Sabbath."[51] This debate, which continued for the next two decades, highlighted the National Council's ambivalent position of wanting to affirm Jewish tradition while remaining open to pluralism within the faith.

The National Council's internal contest about its meaning for culture echoes throughout its records. Some members lamented study circles' lack of focus on Jewish traditions: "To secure the attention of the busy woman of today and to induce her to undertake systematic study is not easy. . . . Browning is more fashionable than the Bible and just as difficult to understand. Art and literature are easier to understand than history. The Bible and history mean work, not absorption. These considerations shut out many who would have joined us in the study of Literature or in our philanthropy."[52] Despite the sort of resistance acknowledged here, National Council yearbooks continued to publish many pages on religious activities and urge an integration of Jewish traditions into the forms of culture pursued in study circles, as this excerpt from the New York Section illustrates: "Biblical characters as created by the different writers, poets, and others have a particular attraction for the women of the Council. . . . Women who were taking a deep interest in literary matters have become desirous of knowing and understanding the position of the Bible in the development of the world, its civilizing influence, and above all the potency of its moral teachings."[53] By positioning the Bible as a resource for women interested in literature, this writer offered yet another way of incorporating religious study into the meaning assigned to culture. The National Council's internal conflicts about the role and meaning of religion in its work thus contributed to the recalibrations of culture in the larger society. As evangelical Protestants' hold on culture relaxed, other traditions entered the picture.

In addition to the internal pressures of their own contests about culture, National Council members faced, as did other clubwomen, criticism from the men of their community. Besides the standard objections that clubwomen threatened home and family life by absenting themselves, there were negative comments about their failure to nurture and perpetuate Judaism. When it appeared that National Council members slighted religion, male critics objected: "Much of the new activity is purely philanthropic in direction, which seems to have diverted the attention of the National Council from more specifically Jewish lines of activity."[54] Since preparing themselves for effective religious education was one of their justifications for venturing outside the domestic sphere, National Council members needed to provide continuing assurance that Jewish traditions were prominent in their deliberations. This external scrutiny, combined with their internal debates about various representations of Judaism, led National Council women to engage in continual complex negotiations about expanded meanings for culture.

Although they did not form an organization like the WEIU, National Council members devoted considerable time, energy, and money to working women, many of whom were recent immigrants. Like other middle-class clubwomen—both white and black—they expressed ambivalence about their relationship with their less affluent sisters, but they recognized that providing aid at Ellis Island did not end their responsibility for helping these newcomers become acculturated. Like adherents to the genteel tradition, these middle-class clubwomen saw culture as a means of distinguishing themselves from recent immigrants, but they also recognized that maintaining their status depended on bringing a degree of culture to the immigrant Jews, by whom they and their more refined peers would be judged. Sadie American, a longtime leader of the National Council who assumed a prominent role in this project of transforming immigrant Jews, explained that she and her middle-class sisters sought not to "go and give" but to find "what there is . . . to lead it forth." Accordingly, American described working women's clubs as self-supporting institutions seeking "mutual improvement and culture." With the guidance of more affluent clubwomen, such groups read "Lamb's Tales from Shakespeare, with frequent passages from the great bard himself" and "entertaining books," or they distributed "good reading among children."[55] By urging Shakespeare (in abbreviated form) and other books upon workers, American and her peers emulated the genteel tradition's hierarchy of standards that assumed only certain texts met the standard of "good" and that this "good literature" was of equal interest and value to all readers. Ironically, in appropriating the status of the genteel tradition to regulate the literacy practices of working women, American and her peers sometimes undercut the broader view of culture their own study circles encouraged.

African American clubwomen embraced a similarly contested and expanded meaning for culture. Some embraced the genteel tradition as a means of entering the larger world outside their racial group and gaining acceptance from whites. Many felt, as the clubwoman Charlotte Hawkins Brown, put it, "'Nordics' would give black people more social recognition if blacks adopted the social practices and customs of 'peoples of refined tastes.'"[56] Armed with the knowledge and practices associated with culture as defined by the dominant society, they could acquire a positive visibility. Brown and the many others who shared her view clearly sought to acquire for themselves some of the social status associated with the genteel tradition. Culture thus became a means for African American clubwomen to transform themselves, and its terms, as Brown expressed them, echoed the principles of the genteel tradition: "Culture is the discipline of the mental and moral powers manifest in the ease, grace and poise one exhibits in the performance of one's life. It is the result of the development of the intellect and the appreciation of the aesthetic. Culture may be achieved through intensive training and continued practice."[57] Brown points to the connection between culture and the moral betterment of persons by describing it as regulating both mind and morality. In seeing culture as something acquired through self-discipline and connecting it with morality, Brown aligned herself with the white Protestant view that linked self-improvement with the doctrine of perfectionism and saw it as extending to the general "performance of one's life." Brown's emphasis on training and practice acknowledges that African Americans could not—given their stigmatized position—claim the culture of the genteel tradition without special effort. With "intensive" and "continued" work, African American women could, in Brown's view, transform themselves into refined people who would merit approving recognition from whites.

Brown spoke for many in assigning a transformative power to culture. Fannie Barrier Williams, in the "Illinois" column of the *Woman's Era,* echoed this claim, arguing that "daughters capable of culture" should receive a college education: "The mental discipline and culture that are the most important furnishings of a university education will save us from many humiliating mistakes in our public lives, and will tend to lessen the small jealousies, petty envies and the general unkindness of woman for womankind." Like Brown, Williams assumes that training, such as that provided by colleges, enables the acquisition of culture, but her reason for seeking it differs slightly. In asserting that culture can reduce "humiliating mistakes" and "general unkindness," Williams constructs culture as a force capable of shielding African American women from pain in their dealings with the (white) "public" outside their immediate communities. Williams, who had recently been rejected for membership by the white Chicago Woman's Club because of her race, knew this pain in very personal terms, but she persisted in her belief that culture belonged to "us" colored women and that it could be acquired through such structured programs as university education. Implicit in Williams's extension from "the daughters" to "womankind" is the idea that culture could not only improve individuals but also, in keeping with the National Association of Colored Women's stated goal of "Lifting as We Climb," could ameliorate the lives of African American women in general. Williams continues, "Oh for some kind of culture or talisman that will save us women from being consumed by each other in our ambitions to be useful in this world of ours." Equating *culture* and *talisman* suggests the enormous power she attributes to culture, yet even as she acknowledges its force, Williams calls the power of culture into question by pointing to its inability, in the face of racism, to transcend the differences among women and unite them into "womankind."[58] Many clubwomen shared Williams's reservations about the capacity of the genteel tradition's version of culture to improve their lives. Certainly women who claimed their purpose was the "improvement of colored women and the promotion of their interests" recognized that culture as defined by white middle-class society could not be wholly theirs or serve socially defined needs.

Accordingly, African American clubwomen's projects of "improvement" took into account the inability of the genteel tradition's version of culture to effect a transformation that would ease their lives. In response, they tried to expand the boundaries of culture. One strategy was to include members of their own race in its tradition, as an excerpt from a *Woman's Era* column demonstrates: "Paul Laurence Dunbar is recognized as a true poet by the first critics of America and his little volume 'Majors and Minors' will be welcomed as a contribution to real literature. There is hardly a recent circumstance which means more to the race than this. As Mr. Howells says it is probably through the arts that nations are to be brought together and hostilities and prejudices to disappear."[59] William D. Howells's support of Dunbar provided African American clubwomen the basis for claiming that Dunbar was a "true" poet who contributed to "real" literature, one who could strengthen national unity. At the same time that the editor of the column acknowledges the authority of the tradition of "real" literature represented by Howells, she urges an enlargement of it to include members of her race without "hostilities and prejudices." A later column in the *Woman's Era* reinforces this view. When Dunbar's *Lyrics of a Lowly Life* appeared, the *Woman's Era* titled a column "Paul Dunbar's New Book," which, after urging colored people to support one of their own by purchasing the new volume, identified it as "among the best poetical contributions of the year." This column concludes with a quotation from William D. Howells's introduction: "Had these poems been written by a white man I should not have found them less admirable. I accepted them as an evidence of the essential unity of the human race, which does not think or feel black in one and white in another, but humanly in all."[60] In emphasizing the unity of humanity across racial lines, the author of this column urges a vision of culture that extends well beyond the boundaries of the genteel tradition.

Medora Gould, editor of the *Woman's Era*'s literature column, supplemented entries about Henry Wadsworth Longfellow, Judge Tourgee, George Cable, James Lowell, W. D. Howells, Thomas Wentworth Higginson, Henry James, and Oliver Wendell Holmes with such notices as "*Harper's Magazine* for March contains an interesting contribution entitled 'The New England Negro' by Miss Jane DeForest Shelton. It treats of the time when slaves were owned extensively throughout Massachusetts and Connecticut, and the period immediately following their emancipation"; "The *Chautauquan* for October last contains an article entitled 'The Southern Negro Women' by Olive Ruth Jefferson"; "Thomas Ewing, in the *Cosmopolitan* for May tells his story of the struggle for freedom in Kansas, giving sketches of the leaders on both sides, and the plans and purposes of John Brown"; "The American Citizen Company also publishes a book by J. Robert Love, M.D. of Port Au Prince Hayti"; "An attractive little volume is that entitled 'Aunt Lindy.' Its author is Victoria, the *nom de plume* assumed by Mrs. Wm. E. Matthews, the President of the Woman's Loyal Union of New York. . . . The heroine is a typical woman of the Negro race, well advanced in years, whose heart is warm, whose hand is skillful and whose life is devoted to the service of her Maker"; and "*The Work of the Afro-American Woman* is a daintily bound volume whose author is Mrs. N. F. Mossell . . . Mrs. Mossell's very commendable object in writing this book was to do for the women of her own race what had already been done for other women more favorably circumstanced."[61] As these notices make clear, Gould expanded the category of literature to encompass a wide variety of historical and literary texts written by and about African Americans. In regularly recommending such authors as James, Lowell, and Longfellow in a literature column read by thousands of African American women nationwide, Gould and her successors demonstrated their desire to acquire high culture as defined by mainstream society. At the same time, by including notices about books and articles by and about people of her race, this columnist highlighted the ways African Americans could supplement if not supplant the genteel tradition's culture with their own unique contributions.

The clubwomen who wrote and read such statements saw culture not just as a means of improving themselves individually—although they certainly approved of that—but also as something that could render racial status irrelevant. The expanded vision of culture these clubwomen espoused included social transformations, as the epigraph on the program for the nineteenth annual convention of the Colored Women's Clubs of Colorado, for example, stated: "How empty learning, and how vain is art, But as it mends the life and guides the heart." Mending life meant eliminating Jim Crow laws and lynchings and creating ways of recognizing and affirming African Americans' contributions. This insistence on addressing life's problems through culture shows the connection these clubwomen saw between their own refinement and transformations outside themselves. Accordingly, they deployed the politics of respectability to counter the descriptions and designations imposed on them by whites and looked to culture as a means of making their self-representations visible to the larger public, even as they recognized how "wholly impossible" it might be.[62]

African American clubwomen also appropriated cultural institutions of the white world for their own purposes. "Colored Chautauquas" represented one such adoption, and clubwomen in many parts of the country participated in study groups that used Chautauqua materials or followed its general program. For example, the Chautauqua Circle of Atlanta was founded by Henrietta Porter, who had hoped to complete the Chautauqua Literary and Scientific Circle course but lost all her books in a fire. As an alternative, she joined with other "earnest and dedicated" women of "unusual ability," who left their stamp on "the social and cultural life of Atlanta."[63] Although they borrowed the name and idea of sustained study from Chautauqua, this circle constructed its own idea of culture, one that honored African American contributions as well as those from the traditional genteel tradition. From the earliest days members regularly sang James Weldon Johnson's "Lift Every Voice and Sing," otherwise known as the Negro National Anthem. Minutes report that at their first reception for husbands, "The Negro in Literature and Art was a master production by Mrs.

Watson. She showed unlimited research. Mrs. Ross read an excellent paper on Gems from Negro Writers. She quoted some of their choice selections."[64] As this report indicates, when called on to display their cultural accomplishments to outsiders, these clubwomen focused on work by members of their own race. Although the Chautauqua Circle included study of John Milton, Sir Walter Scott, William Bryant, and John Ruskin in their program, they also gave papers on William Stanley Braithwaite, James Weldon Johnson, Benjamin Brawley, Charles Chestnutt, W. E. B. Du Bois, and African art. This blending of figures from the genteel tradition with those of African American descent demonstrates how these clubwomen reconfigured the terms of culture.

The gendered terms of culture also preoccupied African American club-women. As Gould wrote in one of her columns, "It is we women who are re-sponsible for the present trend in literature, for it is the women who do the novel reading."[65] Accordingly, African Americans resisted the male dominance of culture. In addition to recommending work by the white men traditionally assumed to represent high culture, the *Woman's Era's* literature columns called attention to the writing of Mary A. Livermore, Mary E. Wilkins, Jane Barlow, Kate Douglas Wiggin, Agnes Repplier, and Mildred Rutherford. The column also included comments about the lack of admirable mother figures in litera-ture, blaming it on women "who were content with too low a standard, and who did not claim the culture which men looked upon as their exclusive right," thus highlighting the gendered as well as racial boundaries of the genteel tra-dition. Just as culture (or rather lack of it) represented the problem, so culture offered the solution: "The woman of the new school . . . [believes] it the duty of the wife and mother to . . . represent the highest culture attainable.[66] These African Americans sought more positive textual representations—including admirable mothers—of themselves and saw their self-culture as a way to claim and reshape a genteel tradition that portrayed women in negative terms.

Mormon clubwomen also appropriated aspects of the genteel tradition to enhance their own status and to regulate the literacy practices of others. The *Young Woman's Journal* included lengthy articles on such writers as Shakespeare, Chaucer, and Milton, and the *Woman's Exponent* featured a column titled "Cur-rent Literature" that recommended books and articles to readers. The prose style of the *Journal's* articles on authors associated with high culture suggests the value assigned to them. The series on Shakespeare, for instance, begins by comparing the bard to "a cloud-piercing teneriffe raised up like magic in the waste of waters; its snow-capped summit crowned by a golden circlet of sun-shine, its feet hidden 'neath a foamy skirt of ocean spray, its sides painted, zone above zone, by nature's own artist in every tint pleasing to the eye of the ever-changing, ever-constant goddess," and it continues in equally hyperbolic terms. Much of the series traces events in Shakespeare's life, linking them to passages in his plays and continually reminding the reader of their "pristine gorgeousness and splendor."[67] This language, which has much in common with the almost parodic prose of Mormon affirmations of patriotism before Utah became a state, suggests the eagerness with which these clubwomen sought to identify themselves with an icon of high culture. Publishing this overblown praise on a figure clearly identified with the genteel tradition, the editor attempted to engender appropriate awe for Shakespeare and simultaneously accrue for Mormon clubwomen some of the status associated with him.

While *Journal* articles familiarized readers with writers of the genteel tradition and instilled an admiration for them, the *Exponent*'s "Current Literature" column pushed at the boundaries of that tradition by recommending as "excellent and useful," as well as "practical, moral and intellectual," texts written by such women as Lilian Whiting, Martha D. Lincoln, Maria Louise Poole, Mary E. Watkins, Fannie Fern, Bernice Harraden, and Sarah Grand. In addition to expanding the definition of culture to include women's writing, this column framed culture in religious terms. A list of "books that can never . . . be surpassed" included "the Bible, Book of Mormon, the Iliad, the Odyssey, Shakespeare, and Milton," and an account of the emergence of literature asserts, "In the literary world alone were born many most glorious spirits, Hugo, Eliot, Dickens, Bancroft. But the brightest star in all this wondrous constellation, the brightest since the sorrowful Nazarene, was the spirit of *Joseph Smith the Prophet*."[68] By juxtaposing the central text and major prophet of their religion with established texts and authors of the genteel tradition, these clubwomen aimed to borrow status through association and expand the terms of culture.

Highlighting the achievements of such Mormon authors as Eliza Snow, Emmeline Wells, Hannah King, Hannah Cornaby, Emily Woodmansee, and Sarah Carmichael furthered this project. In an article describing procedures for establishing and maintaining a club, an author in the *Woman's Exponent* asserted, "All knowledge does not come from books, there is the Great Teacher who inspires us all in a greater or less degree, and none of us knows what may yet be developed in this progressive age of the world, and whether this new truth may be given to a sister woman . . . we may find ourselves wiser and better by living in a condition to receive it."[69] In contrast to the a priori standards of the genteel tradition, where the task of the learner is to absorb the predetermined greatness of books, this author argues for an openness to innovation and a culture inspired by religion.

An account of papers given at a meeting of New York's Sorosis underscored this broad view: "One lady . . . said the whole art of life is to learn real things from shams; to learn how to strip the husks away and get at the kernel; how to absorb that kernel in our own lives; transform its energy by our own individuality in the expression of ourselves in terms of work and conduct. . . . Another lady affirmed that art took in the knitting of a stocking or the making of a loaf of bread, as well as the painting of a picture or the modeling of a bust."[70] The author who selected these statements for her summary and the readers who perused them constructed a culture that included domestic arts rather than more narrowly conceived terms of value. Records of meetings indicate a similar insistence on inclusive meanings for culture. Papers given at the Reapers' Club included topics in current literature as well as suffrage. Intermingled with the Woman's Press Club discussions of Browning, Dickinson, and Shakespeare were sessions on heredity, Indian traditions, and pen names. This array of topics, scheduled by clubs that declared culture central to their mission, offers further evidence of Mormon clubwomen's participation in the project of defining culture in inclusive and relativistic terms.

The *Young Woman's Journal* explored questions of culture in fiction, leading readers to consider its relation to their religious beliefs. Assuming a didactic stance, the editor often directed readers to particular selections with such admonitions as "You may see the results of the two opposite courses pursued by mortals under the temptations of the Evil One. Read well and consider long, thou maiden of blest Mormon parentage!"[71] The fiction itself took an equally pedagogical stance. It its first issue, for example, the *Journal* featured a story with this opening line: "Leonard Fox, if you don't stop reading them trashy novels day and day and day after day you'll go clean crazy." As the romantic plot develops and concludes in a polygamous marriage, Leonard loses out to his less bookish brother, not because he reads but because he reads "trashy" books and does little else.[72] Like the working women on the other side of the continent, Mormon clubwomen incorporated their material circumstances into their concepts of culture, acknowledging that the tired mothers who claimed "I never read, I cannot, I never have time. I have all I can do to bring my children up properly," could not make culture their "whole and sole occupation." Arguing for the importance of reading many kinds of texts, Susa Young Gates, the editor of the *Young Woman's Journal,* claimed that reading just the Bible, the Book of Mormon, and the *Weekly Desert News* did not bring people to "higher views" and "nobler conceptions." Comparing cultural development to the physical nourishment of the body, she continued, "How much more important is the similar nourishment of the spirit—the immortal part. We can take with us no houses, no lands, no jewels, no fine apparel. . . . but every truth, every good and gracious thought goes with you forever and ever."[73] Gates's rejection of materialism is in keeping with the genteel tradition, but she departs from this tradition by highlighting the Mormon emphasis on preparation for eternal life. This attention to the immortal takes her argument beyond the Protestant ethos of the genteel tradition.

Geography as well as religion shaped Mormon clubwomen's concept of culture. Isolated in the intermountain region, they resisted the genteel tradition's tendency to identify a few eastern cities as cultural centers. Music constituted one form of culture advocated in the *Journal,* and Salt Lake clubwomen took a defensive posture about the "musical culture" available in their city: "It would be interesting, perhaps, to those who have believed Salt Lake to be the abode for 'outside barbarians,' to note the repertoire of musical classics which have been rendered by local organizations, and that, too, in a manner to elicit the praise of the most competent of critics." This account continued by reassuring readers that recent local productions demonstrated Salt Lake City possessed a musical culture comparable to that of other cities. After observing that no single metropolis could be designated a cultural center, the columnist remarked, "In these days of rapid transit and universal travel, it is almost impossible to get beyond the culture and advanced thought of our civilization."[74] In her speech at the World's Columbian Exposition in Chicago in 1893, Emmeline Wells assured her audience that "considering the population of the territory . . . Utah had more literary and musically inclined women than any of the older settled states."[75] An annual summary of club work included this statement: "The outlook for literary work among women is encouraging, and it is thought that the West will be equal with, if it does not excel the East in progress and advancement towards the higher education and development of mankind."[76] In these and similar statements, Mormon clubwomen expressed their anxiety about and resistance to geographic boundaries on culture that excluded them and their achievements.

White middle-class Protestant clubwomen had least reason to contest the genteel tradition since it affirmed their social position and conferred high status. To a large extent they embraced it, welcoming the advice of such institutions as Chautauqua and the Bay View Reading Circle. According to its statement of purpose, the Bay View Reading Circle aimed to "provide and direct at the lowest possible expense, a choice course of reading made up after an approved educational plan, and to promote habits of home study. It is for people of too limited time for elaborate courses, and who are yet ambitious to advance in intelligence, and would like to turn their spare moments to good account."[77] Combining the virtues of economy, an "approved" (although the identity of those approving remains unstated) and presumably coherent educational plan, and accommodation to the busyness of readers' lives, this plan, like that of the Chautauqua Literary and Scientific Circle, proposed to define and distribute culture, presuming readers' inability to identify and assimilate it for themselves.[78] Clubwomen who subscribed to this or a similar program demonstrated a willingness to affirm its authority, to confer on others the right to regulate their cultural experiences.

Typically such clubs adhered to a view of culture that drew on the theories of Matthew Arnold, as did this one from the *General Federation of Women's Clubs Magazine:* "Matthew Arnold defined culture as a study in perfection. It is the definition of a master of language. It combines the scientific passion for pure knowledge with the moral and social desire for doing good. It indicates that culture is dynamic; that it consists in becoming something rather than in having something. It does what all real definitions should do; includes all that belongs to the object defined, excludes all that does not."[79] Holding to this Arnoldian construct of a clearly bounded "perfection" or "master language," statements like these earned for white middle-class clubwomen the designation of "genteel." Despite its protestations on behalf of Arnold and its claims for the moral and the good, this statement also contains hints of deviations from the genteel tradition. The observations that culture is "dynamic" and that it consists "in becoming" rather than "being" suggest that even these clubwomen who clung to Arnold created a more expansive version of culture.

In addition to contesting some of the terms of the genteel tradition, white middle-class clubwomen appropriated its authority for themselves by attempting to regulate the literacy practices of others, both within and beyond their groups. National club publications regularly included reviews and recommendations for what to look for in books. Appealing, as the Book-of-the-Month Club later did, to readers' uncertainty and insecurity in the face of an overwhelming number of books and magazines, editors of the *Federation Bulletin* sometimes portrayed clubwomen as "confused, perhaps, by the difficulty of choosing wisely, from the innumerable papers and magazines claiming approval, disheartened by their inability to find time to read all those which enter the homes, thinking and believing that they already have 'more papers than they can afford,' the thought of another added to the list is almost appalling to the average club member."[80] Editors of the *Bulletin,* drawing on the authority of the genteel tradition, positioned their readers as incapable and overwhelmed by the choices required to develop and demonstrate taste. The *Bulletin* editors then asserted their own cultural authority by providing model programs on such topics as "twelve famous novels" and "English poetry in the nineteenth century."

Clubwomen extended their recommendations beyond their own ranks with attempts to regulate the cultural experiences of others, particularly children, immigrants, and the poor, whom they viewed as deficient in some way. Arguing for reading as a form of living, a General Federation article on children's literature asserts, "We want to build up certain powers in the minds of children. For us today these are, imagination, love of natural beauty, chivalry, patriotism: we want to develop in the soul that subtle quality that resists the impact of materialism and scientific reality."[81] In its stand against materialism and science, this statement reinforces the genteel tradition, emphasizing the importance of transmitting it to the next generation. For many clubwomen, then, culture meant imposing their personal values on others as much as achieving new understandings for themselves. As Mary Poppenheim wrote, these clubwomen defined "true culture" in terms of giving to the "less educated sister" from their "wealth of intellectual attainment."[82] The assumption that an individual clubwoman's "wealth" of knowledge would fit the needs of a "less educated sister" reflects the genteel tradition's belief in the value of a fixed set of texts as well as the hierarchy that posited some individuals as possessing greater cultural "wealth" than others.

Clubwomen who wished to regulate the cultural experiences of those outside their immediate group often played on the outsiders' insecurities. Maria Bowen Chapin, a middle-class editor of *Far and Near,* often suggested readings for her working-class audience. In announcing a new column, "Books Old and New," Chapin explained, "The librarians of clubs are often puzzled as to the best manner of spending a donation to their library, and should find here suggestions which shall help them to choose among the many new books which are constantly issued."[83] In addition to attempting to shape the reading choices of individual clubwomen, Chapin tried, as this quotation indicates, to control the materials that would be available to potential readers. Like the *Bulletin* editors, she portrays her readers as unable to select appropriate books and attempts to acquire some of the genteel tradition's power for herself by proposing to regulate the literacy practices of others. Ironically, Chapin and others who used the status of culture to distinguish themselves from others and exert power over them reproduced the hierarchy and the regulation they themselves experienced in a society that feared and resisted a cultural takeover by women.

Like their peers in other social locations, white middle-class clubwomen included women writers in their programs of study, thus transgressing the gendered boundaries of high culture. They also helped shift the meaning of culture by aiding the transition from what has been described as a culture of character to a culture of personality. The genteel tradition emphasized the development of character and such qualities as morality, virtue, and goodness, while the more relativistic and inclusive view of culture gave prominence to individual attributes of personality that did not emphasize the perfectibility of a religiously based view of culture. Echoing psychology's emphasis on egotism, power, and the unconscious, those focusing on the personality reflected a perspective very different from the moralistic view of character propounded by the genteel tradition.[84]

White middle-class Protestant clubwomen considered and expanded on these differences in their literacy practices, as selected papers written across three decades show. In 1881 Julia Ward Howe wrote a paper drawing on common assumptions about character, praising the "courageous souls" who proclaimed the "triumphant progress of truth." For Howe, character and culture remained inextricably bound, reflecting the genteel tradition's fixed standard of morality as grounds for assessing someone. An 1897 paper written for the Olympia Woman's Club explored the influences on character. In examining the effects of environment, heredity, association, and socioeconomic status, it positioned character in much more social terms than did Howe's hierarchically and individually oriented treatment. In 1907 a paper titled "Personality," delivered at the Naugatuck Study Club, raised questions about elements of "temper, attitude, and methods" that distinguished the personalities of Napoleon, Bismarck, and Lincoln.[85] Instead of insisting on a fixed set of approved qualities as Howes did, the author of this paper drew on Freudian-inspired concepts to describe the personalities of three individuals. The progression from character to personality exemplified by these three papers paralleled and helped foster the major cultural shift from religiously based to psychologically derived descriptions of human behavior. In reading and writing about the terms of character and personality, clubwomen participated in the transformation that gave personality precedence over character.

White middle-class clubwomen also resisted the genteel tradition's emphasis on an inward and highly individualized approach to art. Even when they appropriated and promoted other aspects of the genteel tradition, they developed alternatives to the stipulations of silence and solitude that grew out of a definition of culture emphasizing inwardness. During the last third of the nineteenth century musicians, dramatists, and other artists began disciplining audiences to approach cultural performances with respectful silence. In so doing, they gave life to Matthew Arnold's claim that culture was "above all, an inward operation. . . . Culture . . . places human perfection in an *internal* condition." Even the cultural institutions—such as libraries, museums, and symphony halls—that took shape at the turn of the century created spaces where people could, as Lawrence Levine notes, "contemplate and appreciate the society's store of great culture *individually*. Anything that produced a group atmosphere, a mass ethic, was culturally suspect."[86] The "rules" established in such cultural spaces transformed audiences into spectators who practiced "silence in the face of art."[87] Contradicting this norm, clubwomen in all social locations approached culture in lively group contexts, making it a communal as well as individualized experience. Reading texts aloud; interrupting one another to discuss, disagree, and laugh; performing their papers, and even club minutes, orally—in these and other ways, they flaunted the convention of silence before art and conceived of culture in communal terms.

Reflections on their own practices affirmed this communal approach. Edith Howes, a working-class clubwoman, wrote, "One of the best means of culture is the companionship of natures wiser, richer, stronger than our own, whose affectionate intelligence should stimulate both mind and heart."[88] Instead of the individual effort endorsed by the genteel tradition, Howes insists on the value of "companionship" in fostering culture. As the expression "affectionate intelligence" shows, it is a companionship that includes intellectual and emotional connections among clubwomen. Instead of silent contemplators or passive spectators, Howes's clubwomen were actors and participants in culture. In addition to oral renditions of texts and responses to them, clubwomen's activities often included sewing or knitting, petting nearby family pets, or nibbling cookies while discussing texts endorsed by the genteel tradition. This open acceptance of physical need further underscored the transgressive approach clubwomen took to culture. Instead of disciplining their bodies in accordance with the doctrine of self-perfectionism, clubwomen indulged themselves physically, thereby incorporating more of "a whole way of life" into their experiences of culture.

Clubwomen from all social and geographical locations maneuvered to include themselves and the particularities of their class/race/ethnic/religious heritages in an expanded definition of culture. In doing so, they helped refashion the highly standardized genteel tradition into the more inclusive and relativistic version of culture that began to emerge in the early decades of the twentieth century. Adherents to the genteel tradition resisted relativistic incursions furiously, holding to the value of elitism, a priori standards, and antimaterialism, while tagging modifications in culture with such terms as *illiterate*.[89] The shifting meanings for culture engendered conflict and division rather than coherence and continuity. Like the more visible institutions, such as museums, concert and lecture halls, theaters, colleges, and mass market publications, where many of the contests about and reformulations of culture were enacted, women's clubs provided public sites in which new meanings for culture could be explored.

Clubwomen's reading and writing circulated terms, concepts, and approaches that offered sharply different views of culture current at the turn of the century. Unlike George Santayana, who identified two perspectives—the genteel tradition and a more relativistic pragmatism—in order to dismiss one, clubwomen took a more complicated view, often calling principles of the genteel tradition into question even as they appropriated and borrowed from them. As they challenged the gendered construction of culture that excluded them, as they instituted noisy and sometimes irreverent ways of reading and talking about texts, and as they inserted works by women into discussions of art, clubwomen pushed against the gendered boundaries of genteel culture and questioned its definitions and approaches. African Americans who insisted on their own refinements and the inclusion of such writers as Paul Dunbar and Gertrude Mossell under the category of "excellent"; working women and WEIU members who transcended class boundaries to claim the importance of life experiences and knowing people "as they really are"; Mormon women who incorporated their religious heritage and geographical location into statements of value; Jewish women who affirmed their own traditions and social welfare projects as worthy of study—each in their own ways contributed to the development of languages and ways of thinking that made new meanings of culture possible.

In particular, by transcending the boundaries of genteel tradition through reading and writing texts about gender, inclusion, and methods of approach and apprehension, clubwomen rendered culture more accessible. Karen Blair, whose study of clubwomen's work with music, art, theater, and pageants demonstrates some of the material changes clubwomen effected, writes that they operated from the principle "that every American, regardless of economic status or geographical circumstance, deserves access to the fine arts."[90] Blair's work concentrates on white middle-class women, but her point about access can be applied to all clubwomen, since groups everywhere helped challenge the limitations, boundaries, and constraints of the genteel tradition. The textual negotiations of white middle-class, working-class, Jewish, African American, and Mormon clubwomen helped (re)define culture and provided the foundation for such projects as school art displays, junior music clubs, community pageants, and little theater productions. As clubwomen themselves were quick to say, literacy practices carried out in study groups and specialized departments were the basis for their practical work.[91] Contesting, shaping, and reconfiguring meanings o culture through their reading and writing, clubwomen helped shift it away from bounded assertions of value to a more relativistic intellectual method. The reading and writing shared by small groups of women from many circumstances and places did not, by itself, transform the meaning of culture, but it created an environment in which change could be considered and the assessments and standards of culture could be recalibrated.

Gender figured prominently in this recalibration of culture. While woman remained the figure upon whom anxieties and hostilities toward mass culture could be projected, and upon whom blame could be laid for any perceived decline in cultural standards, clubwomen introduced concepts and practices that mitigated against the long-standing assumption that "men create culture and women transmit it."[92] To be sure, those clubwomen who embraced or appropriated aspects of the genteel tradition helped disseminate it, but this transmission tells only part of the story. By participating in clubs, women located themselves where they were more comfortable and where they could become proficient readers and writers, and many clubwomen who appeared in mass circulation publications learned to become producers as well as consumers of culture in women's clubs. Such women as Charlotte Perkins Gilman, Frances Harper, and Agnes Repplier—to name just a few—who addressed clubs across the country, supplementing their incomes as writers and establishing the role of women in public speaking, became more visible producers of culture because of the support of women's clubs. Writers such as these found clubs a nurturing context for developing their skills. The novelist Pauline Hopkins, who published serialized versions of her work in the *Colored American,* read portions of her first novel, *Contending Forces,* to the Woman's Era Club before publishing it.[93] Clubwomen in other social locations read their drafts as they moved toward mainstream publication, and members took pleasure in the literary accomplishments of their peers. As early as 1904 commentators noted the role of women's clubs in fostering the careers of writers. Helen Winslow, for example, observed, "There are writers who are making a name to-day, who got their first taste for literature in the class from club study. . . . It would scarcely be possible in the limits of this article to give the names of well-known women who have to thank the club for their first literary incentive."[94] As Karen Blair's *Torchbearers* shows, clubwomen's support of female composers, musicians, artists, and dramatists also helped make the production of culture easier for women by providing them audiences and financial backing.

In a paper delivered to the Naugatuck Study Club, A. C. Tuttle described culture as "a wand of enchantment" that women could wield to effect changes in their homes.[95] Although Tuttle limited her discussion of culture to the domestic scene, clubwomen used this wand of enchantment to transform the larger world as well. Enchantment, as Mark Schneider explains, exists whenever and wherever we lack sufficient capacity to explain the world's behavior and social control over reports is weak, and it raises "the prospect of an order as yet unfathomed, familiarity with which would fundamentally alter our understanding of the world."[96] At the turn of the century, as the genteel tradition, pressed by major social changes, was losing its capacity to explain culture, clubwomen participated in literacy practices that introduced new meanings for this term. The reports they issued, in the form of minutes, papers, and national publications, were produced without the direct impress of social control. Clubs functioned, then, as sites of production for ideas that could alter understandings of culture because their status as autonomous organizations enabled them to ask questions and raise issues without confronting those most interested in preserving the genteel tradition. Their systems for textual distribution likewise enabled clubs to evade external control. Issues of the WEIU president's report that combined "culture with industrial intelligence and skill," copies of Mrs. Ross's "Gems from Negro Writers," and the list of "books that can never . . . be surpassed" published in the *Young Woman's Journal* remained largely beyond public censure. The literacy practices of clubwomen as they contended with the genteel tradition and reinforced it became a wand of enchantment with which they helped recalibrate the terms of culture.

6

(Un)Professional Reading and Writing

❖⇒◦◦⇐❖

❖⇒ The book has some very interesting minor characters, but the main question is: "Who is the better man, the dreamer or the man of affairs?" The style is excellent, the action rapid, and the characters develop in the most interesting manner. Emma Wolf is not only the best Jewish fiction writer of America, but the peer of the best novelists.

"Book Brieflets,"
American Jewess, 1897

❖⇒ The class of literature embracing treatises, essays, letters, history, journalism, and poetry, has always existed with the people of Utah and is of the highest and best order. In the building of an empire where all the strength and ability of every man, woman, and child had to be spent towards the making of homes, little time could be given towards the cultivation of the talents in the higher refinements, and yet from the foundation of the Church, the Latter-day Saints have been a studious reading people and the records of the Church itself is a literary drama.

ANNIE WELLS CANNON,
"Pioneer Literature and Writers,"
Woman's Exponent, 1908

❖⇒ The most general view is that the old man had no manhood, not the sense, nothing even to suggest to his inner conscience aught that could awaken a comprehension of the word man, much less its rightful price; no moral responsibility, no spirit or, as the Negro-hating Mark Twain would say, no capacity of kicking at real or imaginary wrongs, which in his estimation makes the superior clan. In a word, there was nothing within the old man's range of understanding to make him feel his inalienable rights.

We know the true analysis of the old man's words was that faith, once destroyed, can never be regained, and the blow to his faith in the individual and the wound to his honest esteem so overwhelming, rendered it out of the question to engage further with a fallen idol.

VICTORIA EARLE MATTHEWS,
"The Value of Race Literature," 1895

↦ And behold all the women were sore afraid, and again they said one to another of a surety, this is the place of departed spirits—for we hear sounds of instruments which are not, and we see the form of one who is afar in a distant city. But behold there was one among the women who had much wisdom, and she cried out in a loud voice saying— fools and unbelievers, Know ye not of one Edison who has learned the secrets of the lightning and who can shut up sounds of stringed instruments and of song, that one can command the sounds at will, and the sounds will come forth freely, even as water from a jug?

Minutes of the Friday Club of
Jackson, Michigan, 1891

↦ Most clubs are provided with an abundance of books and papers, but as a rule, these are not used to the best advantage. This is due, in part, to the fact that the members lead such busy lives. Feeling that she has only a few minutes at her disposal, it is the most natural thing in the world for a girl to pick up a paper and read at random whatever happens to catch her eye. By this method she gathers scraps of information, but does not really add to her stock of knowledge. She has no clearer idea of what is really going on in the world, no more grasp of the great movements which intelligent men and women are talking about, than if she had not touched the newspaper. Ask her, an hour later, what she has been reading and ten chances to one if she is able to mention a single item of news. Now, in order to point out a more excellent way, let me describe, briefly, what has been done by a body of bright, intelligent girls, in a Boston club, who meet once a week to discuss current events.

FRANCES J. DYER,
"How to Read the Newspapers,"
Far and Near, 1891

Intimate Practices

↝≡◦ On the topic of the five greatest English novels, those who gave papers agreed on three: THE SCARLET LETTER, ESMOND and IVANHOE. Their criteria included giving a picture of life as well as an ethical idea.... SCARLET LETTER, that artistic record of sin overcome; IVANHOE as a picture of the past; HENRY ESMOND, the tender portrait of another age.... JANE EYRE in her eager strength, ADAM BEDE facing the problems of life. These five represent the art which attempts to realize the ideal which escapes us in life.... Fielding's TOM JONES, which though not refined has one of the best plots in existence and portrays the shrewd, appreciative, good sense of the man of that time as THE MILL ON THE FLOSS. Another argued that great novels must be universal in interest, characters must be human beings, plot within the limits of probability, and we must be carried into its surroundings. Another argued that we can only confess those books which make the deepest impression upon us, such as JANE EYRE and MILL ON THE FLOSS.

Minutes of the Saturday Morning Club
of Boston, 1892

↝≡◦ The central theme of this collection of suggestive essays is "the significance of the amateur spirit in carrying forward the daily work of our modern world." By this Mr. Perry does not intend to say that professionalism, which means method, training, and skill, should be discouraged; but that in all fields, from athletics and politics to science and letters, it should be combined with the individual initiative, the versatility, curiosity, spontaneity, zest, and enthusiasm—even the ardor and gayety and delight—that characterize the spirit of the amateur.

"The Book Table,"
Federation Bulletin, 1904

↝≡◦≡↜

COLONEL THOMAS WENTWORTH HIGGINSON, literary critic and longtime correspondent of Emily Dickinson, wrote in 1880:

It is a curious fact that, away from a few great cities, those Americans who do serious work in the study of literature are generally women. Whether it is due to more ample leisure or to the wish to superintend

the education of their children, or from whatever source, the fact is un-
questionable. Let the most accomplished critic of Shakespeare, as Professor Rolfe or Professor Corson or Mr. H. A. Clapp be announced to give
a lecture on his favorite theme in a hall or a parlor, by day or evening, and
it can be safely guaranteed that three-quarters and probably nine-tenths
of his audience will be women.

Higginson described the clubs in which women studied literature and went on
to speculate that their activities might be explained by the fact that literature
is a thing of the past and women, being more conservative, cling to it while
men turn to science. Alternatively, he proposed that literature still retains "a
little of the sentimental and emotional about it," thereby attracting women.
Then he asserted, "But whatever be the cause, it may fairly be assumed that the
women's clubs have become to some extent the popular custodians of literature in America."[1] In describing clubwomen as custodians of literature, Higginson expressed the considerable cultural, professional, and sexual anxiety that
surrounded women's interactions with literature in the latter part of the nineteenth century. Although his comments did not sound particularly negative,
Higginson's article and others like it took a position that, in addition to ignoring
the diversity of women's clubs by portraying them as white middle-class
groups, challenged clubwomen's right to serve as custodians of literature.

Long an advocate of woman suffrage, Higginson actively campaigned for
woman rights and offered public support of women's clubs when many of his
peers portrayed them as dangerous and subversive. Indeed, in his 1880 article
Higginson examined the program of a typical club and praised it for the "thor-
oughness in [its] schedule" and its "sensible collection of themes." Yet just as
Higginson assumed a proprietary, ambivalent, and finally damaging approach to
Emily Dickinson's poetry even as he promoted it, so his support of women's
clubs conferred a mixed blessing.[2] Higginson insisted on women's "instinctive,
intuitive, and imaginative" qualities, opposed self-supporting women, and
affirmed women's inherent physical and psychological limitations.[3] His approval
of women's club programs in *Harper's* focused on their "modesty" and "moderate
variety," and he left little room for more progressive enterprises.[4] When Laura
Wentworth Fowler, founder of the Abbott Academy Club, proposed that this
new organization take a scholarly approach and "form a sort of postgraduate
course for the graduates of the academy," her proposal was "crushed by Col.
T. W. Higginson." The historian of the Abbott Academy Club goes on to explain,
"Like most studious men, he advised recreation and entertainment for women's
clubs rather than study; and the 'scholarly' idea was abandoned."[5] Higginson's

support of women's clubs extended only as far as they conformed to his conservative views of women's capacities, and although he offered a cautiously approving description of the clubwomen's program of study, he framed women's preeminence in literature as anomalous, as "a curious fact."

In calling attention to clubwomen's custody of literature, Higginson identified literature as a site of contest between the sexes and articulated the male English professors' fear that their field faced the threat of feminization. As Gerald Graff has observed, the "reputation for effeminacy would have to be effaced from the modern languages before they could become respectable in the university," and warnings like Higginson's reminded professors of the need to discredit anything that connected nascent English departments with women.[6] This chapter explores how clubwomen related to the professionalization of the field of English. As Higginson's assertion about clubwomen's custody of literature suggests, these interactions included many complications and contests. Clubs provided sites where women not only listened to such professors as William Rolfe, Hiram Corson, or Henry Austin Clapp but also made decisions about literary merit and performed acts of interpretation. To claim a place in the academy, English had to demonstrate sufficient intellectual rigor, and, in the professorial view, women's clubs offered a cultural other against which a professionalized version of English studies could be established.

As English studies developed between 1880 and 1920, it faced more than the challenge of wresting control of the field away from women; it also confronted an internal dispute between the critics and scholars.[7] Critics emphasized aesthetic approaches and, accordingly, tended to blur distinctions between amateurs and professionals. Scholars, however, drew on philology, emphasized mental discipline, and sought to make English studies intellectually rigorous enough to justify its place in the academy. Rolfe, Corson, and Clapp represented the critic group, much as Higginson himself did. While Rolfe and Corson held positions as professors in the academy, Clapp, Rolfe's student, and Higginson, who briefly held a position at Harvard, supported themselves as critics, writing for popular newspapers and magazines.[8] Although both Clapp and Higginson functioned mainly outside the academy, they maintained close affiliations with such English professors as Corson and Rolfe, who sought to create permeable boundaries between academic and larger public worlds. Corson, who never attended college himself, subscribed to the view that talk about literature should not take the place of literature itself, and he read aloud to his students. Rolfe lectured widely on Shakespeare and produced an edition of the bard's work that was popular with women's clubs as well as academics. Critics like

Corson, Rolfe, Clapp, and Higginson worked to make English studies accessible to a wide audience and valued such qualities as enthusiasm and appreciation. In speaking regularly to women's clubs, these men underscored their interest in extending English studies to groups in parlors and halls outside universities, while those in the scholars' camp aimed to separate the two.

In 1880, when Higginson wrote his article, the battle lines between critics and scholars had begun to take shape, even though they did not emerge in full force until the early 1900s. Scholars trained in German universities urged English departments to focus on systematic methods and develop enough scholarly rigor to "make English as hard as Greek."[9] Critics saw the methods of their scholarly colleagues getting in the way of the literature itself and urged the moral, civic, and nationalistic value of reading and writing. Debates between members at early meetings of the Modern Language Association solidified the separate ranks of scholars and critics. In 1884, for example, the association, having decided to start a journal, struggled over whether it should be one of "popular philology," designed for "a large and growing class of educated men [*sic*] in many walks of life" or one of "scholarly and professional rather than a popular nature." The scholars who preferred the professional publication eventually won the day, but negotiations continued for years.[10] Faced with such internal conflicts, English professors could deflect attention away from their own contending factions by following Higginson's lead in accusing clubwomen of taking over literature.

Academics who sought to strengthen the position of English studies opposed women in both social and cultural terms. The very real limitations imposed on women in higher education by, for example, restricting college admission to men, excluding women from certain courses, or forbidding them to read their own compositions aloud in public, demonstrated their subordinate social position. In cultural terms, the discourses of English studies readily embraced the strategy of associating women with devalued approaches to the field. Herman Brandt, who in 1884 urged a scholarly approach to the field, contrasted the scientific study of language he proposed with a view of language study approached "like dancing, fencing or final touches to be put on (to) ladies in their seminaries at an extra charge."[11] In linking women with the undesirable form of language study, Brandt sounded a theme that echoed throughout the next four decades as English professors, joining the general movement toward professionalism, tried to establish a secure presence for themselves in the academy. As such theorists as Burton Bledstein and Magali Larson make clear, professionals declare themselves by rendering others powerless, by claiming an authoritative knowledge presumed to be unavailable to those outside the professional guild.[12]

To professionalize English studies, then, would-be academics had to discredit clubwomen's literary projects in favor of their own; they stigmatized the literacy practices of women's clubs to enhance those of professors. This tendency of men to take over territory claimed by women when professional interests are at stake has played itself out in other fields. Ridicule, coupled with policies of exclusion, usually enabled male professionals to discredit and diminish female competition.[13] An illustration of the deprecation of clubwomen's literacy practices appears in an 1896 essay Frank Norris wrote shortly after he graduated from Berkeley. Arguing against the methods of his former professors, Norris asserts:

> The "co-eds" take to the "classification" method even better than the young men. They thrive and fatten intellectually on the regime. They consider themselves literary. They write articles on the "Philosophy of Dante" for the college weekly, and after graduation they "read papers" to "literary circles" composed of post-graduate "coeds," the professors' wives and daughters and a very few pale young men in spectacles and black cutaway coats. After the reading of the "paper" follows the "discussion," aided and abetted by cake and lemonade. This is literature! Isn't it admirable![14]

Although the women portrayed here may consider themselves literary, Norris assures his knowing readers that they really are not. The quotation marks around terms such as "papers" and "discussion" signal that this is not *real* literary work. While a few pale men appear in this scene, Norris makes it clear that the proceedings owe their design to the coeds, wives, and daughters—all women who mistake the form of literature for its substance. Attributing this deprecated form of "classification" to women's clubs serves to obscure the conflict within English studies and to devalue the literacy practices of clubwomen. Norris, who opposed the classification method that lay at the heart of Brandt's scholarly approach, joined Brandt in undermining women's literacy practices. Even though the critic Norris and the scholar Brandt disagreed profoundly about the goals and methods of English, they created a united front by *both* attacking (club)women. Scholars like Brandt believed that such critics as Norris made English vulnerable to feminization, thereby endangering the discipline's place in the academy. Critics like Norris—and Higginson—who feared scholars would tar them with the brush of feminization deprecated clubwomen's literacy practices to protect themselves. Gendering those responsible for the vulgarization of literature as female aided the professionalization project because academics could enhance their own standing by contrasting themselves with a feminized and uncritical readership. The emerging professionalized readership represented by English professors cast itself as intelligent, critical, reflective, and male.[15]

At the turn of the century, professionalism offered a new source of authority in a society where change had unsettled traditional patterns. For those seeking professional authority for English studies, women's clubs offered a pervasive if not forceful challenge. Although clubwomen participated in many kinds of projects, literacy practices remained at the center of their work, fostering their intimacy with one another, intellectually preparing them for service projects, and reinforcing their image of themselves as readers and writers. As Helen Winslow put it, "Even those [clubs] most active in public or civic work, like the Denver Woman's Club of a thousand members . . . [maintained] literary classes."[16] Charlotte Emerson Brown elaborated on this view in her address to the St. Paul Biennial of the General Federation of Women's Clubs in 1906:

> The influence of the club, which is felt so helpfully in its efforts to improve existing conditions, could never have been so potent without the preparation and study which had gone before, for thought and knowledge must ever precede practical work. A knowledge of nature and nature's laws, a study of the experience of the race, a comprehension of the development of the human soul, with its ideals, its aspirations, its temptations, its limitations, must be reached before there can be a sympathetic understanding of conditions or effective work in philanthropy or reform.[17]

Brown spoke for women in many social locations who saw reading and writing as the foundation on which other club activities could be built. The "thought and knowledge" gained from their study gave clubwomen the wisdom to carry out their "practical work." Their ability to "improve existing conditions" depended on "preparation and study." Located in nearly every town and city and dispersed among various racial, religious, and class groups, women's clubs challenged the emerging norms of English departments by their very existence, by their orderly self-perpetuation, and by their alternative approaches to texts.

Women's clubs represented an alternative means of approaching literature as well as an alternative public institution. Seeing literature as a means for understanding "nature and nature's laws" and "the development of the human soul" represented a view very different from that held by most English professors. In accordance with the goal of making "English as hard as Greek," members of the academic community emphasized mental discipline rather than self-development. Writing in 1894, Professor Albert Cook of Yale asserted, "The larger number of courses in English are intended to be disciplinary as well as instructive: in other words, they have in view the development of insight and power no less than the conveyances of information."[18] For Cook, like most of his scholarly peers, *disciplinary* connoted a development of mental rigor along with "insight and power." Information—about the nature of human development or any other aspect of life—conveyed through literature mattered much less than fostering the desired mental capacities.[19] Clubwomen's emphasis on literary study as a means of informing philanthropic projects by enhancing their understanding of humanity stood in sharp contrast to professors' insistence on mental discipline and scholarly rigor. Each presumed different purposes and basis of knowledge. For clubwomen, learning about life and the world could provide the basis for more effective benevolence and enhanced life experiences, while for professors of the scholarly tradition, literary study existed to strengthen the mind and develop intellectual capacities. Drawing on philology to study English "like Greek," professors privileged knowledge of language, while clubwomen often looked to the knowledge of their own experience.

Academics who projected onto clubwomen the anxieties and conflicts of English studies also reduced them to a single type—white, middle-class, and educated—thereby ignoring the groups of women from diverse racial, ethnic, and class backgrounds who regularly met to share reading and writing. Erasing clubwomen's class, racial, and religious diversity made it easier to portray English studies in monolithic terms, because it ignored ways clubwomen from various social backgrounds both aided and resisted its professionalization. Similarly, most contemporary narratives of professionalization give little attention to the many extra-academic social practices that prefigured English studies, and they ignore women's groups entirely. While some accounts identify college men's literary societies as one antecedent of English studies, clubwomen's contributions are not mentioned. Current representations of professionalism in English studies restrict themselves to social formations already allied with institutions of higher education and pay remarkably little attention to the culture of amateurism that flourished at the turn of the century.[20] These accounts ignore or are institutionally blinded to the fact that when English professors were claiming their professional territory in higher education, thousands of women's clubs conducted, outside the academy's walls, projects of consuming and producing texts.

Although such national organizations as the General Federation of Women's Clubs and the National Association of Colored Women provided a certain amount of institutional force, they could never grant clubwomen the sort of legitimation universities accorded professors.[21] As the emerging center for credentialing professionals in American society, higher education conferred enormous social status on English professors, and they succeeded, as Paul Lauter has explained, in supplanting clubwomen's community-based literacy practices with university-sanctioned ones.[22] By emphasizing the scholarly respectability of their approach, professors simultaneously deprecated clubwomen's literacy practices and strengthened their own position in the academy. Furthermore, the culture of professionalism, which English studies shaped and was shaped by, produced much of its currency by what Samuel Weber describes as "the cultivation and exploitation of anxiety."[23] Taste, conceived as central to the cultivated mind, depended on being exposed to the right texts. In seizing the authority to serve as arbiters of culture, English professors claimed for themselves the right to dictate its terms, making nonprofessionals fearful they were reading the wrong books or reading them in the wrong ways.

Anxieties engendered by professionalized English studies led many clubwomen, particularly those in white middle-class groups, to emulate the practices and terms of the academy. In the 1890s most English departments took a chronological approach to literature, dividing authors into designated periods and contextualizing their work in terms of historical events, thereby creating the outlines of the familiar coverage model of English studies. Many clubwomen's programs from the same period show a similar emphasis on literary history with such topics as "the Victorian Age," including selections by Walter Savage Landor, Mary and Charles Lamb, Thomas Carlyle, Thomas Macaulay, Edwin Bulwer Lytton, Alfred Lord Tennyson, and Jane Austen. Another feature of English department approaches that clubwomen emulated centered on the kinds of questions posed. In keeping with the goal of disciplining the mind, English professors preferred factual questions that required attention to detail. Clubwomen followed suit with such questions as "What character has been called Shakespeare's 'perfect woman'?" and "Which character figures in three plays?" Some clubwomen also echoed a version of the English department's reverent stance before texts with such claims as "Taste in fiction can be cultivated only by reading and rereading the works of the great masters, with docile attention always and sometimes with distinct effort and study."[24] Structuring their programs around historical periods, asking questions that required readers to focus on details, and emphasizing such behaviors as "docile attention," these clubwomen reinforced through imitation the classroom practices of professors.

At the same time, other women's clubs often adopted the language of critics to describe texts as sources of imaginative power and spiritual enlightenment.[25] Mormon clubwomen, for example, described Shakespeare as "the world's greatest poet," claiming that knowledge of "his mighty works is indispensable to every young woman," and they portrayed Chaucer as "a new star, which by its mellow radiance, revealed to that world, beauties and pleasures it never dreamed of before."[26] Members of the General Federation of Women's Clubs espoused the view that "the spiritual and immortal in literature" should be "exalted" and that literary study should "emphasize spirit rather than form, and . . . convert dead fact into quickened thought, for literature is for nothing but to inspire."[27] Jewish clubwomen, for whom religion and literature were closely allied, described their work as aiding a "visible, spontaneous evolution of old truths [permeating] the religious atmosphere."[28] Members of working women's clubs asserted, "Surely it is worth while to know something of such writers as Shakespeare, Tennyson, and Longfellow. Though we may have been able to touch but the hem of their garments, we feel that some virtue has passed from them to us, helping us to nobler living."[29] African American clubwomen wrote and read discussions of literature that featured "elevated minds" and "high purpose."[30] Echoing the critics' emphasis on enthusiasm for and appreciation of literature, such clubwomen departed from the more professionalized approach of scholars.

While white middle-class Protestant clubwomen may have been motivated to imitate the language of both scholars and critics as a way of securing their own class status, clubwomen from other social locations often appropriated the terms and practices of professors to resist the definitions imposed on them. African American women who confronted racist denigrations, Jewish and Mormon women who faced deprecations based on religion, and working women who were frequently dismissed as illiterate or uncultured all used sanctioned texts to challenge the negative stereotypes assigned to them. Despite the differences in their motivations and enactments, all clubwomen appropriated the language of the sacralized text to confer (borrowed) authority on their literary practices and lend dignity to them.

Identifying literary texts as sacralized introduced the possibility of profaning them. Even as they accepted and enacted a view of literature that venerated texts and practices sanctioned by the authority of English professors, clubwomen transgressed the boundaries of this authority in several ways. For one thing, clubwomen in all social locations regularly included on their reading lists women writers, often living ones. While the scholars and the critics disagreed slightly about which authors should be studied—the critics tended to give more credence to American writers—they closed ranks on the subject of women writers. Authors that professors deemed appropriate for classroom treatment included Chaucer, Spenser, Shakespeare, Milton, Bunyan, Macaulay, Carlyle, Newman, and Arnold, with Emerson or Hawthorne occasionally making the list, but women writers and most living authors, male or female, generally remained outside the curriculum.[31] In contrast, clubwomen paid considerable attention to living women authors.

One of the most extensive displays of women authors appeared in the library of the Woman's Building at the World's Columbian Exposition in Chicago. Organized by the clubwoman Bertha Palmer—who wanted a library of "women's writing from everywhere and every time"—with assistance from the Wednesday Afternoon Club and Sorosis, this library included over four thousand books written by women from all over the United States and many foreign countries. Carefully catalogued and housed in a tastefully designed room flanked by an exhibition of statistics on women's work, the library roused "amazement and delight" among its (largely female) visitors, who marveled that "so many women had written so many books and contributed so greatly to the pleasure and knowledge of the world."[32] Other displays of women's writing appeared regularly in local and national club publications. Such names as Margaret Deland, Charlotte Perkins Gilman, Sarah Grand, and Lilian Whiting appeared in literary discussions of white middle-class and Mormon clubwomen. Deland and Gilman, in particular, also spoke at many club meetings. Gilman, who wrote about and embodied the "new woman," challenged the status quo in both her prose and her lifestyle.[33]

Sarah Grand's *Heavenly Twins* (1893) appears in the minutes of clubs in every social location. African American, Mormon, working-class, Jewish, and middle-class white Protestant clubwomen all appear to have read (or at least read about) Grand's novel, which, in addition to being composed by a "new woman writer," features a number of transgressive qualities.[34] Grand, who is generally credited with coining the term *new woman,* included in her narrative such issues as the unequal education of men and women, the double sexual standard, and the burdens and depression marriage brings to women.[35] The ubiquitousness of *The Heavenly Twins* among clubwomen suggests their subtle but pervasive subversiveness in maintaining a conventional facade behind which to consider unconventional issues, such as marriage-induced depression, sexually transmitted diseases, and new roles for women. Even though they employed the language of the sacralized text and included many canonical works in their programs of study, clubwomen used literary study to explore controversial and unconventional territory.

Such subversive moves took on additional energy among clubwomen who occupied more stigmatized social positions, particularly when they looked to female writers with whom they shared a common heritage. African American clubwomen fastened their literary gaze on such figures as Phillis Wheatley, Frances Harper, Ida B. Wells, and Anna Cooper. Not only did they study these writers' texts, but they honored them with club names. Phillis Wheatley clubs were founded in Cleveland, Ohio; New Orleans, Louisiana; Buffalo, New York; Chicago, Illinois; Albuquerque, New Mexico; Jacksonville, Florida; and Greenville, Mississippi, among other places. The Harper clubs of St. Paul, Minnesota, and Jefferson City and St. Louis, Missouri, honored the poet and novelist Frances Harper. Like their white counterparts Gilman and Deland, Cooper, Harper, and Wells often spoke at club meetings. As the members of the Harper Union of Jefferson City explained, "Our much beloved and esteemed Mrs. F. E. W. Harper was brought to Jefferson City to lecture, and the great zeal and inspiration of this race-loving woman is still bearing fruit, from seed sown when she was with us years ago. In fact any zeal . . . the colored women of Missouri have today for the uplifting of humanity, we owe to Mrs. Harper."[36] Harper, who served as a vice president of the National Association of Colored Women, addressed clubs across the country, as did Ida B. Wells, the antilynching advocate. Harper's novel *Iola Leroy; Or, Shadows Uplifted,* published in 1892—the same year that Anna Cooper's *Voice from the South* and Ida B. Wells's *Southern Horrors* appeared—broke the silence surrounding white men's sexual exploitation of African American women and offered a nonwhite perspective on the Civil War and Reconstruction.[37] By adopting the names of activist women writers and reading their texts, African American clubwomen deployed some of the prestige and methodology of literary study to foster, in socially acceptable ways, their political agenda of working against the powerful racism unleashed at the turn of the century. Simultaneously, they helped create an audience for women writers of their race by reading, discussing, and writing about their novels.[38]

Such writers as Grace Aguilar, Emma Lazarus, and Emma Wolf appeared regularly on the reading lists of Jewish women's clubs. Even though these clubwomen embraced writers sanctioned by English professors, they extended the terms of literature to include women with whom they could identify. As members of the Quincy Section of the National Council of Jewish Women put it, "While we are working with heart and might to uphold the good cause in our community we are ever mindful of the great object in view, 'Judaism and Jewish Literature.'"[39] In its report at the first convention of the National Council of Jewish Women, the St. Paul Section listed the Bible selections read and added this: "The following are a few of the noted authors used in giving interest to these Bible studies: Byron, Browning, Milton, Racine, and Grace Aguilar."[40] Including Aguilar, a Jewish author of short stories and poems, in this list of male authors whose texts fall into the category of sacralized signals the section's willingness to transgress the established boundaries of literature. A description of Aguilar published in an 1892 issue of the *Ladies' Home Journal* suggests the motivations for listing her: "Hers was a higher aim than merely to amuse. . . . she strove to raise her race to a loftier consciousness of their duty and mission, and to educate the general public as to the character of her creed, so often misjudged and caricatured."[41] As this reviewer suggests, Aguilar provided important cultural education to non-Jews and validated the religious lives of her Jewish readers.

An 1897 review of Emma Wolf's novel in the *American Jewess* concludes that Wolf is "not only the best Jewish fiction writer of America, but the peer of the best novelists," thus placing Wolf alongside more canonical authors. The 1906–7 Yearbook of the New York Section of the National Council of Jewish Women includes this: "It was also considered appropriate to honor the memory of Emma Lazarus, a writer of our race, whose poems and translations are the source of great enjoyment, and whose efforts to help and to welcome the first Russian refugees ought never to be forgotten. The following program was presented on the Occasion of the 'Memorial Meeting in Honor of Emma Lazarus.'" The full program, including a biography of Lazarus, a literary appreciation, songs, a statement on Lazarus's work for the Jewish community, and readings of her poems, follows.[42] In honoring Lazarus and categorizing Emma Wolf and Grace Aguilar with established authors, these clubwomen expanded the terms of literature to include Jewish women writers.

Working women pushed at the boundaries of literature from a different direction. Like clubwomen in other social locations, they expanded on the Arnoldian emphasis on literature's capacity to form character and criticize life. Viewing texts as informing philanthropic projects, providing insights into domestic situations, or providing instructions for life, many clubwomen took a didactic perspective on literature.[43] For working women the didactic aspect had particular urgency because of their precarious economic circumstances, and they expanded literature to include books by such writers as Jane Addams, settlement house worker; Florence Kelley, director of the National Consumers' League; and Annie Nathan Meyer, editor of *Women's Work in America*. A clubwoman's review of Meyer's book demonstrates how working women's critical assessments reflected their own social positions. Beginning by describing the book as one about which one "could write a volume," the author observes that "the same old objections which are now urged against any new step forward of women were advanced 'in ye olden tyme' against those things which everybody now considers a matter of course," and she goes on to underscore the book's point that "the theory that women should not work is a corruption of the old aristocratic system. Slaves and servants, whether male or female always worked."[44] This review, written by and for working women, sees reading as a means of validating their labor and looks to the text as a didactic guide for living as much as an aesthetic object of study. Reading and writing about books like these offered working women textual validation for their status and provided explicit suggestions and information regarding the material conditions of their lives.[45]

For Mormon clubwomen, literature included such authors as Eliza R. Snow, Emmeline B. Wells, Hannah T. King, and Emily Hill Woodmansee. Each of these women was revered as much for her religious orthodoxy as for her literary production, as this homage to Snow demonstrates: "She was a true Saint, as her long life of vigorous spiritual teaching proves, and bears out her own words when she so beautifully writes." Even though they recognized that Utah's "writers had made no fame outside her boundaries," these clubwomen lavished attention on them and applied to them the same careful reading they accorded to Shakespeare, Chaucer, and Tennyson, thereby moving beyond the "standard texts" English professors authorized. In addition, by including, as does the *Woman's Exponent,* "treatises, essays, letters, history, journalism, and poetry" and even "the records of the Church itself" as literature, members of Mormon clubs profaned the literary canon English professors sought to establish.[46]

As they read texts by such authors as Sarah Grand, Frances Harper, Emma Wolf, Emily Hill Woodmansee, or Annie Nathan Meyer, clubwomen from various social backgrounds had the opportunity to explore alternatives to domestic femininity and scrutinize female figures with whom they shared racial, ethnic, or religious heritages. Because they consumed these works with other likeminded women, they developed interpretive communities in which they could examine their own experiences and opportunities for change—women's groups to explore women's lives. As Julia Ward Howe put it, "What did club life give me? Understanding of my own sex."[47] Although a majority of clubwomen readily listed the books read, a much smaller number provided detailed accounts of their responses. Like their predecessors from an earlier era, whom Susan Harris describes as on the one hand acutely aware of the "needs and censures of the public" and on the other "intensely aware of *other* possibilities for female protagonists than the ones they publicly espouse," they often kept their thoughts and discussions to themselves.[48] Yet their choices of books by and about women—often strong or unconventional women, such as the characters in Sarah Grand's *Heavenly Twins*—show how gender shaped their literacy practices.

In addition to embracing women writers with whom they could identify, clubwomen gave prominence to authors who represented people and issues important in their social positions, thus further highlighting the didactic aspects of their readings. Besides considering texts by such writers as Phillis Wheatley, Frances Harper, Ida B. Wells, and Anna Cooper, African American clubwomen regularly read the prose and poetry of other members of their race. Minutes of Atlanta's Chautauqua Circle include discussions of works by James Weldon Johnson, W. E. B. Du Bois, Frederick Douglass, and William Stanley Braithwaite, along with articles from the *Crisis.* Papers by members included "The Negro in Literature and Art" and "Gems from Negro Writers."[49] The Woman's Improvement Club of Indianapolis featured papers on Amanda Smith, Benjamin Banneker, Sojourner Truth, Paul Dunbar, and William Stanley Braithwaite. The Detroit Study Club read the work of W. E. B. Du Bois, Paul Dunbar, and F. Moss Clark.[50] Minutes of black women's clubs include discussions of texts dealing with such issues as lynching and Jim Crow laws as well as other concerns produced by the racist society in which they lived.

For African American clubwomen, literature occupied a site of dispute for the rival philosophies of Negro education articulated by Booker T. Washington and W. E. B. Du Bois. Washington, who advocated practical education to prepare members of his race to serve as maids, manual workers, and agrarian laborers, expressed a distinct antipathy toward literature, arguing that it might widen class divisions in the race. In contrast, Du Bois, who held that members of his race should have a full classical education to learn the pleasure and power of reading and writing as well as prepare them for careers as teachers, argued for the centrality of literature in Negro education. Indeed, Du Bois described literature as a haven from the racism that engulfed African Americans of all classes. Margaret Washington's prominence in the movement (she served as president of the National Association of Colored Women from 1914 to 1918) no doubt complicated clubwomen's responses, but they managed to steer a middle course between the two. Embracing the world of possibility Du Bois suggested and the racial solidarity Washington urged, African American club-women negotiated an approach to literature borrowed from both perspectives without fully embracing either, somehow serving both aesthetic and pragmatic ends.

Learning more about the accomplishments of their race represented aesthetic as well as pragmatic goals for African American clubwomen. Victoria Earle Matthews, essayist, short story writer, founding president of the Brooklyn Woman's Loyal Union, and frequent contributor to the *Woman's Era,* undertook a survey of teachers, ministers, and other representatives of the race to determine "the true statistics of our people." She also planned a history to demonstrate African Americans' contributions to "every phase of this country's history."[51]

In a paper delivered at the 1895 convention of clubwomen convened by Josephine Ruffin in Boston, Matthews articulated her desire to include a wide range of texts—"History, Biographies, Scientific Treatesses, Sermons, Addresses, Novels, Poems, Books of Travel, miscellaneous essays and contributions to newspapers and magazines—under the term 'race literature.'" This essay, titled "The Value of Race Literature," argues for both the uniqueness ("different in all essential points of greatness") and the wide range ("in the broader field of universal literature") of a race literature, which would serve a pragmatic goal (the "supply of influential and accurate information, on all subjects relating to the Negro and his environments, to inform the American mind") and an aesthetic one (not "thoughtless praise of ourselves" but "true culture"). Although she begins by framing the issue in terms of race, Matthews adds gender by asking, "What part shall we women play in the Race Literature of the future?" Answering her own questions brings Matthews to the *Woman's Era,* edited by Josephine Ruffin, and the assertion, "If the brothers of the press have had their difficulties, to contend with their task has been an easy one compared with that of the colored woman in journalism." Despite this, claims Matthews, "Woman's part in Race Literature, as in Race building, is the most important part and has been so in all ages."[52] Even as she acknowledges the difficulties clubwomen face, Matthews insists on the centrality of their developing alternative constructions of the race through their literacy practices. Simultaneously, Matthews urges an approach to literature that addresses readers' needs for both information and pleasure. This formulation moves well beyond the approaches to sacralized works that English professors promoted.

Iola Leroy by Frances Harper numbered among the novels Matthews recommended. Such domestic narratives enabled clubwomen to exercise, as Claudia Tate put it, "political self-definition in fiction at a time when the civil rights of

African-Americans were constitutionally sanctioned but socially prohibited."[53] Gertrude Mossell, whose *The Work of the Afro-American Woman* appeared in 1894 and was soon reviewed by the *Woman's Era,* paid particular attention to Frances Harper, claiming that she and Anna Cooper "have always been, not primarily makers of literature, but preachers of righteousness."[54] This praise, which disqualified Harper and Cooper from study by scholars and critics alike, centers on presenting "a vivid and truthful aspect of . . . Negro character," not only to whites but to blacks who could, as a result of gaining information about their own people, become more active agents on behalf of the race. African American clubwomen, who constituted the primary audience for Frances Harper and her contemporaries, could discuss the literary features of novels while drawing on their power. Their reading, which contained aesthetic and functional dimensions, empowered them to counter racism as they shaped and were shaped by the politics surrounding them.[55] Moving from the pragmatics of resisting racism to transcending it in aesthetic terms, these clubwomen negotiated with both belletristic and utilitarian forces to construct alternative subjectivities for themselves.

Those working women who read and wrote selections in *Far and Near* and the *Club Worker* stretched "literature" to include a wide range of self-help books.[56] Under the title "Literary Criticisms," for example, appeared a book called *The Child Housekeeper,* which outlined, in poetic form, techniques for washing laundry, doing spring housecleaning, and performing other domestic chores. In 1908 the *Club Worker* offered a list of books designed to help clubwomen explore their "broad relations to society," including such topics as consumerism, immigration, and working conditions. These texts demonstrated working women's desire to inform themselves about the issues surrounding their labor.[57] For these clubwomen, exploring "broad relations to society" meant beginning with the practical issues of their own lives and expanding the terms of literature to include texts that addressed the material concerns of their lives.

Like their African American peers, Mormon clubwomen saw broader definitions of literature as a means of addressing the "prejudiced world" that looked askance at the Latter-day Saints and remained "reluctant to give merit even where merit [was] due."[58] They also defined literature in religious terms, naming poetry, for example, as the language of the soul and the inspiration of humankind, a language suitable for singing the praises of nature and God. The poetry of such Mormons as Eliza Snow and Emily Woodmansee received special acclaim for its affirmation of Mormon views on the afterlife and the importance of maternal love. In calling on literature to redress the religious prejudice that dogged their lives, these clubwomen emphasized its capacity to transform the identities others imposed on them.

Jewish clubwomen likewise focused on texts that addressed their concerns, as this report indicates: "The agenda of the meetings in the early years were dominated by discussions on such themes as women of the Bible, Jewish authors like Emma Lazarus and Israel Zangwill, and literary works like *Ivanhoe* and *The Merchant of Venice* that contained Jewish characters."[59] In addition to focusing on topics important to them, these clubwomen asserted the value of literature produced by Jewish writers. For example, the 1904–5 yearbook of the Detroit Section of the National Council of Jewish Women introduced its literary program with this: "Our race has made characteristic and supreme contributions to the progress of civilization. . . . we have chosen for study this coming year, such soul-pictures in the world's great gallery of human life, as we believe will make for our larger character as members of the Jewish community and the world in general."[60] According to this writer, clubwomen were responsible for informing themselves about "topics distinctively Jewish" and at the same time teaching the gentile world about Jewish contributions to literature. This explicitly didactic goal that extended to both Jewish and non-Jewish readers invested literature with qualities foreign to the increasingly belletristic emphasis of English professors.

Their concern with didactics and aesthetics in literature led clubwomen to extend the boundaries of *how* they read as well as *what* they read. Here, for example, is an excerpt from the minutes of a white middle-class group that had been reading Emerson. "Objection was raised to the statement 'There is a time in every man's education when he arrives at the conviction that envy is ignorance and imitation is suicide.' Other truths came up for discussion and were thrown in new lights."[61] On another occasion members of the same group made this observation: "The Realist doubtless had its attractions for those among us competent to 'scrut the inscrutable and poss the impossible,' but for the student of Emerson's more obvious truths, there was something too much about it of the 'whichness of the what' style of philosophy."[62] Even as they acknowledged Emerson's value to their thinking, these women were willing to joke about his opaque language and pit their own authority against Emerson's views on education, thereby testing the boundaries of authorized interpretation. In doing so, they adhered to a way of reading recommended by another clubwomen, who urged readers of the *Federation Bulletin* "to study, with open minds, not with the spirit of the Latin scholar, who, when dying, wished he had given his whole life to the study of the dative case; nor with the plodding, narrow soul of George

Eliot's Casaubon, who seemed to extinguish every spark of warm and genuine life with which he came in contact; nor, in a word, with a thumb-nail dissecting view, which is technical, critical, or abnormal," implying a direct criticism of philologists with the reference to studying the dative case.[63] Clubwomen who read with the recommended "open mind" clearly challenged scholars' ways of reading by subjecting texts to scrutiny, questioning central points, and insisting on the validity of their own perceptions.

African American clubwomen who wrote for and read the *Woman's Era* gave and received similar advice. Although they emphasized the importance of choosing the "best novels" and studying "carefully," they claimed that "the chief benefit derived from [literary] study was through this discussion and being able to form and hold one's own opinion," thus privileging their own rhetorical development over the scholar's emphasis on mental discipline and critical capacities. The phrase "through this discussion" affirms the importance of the *process* of talking about literature rather than the conclusions arrived at. Indeed, the author goes on to explain that even though the *Woman's Era* will occasionally raise questions about literature, "No answers will be given, for many can simply be a matter of personal opinion."[64] Encouraging women to express their own opinions rather than look to scholarly authority reinforces the earlier point about literary study being useful for learning "to form and hold one's own opinion" and undercuts the academic hierarchy of value.

Victoria Earle Matthews's interpretation of a popular story in her essay "The Value of Race Literature" illustrates a way of reading to counter racist representations of her people. Matthews outlines the plot: A "darkey" who was cheated by "Marse Wilyum" leaves the cabin for which he had paid triple the actual price and later, when asked why he had not stood up for his rights, responds, "Wid White folks dat's de way, but wid niggers it's dif'unt." Then she considers the meaning of this sentence, contrasting "the most general view" with "we know the true analysis." She counters the standard (racist) interpretation that positions the old man as lacking moral spirit with (a more sympathetic) one that shows him so full of integrity as to make it "out of the question to engage further with a fallen idol."[65] By showing her peers how to read in ways that affirm African American beliefs and traditions, Matthews moves literature into the realm of racial politics, thus revealing the power inherent in literary interpretation.

Clubwomen also transgressed the emerging norms of English studies by reading to reinforce their religious beliefs. While sacralized literary texts replaced the Bible in English classes, some clubwomen made sacred texts a primary object of study. Members of the National Council of Jewish Women, which took religion, philanthropy, and education as its three central activities, devoted considerable time to their Bible and reported regularly on its role in their programs of study. The New York Section included this in its 1896 report: "Biblical characters as treated by the different writers, poets, and others have a particular attraction for the women of the Council. . . . Women who were taking a deep interest in literary matters have become desirous of knowing and understanding the position of the Bible in the development of the world, its civilizing influence, and above all the potency of its moral teachings."[66] Assertions like these echoed across the country, showing how Jewish clubwomen adapted literary study to serve their own (moral) purposes. Positioning their Bible as central in the "development of the world," they gave it priority in their projects of interpretation, applying to it the same strategies that guided their reading of literature.

The Book of Mormon figured prominently in the study of clubwomen belonging to the Church of the Latter-day Saints and informed their reading of other texts. In describing a character in Sarah Grand's *Heavenly Twins,* a member of the Mormon Reapers' Club asserts, "She holds up a perfect moral, ideal standard to guide humanity, shows that man *must* and *can* bring to the marriage altar as unspotted a record as he demands from the bride. It is the doctrine of our *own* church as well all know, though the world will not receive it from a 'Mormon.'"[67] The terms of interpretation, shaped by religious doctrine, thus extend to consideration of morality, and the sexual double standard comes under scrutiny in a discussion of literature.

Affective responses also helped shape clubwomen's terms of interpretation. A Mormon's advice on reading Shakespeare, for example, included this: "To sense such passages fully the mind must be worked up to a white heat, as was his mind who wrote it."[68] Contrasting this invitation to emotion with the assertion by Professor Theodore Hunt that although "the purely disciplinary value of English literary study has been greatly underrated," it should "take its place . . . with all other studies of a philosophic order and the result will be mental breadth and vigor" illustrates the distance between the two.[69] The clubwoman's attention to feelings, both the writer's and the reader's, finds no place in the professor's concern with "rational method" and "critical sensitiveness." For clubwomen emotions could be playful as well as "worked up to a white heat," as evinced by the following excerpt from minutes recorded on a hot August day about a white middle-class club reading Edward Emerson:

The meeting was called to order and reading commenced by Mrs. Robb, and after reading a few pages she pantingly resigned the book to Mrs. Mathison who heroically began her struggle to keep in breath to the end of one of Dr. Edward's sentences. The excitement of the club was intense as idea after idea were tacked together with no sign of a period, the club dropped their work and leaned forward straining every nerve to catch every new thought, on, on she went, could she, would she hold out, the club were wild with agitation, but at last she conquered, flushed with the effort so nobly accomplished she resigned the book, and the club tremblingly resumed their work. A short discussion upon the difference between the style of Emerson and his son followed.[70]

This irreverent recounting of the impossibility of reading one of Emerson's sentences in a single breath not only profanes a potentially sacralized text but also gives precedence to the group's amusement over its erudition by foregrounding the joke about Emerson's long-windedness and leaving out details about the discussion of style. The secretary who composed this account knew she would read it aloud at the next meeting, and by inscribing a sentence that imitates Emerson's in length, she creates for herself a script with which to amuse and delight the members of her club, performing her argument about Emerson by playing with his prose and style.

English professors at the turn of the century ranked systematization high among their priorities. With such phrases as "in the sophomore year the following authors are read," with careful sequencing of courses, and with delineations of topics to be covered, catalogues announced an emphasis on teaching literature methodically. Clubwomen both adopted and resisted such systematized approaches. Some clubwomen gave and followed such advice as "An important feature of the account ought always to be a full list of the author's writings with the date of their appearance, so that a clear view of his or her development may be had," while others assumed an opposing stance.[71] Writing in 1904, Helen Winslow articulated the differing priorities of clubwomen regarding systematization:

In a small Western college a certain professor about to open a new course of lectures was accosted by the president with:

"I suppose, Professor, you will begin your lectures on zoology by laying down the fixed laws and rules that govern that science."

"No," replied the Professor, "I shall begin with a bushel of clams."

The earlier clubs started out with the president's way; but those of to-day are more content to begin with the bushel of clams.[72]

Winslow's bushel of clams signifies clubwomen's resistance to following the sort of "method" English professors advocated. Rather than begin with fixed principles, they preferred to plunge into a subject, developing their own program for intellectual development along the way. As Winslow makes clear, clubwomen were not averse to systematic work, but it often took a more organic form, evolving out of the material studied instead of being imposed at the outset.

Clubwomen's ubiquitous yearbooks provide pervasive evidence of their systematic approaches. By laying out topics, texts, and speakers a year in advance, yearbooks demonstrated members' ability to regulate their own behavior. Frequently, yearbooks included assignments for club papers, thus ensuring that members had nearly a full year to prepare their written presentations. A history of the white middle-class Fortnightly of Chicago reports that "topics of papers to be delivered each year were printed in advance and sent to members, complete with a suggested reading list. In 1885 . . . twenty-five books were included on the list. . . . in 1906–07 there were thirty-two books on the reading list, and in 1909–10, when the focus was on seventeenth-century France, a third of the books in the bibliography were scholarly works written in French."[73] As this account shows, clubwomen did not shrink from intellectual work, but their methods and goals often differed from the academy's. Rather than emphasize rigorous procedures to foster mental discipline or the development of critical capacities, clubwomen employed more collaborative approaches to do the research and writing required by the systems of study they established for themselves, as their creation of the office of critic shows. Many clubs elected as critic a member who listened carefully to papers and noted all mistakes in pronunciation, grammar, and factual information. Then the critic, either immediately after the speech or at the next meeting, reported all the errors.[74] Providing disciplined assistance in the context of a nurturing environment that fostered the development of writers, the critic exemplified clubwomen's capacity to combine self-regulation with supportive encouragement.

An article published by an African American clubwoman in the *Woman's Era* shows another form of self-regulation. Written as a dialogue between two women, the article begins with one woman expressing amazement at the second's ability to carry out a program of study: "What becomes of your house, your children, and your sewing? I've neither chick nor child, and I haven't one minute to spare after the monotonous household affairs have been dispatched." The second explains, "I systematize my work, for in the long run it is much more satisfactory to map out a schedule of work and go by it." She continues by detailing how she organizes her work and concludes, "I simply arrange my work so as to leave a certain amount of time each day for study, and whether I feel like it or not I go at it religiously, unless I am positively ill."[75] The second speaker's use of the term *systematize* echoes the professional's concern with ordered approaches to literature. In the culture of professionalism, as Bledstein puts it, "genius was an act of concentration" enabled by self-discipline.[76] The self-regulated life described by the second woman draws on the "concentration" of professionalism but directs it toward a more personalized goal. She makes it clear that system enables study, but, like the zoology professor, she allows her intellectual work to develop organically instead of imposing a preconceived structure on it. By regulating herself and her household tasks, she creates a space in which she can study freely.

An emphasis on accessibility rather than difficulty contributed to the more organic systems of study clubwomen developed. While the academic model of literary study prized rigor, seeking to make English as hard as Greek, clubwomen frequently gave priority to texts that a wide audience could understand. The *Club Worker,* for example, regularly published such poetry as Ela Wheeler Wilcox's "Which Are You?" William Wordsworth's "I Wandered Lonely as A Cloud," Mary Low Dickinson's "If We Had But a Day," and Belett Burgess's "Childhood," with no directives on how they might be read. Signaling its importance by putting it in large print on the front of the paper, the journal made poetic language readily available to its working-class readership, leaving the details of interpretation to the readers.

Communal reading provided another way for clubwomen to foster accessibility and resist the norms of "difficulty." As a member of the Earnest Workers of Bridgeport, Connecticut, put it, she and her peers "had much pleasure in the past few years reading together."[77] In the face of a dominant aesthetic that emphasized individual contemplation of a work of art, communal reading represented deviance, although it was a deviance clubwomen could hide under the protective coloring of domestic practices that had emerged earlier in the nineteenth century in response to social concern about the dangerous delights of solitary reading for women. Unlike the socially sanctioned parlor reading of an earlier era, the communal reading done in women's clubs provided women intense and intimate ways of approaching texts in a single-sex environment.

Barbara Sicherman has argued that reading has practical and positive conse-
quences for women and particularly in the late nineteenth century "encouraged
vital engagement with the world, a world many thought would be transformed
by women's special sensibilities, and oral reading heightened this effect by uniting women temporally and physically."[78] Clubwomen who listened together to
a text, as the Earnest Workers did, stopping to discuss passages and offer various interpretations, made reading more accessible to all while also helping
clubwomen develop a keener sense of their own needs and desires. This oral
reading challenged the growing prominence of university-based approaches to
reading that encouraged passivity and appreciation, eschewed emotion, and
prized the "idea above the expression."[79] Oral reading fostered an analysis of the
effects of language, encouraging readers to develop a broader understanding of
the tools of discourse. While English professors aimed to institutionalize their
own highly aestheticized interpretation in the academy, clubwomen resisted by
engaging in oral reading.

The elocutionary roots of oral reading also lent it a performative quality that
clubwomen frequently exploited, as this excerpt from records of the Mormon
Utah Woman's Press Club shows: "Mrs. Lizzie Wilcox recited, very impressively,
'O My Father,' E. W. Hyde read 'God Knows Best' from Ella Wheeler Wilcox,
and L. T. Freeze read a beautiful selection from the same author. Mrs Lydia Alder read 'The Golden Curl' from Browning. The President then charmed the
club with her feeling rendition of Jean Ingelow's beautiful poem 'Seven times
Seven.' Mrs. Lawler read the 'Deserted Mining Camp' which awakened an animated discussion of the silver question and Kate Field's unjust criticism of the
Women of Utah."[80] The adjectives and adverbs used to describe the various performances here show the evaluative calculus that undergirded clubwomen's oral
interpretations of texts. Such terms as *impressively* and *feeling rendition* indicate
that dramatic renditions were expected and appreciated. These oral performances also led clubwomen to respond actively to texts, as the reference to
"animated discussion" shows.

In addition to reading from or reciting texts, clubwomen performed them
in other ways, as this report from the African American Charleston Women's
Improvement League explains: "At the completion of the study of Longfellow
a Longfellow's evening was given in the home of one of the members, to which
the public was invited. A program was rendered, the recitations and music were
taken from that author, an essay giving the conditions under which certain poems were written and an essay with a description of his life. The quotations
were from Longfellow."[81] This account of recitations, music, essays, and quo-

tations suggests a lively interaction with literature that emphasized performance. "The quotations" refers to a common practice that required clubwomen to memorize and recite a selection from the author being studied, so the performance of Longfellow involved all members of the Charleston Women's Improvement League rather than just the individuals who wrote about his life and the context of his writing or those who sang songs or gave oral interpretations of his work. Clubwomen's widely dispersed and differing set of performances acknowledges the need to develop some of the capacities English professors advocated. At the same time, these performances assert the value of becoming physically engaged with literary texts, producing texts in response to those consumed, and rendering literature performative.

Clubwomen from other social locations similarly connected performance with literature. Groups that concentrated on Shakespeare frequently mounted performances of the bard's work.[82] Plays "suitable for acting in our clubs" appeared regularly in the pages of *Far and Near* and the *Club Worker,* along with suggestions for rehearsals, and the secretary of the League of Women Workers advertised a collection of about twenty scripts that could be "sent to club members in search of a play."[83] On celebratory occasions clubwomen's performances included toasts and epideictic speeches. When the Omaha Section hosted the 1898 meeting of the National Council of Jewish Women, a meeting that included the suffragist Susan B. Anthony, the General Federation's President May Wright Sewall, and the National Council leader Hannah Solomon, delegates offered encomia that drew on literary texts to celebrate women's recent accomplishments and affirm the importance of women's clubs in advancing them "from the seclusion of the past."[84] Similarly, the report of a celebratory meeting of the Utah Women's Press Club includes this: "The literary feature of this charming social function was the toasts given at table," and the list of toasts offered includes "Utah Woman's Press Club, Its Origin, Its Present, Its Future," "Utah's Pioneer Women," and "The Freedom of the Press."[85]

In both content and method, such performances transgressed the boundaries of academic English studies. Appropriating literature to celebrate women's achievements countered professors' tendency to locate texts as objects of admiration. The physicality of movement, song, and oral rendition borrowed from the declamations and recitations of the academy but simultaneously undercut them. Instead of rendering literature as objectifiable, as the focus of the gaze, this performative approach to literacy immersed the self in the text so that the individual became physically connected with it in a way impossible in college classrooms overseen by scholars.[86] This transgression of the norms of disciplined attention made literature more accessible and better able to express and address women's desires because it took form in the somatic symbols of voice and movement. Ironically, of course, clubwomen's transgressions only strengthened the position of professors who sought to distance themselves from the behaviors and people that threatened to feminize and thereby deprofessionalize English studies.

Clothing provided another means for clubwomen to transgress boundaries. Dress reform, a highly controversial topic in the late nineteenth century, frequently appeared on club agendas, and clubwomen demonstrated considerable awareness of the relationship between dress and status.[87] In the light of this sensitivity, cross-dressing among clubwomen in all social locations represents a significant form of deviation. It is worth noting that Sarah Grand's *Heavenly Twins,* a novel many clubwomen read and commented on, features a central female character who frequently dresses as a man. Clubwomen of this period regularly wore men's clothing for author parties and club plays or pageants. For author parties at their clubs, members arrived dressed as their favorite authors, and the many photographs of women dressed as Charles Dickens or William Shakespeare testify to the importance clubwomen attached to this form of transgression. When they performed plays, clubwomen took both male and female parts. The white middle-class Saturday Morning Club of Boston, for example, mounted an all-female production of *Antigone,* which played to three sell-out audiences—of women only.[88]

Clubwomen regularly donned men's clothing for club dramatics at their meetings. A member of the working women's Steadfast Club no doubt spoke for many when she expressed her desire to screen this activity from the view of outsiders: "I have always thought that there was no harm in our dressing up as men in our own clubrooms, when only girls see us, but I don't like to do it myself or to see the other girls do it, when there are gentlemen in the audience."[89] Reading about this young woman's concern in *Far and Near* provided clubwomen a way of exploring the implications of their own (deviant) behavior. In particular, her desire to protect cross-dressing from the male gaze suggests an awareness of the power inherent in this act. By putting on men's clothing, clubwomen called the binary categories of male and female into question, creating for themselves what Marjorie Garber calls a "space of possibility" where they could try out novel roles and see themselves in new ways.[90] Cross-dressing explored and expressed the blurring definitional distinctions between women and men elsewhere in society because this form of transgression simultaneously underscored and questioned the gendered hierarchy of male and female.

Clubwomen's writing, like their reading and performing, transgressed the boundaries taking shape around professionalized English studies. Academic approaches to writing were, as Miriam Brody has shown, gendered male, and only a few professors acknowledged extracurricular writing.[91] Clubwomen, in contrast, assigned themselves topics central to their lives, such as suffrage, dress reform, and the status of women.[92] Papers also reflected the more specific concerns of particular groups. Jewish women, for instance, wrote about their religion's role in women's lives, Jewish educational programs, and religious questions.[93] In a culture where women had within recent decades been prevented from reading their own compositions aloud, clubwomen established writing practices that put performance at the center.[94] Clubwomen in all social locations followed the practice of giving papers or oral presentations on assigned—or self-selected—topics. Often the audience for these papers extended beyond the club. While reading *Middlemarch,* members of the working-class Wiltse Literary Club chose individual characters for special observation and reported, "At the end of the year we wrote essays about these characters, and our friends came to hear them read."[95] In addition to writing and reading their work aloud, not just for members but also for friends outside the club, several of these authors displayed their textual performances to the wider audience of the *Club Worker.* Reciprocity days and other club exchanges further extended the reach of textual performances. Papers written for the national convention of the League of Women Workers constituted another kind of performance, and these often appeared subsequently in the national journal. The *Young Woman's Journal, Far and Near,* the *Club Worker,* the *Federation Bulletin,* the *Woman's Era, National Notes*, and the *American Jewess* all included many articles prefaced with the statement "delivered at national convention." In contrast to an academy that frequently discouraged women's oratory, clubs offered members opportunities to develop and enact literacy practices that demonstrated their capacities as writers and public speakers.

Lively and fun-filled performances accompanied the parodies and playful verses clubwomen wrote. Sometimes members wrote parodies as part of their minutes. Because minutes were read aloud (and sometimes applauded) at the next meeting, the recorder had reason to make her account as entertaining as possible. The women who recorded the club's "sore afraid" encounter with a victrola appropriated the Bible to describe her peers' response to new technology.[96] More commonly, clubwomen wrote playful verses for special occasions, such as the Valentine's Day breakfast organized by the New York Section of the National Council of Jewish Women. This metrical sketch, written to summarize the year's accomplishments, offered poetic tributes to such committees as religion and philanthropy. Members celebrate their accomplishments and put poetry to new uses with such lines as:

> the lonely child to sorrow's heir
> now taught to hope, your bountless share
> the immigrant and the home-born lass
> that needs your help, your care and free
> that each may better, nobler be.

The 1911 yearbook published the entire text with a full-page preface explaining the composition and circumstances of this poetic drama and concluding: "The little play is incorporated in this report because it is felt that many may like to preserve it as a souvenir of an agreeable occasion."[97] This display of a text marking "an agreeable occasion" suggests that the value of such playful verses lay more in their group-building qualities than in their aesthetic ones. It also offers tangible evidence of clubwomen's willingness to write for pleasure rather than exclusively intellectual purposes.

Clubwomen in all social locations wrote plays for their peers. Some of these dealt with issues of women's lives, as did "The Enthusiastic Club Member," composed by Esther Nyskenk for her working-class Friendly Club of New York. This play, performed by the club and later published in *Far and Near,* asserts the value of clubs and concludes, "If you knew how the long working hours are shortened by bright thoughts of the club, then you would indeed understand what a great blessing to us girls is the Friendly Club."[98] Jewish clubwomen frequently wrote scripts and plays based on themes and experiences drawn from helping immigrants.[99] Drawing on the material of their experiences, these clubwomen composed texts that commented on their own circumstances. Frequently the club itself figured as the main character in plays written to celebrate anniversaries or recount club history.[100] In addition to historicizing the clubs, these women transgressed prohibitions against their performing their own texts, calling another dimension of masculine privilege into question.

Pageants as well as plays occupied club writers. The most ambitious pageant the League of Women Workers undertook was performed by the New York Association at its annual convention in 1914. Paulina Brandeth described it: "There will be four Episodes embodied in the Pageant, each picturing some distinctive period in the history of woman's labor, and each followed by a symbolic Dance of a charming and original character. The final Tableau will depict the equalization of man and woman and the Pageant will close with a festival song and procession." Explaining the pageant's goals, Brandeth observed, "Fellow workers from all parts of the country will be gathered in the city and the instructive influence as well as enjoyment derived from the performance will, therefore, be far-reaching." Emphasizing the theme of cooperation, Brandeth concluded, "In the past, woman toiled very much alone. Now, however, she is working side by side with her fellowmen and women, and thus attaining development of capacity and a consequent place in the activities of the world hitherto undreamed of."[101] Through music, dance, costumes, and scenery, as well as language, these clubwomen enacted and affirmed their worker status in a culture that sought to marginalize and deprecate them.

Similarly, Mary Church Terrell, the president of the National Association of Colored Women, wrote a pageant based on the life of Phillis Wheatley, prefaced with the statement, "Phyllis Wheatley, an African-born slave, was educated in America and became a poet of such note as to attract the attention of George Washington, who wrote her a letter commending her 'poetic Talents' and 'elegant Lines.'" The pageant begins with a scene of slave catchers and concludes with Phillis's European tour and wedding. The action and dialogue trace the writing and reception of Phillis's poetry, showing her as an established historical figure who is part of the literary tradition. This production highlights, in a relatively noncontroversial way, an African American woman's contribution to society.[102] Encouraging wide participation and engendering close cooperation among members, the literacy practices associated with papers, plays, and pageants rehearsed important events in club history and invested clubwomen's experiences with a bracing physicality. In their use of the universal languages of music and image, these performances enacted resistance to what Thomas Strychacz describes as a key source of professionalism's power, "a mastery of discourse that is not readily accessible to a wide range of people." Instead, clubwomen deployed languages easily comprehended by all.[103]

In contrast to college, where students wrote papers read only by the instructor, clubs provided rich opportunities for members to develop a sense of audience. To be sure, clubwomen did not always begin by writing; more frequently they started with reading and turned to composition somewhat later, as was true for the Cambridge Mother's Club: "We began with reading from well-known authors. Then one of our number told us of a similar club in Boston in which the members wrote original papers, and she offered to borrow one of them for us. As we listened to the article on 'The Choice and Use of Books by Children,' we were stimulated and delighted. We became less timid and began to write our own views."[104] Emboldened by another group's model of writing, these women expanded their repertoire to include composing as well as reading. Clubwomen evidently became "less timid" and better able to express their "own views" as a consequence of writing. Even though writing evoked anxiety, procrastination, and resistance among some clubwomen, it empowered them by enhancing their confidence and self-esteem. An awareness of the power in writing no doubt strengthened the resolve to require it.[105] The historian of the World Research Club in Ponca City, Oklahoma, reported that "sometimes assigned topics seem hard; however, no one refuses but delves into her subject and emerges with a paper that not only holds our interest but challenges our efforts," thus confirming that writing's rewards.[106] Lucy Anna Warner, a member of the working women's Help Each Other Club, wrote about her experience of submitting an article to *Far and Near*: "My audience must have been an audience of friends and not of critics. . . . that was a result I did not hope for when I sent my article away with many fears and forebodings that it might not even be published." Warner explained that she submitted her article in an attempt to "prove to all New York that working girls are not stupid" and to counter the assertion that working women "have too high aspirations."[107] In addition to enhancing her self-esteem, Warner's experience as a writer increased her rhetorical awareness by giving her a greater sense of audience, as it did for clubwomen in all social locations. Clubs provided immediate responses to writers, helping them develop their capacities to persuade or entertain readers, and members wrote with the expectation that many other people would read and hear their words.[108]

Because clubwomen saw themselves as writers, their national journals regularly included advice to women about publishing their work. A column titled "Advice for Young Writers" published in the *Young Woman's Journal* urged writers to take their time between books and to avoid writing too quickly: "Because the critics pronounce some early work by you as indicative of reserved strength don't spoil everything and misconstrue their remark by writing your next piece the same day and rushing it into print."[109] In addition to providing opportunities for women to produce and perform their texts, clubs encouraged writing by holding writing competitions. National publications such as *Far and Near* regularly invited working-class clubwomen to contribute articles on such topics as "How Can We Best Cultivate Club Feeling," "Domestic Service," "The Ideal Club," and "Would Members Like to Have Lectures on Cooking, Nursing etc.

at the Vacation Houses Next Summer?"[110] In addition to publishing in national journals, working women instituted publications in their local clubs. The Help Each Other Club, for instance, founded a journal, asking each member to "send in an original article" once a month.[111] White middle-class women's clubs also sponsored writing contests. The Literature Department of the North Carolina Federation held an annual competition for the best paper, and the reading of the written essay constituted a major event at the annual convention.[112] Such competitions reinforced clubwomen's awareness of the larger audience for whom they wrote and blurred the distinctions between amateur and professional writers. Clubwomen saw themselves as producers as well as consumers of texts. Although the tacit bargain between clubwomen and their suspiciously disapproving culture stipulated that they reinvest the cultural capital of their literacy into the domestic economy, authors nurtured by clubs clearly made other allocations. Instead of focusing all their self-improvement efforts on maternal skills, they used the opportunity to enhance their own capacity as readers and writers.

Not surprisingly, the textual transgressions of women's clubs were met with attempts at containment. Thomas Higginson's 1880 warning that women had become the custodians of literature ushered in four decades of regulative language surrounding women's literacy practices, supplemented by the sort of deprecation Frank Norris fostered. Women's reading, a topic of debate since at least 1540, when women were first recognized as an identifiable readership, received increased attention.[113] As women's clubs became a more distinct and prominent cultural feature, the language of containment grew. English professors, such as Hiram Corson and William Rolfe, who performed the critic's role of making literature accessible by lecturing frequently to a public that included—prominently—women's clubs, exerted their considerable authority to reinforce the sacralized text and extinguish transgressive readings. Ironically, as James Machor has noted, such admonitions often had the opposite effect, so that language designed to regulate clubwomen's literacy practices actually led them to be more active readers and writers.[114]

As often happens with subjugated populations, clubwomen reinforced the language of containment by circulating it among themselves and profiting from what Pierre Bourdieu calls its cultural capital along the way.[115] Making recommendations about the literacy practices of children, women of different social classes, and one another, clubwomen appropriated some of the cultural authority assigned to those (males) who attempted to control women's reading. As noted in chapter 3, establishing libraries provided middle-class clubwomen one means of regulating the reading of others.[116] Assuming a panoptic view of working women's desires and literacy practices, middle-class clubwomen attempted to regulate the literacy practices of their less affluent peers. The excerpt from Frances J. Dyer's "How to Read the Newspapers" at the beginning of this chapter typifies the way middle-class clubwomen constructed their working-class peers. Girls who "pick up a paper" to "read at random," gathering "scraps of information" but having no understanding of "what is really going on in the world," are contrasted with the "intelligent men and women" with whom the author identifies. Book reviews written by middle-class contributors often included such condescending comments as "And now, girls, when you make your good resolutions for the new year, come two very inspiring and helpful books to your assistance," thus playing on working women's desire for self-improvement.[117]

Despite their assumption that intelligence correlated with social status, middle-class women often had to confront its falseness: "Coming together one evening to consider what course of reading might be helpful for the winter, the leader of the class was surprised to find how many, and what excellent books the girls had been accustomed to peruse. They showed a familiarity with good authors which would have done credit to those who have enjoyed larger educational advantages."[118] This surprise at the quality of working women's reading and writing appeared frequently in middle-class clubwomen's prose. In one way it registered a genuine delight that working women had similar tastes. In another it helped preserve class distinctions by casting the surprising case as an exception that proved the rule of class-determined accomplishment. Both in attempting to direct the reading of working-class women and in assigning them to predetermined categories of literacy, middle-class clubwomen imposed on others the same kinds of constraints they themselves faced.

More affluent clubwomen also encouraged their working-class peers to read texts that served middle-class interests. "Mary's Room," for example, describes the central character's efforts to make habitable the room she is assigned when she takes a position as a maid. With such directions as "stretch each spread, and especially the outside one, as tightly as possible" and "the back porch is the place for cleaning up muddy clothes," the narrative offers instructions to domestic workers at the same time that it argues for the benefits of cleanliness.[119] Written from the viewpoint of the prospective middle-class employer of domestic servants, these claims for the virtues of neatness treat wage work as a temporary condition prior to women's making "homes of their own" and reflect the middle-class desire to produce domestic workers who would solve the "servant problem."

While middle-class clubwomen often disguised their attempts to regulate the reading of their working-class peers in the language of assistance, they themselves encountered attempts at containment in proffered help. The North Carolina Federation of Women's Clubs received "an offer from the State Literary and Historical Association to cooperate in arranging programs for use in Study Clubs."[120] The American Library Association published *A List of Books for Girls and Women and Their Clubs* (1895), and such journals as the *Ladies' Home Journal* regularly published recommendations for what and how to read.

Despite the attempts by others to regulate their literacy practices, clubwomen's textual transgressions had a lasting impact on English studies. Seeing this impact, however, requires changing the position from which we commonly view the emergence and growth of the field. Specifically, discussions of professionalism in English usually begin from inside the academy, presuming that the desire for and fulfillment of English studies blossomed within ivied halls. For instance, Michael Warner, an insightful commentator on professionalism, points to the difficulty of understanding English studies in relation to its clients, asserting that the transformation of literature into a "knowledge subject" was "not the satisfaction of a public demand (as the answer, say, to a pervasive uncertainty about literature)."[121] He explains, "It is not the case that the literary profession arose as a response to a general demand for literary interpretation. No one was sitting around wondering what *The Faerie Queene* meant, waiting for someone to come along and explain it." As he sorts out the struggles between the critics and scholars of the academy, Warner, like most of those who consider the professionalization of English, does not step outside the academy to look at the literacy practices of women's clubs.[122] Instead, Warner and many others point to self-interest and a desire for control or limitation of access as inherent to the professionalizing of literary critics. If interpretation did not emerge from social need, such commentators argue, then it must have been the product of professional ambition. This view of professionalization overlooks the clear need for interpretation demonstrated in women's clubs. Members were, in fact, sitting around wondering what *The Heavenly Twins* and *The Faerie Queene* meant, even as they recognized the differences between the two texts. Although educational institutions ultimately constituted the site where the goals of English studies would be presented and enforced, the intellectual activities of women's clubs contributed to the development of the discipline.

In fairness, clubwomen's need for interpretation looks different from the academy's. The insistence on an open mind, the attention to didactic features in literature, the receptivity to personal opinion, the prizing of affective and spiritual responses to texts, the organic approach to system, the emphasis on accessibility instead of difficulty, and the foregrounding of performance create an image quite distinct from academic interpretation. A bushel of clams does not look much like a set of fixed principles. Theory tells us that the production of texts by readers varies with the readers themselves, and women's clubs constituted social institutions quite different from universities. Furthermore, most histories of women's clubs have minimized their religious affiliations. Their common hermeneutical heritages gave clubwomen a vocabulary for interpretation as well as an additional source of kinship. Knowing how to ask and answer questions requires readers to look closely at the text, to consider meanings, and to explore (aesthetic/spiritual) implications, the very skills clubwomen's religious studies had provided. At the same time, clubwomen reserved the right to posit their own lives as a source of knowledge, and interpretation did not always lead to a single meaning: "We decided once or over again, singly, doubly, in groups, all together by turn in season and out of season (especially sister Ruth) that the hero [of Margaret Deland's "Where Ignorance Is Bliss"] was a fool and so was she, that the hero was indeed a moral hero, but the girl a fool, that the hero was a fool, and the girl wise."[123] Rather, it frequently embraced multiple perspectives and valued the expression of individual opinions.

Interpretation includes, along with exploring meanings, making value statements, and clubwomen enacted this also. As the excerpt from the Saturday Morning Club minutes at the beginning of this chapter shows, debates about what constituted the "greatest English novels" occupied many clubwomen. In developing the criteria of "universal interest," probable plots, human characters, "a picture of life as well as an ethical idea," and the capacity for making "the deepest impression" to evaluate such works as *The Scarlet Letter, Ivanhoe, Henry Esmond, Jane Eyre, Adam Bede, Tom Jones,* and *Mill on the Floss,* these clubwomen articulated their own concepts of value in literature.[124] Even though many English professors of the time would probably have disagreed with their criteria, the very existence of such discussions shows how clubwomen helped create the social need for interpretation. Similarly, minutes of the Naugatuck Study Club include this:

The novel was conceded by all to hold an important place in education. Its value was summed up in the following terms:
It teaches correct English, is authentic in descriptions of scenery and modes of living, reproduces life and customs of earlier times, is a teacher of ethics, a promoter of reforms educational and industrial, cultivates

imagination, discloses true social ideals, influences individual character, thus influencing humanity, stimulates wholesome living, touches the emotions and spiritual nature, lessens distinctions between classes in society and in many other ways is a positive influence for good. . . . Question was raised for informal discussion concerning the advisability of allowing children to indulge freely in reading. . . . All agreed that parents should take an interest in and direct the reading of their children until they were old enough to choose for themselves.[125]

As they considered the value of regulating children's reading and explored the educational merits of novels, these clubwomen, like their peers in other social locations, insisted on relating literature to their own lives. They saw novels as teaching and improving readers, connecting them with remote places and persons, and touching hearts and minds. For all clubwomen, the relationship between literature and life depended on interpretation—asking questions about literature and developing ways to address those questions. In articulating the demand for interpretation and exploring ways of responding to it, clubwomen carried out cultural work that most narratives of professionalization fail to take into account because they proceed from the assumption that English studies did not respond to social need. Clubwomen across the country who sought answers to questions about the meaning of Deland or *Ivanhoe* or about the quality of certain novels created the preconditions for professionalizing literary study while offering an alternative to its university instantiation.

The narratives of professionalization in composition have similarly focused on its relation to higher education and its continuity with classical rhetoric. James Berlin, who closes his examination of college writing in this century with an optimistic listing of such markers of professionalism as graduate programs and new scholarly journals in composition, frames his discussion in terms of the academy. He cites curricular shifts at the turn of the century as the cause for the change in the status of rhetoric. Although Susan Miller's account of composition's role in English studies refers to extracurricular textual production, it focuses on writing's position in colleges and universities. John Brereton acknowledges the limitations of excluding extra-academic writing, but his collection also focuses on composition in colleges.[126] Such narratives of professionalization overlook the Mormon clubwomen who saw invention as the most important part of writing, the working-class women who read their papers at local and regional meetings, and the women from all social locations who entered essay competitions or became published authors.[127] Even though their location outside institutions of higher education makes them less visible, the clubwomen who produced these texts helped shape the history of writing instruction. In particular, they offered a rhetorically based alternative to the more reductive and mechanical approaches to writing instruction common in English departments at the end of the nineteenth century.[128]

A more complex and nuanced view of professionalization emerges with the recognition that contributors to professionalization can appear outside the academy as well as within it. As Robin Muncy has argued, professionalism is not a monolith, and gender, social location, and variations across fields lead to multiplicity in the professional code.[129] Clubwomen's literacy practices helped broaden English studies by circulating alternative texts and readings. Similarly, by taking exception to the race, gender, and class assumptions that dictated *what* women should read and focusing on texts by women writers (including Sarah Grand, Frances Harper, Annie Nathan Meyer, Florence Kelley, and Emily Hill Woodmansee) and on texts that extended the boundaries of literature (including those dealing with religion, working conditions, lynching, and domestic economy), clubwomen created and maintained discourses distinctly different from those prominent in nascent departments of English. Specifically, clubwomen transgressed the boundaries of professionalized literature to include literacy practices that reflected their own comprehension of the social world. Similarly, their writing resisted the norms of English studies. Instead of embracing theme topics professors assigned, clubwomen wrote papers on such issues as woman suffrage, the indignities of anti-Semitism, the dangers of factory life, and the educational liabilities of racism; they wrote histories that lent authority to club traditions; they wrote petitions, resolutions, and letters addressing concerns that extended outside their circle; and they wrote plays, masques, and pageants that celebrated events in club life. In reading and writing, clubwomen inscribed alternatives to the professional model college English departments offered.

Although they sometimes enacted the sanctioned schematized readings that positioned sacralized texts in historical epochs and attended to them through catechism-like questions about their details, clubwomen also resisted such readings with performances, cross-dressing, and parody. The playfulness and irreverence with which they treated reading and writing, their emphasis on accessibility rather than difficulty, and their collaborative and highly social approaches to texts constituted a pedagogy quite different from that promulgated by universities.[130] Likewise, the nurturing didactics of women's clubs contrasted sharply with the instruction women received in colleges, where sympathy and help were in short supply.[131] Developing their alternative pedagogies, clubwomen transgressed the boundaries of professionalized English studies.

These forms of resistance suggest a more complicated view of professionalism, one that addresses what Bruce Robbins calls the "undynamic quality of professionalization stories." As Robbins observes, a lack of dynamism reflects the complacency inherent in professionalization narratives written by professors unwilling to step outside the ivory tower. Looking at the politically polyvalent relationship between the university and the world outside disrupts this complacency. The appropriations and transgressive moves of fin de siècle clubwomen reveal how power moves between the professionalized English studies of the academy and the club parlors and meeting rooms in the world beyond its gates. It can be instructive to read the professionalization of English as a complex response to women's clubs, just as clubwomen's literacy practices can be seen as both supportive and transgressive reactions to the nascent discipline of English. Recognizing these complicated political dynamics opens the way for aligning professionalism with what Robbins calls "the new world of compromise formation," one in which many concrete groups carry out various responsibilities.[132] This more nuanced view of professionalism also takes into account the different meanings that have been assigned to the term over time.[133]

While Robbins proposes a professionalism that accommodates "practical aesthetics," an aesthetics that links with real groups struggling in the real world, my proposal moves in a slightly different direction by reconsidering the relation between the professional and the amateur, a reconsideration that profits from Michael Bérubé's observation that the idea of "the public" is not always already internal to the discipline of English.[134] At the turn of the century, when English departments were trying to establish themselves in the academy, dichotomizing professional and amateur might have helped delineate the new field of study, but at the dawn of the twenty-first century this division merits reconsideration. In particular it is worth thinking about how the rigid and gendered separation of professional and amateur in the discourses of such commentators as Herman Brandt reinscribes itself in professors' relations with the amateurs who inhabit classrooms—the students. The resistance academics frequently encounter to their ways of reading and writing, particularly in introductory composition and literature classes, draws much of its energy from the worn dichotomy of professional/amateur or professional/personal. Bracketing the *un* of *unprofessional*—through recognizing the multiple and complicated relationships between amateurs and professionals, such as clubwomen and English professors—can open new ways to enhance both sides' engagement with English studies and reduce the agonistic relationships that often develop between professors and their students.

One route to this recognition lies in elaborating on the history of what William Cain calls anti-criticism. As defined by Cain, anti-criticism is not the anti-intellectual response that resists any attempt at interpretation. Rather, it encompasses the more complex position of affirming the need for criticism while acknowledging its impossibility. Cain asserts that such critics as Thomas Higginson and Hiram Corson, whose descendants eventually, with the advent of New Criticism, wrested English studies away from the scholars, enacted a form of anti-criticism. Corson, in his insistence on vocalizing instead of analyzing literature, embodies anti-criticisms's unwillingness to explain as well as its insistence on interpretive authority.[135] Although Cain does not include clubwomen, I argue that they represented another, more pervasive, instantiation of anti-criticism. They resisted academic method and held to their own unchallengeable intuitions about literature while asserting the need for their own forms of interpretation and enacting them. Recognizing a related form of anti-criticism among students can recast the professional-amateur relationship in less agonistic terms.

As the 1904 excerpt from "The Book Table" at the beginning of this chapter demonstrates, clubwomen resisted the separation of amateur and professional even as it took shape. Giving prominence to Bliss Perry's claim that the "versatility, curiosity, spontaneity, zest, and enthusiasm—even the ardor and gayety and delight" of the amateur be combined with the method, training, and skill of the professional shows how this clubwoman and her thousands of readers sought to merge the two.[136] The ardor or desire animating the literacy practices of clubwomen made space for the personal so that women could examine the conditions of their own lives while appropriating many of the practices and terms of professionalized English studies.

Recent developments in English studies reflect a reconsideration of the current terms of its professionalism. Sandra Gilbert's claim that the professional is the personal, because feminist criticism aims at individual as well as sociocultural transformations, challenges a central dichotomy. Gilbert, who describes feminist criticism as a "home industry" or a "fundamentally confessional enterprise in which each participant inevitably begins her intellectual work with a careful study of the house of fiction(s) in which she herself has, perhaps unwillingly, dwelt all her life," is not, of course, unusual.[137] Feminist theorists, such as bell hooks, Ann Snitow, Jane Tompkins, and Patricia J. Williams, have extended academic forms to create new relationships between personal and professional while expressing general dissatisfaction with a professionalism that maintains its authority by the contingency of knowledge.[138] Literary critics, such as Henry Louis Gates and Michael Bérubé, have appeared in popular journals like the *New Yorker* and *Harper's;* Louis Menand has pointed to the inadequacies of some versions of critical theory; and Morris Dickstein has made an appeal for the common (as opposed to the professional) reader.[139] The memoir has attained significant popularity among academics, collaborative pedagogies and personal writing have begun to flourish in composition classes, and theorists in rhetoric and composition urge opening the boundaries between professional and amateur writers. All of these represent attempts to integrate the personal and the scholarly, the amateur and the professional. Such attempts reflect the intradisciplinary tensions that inform work in English studies today. Understanding—and perhaps mitigating—these tensions depends on reconceiving professionalization narratives of the field.

The literacy practices of clubwomen not only created many of the preconditions for professionalized English studies but also embodied and enacted many of the differences between the amateur and professional; between sacralized/canonical and noncanonical texts; between pedagogies emphasizing "difficulty" and those fostering accessibility; between institutionally sanctioned and community-developed composition and interpretation. They contained, in other words, most of the dilemmas that preoccupy present-day considerations of English departments' relations with the society that supports them. Narratives of English studies will be richer and more incisive for considering how women's clubs instantiated and contended with these tensions at the dawn of professionalization.

7

Images and Public Memory

❖❖❖

❧ The clubs among the women are a blessing to the world and more so among our race. . . . I feel as though God is blessing every effort put forth by the women in this work, which may seem small at the present time, but in the future it will grow and broaden until the nation will awaken to its power.

MRS. J. H. YOUNG,
"Among the Women's Clubs,"
National Association Notes, 1899

❧ Perhaps no club in the state or nation has been represented like the U.W. Press in the congresses of the world. The great congress and fair held in Chicago in 1893 had delegates from Utah, both of the Club and other women's organizations.

"History of the U.W. Press Club,"
Woman's Exponent, 1907

❧ We, the twentieth century daughters of Israel, hold in the balance not only our own welfare and the world's opinion of us, but the name and fame of those greater than we, whose deeds we pass on to their ultimate fulfillment or final oblivion.

Yearbook of the Detroit Section of the
National Council of Jewish Women, 1904

❧ The Federation may become a mighty factor in the civilization of the century, if wielded as a whole,—an army of builders, ready alert, systematic, and scientific, not only a potent force in this generation, but transmitting to the next a vigor and strength which have never been given by any race of women to their inheritors.

SARAH S. PLATT DECKER,
"The Meaning of the Woman's Club Movement,"
*Annals of the American Academy of Political and
Social Sciences*, 1906

↢≡◉ As riches increase on one hand and the ranks of labor on the other, organizations like our clubs become of greater value to our nation. By their quiet and persistent work they are helping forward that ideal commonwealth which shall be worthy to be called the Kingdom of God.

EDITH HOWES,
"The Club Spirit,"
Club Worker, 1906

↢≡◉ Answers to the Biblical test questions that were propounded at the last meeting were given by the ladies, after which Mrs. Mendes, the President introduced Mrs. Julius Mortimer Alexander of Atlanta, President of the Section in that city. Mrs. Alexander read an interesting paper that she recently presented in Atlanta, on "The Sabbath."

The report of the mission school, which is the pride of the members of the Section, was presented by the teacher, Mrs. Amram. It showed that excellent work in the school is being done under the able management of Mrs. Amram. Many small children attend the school, and they have progressed greatly since they were enrolled. A number of the little ones were not able to speak a word of English when they were received, having but lately arrived in this country from abroad, but they have now advanced sufficiently to enable them to enter the primary classes of the public schools.

"Council of Jewish Women: Savannah, GA.,"
American Hebrew, 1898

↢≡◉ One of the notable things about the woman's club movement in the United States is that it has for many years commanded the serious attention of the press and is now widely accepted as one of the important sociological factors of the time. . . . Miss Winslow, who knows whereof she speaks sketches the rise of the club movement in America, and its almost simultaneous acceptance throughout the country as a means of education and development. She regards the club as an important phase of the great popular educational movement which has swept the country like a tidal wave.

"The Book Table,"
Federation Bulletin, 1904

⌐⇒ I think that the chairman of this Department indulges inside the thought that our program is looked upon as very dull and that we are viewed as a gathering of cranks studying subjects outside the realm of women. I was confirmed in this idea as I went to call upon one of our numbers a few weeks ago. Accidentally the club husband came in and was introduced. After that trying ceremony, the gentleman sat down with a sort of gasp saying "Well at last I have seen Mrs. Conant the Social Reformer." I could echo the gasp when I discovered that I bore such a title as that in anyone's mind. This innocent gentleman declared he had pictured a woman over fifty (oh the tact of the masculine sex—when he meant over 70) with a wild unkempt look—green umbrella and all the paraphernalia that a social reforming woman (with a capital W) is considered to claim as her natural adjoinments. Much to this man's astonishment, he beheld a mortal quite like other women that he knew.

EMILY CONANT,
Annual Report of the Nineteenth Century Club, 1900

⌐⇒ This is the age of organization among women. "What is the matter with them all?" cry the men aghast. "They used to be contented to take their opinions from us (when we had time to explain things to them); but now they must be examining everything, trying everything, having a finger in everything; where is it going to stop?"

ELIZA TURNER,
"The Uses of Guilds,"
Far and Near, 1894

⌐⇒ The most interesting and curious part of this little book, however, is its extended reference to colored women. The comparisons drawn between white and colored women with reference to club life, marriage, and maternity are certainly not to our discredit, although some of her reasoning and conclusions show an unwarrantable ignorance of our social status.

After stating that colored women do not take to club life and have very little social life, she says: "Among the Negroes, there is an unwritten law, seldom broken, except in a very few large cities, notably Washington, D.C., that arbitrarily compels married couples to consider themselves outside the pale of society. Marriage to the Negro means settling down, and thus in 82 cases out of 100 a Negro woman begins to raise a family within twelve months after her marriage." This will seem strange to those of us who know what we really are.

FANNIE BARRIER WILLIAMS,
"Some Perils of Women's Clubs,"
New York Age, 1905

⋅→⋅═◉═⋅←⋅

A S the tracings of their literacy practices show, fin de siècle clubwomen's cultural work extended in many directions and had significant implications for them and the society in which they lived. Through their reading and writing they engaged with important texts and compelling questions of their time, altering their own perceptions and those of people around them. These ordinary women shaped and were shaped by extraordinarily complex interactions in civic and economic life, negotiation of gender roles, calibration of culture, and professionalization. Practiced differently according to clubwomen's specific circumstances, literacy enabled women to address the various class, race, and religious constraints in their lives. They thereby enacted cultural work that alternately fostered and modified dominant conceptions of citizenship, capitalism, womanhood, culture, and English studies. A quick summary of this cultural work leads to the obvious question of why it remains largely unacknowledged.

African American clubwomen called on literacy's transformative powers in their attempt to change the way they and others of their race were perceived and portrayed by whites. Defining *American* in terms of behaviors rather than inherent qualities, they challenged racist principles by appropriating the discourse of Americanization for their own purposes. They adapted the rhetoric of female benevolence to include their own efforts to redress the poverty, discrimination, and cruelties that dogged members of their race. They read and wrote texts in which they used the politics of respectability to reconfigure the ideology of womanhood and construct a version of culture that included African American contributions. Giving race literature and African American women writers a central place in their literacy practices, they extended the terms of literary study.

For middle-class white Protestant clubwomen, literacy offered a means of preserving class position while resisting several of its gender-imposed constraints. These women inscribed themselves into Americanization projects that reinforced their white Anglo-Saxon heritages, into philanthropic projects that distanced them from the recipients of their charity, into ideologies of consumption and motherhood that supported their domestic patterns, into constructions of culture that emphasized their identification with the genteel tradition, and into attempts at controlling the literacy practices of others less affluent. At the same time, their reading and writing on America turned to identifying and celebrating the roles of women, thereby expanding the boundaries of national history and identity. They circulated texts and established social institutions to undercut the expanding forces of capitalism, and they rewrote the ideology of motherhood into a peace movement that challenged imperialism as well as many aspects of industrialism. They contested the male-defined genteel tradition of culture, and they instituted reading and writing practices that highlighted women authors and contended with issues central to the emerging professionalization of English studies.

Working women inscribed an Americanization that alternated between trying to become more "white" and/or middle-class and seeking improved material conditions and textual affirmations of their status as workers. As frequent recipients of benevolence, they resisted middle-class attempts to position them as victims and sought from consumer society the means to function independently. Their ideology of womanhood included earning wages, and in the early twentieth century women from other social groups found many aspects of workers' lifestyles attractive enough to imitate. Attending to the material conditions of their lives, working-class clubwomen helped shift the terms of both culture and literature.

Jewish and Mormon clubwomen, similarly constrained by gendered precepts in their religious communities and subject to hostility and prejudice outside them, enacted literacy practices calculated to address their complicated positions. Simultaneously supporting and resisting aspects of their faiths, they tried to renegotiate gender relations to bring them closer to mainstream norms without invoking male/religious censure. Their inscriptions of Americanization displayed a sometimes overzealous patriotism calculated to stifle any doubts about their loyalties to the nation. Middle-class Jewish clubwomen frequently embraced consumer culture, with its "store clothes," as part of that loyalty, while their Mormon sisters took more entrepreneurial approaches. Both groups tried to construct ideologies of womanhood that simultaneously extended their rights and adhered to religious precepts. They also shared an interest in including the ideas and people of their own religious communities in culture and literature.

Clubwomen's pride in their cultural work is evident in an article by Martha White: "When the history of this period comes to be written, it will be recognized that from 1870 to 1900 was a period of greater significance than any former two hundred years; and out of that whole time of thirty years, that which will be recognized as the most significant, as the most far-reaching, will be the movement that is represented by the women's clubs."[1] This was not an isolated prophecy; clubwomen regularly made optimistic and generous claims about the effects of their organizations. Like the African American clubwoman Mrs. J. H. Young of the Sierra Leone Club who contributed to the column "Among the Women's Clubs," they expected the United States to "awaken to [the] power" of their work. Like members of the Mormon group who published in the *Woman's Exponent,* they saw themselves participating in "the congresses of the world." Like members of the Detroit Section of the National Council of Jewish Women, they portrayed themselves as wielding power over "ultimate fulfillment or final oblivion." Like Sarah Platt Decker and other members of the General Federation of Women's Clubs, they conceptualized clubs as "a mighty factor in the civilization of the century." Like the working women represented in the *Club Worker,* they looked forward to becoming "of greater value to our nation." These authors, like the parliamentarian Emma Fox who dedicated her book to "the club women of America, a potent factor in the progress of civilization," expressed a widely shared belief that their organizations had an importance and value that extended beyond a particular time or location, and they looked to the future with hope and optimism.[2]

The history of the 1870–1900 period to which Martha White referred *has* been written, and the twentieth century has nearly wound to a close, but this book cannot conclude with a ringing echo of White's description of women's clubs as "the most significant . . . far-reaching . . . movement" or Decker's depiction of clubs as "a mighty factor" in the civilization of the twentieth century. The past, as we have received it, does not include long chapters on the club movement. From the perspective of the late 1990s, women's clubs occupy a very small corner of U.S. history, despite the enormous number of women involved, their geographical and social diversity, and their wide-ranging projects.

The numbers, of course, began to drop in the 1920s. Although statistics vary—the General Federation of Women's Clubs, for example, claimed two million members in 1925, but Karen Blair reports that membership was probably closer to one million—all clubs began to lose members after World War I, following more than a decade of growth.[3] The National League of Women Workers vanished entirely shortly after the *Club Worker* published its last issue in 1921; the National Council of Jewish Women lost nine thousand members in 1929 alone; the *Woman's Exponent* ceased publication in 1914 and the *Young Woman's Journal* in 1929; and the National Association of Colored Women faced a series of financial crises precipitated by declining membership and cut its departments from thirty-eight to two in 1930.[4] Despite decreased club dues, efforts to revitalize programs, and less stringent membership requirements, women's clubs no longer attracted as many members as they once had.

Explanations for the declining memberships in women's clubs vary. Paula Giddings asserts that the National Association of Colored Women (NACW) had become anachronistic because "the civil rights and welfare organizations that . . . it had helped to spawn were by then doing many of the things the NACW had done in the past."[5] Certainly such organizations as the (male-dominated) National Association for the Advancement of Colored People assumed many of the projects African American clubwomen had initiated, and by 1938 Mary McLeod Bethune, a former NACW president, established a new clearinghouse for clubwomen because she found that organizations run by men (or white women) did not give black women a sufficient hearing.[6] Faith Rogow observes that the post–World War I decline in immigration deprived the National Council of Jewish Women (NCJW) of one of its central missions, and the variation in the National Council's strengths from community to community created confusion: "Even within the Jewish community, a significant number of people were unsure of NCJW's purpose or what differentiated it from the organizations with which it frequently cooperated."[7] Nancy Tate Dredge describes Mormon women as victims of "an unbending Church" in the years after Utah achieved statehood. The increasingly conservative stance of the Mormon church in the early years of the twentieth century undoubtedly took its toll on Mormon women's clubs.[8] Alice Kessler-Harris reports that the percentage of married women in the work force increased more than 25 percent between 1920 and 1930. This demographic shift, combined with the establishment of the Women's Bureau in the U.S. Department of Labor in 1919, rendered many activities of the National League of Women Workers irrelevant.[9] Many aspects of working women's culture—including clothing, entertainment, and public behavior—were appropriated by middle-class women, making working women a less identifiable and cohesive group. Karen Blair argues that for many groups in the General Federation of Women's Clubs, "the enthusiasm for building women's clubhouses did considerable damage to the club movement" because financing and maintaining these houses "diverted them from other issues they might have addressed, new programs they might have invented, and new goals they might have set for their membership and for society in general."[10]

The Great Depression reduced the number of women willing or able to pay dues, and the decreased revenues forced many clubs to limit their philanthropic activities, cut back on printing, and recruit members for financial rather than affinitive reasons. Carroll Smith-Rosenberg observes that the close mother-daughter ties of the nineteenth century gave way to more conflicted relationships because "greater options were available for daughters than for mothers" after World War I.[11] Woman suffrage, increased coeducation in colleges and universities, and opportunities for middle-class women to work outside the home opened the possibility that daughters' life experiences would be significantly different from their mothers', thereby diminishing the intimacy and intergenerational affection long prominent among club members. Estelle Freedman proposes that women abandoned female institutions (such as women's clubs) in favor of male-dominated ones after the Nineteenth Amendment passed, vainly "hoping to become equals by adopting men's values and integrating into their institutions."[12] Nancy Cott underscores the fact that women of the 1920s did not share political consensus. As such issues as prohibition and the growth of the military cut into gender solidarity, women's clubs suffered.[13] Such explanations, some tied to the circumstances of particular clubs and some extending across the entire nation, offer ways of comprehending why the numerical and institutional force of clubs declined during the late 1920s.

It is more difficult to understand how the contributions of clubwomen came to be largely erased from public consciousness. Clubwomen's roles in establishing libraries and art museums, instituting such professions as social work or kindergarten teaching, introducing juvenile justice systems and pure food legislation, and preserving such national treasures as the Palisades and Mesa Verde receive only a tiny footnote—if that—in narratives of national history.[14] The cultural work described here—negotiating various forms of Americanization, introducing discourses of compassion in a society driven by capitalistic consumption, fashioning new meanings for *woman,* helping reconfigure the terms of culture, and interacting with the professionalized model of English studies—remain largely unrecorded in the public memory, that shifting mass of perceptions and enactments shaping the way the nation thinks about itself.

This chapter argues that reductive and distorted images of clubwomen helped erase their cultural work from the public memory. Representations imposed by uninformed and often hostile outsiders created damaging stereotypical images that frequently overpowered the memory of clubwomen's archives. Positive self-representations created by clubwomen thus gave way to negative spectacles developed by others. As Alice Kaplan explains, an image or spectacle "creates an eternal present of explanation: memory ceases to be necessary or desirable."[15] When a nation wants or needs to forget, the static image can stand in for memory, rendering other aids to recollection irrelevant. In the case of women's clubs, images created by hostile critics replaced memories of clubwomen's actual projects, thereby helping the nation forget the cultural work clubwomen carried out at the turn of the century. The weakened status of clubs themselves aided this because institutions help sustain memory; the diminished clubs offered little resistance to the powerfully reductive and negative images circulating in U.S. society. The practice of shielding their literacy practices from the gaze of outsiders also made it very difficult for clubwomen to circulate their own representations of themselves and their work within the larger society. Articles appearing in *National Association Notes* or the *General Federation of Women's Clubs Magazine* reached only a small percentage of the audience available to, say, the *Ladies' Home Journal*. This combination of limited access to the most powerful technologies of literacy, diminished numbers and institutional force in clubs, and the production of derogatory images by outsiders reduced the presence of women's clubs in the national memory.

During the same period that women's clubs coalesced into what could be described as a movement, the United States began, according to Michael Kammen, to develop a national public memory. "Between 1871 and 1907, American memory began to take form as a self-conscious phenomenon," he claims, citing among his evidence the appearance of a 1909 article in the *New York Times* that described the progress of the nation in five stages, including "the wonderful quarter century" from 1885 to 1908. Acknowledging the tension between national memory and local allegiance, which generates more enthusiastic responses, Kammen affirms the ideological role of public memory in shaping the national ethos and sense of identity.[16] Public memory, like all memory, is always selective, and its selections shift with the politics of the present. Within memory, myths and legends flourish despite the accessible bodies of information that contradict them. Accordingly, to the extent that the public memory includes women's clubs, it is shaped by myths that bear little relation to the available information from clubwomen's own texts. Rather, public memory draws on the spectacle or images that evolved from (largely hostile) representations of club-women at the turn of century. These images, constructed from popular anxieties, misconceptions, and distortions circulating at the time, contended with and eventually crowded out the accounts of cultural work available in clubwomen's own records. With these negative images firmly established in the public consciousness, the memory encoded in club texts became unnecessary and undesirable.

A July 1995 cartoon demonstrates the longevity and pervasiveness of one of these images. It features a child asking his father what his mother does at the women's club and then cuts to the club where a woman poised like a batter advises her audience: "So when he comes home five hours late, you take your club back like this. . . ."[17] This scene, which echoes the 1868 claim of the *New York World* that "woman has laid down the broomstick to pick up the club" and assigns masculine physical force to women, demonstrates the enduring power of the image of the gendered world turned upside down by clubwomen. The 1868 article begins, "Women have long been accorded the privileges which were once thought to be prerogatives and proper to the masculine gender only to vote, to shave, and to sing bass," then describes clubs as men's last citadel, and announces the "authentic though disgusting fact" that a group of women have formed a club. Connecting voting, shaving, and singing bass with the advent of women's clubs creates the image of the gendered world turned upside down by women seeking to assume all forms of masculine privilege—including the right to "get drunk and warble convivial carols on the way home" from club dinners. The author suggests the negative spectacle inherent in this image by beseeching women "to refrain from entering on a course which leads inevitably to such dreadful things."[18] This author also expresses, albeit humorously, the anxiety that surrounded any single-sex gathering of women in the late nineteenth century.

This image of the gendered world turned upside down recurs throughout representations of women's clubs at the turn of the century. A 1904 article in the *Critic*, for example, asserts, "I am certain that women do not need clubs. All a woman wants is someone, and it must be a man, who will take care of messages and letters which postmen and boy messengers bring, and forward them upon the days only when she directs. Thus it is that the hall-porter becomes the woman's club, and as far as the members care, the hall-porter is the President, the Committee and the Secretary rolled into one."[19] The masculine model of clubs—places where men could retreat to be pampered and relax—dominates this critique, completely overlooking the fact that by 1904 women's clubs had established themselves as sites where women worked, with very little relaxation, on self- and community-improvement projects. Portraying women's clubs in terms of the male model, with women "becoming" men, left no space for an alternative, feminized, image of clubs.

The animosity spawned by the prospect of a shift in gendered power arrangements found its way into George Rugg's 1896 script for *The New Woman: A Farcical Sketch with One Act, One Scene and One Purpose.* The sketch opens with Maria, a self-important clubwoman with a busy schedule, and her husband, Darius, who whines for pocket money and help wringing out the clothes. When Maria and her women friends see a mouse, they jump on chairs, and Darius seeks revenge: "'Maria Simpkins, listen to me. Will you help me wring out the clothes or shall I set this ravenous beast upon you to fasten its fierce fangs in your quivering flesh?'" After winning concessions from his wife, Darius asserts, "'Henceforth the "Old Man" will divide honors with the "New Woman" in this household.'"[20] The figure of the man reduced to the harassed, underappreciated, and overworked position of the female homemaker generated loathing as well as fear of disrupting gender roles.

Cartoons offered an accessible and inexpensive medium for displaying the image of the world turned upside down by clubwomen. A typical representation appears in Charles G. Bush's 1869 rendering of a crowded meeting of Sorosis in a space that resembles a schoolroom, where grim and masculine-appearing clubwomen push against one another in rowdy disarray and members point umbrellas, wave their arms, assume wide-stance poses, and ignore the president. On the stairs outside the meeting room sit two men, each holding a small child.[21] An 1893 cartoon features a man with a nose ring and chain being led by a woman, and the caption reads, "The wedding ring, as Sorosis would like to see it worn." Another version of the same concept portrays a stout "lady manager" leading her undernourished husband on a leash down the Midway Plaisance.[22] The image of the feminized man also appears in an 1869 cartoon that features two men facing one another in rocking chairs, one with knitting in his hands and the other holding a crying baby. The cartoon's caption reads, "First Gent: 'As Mrs. Nettlerash has gone to the Sorosis Club, I tho't I'd just come over with my knitting. Baby not well, eh?' Second Gent: 'No, poor thing, he requires so much care that I really don't get time to do my mending!'"[23] This cartoon builds on the image Bush introduced by adding knitting and mending to the array of feminized symbols. Including children in these cartoons also served as a reminder of another fear implicit in the image of the world turned upside down—the dropping fertility rate. Olga Louise Cadija, who described women's clubs as destructive to home and family, a curse to the home, and "one of the strongest promoters of race suicide," supported her claims by comparing the fertility rates of nonclubwomen and clubwomen and urged whites to "save America from becoming a black-peopled country."[24] Like most other critics of clubwomen, Cadija portrayed clubs as peopled only by white middle-class women, and in calling on racism, she added new force to the image of the upside-down world.

Another of the negative images attached to clubwomen emphasized the triviality of their projects. An 1868 *New York World* article, for example, acknowledged Sorosis as "an accomplished fact," but describing the club's larger purposes as "not quite so clear," it urged the club to focus on "the destruction of gossip and the due restraint of dress," thus portraying its work as both silly and impossible.[25] This move toward minimizing or mocking the work of clubwomen became an increasingly popular way of representing them, and an 1873 cartoon published in *Harper's Weekly* features this caption: "This gathering of Ladies (bless 'em) is not caused by some one having fallen in a fit, nor has a robbery been committed; it is merely a social group discussing how a certain New Hat ought to be Trimmed."[26] Clubwomen's literacy practices became a particularly popular target of mocking critics, which is not surprising in a culture where women had long been prohibited from writing or at least from making their writing visible.[27]

Edward Bok, editor of the best-selling *Ladies' Home Journal* from 1889 to 1919, carried out a vigorous campaign against women's clubs. He was especially contemptuous of their study programs, arguing that "to inculcate the love of the beautiful and the pride of home in the mind of the young is far more important to us in the immediate present than what Caesar did or Rameses stood for." Whereas Louisa Knapp Curtis, the founding editor of the *Ladies' Home Journal,* had supported the self-improvement projects of women's clubs, Bok actively opposed them for both philosophical and economic reasons. Philosophically he disapproved of women in public life. Economically he depended on plentiful advertising for the success of his magazine, and women who saw themselves as practical consumers served this end better than those who focused on art or literature. In addition to publishing such articles as Grover Cleveland's attack on women's clubs for threatening the family and home, Bok regularly editorialized against clubs himself: "This magazine is writ in large and angry letters in the minds of many estimable women as being opposed to women's clubs. And it is."[28]

Bok's critique, particularly since his tenure as editor coincided with the emergence of women's clubs, did much to foster the image of clubwomen engaging in superficial and silly study programs. Henry James, in a series of essays published in *Harper's Bazaar* in 1906 and 1907, castigated "an unprecedented system of clubs and congresses" for promoting culture without any consideration of the "*effect* of the cultivated feminine consciousness," thus elaborating on the image of the frivolous and anti-intellectual clubwoman.[29] Edith Wharton's short story "Xingu" further strengthened this image. The narrative begins, "Mrs. Ballinger is one of the ladies who pursue Culture in bands, as though it were dangerous to meet alone," and it goes on to recount the Lunch Club's fumbling attempt to entertain Osric Dane, a visiting author. Wharton's clubwomen include Mrs. Leverett, who comes to meetings armed with her book of "Appropriate Allusions," even though its quotations "deserted her at the critical moment, and the only phrase she retained—*Canst thou draw out leviathan with a hook?*—was one she had never yet found occasion to apply"; Mrs. Plinth, whose "mind, like her house, was furnished with monumental 'pieces' that were not meant to be disarranged" by any detailed questioning; and Mrs. Ballinger, whose "mind was an hotel where facts came and went like transient lodgers, without leaving their address behind, and frequently without paying for their board." Wharton explains that the club, "when fresh from the 'Encyclopedia Britannica,' the 'Reader's Handbook' or Smith's 'Classical Dictionary,' could deal confidently with any subject; but when taken unawares it had been known to define agnosticism as a heresy of the Early Church and Professor Froude as a distinguished histologist."[30] This series of satirical indictments, showing clubwomen as incapable of true intellectual work, unable to distinguish the appearance from the substance of learning, and unwilling to engage in significant thought, strengthed the spectacle of clubwomen focusing on trivialities.

The image of clubwomen as silly and superficial has endured alongside that of the gendered world turned upside down. This image appeared in cartoons as clubs took shape in the 1870s and continued to appear through the early 1950s in Helen Hokinson's work. Typical of the early cartoons is one titled "Sorosis Opens the Winter Season. . . . In a Forest of Millinery." Echoes of the world turned upside down remain in the corners, with a female figure guarding the door and ordering a well-dressed man to "go away please," while in the other corner "the only man" stands at attention in a butler's uniform. The center of the cartoon, however, focuses on an array of women, each dressed in an ostentatiously decorative hat with identifications, such as "lady with monocle" and "defiant," attached to each. Prominent in the upper center with the label "outside" stands a small winged urchin, symbolizing the real needs being ignored by the hat-flaunting women.[31] With this last figure, the cartoon adds the indictment of "selfish" or lacking in compassion to that of "trivial," thus echoing Edward Bok's attack on clubwomen for attending to meaningless activities while ignoring the social problems around them.

Helen Hokinson, whose first *New Yorker* cartoon appeared in 1925, took a less accusatory stance, but she gave new life to the trivialized image of the clubwoman. Drawing her overweight and matronly clubwomen's figures in opulent settings, Hokinson strengthened and perpetuated the image of the clubwoman as a well-intentioned but ill-informed bumbler. In a typical portrayal, hatwearing matrons sit in a room with high ceilings, chandeliers, and generous drapery and listen intently to the spectacled woman reading from the dais. The caption reads, "The Garden Committee reports that Mrs. Bernard Thayer, Mrs. Harrison S. Quigley, and Mrs. Thompson Sperry have all seen pussy willows." In a similar scenes, the captions read, "*Life* says that it will send a photographer to our cake sale if it possibly can," and "I just want to say that I'm perfectly willing to serve as treasurer, provided every penny doesn't have to come out exactly even."[32] By portraying clubwomen as financially incompetent, possessed of unrealistic expectations for public notice of their work, and unable to distinguish casual observation from substantive reporting, Hokinson for three decades reinforced an image of club work as trivial.

As clubs began to take on social reform projects, such as providing aid to the indigent, developing parole programs, and improving sanitation, critics added the image of the self-righteous reformer to their repertoires. An 1895 sketch in *Life* typifies this critique by portraying the president of a woman's club as wearing "her husband's best necktie" and "his new imported collar" while asserting, "We would sooner imitate our ancestral apes than the modern member of the masculine sex" because he hasn't "a single trait worthy of even half-hearted admiration in his mental and moral nature that is not derived directly from his mother." She continues, "Now that the progress of science and civilization has indisputably shown his inferior nature, we, Advanced Women, feel that *we* are entitled to the best, and we are going to wrest it from him."[33] Playing on the female reformer's claims to a superior morality, this sketch points out the incongruity of simultaneously imitating and condemning men.

Even when clubwomen employed the socially sanctioned strategy of trying to influence others instead of attempting to wield power themselves, their critics produced negative images of the clubwoman reformer. In 1904, for example, a U.S. congressman observed:

This is fast becoming a government of the women, for the women's clubs, and by the women's clubs. Strange that the men do the voting and elect us to these positions, while the women assume the duty of telling us afterward what they want us to do. . . . why, if the women of the country should suddenly decide that they wanted the tariff revised, or a rate bill passed, or the coal mines nationalized, we should have it before the men would wake up to know what had happened. The petitions from the women's clubs would do the work. . . . And they have never been known to quit.[34]

Women's capacity to influence (the argument used most frequently against woman suffrage) thus becomes a source of mockery, and clubwomen are belittled for using the very strategies assigned to their gender. By using examples from international trade and industry, this critique ignores and undermines the largely domestic and socially oriented legislation to which clubwomen actually devoted most of their time.

The image of clubwoman as reformer owed much of its power to the antimaternalist forces of the early twentieth century. The novelist and satirist Edward Beer created the "Titaness" as an emblem of these forces. He described her as a midwestern woman, "a terror to editors, the hope of missionary societies, and the prey of lecturers," "a grotesque shape in hot black silk, screaming threats at naked children in a clear river" who uttered such phrases as "the nobility of democracy" and "social purity," confused "morals with manners," and "hovered upon shoals of women shuffling and cawing in the congresses of the World's Fair in 1893," where "congress after congress for the correction of mankind drew ladies to galleries."[35] With specific references to Bertha Palmer as well as to the clubs gathered at the World's Columbian Exposition in Chicago, Beer equates the Titaness with clubwomen. Lamenting the absence of a more "masculine" literature, Beer charged, "It is not alleged against the women of the Mauve Decade that they invented cheap cruelty and low social pressures, but they erected these basenesses into virtues by some defensive sense of rectitude, and a generation of sons was reared in the shadow of the Titaness, aware of her power, protected by nothing from her shrill admonitions."[36] John Erskine's 1936 attack on women reformers repeats the refrain: "The influence which women exercise in mass is funny when not distressing, distressing when not pernicious. To realize her true talent for inspiration, woman should be isolated."[37]

As Ann Douglas has observed, "The slaying of the Titaness, the Mother God of the Victorian era, was the most important instigation of the modern urban era, and the basis for its central ethos, 'terrible honesty'. . . . Cultural matricide gave fresh access to an adventurous new world of uninhibited self-expression and cultural diversity, a world the Titaness's bulk had seemed designed expressly to block."[38] This powerful cultural impulse to exorcise the matriarchal ethos of the late nineteenth century helps explain the tremendous impact of the (negative) image of the clubwoman as reformer. The essentialism that argued for women's superior morality engendered the hostility that created and promoted the Titaness. The "bulk" of the Titaness took literal form in a statue displayed at the 1915 San Francisco Exposition. Standing ninety feet tall in the midway, this wooden caricature of a banner-waving, drum-beating suffragist was named "Little Eva" because, as Robert Rydell points out, "the directors feared 'Panama Pankaline Imogene Equalrights' would offend women."[39] Looming over the section of the exposition that displayed freaks and distortions, this figure conflated clubwomen and suffragists to create a grotesque image of women reformers.

Motion pictures joined cartoons, prose, and statues to create images of clubwomen in the early years of the twentieth century. D. W. Griffith's 1915 *Birth of a Nation* marked the emergence of the movie industry, and his 1918 *Intolerance* offered a particularly compelling image of the clubwoman as reformer. Budgeted for ten times more than *Birth of a Nation,* this was the most ambitious silent film ever made, and Griffith aimed his extraordinarily expensive vehicle at reformers, whom he regarded as potential threats to his artistic freedom. Labeled "Uplifters," the suit-wearing, calculatedly unattractive women in this film meddle ineffectively and disastrously in the lives of poor factory workers, and one heavy-handed caption reads, "When they no longer attract men, women turn to reform." Even though *Intolerance* was not a commercial success because Griffith misjudged his audience, it influenced subsequent films.[40] This new medium—like the newspapers, magazines, and books that conveyed cartoons and prose images of clubwomen—added to the spectacle, the visual rendering of the reformer clubwomen in reductively static terms.

Indeed, the image of the clubwoman as reformer became so powerful that it defined members in absentia, as Emily Conant of the Nineteenth Century Club discovered when she was introduced to the husband of one of the club members. Long before she met the "club husband," he had assigned her to the category of "the social reformer," assuming her to be possessed of "a wild unkempt look" and a "green umbrella." His delighted surprise at finding Conant to be "a mortal quite like other women that he knew" might have reduced his wariness about this particular woman, but the image of the unkempt, umbrella-wielding social reformer remained intact.[41]

All of the distortions and deprecations associated with the image of the clubwoman reformer, trivialized club activities, and the gendered world turned upside down pale before the portrayal of the reformer as a subversive and a threat to the nation. Clubwomen's work in the peace movement attracted the ire of right-wing political groups as well as the government, and their hostility sparked a merciless attack on all women's organizations. Perhaps the most vicious rendering of the clubwomen as reformer appeared in the infamous Spider-Web Chart. Developed by the office of Brigadier General Amos A. Fries of the Chemical Warfare Service (Fries was a frequent target of the women's peace campaign), this chart described twenty-nine women leaders and fifteen women's organizations—including the General Federation of Women's Clubs, the National Council of Jewish Women, and the National Consumers' League—under the title "The Socialist-Pacifist Movement in America Is an Absolutely Fundamental and Integral Part of International Socialism." Between 1923 and 1924 this chart circulated among governmental agencies, including J. Edgar Hoover's FBI, and hyperpatriotic groups, such as the American Defense Society. Henry Ford's reactionary *Dearborn Independent* published it, and to further demonstrate the culpability of clubwomen, this journal subsequently published an article titled "Are Women's Clubs 'Used' by Bolshevists?" which portrayed reformers as the unwitting dupes of "radicals" who "through teamwork on interlocking directorates . . . dominate the legislative program in most of the women's organizations."[42] Tarring women's clubs with the brush of socialism or accusing them of being under the control of the Soviet government significantly undercut their reform efforts. While no one force can be credited with erasing clubwomen's cultural work from the national memory, the virulence, longevity, and concerted nature of this attack did a great deal to foster negative images of clubwomen.

Although they could not muster a force sufficient to counter images of them as turning the world upside down, engaging in trivial activities, and carrying out social reform, clubwomen responded to the portrayals of them and their work. In part, however, their retorts were muted by the screens they had erected as protection against the gaze of outsiders. Because clubwomen had been careful to shield their reading and writing from public view to avoid the accusation of selfishness, little information about their literacy practices reached commentators outside clubs. The system of circulating club texts that had served to inform clubwomen about one another's activities did not offer them a means of addressing a wider public, and since their access to the powerful technologies of the mass media was severely limited, clubwomen had few ready avenues for countering inaccurate representations of their activities. Many of their rebuttals appeared in publications distributed to other clubwomen. The General Federation's full response to Grover Cleveland's attack appeared not in the best-selling *Ladies' Home Journal,* where Cleveland had launched his salvo, but in a 1905 issue of the *Federation Bulletin,* where it reached a much smaller group of readers, few of whom supported Cleveland's views.[43]

Clubwomen also had difficulty countering critical images because so many were couched in humor. Cartoons and satirical prose did not lend themselves to easy refutation. As Mrs. Tuttle of the Naugatuck Study Club observed, "Nothing kills like ridicule, and the new woman is being put to death in this way."[44] By using humor, critics increased their own effectiveness and limited the possibility of response. Humor, as Regina Barecca writes, "occupies a different space emotionally and socially" for men and women.[45] While humor is expected and reinforced among men, women have much less access to it. Accordingly, clubwomen often had to rely on other (usually less effective) means for responding to the jokes made about them.

A report of a section meeting published in the *American Hebrew* illustrates one such strategy. Writing in a newspaper widely distributed in her religious community and aware of the criticism that Jewish clubwomen were shirking their responsibilities for preserving Jewish religious traditions, the author begins with an account of biblical questions and a paper titled "The Sabbath" to reassure her audience of clubwomen's piety. With this credential established, she moves on to detail the club's educational program, showing how members contribute to the Americanization of immigrants by teaching English to the small children of recently arrived families. By publishing accounts such as this in the *American Hebrew* rather than, say, the *American Jewess* or a section publication, clubwomen ensured a wider audience for their reports. While such accounts did not erase all the negative commentaries about women's clubs, they offered another more positive perspective.[46]

Some clubwomen, such as Eliza Turner, appropriated humor. Even as she makes a serious assertion about women's organizations, Turner makes fun of men's "aghast" reaction to clubwomen's insistence on examining, experimenting, and exploring instead of waiting for men to "explain things to them." By making this a point of humor, Turner creates a rhetorical space in which to claim that the working woman's club, like that of the middle-class woman, addresses the "new longing to be all and to do all that her Creator has made it possible for her to be and to do."[47] Turner thus claimed the right of working-class clubwomen to define themselves in their own terms, but publishing in the national association journal automatically minimized its effect because it had only limited circulation.

The representations of Mormon, as well as African American, working-class, or Jewish, clubwomen posed special challenges. Although the negative images of clubwomen were often assigned to them by males from their own social locations, the images circulating in the dominant culture excluded them. Cartoons of clubwomen included few black faces, and images of the world-inverting, trivial, or reformer clubwoman usually portrayed only white middle-class women of Protestant stock. Recognition of other clubwomen nearly always carried negative implications. In Edward Beer's diatribe against the Titaness who ignored the needy people around her, he makes a passing reference to the National Council of Jewish Women: "Female workers in the industrial centers were abominably paid although associations mostly organized by foreign Jewesses had a little improved the condition in New York and Chicago."[48] Dismissing National Council members as "foreign" underscores their marginal status in the nation and completely ignores their participation in the larger "movement" of clubwomen. Jewish women thus paid a double price—one extracted by the men of their own religion and one by the mainstream press—for their involvement in clubs.

African American clubwomen faced similar marginalization, with most commentators ignoring them completely or misrepresenting or maligning them. Olga Louise Cadija typifies this practice when she exhorts white clubwomen to emulate their African American sisters who, according to Cadija, "do not take to club life." Fannie Barrier Williams, an active member of the National Association of Colored Women, responded to Cadija's claims in the *New York Age,* where she could reach a broader audience. In addition to defending the women of her race against the assertion that they did not participate in clubs, she had to reassure her (male) readers that black women did not neglect their duties as wives and mothers. Accordingly, after she dispenses with the inaccuracies born of Cadija's "unwarrantable ignorance," she concludes, "The women's clubs have undoubtedly a part to play in our social development. We are scarcely open to the charge that colored women's clubs have had the effect of making us neglect the precious interests of home and motherhood." Williams goes on to warn her (female) readers that the situation Cadija laments among white women could occur in the black community as well. Then, in a move calculated to reassure her (male) readers, she proclaims, "Our women must keep in mind that a woman's club is not an end but a means towards our social and economic development and uplift. When it ceases to make home, and everything contained in that name, the most important and precious of all our thought and effort, it has lost forever its power for usefulness."[49] Because her complicated rhetorical stance required her to address the image of the gendered world turned upside down by affirming that clubwomen posed no threat to domesticity at the same time that she asserted the vitality and significance of clubs among women of her race, Williams could not counter the claims about African American clubwomen as forcefully as she might have had she occupied a less contested position.

In addition to the distortions of whites, African American clubwomen faced misrepresentations by members of their own race, particularly those who attacked their politics of respectability. Writing about the black aesthetic, Langston Hughes, for instance, called on the image of the "Philadelphia clubwoman [who] is ashamed to say that her race created [jazz]," charging clubwomen with trying to emulate whites instead of valuing and promoting the accomplishments of African Americans.[50] As portrayed by Hughes, clubwomen's attempts to enact the politics of respectability and to define themselves outside the prevailing racist discourses constituted disloyalty to the race. Such claims ignored the significant support clubwomen lent to artists and writers of their own race (including Hughes himself). This distortion of clubwomen's relation to race-specific creativity made it easier to promote an image of the African American clubwomen as engaged in trivial activities.

White middle-class clubwomen, who occupied a more privileged social position, often took a slightly different approach in responding to the media's portrayals of clubwomen. One writer, for example, dismisses negative portrayals of British clubwomen as "utterly irrelevant" to the U.S. context. Instead, she avers, the club movement in the United States is recognized as "one of the most important sociological factors of the time." To support her claim, she turns to an article by a more favorable commentator, who affirms the club movement's "almost simultaneous acceptance throughout the country as a means of education and development" and places it within the context of the great popular educational movement which has swept the country like a tidal wave, manifesting itself in Chautauqua, Summer Schools, University Extension and Societies for Home Study.[51] This tendency to dismiss club criticism as belonging to another era or another place recurs in the publications of white middle-class clubwomen.

Though the media derided them, these clubwomen continued to represent themselves in positive terms. In her history of the North Carolina Federation, for example, Sallie Southall Cotten asserts, "Man has been hard to convince of the difference between men's clubs and women's clubs—one being for pleasure and self-indulgence—the other for culture and reform." She then describes women's clubs as "first derided, then tolerated as a passing fad, then acknowledged as good for women and for the world," with no hint of the negative portrayals that shadowed women's clubs.[52] In 1918, at the fiftieth anniversary of the New England Women's Club, a member looked back on "the sneers and jeers, the hoots of derision and floods of ridicule which greeted the suggestion of such a society," explaining that "many women, who were naturally in favor of this new movement, were deterred from joining the association by the violent opposition of the masculine members of their families." But this woman assigns these attitudes to a distant past, when they were "so universal as to be almost comical" and are "quite so as we look back upon them."[53] While such attempts to ignore or downplay criticism undoubtedly were psychologically valuable to club members, they had little impact on those who created and promulgated negative images of clubwomen.

Even if clubwomen had mounted a more effective counterattack, it is doubtful they could have overcome the forces arrayed against them. The images of clubwomen turning the gendered world upside down, engaging in trivial activities, and attempting to reform the world to conform to their (feminized) vision served a cultural function that extended well beyond any club members. These images aided a process of forgetting essential to the (re)development of the nation.

The substitution of image for memory served the national ethos because it erased the *processes* by which cultural change was effected at the turn of the century. Just as good sewing requires one to pull out the basting after stitching the sleeve into place, so effective cultural work concludes by removing the means by which it was achieved. Forgetting is, as Philip Fisher explains, the last stage in cultural work. Once changes have been effected, "the highest work of culture has been done, but because the last step involves forgetting both the process and its very openness to alternatives or to failure, the history of culture has trouble in later remembering what it is socially and psychologically decisive for it to forget."[54] It became essential for Americans to forget the cultural work of women's clubs in constructing a new ethos and sense of identity for the nation in response to the forces of industrialism, urbanization, and immigration; in fashioning new meanings for *American* and *woman;* in developing responses and alternatives to the commodification that accompanied an expanding capitalism; in (re)negotiating the terms of culture; and in providing a precursor to and exploring the conflicts in the professionalization of English studies. Forgetting the processes by which the nation came to new perspectives on its population(s), economy, position in the world, culture, and professionalization was necessary to incorporate the fruits of that cultural work into the ongoing national life.

Representations of former ages, of course, change with the times. History or what we say about the past has to do with the present more than with what happened at another time. The ways we think about the cultural work of women's clubs reveal more about us than about the thousands of women who inscribed themselves—in spidery tracings in leatherbound books, in typescript on "sermon paper," in calligraphy on rich vellum, in slanted letters in spiral notebooks, in printed yearbooks bound with satin ribbons, in newspapers, magazines, or books, and in scrapbooks filled with photographs and clippings. Living, as we do, in a time when feminism has given new prominence to women's organizations, when literacy plays an even more important and complex role in American culture, and when class, race, ethnicity, and gender figure significantly in discussions of any social formation, we find the texts in clubwomen's records look very different than they did to the women who produced and consumed them. Still Martha White's prophecy that "that which will be recognized as the most significant, as the most far-reaching, will be the movement that is represented by the women's clubs" echoes across time, leaving the question of how new perspectives on clubwomen's cultural work might contend with static images to reshape the public memory about these clubs.

Notes

INTRODUCTION

1   Although some clubs were organized well before 1880, this decade brought the kind of growth that led to the formation of several national associations by the early 1890s. Many clubs have, to be sure, survived to the present, but their numbers and social influence began to dwindle in the 1920s.

2   Mary E. Woolley, "The Woman's Club Woman," *Good Housekeeping* 1 (May 1910): 559–65. Woolley's list of tangible accomplishments includes promoting pure food legislation, establishing programs in domestic science, improving home life, enhancing educational opportunities for children, establishing libraries, advancing the work of juvenile courts and probation officers, supporting the arts, fostering child labor laws, and helping preserve historic and natural landmarks.

3   Karen Blair, *The Clubwoman as Feminist: True Womanhood Redefined, 1868–1914* (New York: Holmes and Meier, 1980), shows how clubwomen redefined womanhood, thereby inserting them into the feminist tradition. Theodora Penny Martin, *The Sound of Their Own Voices: Women's Study Clubs, 1860–1910* (Boston: Beacon, 1987), illustrates how clubs contributed to women's education. Karen Blair, *The Torchbearers: Women and Their Amateur Arts Associations in America, 1890–1930* (Bloomington: Indiana University Press, 1994), documents clubwomen's aesthetic improvements in communities across the country and highlights their insistence that art should be accessible to all. While these books focus on white middle-class groups, Anne Firor Scott, *Natural Allies: Women's Associations in American History* (Urbana: University of Illinois Press, 1991), traces the history of both black and white women's groups that identified and addressed social problems beginning in the late eighteenth century. Such accounts as Faith Rogow, *Gone to Another Meeting: The National Council of Jewish Women, 1893–1993* (Tuscaloosa: University of Alabama Press, 1993); and Paula Giddings, *When and Where I Enter: The Impact of Black Women on Race and Sex in America* (New York: Bantam, 1984), describe the work

271

of specific groups, but they do not consider the larger club movement. In addition to these examinations of women's clubs, such studies as Robyn Muncy, *Creating a Female Dominion in American Reform, 1890–1930* (New York: Oxford University Press, 1991); Glenna Matthews, *The Rise of Public Woman* (New York: Oxford University Press, 1992); and Kathleen McCarthy, *Women's Culture: American Philanthropy and Art, 1830–1930* (Chicago: University of Chicago Press, 1991), assert the historical importance of women's organizations more generally.

4   Nancy Cott, ed., *A Woman Making History: Mary Ritter Beard through Her Letters* (New Haven, Conn.: Yale University Press, 1991), 233.

5   Although such archives as the Sophia Smith Collection and the Radcliffe College Archives were created in the 1940s, they assumed their current shape and status two decades later. The Sophia Smith Collection, with an increasingly large proportion of its holdings taking the form of unpublished records, moved to new quarters in 1962, and the Radcliffe Collection, renamed the Schlesinger Library, similarly expanded its collection of unpublished papers and moved to its present location in 1967. These material changes signaled a larger intellectual trend toward feminist perspectives that transformed such unpublished materials as club records into historical documents essential in considering women's cultural roles. Numbers illustrate the increased scholarly value assigned to such archives. Research visits to the Schlesinger, for example, increased from 7 in 1949, to 247 in 1969, to 4,400 in 1983, and over 6,000 in 1992. Schlesinger Library, Fiftieth Anniversary Report, 1983, 2, 7, Schlesinger Library, Radcliffe College, Cambridge, Mass.; Jane Knowles, Letter to Anne Gere, August 6, 1992. The number of accessions by archives themselves also grew as women, newly aware of the historical value of their materials, deposited them with increased frequency.

6   Michel de Certeau, *The Practice of Everyday Life,* trans. Steven Rendall (Berkeley: University of California Press, 1984), argues that everyday practices (a category in which club literacy practices might be included) usually constitute the obscure background of social activity and thereby remain more or less invisible (xi). In conducting the research for this book, I encountered this as well as pride in and neglect of materials. In response to chance remarks, I was led to closets or basements where records were stuffed, with no apparent sense of their value, in paper bags or stacked in heaps. Conversely, through special intercessions, I was allowed to read records still held by clubs that wished their carefully catalogued records to remain private.

7   Helen Hooven Santmyer, *And Ladies of the Club* (New York: Putnam, 1984), reinforced the racist and classist stereotype for contemporary readers. Passing reference to Native American and Catholic women's clubs is included here, despite only a small number of the former and the post-1920 establishment of the latter. As Paula M. Kane, *Separatism and Subculture: Boston Catholicism, 1900–1920* (Chapel Hill: University of North Carolina Press, 1994), shows, Catholic wom-

en's clubs remained largely under the control of male religious leaders until the formation of the National Council of Catholic Women in 1920. Clubs formed by German, Hispanic, Slavic, and other groups of women who conducted most of their work in a language other than English are not included. For consideration of such groups, see, for example, Nancy A. Hewitt, "Varieties of Voluntarism: Class, Ethnicity and Women's Activism in Tampa," in *Women, Politics, and Change,* ed. Louise A. Tilly and Patricia Gurin (New York: Russell Sage Foundation, 1990), 63–86; and Diava Markelis, "Union Halls and Church Pews: Language and Literacy among Early Chicago Lithuanians" (Ph.D. diss., University of Illinois at Chicago, forthcoming). Single issue groups, such as the Woman's Christian Temperance Union and the National American Woman Suffrage Association, also fall outside the purview of this study.

8   Evelyn Brooks Higginbotham, *Righteous Discontent: The Women's Movement in the Black Baptist Church, 1880–1920* (Cambridge, Mass.: Harvard University Press, 1993), shows that the Baptist Women's Convention did not achieve the fiscal and programmatic autonomy of women's clubs.

9   Deborah Golomb, "The 1893 Congress of Jewish Women: Evolution or Revolution in American Jewish Women's History?" *American Jewish History* 70 (September 1980): 65.

10   Mary McCleary, "100th Anniversary," Naugatuck Study Club of Naugatuck, Connecticut, privately held. Topics in the 1915–16 Yearbook of the Detroit Catholic Study Club, Burton Collection, Detroit Public Library, Detroit, Mich., include "Science and Invention by Catholics" and "Why We Celebrate St. Patrick's Day."

11   Jane Tompkins, *Sensational Designs: The Cultural Work of American Fiction, 1790–1860* (New York: Oxford University Press, 1985), defines cultural work as "expressing and shaping the social context" (200); and Philip Fisher, *Hard Facts: Setting and Form in the American Novel* (New York: Oxford University Press, 1985), asserts that it "stabilizes and incorporates nearly ungraspable or widely various states of moral or representational or perceptual experience" (3). Although both Tompkins and Fisher focus on the cultural work accomplished by literature, I extend the term to include the literacy practices of clubwomen.

12   Clubs explored suffrage, but they gave it little public support. The General Federation of Women's Clubs did not endorse woman suffrage until 1914, the National Council of Jewish Women defeated a resolution in favor of suffrage in 1917, and racism prevented full cooperation between the National Association of Colored Women and the National American Woman Suffrage Association. Mormon clubwomen, who obtained the vote in 1870 when Utah was still a territory, did, however, assume leadership in suffrage work.

13   The General Federation of Women's Clubs claimed a membership of two million in the early 1920s, but Blair, *Torchbearers,* estimates that the actual membership was closer to one million (200). Rogow, *Gone to Another Meeting,* puts coun-

cil membership at 50,000 during the same period. Giddings, *When and Where I Enter,* estimates another 50,000 for the National Association of Colored Women. Joanne Reitano, "Working Girls Unite," *American Quarterly* 36 (Spring 1984), claims that membership in the National League of Women Workers reached approximately 14,000, with most of it concentrated in eastern cities (115). At least an equal number of women from these various backgrounds, plus smaller numbers of Mormon, Catholic, and American Indian women, belonged to clubs that maintained no national affiliation.

14 Ruth Frankenberg, *White Women, Race Matters: The Social Construction of Whiteness* (Minneapolis: University of Minnesota Press, 1993), argues that race shapes white women's lives just as it does those of other populations. Other commentators on whiteness as a racial category include Noel Ignatiev, *How the Irish Became White* (New York: Routledge, 1995); David Roediger, *The Wages of Whiteness: Race and the Making of the American Working Class* (London: Verso, 1991) and *Towards the Abolition of Whiteness* (London: Verso, 1995); and Vron Ware, *Beyond the Pale: White Women, Racism and History* (London: Verso, 1992).

15 Josephine Ruffin represented the Woman's Era Club, which had been accepted into the General Federation before the board realized it had an African American membership. The acceptance was subsequently rescinded, and Ruffin was denied admission as the Woman's Era Club's representative, although she could have entered as an individual. Apologists for the General Federation's actions argued that the new and relatively fragile organization would face a mass exodus by clubs from the South if an African American club were admitted.

16 Mary Gay Humphreys, "The New York Working-Girl," *Scribner's Magazine* 9 (October 1896), portrays Jews as nonwhite (507).

17 Josephine St. Pierre Ruffin, "Address," *Woman's Era* 2 (August 1895): 14.

18 Luretta Rainey, *History of Oklahoma State Federation of Women's Clubs* (Guthrie, Okla.: Co-Operative Publishing, 1939), 275–76.

19 Grover Cleveland, "Woman's Mission and Woman's Clubs," *Ladies' Home Journal* 22 (May 1905): 3–4. Cleveland misnamed the General Federation of Women's Clubs as the "National Federation of Women's Clubs" and described it as primarily concerned with suffrage.

20 Fannie Barrier Williams, "Some Perils of Women's Clubs," *New York Age,* December 28, 1905, 3; Rogow, *Gone to Another Meeting,* 33.

21 Quoted in Abbie Graham, *Grace H. Dodge: Merchant of Dreams* (New York: Woman's Press, 1926), 84–85.

22 Edith Howes, "History of the League," *Club Worker* 7 (January 1906): 555. Known as the Association of Working Girls' Clubs from 1885 to 1897, from 1897 to 1899 it was called the National League of Associations of Working Women's Clubs. Here, for simplicity, the National League of Women Workers refers to the league after 1897.

23 "Opinions about Names," *Woman's Exponent* 21 (April 15 and May 1, 1893): 153 (quote); Rogow, *Gone to Another Meeting,* 93.

24 Ella Giles Ruddy, *The Mother of Clubs, Caroline M. Seymour Severance: An Estimate and an Appreciation* (Los Angeles: Farmgardt, 1906), 24.

25 To be sure, some groups retained the more prestigious term with names like the Ladies' Literary Society, but the great majority used the term *woman* to designate themselves.

26 Michael J. Shapiro, *The Politics of Representation: Writing Practices in Biography, Photography, and Policy Analysis* (Madison: University of Wisconsin Press, 1988), ix.

27 Mary Jean Houde, *Reaching Out: A Story of the General Federation of Women's Clubs* (Chicago: Mobium, 1989), 58.

28 Joan G. Zimmerman, "Daughters of Main Street: Culture and the Female Community at Grinnel, 1884–1917," in *Woman's Being, Woman's Place: Female Identity and Vocation in American History,* ed. Mary Kelley (Boston: G. K. Hall, 1979), 162.

29 The *Woman's Exponent* contains several references to favorable notice in the *Woman's Cycle.* See also *Far and Near* 3 (February 1893): 83. The *Woman's Exponent* was clearly the more progressive publication and included regular reports of Cleophan and meetings of the Reapers' Club and the Utah Woman's Press Club, but the *Young Woman's Journal* also published accounts of General Federation clubs and members, and both actively encouraged women to write and publish in their pages. Neither the *Exponent* nor the *Journal* survived long into the twentieth century. The *Exponent* was replaced by the church-controlled *Relief Society Magazine* in 1914, and the *Journal* was merged with the church's *Improvement Era* in 1929. The growing conservatism of the Mormon church after statehood was achieved in 1896 may help account for the demise of these two publications.

30 *Federation Bulletin* 3 (January 1906): 201.

31 The 1906–7 Yearbook of the New York Section, Papers of the New York Section of the National Council of Jewish Women, privately held, includes this report from the Press Committee: "During the past year two hundred notices were sent to the press and your Committee wishes to express its appreciation of the uniform courtesies extended to it by all the papers, in particular, *The Post, The Evening Mail, the Tribune, the Times, The Herald, The Globe*" (45). The 1913–14 Yearbook contains this: "From the press we have received courteous treatment, for which we heartily express our thanks. Our Committee has worked hard, and I hope that next year we will have even more extended notice. We need it" (37).

32 Ann Mauger Calbert, "New Women and New Journalism: A Look at Women's Editions" (Paper presented at Association for Education in Journalism and Mass Communication History Division, Kansas City, Mo., August 11, 1993).

33 "The League," *Club Worker* 4 (January 1903): 67.

34 *Federation Bulletin* 1 (November 1903): 2.

35 Michael Warner, *The Letters of the Republic: Publication and the Public Sphere in Eighteenth-Century America* (Cambridge, Mass.: Harvard University Press, 1990), xiii.

36 Ellen DuBois, "Politics and Culture in Women's History: A Symposium," *Feminist Studies* 6 (Spring 1980): 26–36, distinguishes between women's culture and fem-

inism, warning that questions of culture may replace questions of politics. My use of the term *culture* here does not mean women's culture in the apolitical sense; rather, it conceives of clubs as a force for social change.

37   See Mary S. Cunningham, *The Woman's Club of El Paso: Its First Thirty Years* (El Paso: Texas Western Press, 1978), ix; Jennie June Cunningham Croly, *The History of the Woman's Club Movement in America* (New York: Henry G. Allen, 1898); and Julia Ward Howe, "Culture," Minutes of the Saturday Morning Club, December 2, 1871, Papers of the Saturday Morning Club of Boston, Schlesinger Library, Radcliffe College, Cambridge, Mass., for early affirmations of women's self-improvement. Croly and Howe were founding members of Sorosis and the New England Women's Club respectively (both clubs were founded in 1867). Howe, in the 1871 club paper titled "Culture" defined "selfish culture" as "solitary study" and encouraged clubwomen to make culture the special object of club work.

38   Croly, *History of the Woman's Club Movement in America*, 9.

39   Ibid., 2, 11, 13.

40   Contemporary historians often emulate Croly's model by describing clubs as moving from the selfishness of self-improvement to the altruism of community service. As Mary Ryan, *Womanhood in America: From Colonial Times to the Present* (New York: Viewpoints, 1975), traces the "progression" from textual focus to community projects, she writes, "The little bands of women's reading groups across the country were organized into the massive General Federation of Women's Clubs in 1890. Within a few years the GFWC leaders were asking 'Is there not room in the clubs for outlook committees whose business it should be to investigate township affairs, educational, sanitary, reformatory?'" (230). Similarly, Golomb, "The 1893 Congress of Jewish Women," writes, "Originally a literary society, the women's club later evolved into an organization that sponsored a vast array of reform programs" (57).

41   Three articles, written between 1892 and 1909, trace the changing terms in which clubwomen's literacy practices were represented. Julia Holmes Smith, "The Woman's Club as an Agent of Philanthropy," *Arena* 6 (August 1892) describes the evolution from reading and writing to community service this way: "A club is formed in somebody's parlor for mutual council, for higher culture, for art, for literature; and after a while, the leaven of association working, results began to appear, not merely in the betterment of the individuals composing the club, but in the philanthropics which were the outgrowth of the organization" (383). Although Smith acknowledges a progression from one set of activities to another, she portrays philanthropy as an outgrowth of, not a replacement for, the activities fostering "the betterment of the individuals" in the club. Mary S. Gibson, *A Record of Twenty-Five Years of the California Federation of Women's Clubs, 1900–1925* (Los Angeles: California Federation of Women's Clubs, 1927), takes an approach more in keeping with Croly's model. Noting that in 1892 clubwomen had emphasized intellectual development and describing the club that pursued such lit-

eracy practices as a "resting place from the absorbing activities of life," she continues, "And now, just eight years after this restful decision by the General Federation of Women's Clubs, the far western California women found themselves listening to a strenuous program which offered much responsibility and no period of rest" (11). By describing literacy practices as preceding service and remaining passive compared with its "strenuous program," Gibson creates a dichotomy between study and service activities, implying the superiority of the one over the other. Mary Bronson Hartt, "Work for Women's Clubs to Do," *Good Housekeeping* 49 (September 1909), writes, "Clubwomen are not yet doing a thousandth part of what they might do. Self-culture clubs still linger complacently in communities where they are no longer needed. But they are distinctly on the wane and in their place spring up organizations which mean business" (245). Hartt continued with a long list of possible projects, including improving the ethics of domestic service, enacting pure food laws, enhancing police and fire protection, establishing traveling libraries, and improving arts and crafts. Gibson's implied dichotomy between study and service clubs finds full expression here, with the former denigrated as useless while the latter offers tangible benefits to the larger community. In urging that study clubs be replaced by organizations devoted to service, Hartt typifies a form of self-representation that had gained a firm footing by 1909. Realizing that social approval accrued from their tangible contributions to the community, most clubwomen highlighted their service and said little about their literary practices.

42 Edith Isaacs, "What American Jewesses Are Doing for America," *Watson's Jeffersonian Magazine* 2, no. 7 (1912): 355.

43 Kate Rotan, "Of What Use Is a Federation Organ?" *Federation Bulletin* 3 (March 1905): 194. "Editorial," *Federation Bulletin* 3 (December 1905), observed that self-culture upholds the other activities of clubs: "It is possible that nearly all our organizations were study clubs to begin with, and it is more than probable that many of them will best be held together by continuing the policy by which they first attracted the attention of their members" (100).

44 True Worthy White, "Report of Literature Department," *General Federation of Women's Clubs Magazine* 17 (September 1918): 11.

45 Roger Chartier, "The Practical Impact of Writing," in *Passions of the Renaissance*, vol. 3 of *A History of Private Life,* ed. Roger Chartier (Cambridge, Mass.: Harvard University Press, 1989), 137.

46 Nancy Fraser, "Rethinking the Public Sphere: A Contribution to the Critique of Actually Existing Democracy," *Social Text* 8/9, no. 3/1 (1990): 56–80.

47 Amanda Vickery, "Historiographical Review: Golden Age to Separate Spheres? A Review of the Categories and Chronology of English Women's History," *Historical Journal* 36, no. 2 (1993): 383–414, calls into question the systematic use of "separate spheres" as the organizing concept in the history of middle-class women.

48 Lauren Berlant, *The Anatomy of National Fantasy: Hawthorne, Utopia, and Everyday Life* (Chicago: University of Chicago Press, 1991).

49 Raymond Williams, *Culture and Society, 1780–1950* (1958; reprint, New York: Columbia University Press, 1983), 233.

CHAPTER 1: LITERACY AND INTIMACY

1 The Chinese Exclusion Act (1882), the Foran Act (1885), and the 1888 order to deport all alien contract laborers within one year of entry exemplify the restrictions imposed on immigration beginning in the 1880s.

2 *Congressional Record,* 64th Cong., 2d sess., 1917, 54, pt. 1:877.

3 The 1906 Naturalization Act established procedural standards for transforming aliens into citizens, and it required the alien to file a petition "in writing, signed by the applicant in his own handwriting." Prior to 1906 the variation in procedures made immigrants vulnerable to manipulation by political party bosses. Arnold H. Leibowitz, "The Official Character of Language in the United States: Literacy Requirements for Immigration, Citizenship, and Entrance into American Life," *Azlan* 15 (Spring 1984), argues that proponents of the 1917 bill, "unwilling to argue for racial restrictions . . .struck upon the device of a literacy test" to promote their desire to restrict immigrants who were "unlike the British, German, and other peoples who came during the period prior to 1880"(35, 36).

4 Benedict Anderson, *Imagined Communities: Reflections on the Origin and Spread of Nationalism* (London: Verso, 1983), 49.

5 Rita J. Simon, *Public Opinion and the Immigrant: Print Media Coverage, 1880–1980* (Lexington, Mass.: D. C. Heath, 1985), 72.

6 The first Morrill Land Grant Act, passed in 1862, provided land for agricultural colleges, but the 1890 version added funding for coeducational institutions and colleges serving African Americans.

7 Janet Duitsman Cornelius, *When I Can Read My Title Clear: Literacy, Slavery, and Religion in the Antebellum South* (Columbia: University of South Carolina Press, 1991), quotes the Louisiana slave code of 1830: "all persons who shall teach or permit or cause to be taught, any slave in this State to read or write, shall be imprisoned not less than one or more than twelve months"; she also notes that an 1830 North Carolina law forbade teaching or giving books to slaves because such teaching "has a tendency to excite dissatisfaction in their minds and produce insurrection" (32).

8 Michael Warner, *The Letters of the Republic: Publication and the Public Sphere in Eighteenth-Century America* (Cambridge, Mass.: Harvard University Press, 1990), 12.

9 Thomas Holt, "'Knowledge is Power': The Black Struggle for Literacy," in *The Right to Literacy,* ed. Andrea A. Lunsford, Helene Moglen, and James Slevin (New York: Modern Language Association, 1990), 91–102. Holt draws on James Anderson,

The Education of Blacks in the South, 1860–1935 (Chapel Hill: University of North Carolina Press, 1988). Cornelius, *When I Can Read,* writes that "black people themselves were responsible for founding and perpetuating most of their educational efforts in the South" (150).

10   S. Elizabeth Frazier, "Mrs. Wm. E. Matthews," *Woman's Era* 1 (May 1, 1894): 1.

11   Minutes of the Women in Council, November 26, 1907, Papers of the Women in Council of Roxbury, Manuscript Division, Boston Public Library, Boston, Mass.

12   François Furet and Jacques Ouzouf, *Reading and Writing: Literacy in France from Calvin to Jules Ferry* (Cambridge: Cambridge University Press, 1982), 308, 310.

13   E. Jennifer Monaghan, "Literacy Instruction and Gender in Colonial New England," in *Reading in America: Literature and Social History,* ed. Cathy N. Davidson (Baltimore: Johns Hopkins University Press, 1989), explains that beginning in the seventeenth century instruction in reading always preceded and frequently precluded the teaching of writing, comprehension was ignored or assumed, and "since the child did not write in the course of learning to read; the teacher did not need to know how to write either" (58).

14   Minutes of the Saturday Morning Club, November 28, 1874, Papers of the Saturday Morning Club of Boston, Schlesinger Library, Radcliffe College, Cambridge, Mass. The importance attached to Gray's speech is indicated by the fact that it appears in its entirety in the minutes, whereas the secretary usually summarized the major points of club speeches.

15   Margaret Sanger, "Women's Clubs," *Harper's Bazaar* 26 (July 8, 1893): 547.

16   Margaret Manton Merrill, "Sorosis," *Cosmopolitan* 15 (June 1893): 158.

17   Bylaws of the Saturday Morning Club, 1885, Papers of the Saturday Morning Club of Boston. This item remains in the bylaws.

18   *Young Woman's Journal* 1 (December 1889): 83. The essay contest was instituted in 1896. This publication also featured such columns as "Advice for Young Writers" and "Helps for Young Writers," which encouraged readers to see themselves as writers. *Young Woman's Journal* 1 (February 1890): 191; 3 (April 1892): 266; 8 (September 1897): 519–21.

19   "Thoughts from Club Members," *Far and Near* 2 (April and May 1892): 115, 146.

20   Quoted in Lillian D. Wald, *The House on Henry Street* (New York: Henry Holt, 1915), 305–6.

21   Wald, *House on Henry Street,* 305.

22   Quoted in Abbie Graham, *Grace H. Dodge: Merchant of Dreams* (New York: Woman's Press, 1926), 132.

23   "The Value of a Public School Education," *Club Worker* 3 (June 1901): 5; "Why Women Earn Smaller Wages than Men," *Club Worker* 4 (January 1903): 63; "What Is Domestic Science?" *Club Worker* 4 (June 1903): 158; "Women and Men as Employers," *Club Worker* 7 (May 1906): 465–69.

24   "What Makes a Club Most Enjoyable," *Club Worker* 6 (June 1904): 370.

25 "Illiterate Children," *Club Worker* 4 (July 1903): 171.

26 "Report of Housing Conditions in Massachusetts," *Club Worker* 7 (May 1906): 485–86.

27 Cornelius, *When I Can Read,* 102.

28 Florida Ridley, "Opportunities and Privileges of Club Life," *Woman's Era* 3 (October/November 1896): 10.

29 Quoted in Cynthia Neverdon-Morton, "The Black Woman's Struggle for Equality in the South, 1895–1925," in *The Afro-American Woman: Struggles and Images,* ed. Sharon Harley and Rosalyn Terborg-Penn (Port Washington, N.Y.: Kennikat, 1978), 46. See also Cynthia Neverdon-Morton, *Afro-American Women of the South and the Advancement of the Race, 1895–1925* (Knoxville: University of Tennessee Press, 1989).

30 Minutes of the Detroit Section, November 5, 1905, Papers of the Detroit Section of the National Council of Jewish Women, Reuther Collection, Detroit Public Library, Detroit, Mich. (Although the club was originally called the Jewish Woman's Club of Detroit, I use the contemporary designation.)

31 This alternative form of publication can be seen as parallel to the alternative construction of professionalism such settlement movement women as Jane Addams, Lillian Wald, and Florence Kelley effected. As Robyn Muncy, *Creating a Female Dominion in American Reform, 1890–1935* (New York: Oxford University Press, 1991), has shown, these women and their colleagues created a female professionalism that endured from the turn of the century to the enactment of New Deal legislation.

32 During World War I many clubs adopted alternative means of conveying information about their annual program. Some, such as the Decatur Art Club, produced handwritten yearbooks, while others sent members postcards about upcoming meetings. Mary S. Cunningham, *The Woman's Club of El Paso: Its First Thirty Years* (El Paso: Texas Western Press, 1978), writes that in 1918–19 the Woman's Club of El Paso did not print a yearbook "but used the one from the previous year with a small leaflet inserted with a list of the programs for the current year" (179).

33 Warner, *Letters of the Republic,* 8.

34 Eleanor Benson, "History of the Monday Club," Papers of the Monday Club of Clinton, New York, Archive Division, Hamilton College Library, Clinton, N.Y.

35 Minutes of the Chautauqua Circle, October 10, 1913, Papers of the Chautauqua Circle of Atlanta, Robert W. Woodruff Library, Atlanta University, Atlanta, Ga., include this: "Mrs Johnson spoke of the yearbook which was mentioned at the last meeting. It met with the approval of the Circle and it was voted that we have them." Minutes for November 25, 1913, report, "A motion was carried that the secretary send a yearbook to the honorary members of the circle." Minutes for December 19, 1913, report, "A vote of thanks was extended the program committee for the excellent yearbooks."

36   Minutes of the Woman's Improvement Club, September 24, 1909, Papers of the Woman's Improvement Club of Indianapolis, W. H. Smith Memorial Library, Indiana Historical Society, Indianapolis.

37   "Women's Papers," *Woman's Exponent* 21 (January 15, 1893): 111. *Stake* is the term used to describe the area served by a given church.

38   "Club Notes," *Far and Near* 1 (November 1890), includes a report from the New Century Guild of Working Women in Philadelphia that "all the type-setting for our own paper is now done by our own compositors" (16). Ava Baron, "The Masculinization of Production: The Gendering of Work and Skill in Newspaper Printing, 1850–1920," in *Gendered Domains: Rethinking Public and Private in Women's History,* ed. Dorothy O. Helly and Susan M. Reverby (Ithaca, N.Y.: Cornell University Press, 1992), explains that the printing industry was the site of considerable dispute between men and women during the 1890s, which makes this form of textual production particularly significant.

39   Grover Cleveland, "Woman's Mission and Woman's Clubs," *Ladies' Home Journal* 22 (May 1905): 3–4.

40   "Mr. Cleveland and Club Women," *Federation Bulletin* 2 (May 1905): 251–53.

41   "Men's Views of Women's Clubs: A Symposium by Men Who Are Recognized Leaders in the Philanthropic and Reform Movements of America," *Federation Bulletin* 2 (June 1905): 289, 292–96. The list of prominent men included Josiah Strong, president of American Institute of Social Service; William Dudley Foulke, U.S. Civil Service commissioner; E. G. Routzahn, secretary of the Civic Cooperation, Chicago; Samuel McCune Lindsay, secretary of the National Child Labor Committee; Homer Folks, vice-chairman of the National Child Labor Committee; Ben B. Lindsey, judge in the Denver Juvenile Court; Clinton Rogers Woodruff, secretary of the National Municipal League; Thomas Balliet, dean of the School of Pedagogy, New York University; James B. Angell, president of the University of Michigan; W. L. Bodine, superintendent of Compulsory Education, Chicago; and Calvin Milton Woodward, president of the Board of Education, St. Louis.

42   "Editorial," *Federation Bulletin* 4 (October 1906): 1.

43   Olive M. Foltz, "Eightieth Anniversary—Women's Study Club" (Paper presented at the Naugatuck Study Club, September 19, 1974), Papers of the Naugatuck Study Club of Naugatuck, Connecticut, privately held.

44   *National Association Notes* 3 (April 1900): 1.

45   National Association of Colored Women, *Press Comments: The Second Convention of the National Association of Colored Women Held in Quinn Chapel, Chicago Ill., August 14, 15 and 16, 1899* (Washington, D.C.: National Association of Colored Women, 1900), Papers of Mary Church Terrell, Moorland-Spingarn Research Center, Howard University, Washington, D.C.

46   Kate Flint, *The Woman Reader, 1837–1914* (Oxford: Oxford University Press, 1993), 22.

47 Monaghan, "Literacy Instruction," discusses the gendered literacy pedagogy during the colonial period.

48 Edward H. Clarke, *Sex in Education: A Fair Chance for Girls* (Boston: Osgood, 1873), made a widely imitated argument about the dangers of extended study to the female reproductive system. The "Pastoral Letter" of the General Association of Massachusetts Preachers argued that education would estrange women from their Christian-defined role of dependence, "from the consciousness of that weakness which God has given for her protection," and move her away from helping to "form the character of individuals and of the nation." This move would, in addition to threatening her salvation, lead a woman to abrogate her responsibilities to her family and to the development of her children's characters. Quoted in Thomas Woody, *A History of Women's Education in the United States* (New York: Science, 1929), 423.

49 Flint, *Woman Reader,* 57.

50 *Proceedings of the First Convention of the National Council of Jewish Women, New York, 1896 Nov. 15–19* (Philadelphia: Jewish Publication Society of America, 1897), 67.

51 Elise M. Wilbor, ed., *Delsarte Recitation Book and Directory* (New York: E. S. Werner, 1897); Anna Morgan, *An Hour with Delsarte: A Study of Expression* (Boston: Lee and Shepard, 1895); Charles Darwin, *The Expression of the Emotions in Man and Animals* (New York: Appleton, 1896).

52 "U. W.P. Club," *Woman's Exponent* 22 (September 15, 1893): 35. "The Cleofan," *Woman's Exponent* 26 (March 15 and April 1, 1898), states that members of the Cleofan Club frequently enjoyed "character readings" from Shakespeare's plays (259).

53 "Charleston, W. VA. Club Notes," *National Association Notes* 3 (April 1900): 3.

54 "Plays for the Asking," *Club Worker* 1 (February 1899): 4.

55 Martha Banta, *Imaging American Women: Ideas and Ideals in Cultural History* (New York: Columbia University Press, 1987), 643.

56 Elizabeth Long, "Textual Interpretation as Collective Action," in *The Ethnography of Reading,* ed. Jonathan Boyarin (Berkeley: University of California Press, 1993), 191.

57 Linda Brodkey, *Academic Writing as Social Practice* (Philadelphia: Temple University Press, 1987), vii.

58 Deborah Brandt, *Literacy as Involvement: The Acts of Writers, Readers, and Texts* (Carbondale: Southern Illinois University Press, 1990), 126, 114.

59 Minutes of the Friday Club, September 20, 1889, Papers of the Friday Club of Jackson, Michigan, Bentley Historical Library, University of Michigan, Ann Arbor. Comparisons can be drawn between women's clubs and the medieval textual communities described in Brian Stock, *Listening for the Text on the Uses of the Past* (Baltimore: Johns Hopkins University Press, 1990). Stock stipulates oral contact, educative process, and self-historicizing as the central features of such communities, and women's clubs have all of these features.

60 Minutes of the Monday Club, 1917–18, Papers of the Monday Club of Clinton, New York. The Friday Club of Jackson, Michigan, always read texts aloud, stopping to comment and question.

61 Barbara Sicherman, "Sense and Sensibility: A Case Study of Women's Reading in Late-Victorian America," in *Reading in America: Literature and Social History* (Baltimore: Johns Hopkins University Press, 1989), 202.

62 Willis Buckingham, "Poetry Readers and Reading in the 1890's: Emily Dickinson's First Reception," in *Readers in History: Nineteenth-Century American Literature and the Contexts of Response,* ed. James L. Machor (Baltimore: Johns Hopkins University Press, 1993), 173.

63 Charles Harris Wesley, *The History of the National Association of Colored Women's Clubs: A Legacy of Service* (Washington D.C.: National Association of Colored Women, 1984), 9.

64 Muriel Beadle and the Centennial History Committee, *The Fortnightly of Chicago: The City and Its Women, 1873–1973,* ed. Fanny Butcher (Chicago: Henry Regnery, 1973), 155.

65 Minutes of the Friday Club of Jackson, Michigan, November 8, 1889.

66 Julie Innes, *Privacy, Intimacy, and Isolation* (New York: Oxford University Press, 1992), 90.

67 Anthony Giddens, *The Transformation of Intimacy: Sexuality, Love, and Eroticism in Modern Societies* (Stanford, Calif.: Stanford University Press, 1992), asserts that "intimacy is about sex and gender, but it is not limited to them" (96). I am grateful to Walter Mignolo for calling Giddens's work to my attention. Judith M. Bennett, "The L-word in Women's History" (Paper presented to Feminist Women in History, University of North Carolina, September 1993), describes as "lesbian-like," behaviors including cross-dressing, having profound attachments to other women, and remaining unmarried. Bennett's insistence on a more complicated meaning for lesbian or lesbian-like behavior stands in contrast to the perspective articulated by Helen Horowitz, *Alma Mater: Design and Experience in the Women's Colleges from Their Nineteenth-Century Beginnings to the 1930's* (New York: Alfred A. Knopf, 1984), who argues against defining women who choose to nurture women as lesbian: "The approach distorts the past. It poses a dichotomy unfamiliar to the late nineteenth and early twentieth centuries, dividing human beings into those who are heterosexual and those who are homosexual. It presumes that within each category those who choose each other as loving partners freely express themselves sexually" (188).

68 Innes, *Privacy, Intimacy, and Isolation,* 82, 90.

69 Solomon quoted in Deborah Golomb, "The 1893 Congress of Jewish Women: Evolution or Revolution in American Jewish Women's History?" *American Jewish History* 70 (September 1980): 58; "The Clubable Woman," *Harper's Bazaar* 8 (April 24, 1897): 338.

70   Jennie June Cunningham Croly, *The History of the Woman's Club Movement in America* (New York: Henry G. Allen, 1898), lists the Reverend C. C. Shackford, the Reverend Jacob Manning, Thomas Wentworth Higginson, and Ralph Waldo Emerson among those attending the first annual meeting of the New England Women's Club (38). Records of the Ladies' Literary Club of Ypsilanti, Bentley Historical Library, University of Michigan, Ann Arbor, include a history of the club written by the Reverend Harvey Colburn in 1922.

71   Florence Randolph, "An Appeal to Our Club Women to Observe the Fourth Sunday in January and July as Days of United Prayer," *National Association Notes* 19 (January 1917): 5–6.

72   "U.W.P. Club," *Woman's Exponent* 21 (April 15 and May 1, 1893): 155. Heather Symmes Cannon, "Practical Politicians," in *Mormon Sisters: Women in Early Utah,* ed. Claudia L. Bushman (Salt Lake City: Olympus, 1976), suggests that the liberal Mormon attitudes toward woman suffrage and education might have been part of the church's strategy to overcome antipathy toward polygamy (170–74). My own reading of Mormon clubwomen's complicated position in relation to the church supports her claim. Mormon clubwomen simultaneously supported and chafed against the church patriarchy, but when faced with external discrimination, they rallied to support their faith by demonstrating that its doctrines did not render them passive and subservient. Woman suffrage in Utah did, of course, increase the number of voters in the territory who supported Mormon doctrine.

73   "Spiritual Side of Club Life," *Club Worker* 10 (June 1909): 927.

74   May Wright Sewall, "The General Federation of Women's Clubs," in "Women's Clubs—A Symposium" *Arena* 6 (August 1892): 364.

75   The tenacity of these divisions is evident in my recollection that my mother's white middle-class Protestant club described itself as "integrating" when it invited a Catholic woman to join the group in the 1950s. Paula Kane, *Separatism and Subculture: Boston Catholicism, 1900–1920* (Chapel Hill: University of North Carolina Press, 1994), observes that religious leaders discouraged Catholic women from "joining non-Catholic clubs such as Sorosis, from affiliating with labor groups such as the Women's Educational and Industrial Union, and from membership in political societies such as the New England Woman's Suffrage Association" (206).

76   Carla L. Peterson, *Doers of the Word: African-American Women Speakers and Writers in the North, 1830–1880* (New York: Oxford University Press, 1995), 9. The blurred class lines among African American clubwomen are evident in the strained economic circumstances of many "middle-class" members. Records show wide disparities between the financial resources of white and black "middle-class" clubs, and such accounts as Alice Dunbar-Nelson's (see Gloria T. Hull, ed., *Give Us Each Day: The Diary of Alice Dunbar-Nelson* [New York: W. W. Norton, 1984]) indicate the precarious economic lives of many African American clubwomen.

77   "Editorial," *Far and Near* 2 (April and May 1892): 107.

78   Baron, "Masculinization of Production," details how unions effected this masculinizing process in one industry.

79   For example, Ronald Story, *The Forging of an Aristocracy: Harvard and the Boston Upper Class, 1800–1870* (Middletown, Conn.: Wesleyan University Press, 1980), asserts that "religion was a factor in the development of a culturally coherent . . . elite" as he recounts the emergence of leading families in Boston (7).

80   Minutes of the Women in Council of Roxbury, February 9, 1889, December 30, 1892, November 12, 1919. Minutes of April 22, 1892, include the assertion that "Christianity makes our condition what it is today."

81   Lydia D. Alder, "For My Dear Friend, Camilla C. Cobb, on the Death of Her Darling Gracie," *Woman's Exponent* 21 (April 15 and May 1, 1893): 166.

82   "Biographical Sketch of Mrs. Elmina S. Taylor, President of the Y.L.M.I. Associations," *Young Woman's Journal* 2 (October 1890): 1.

83   "Personals," *National Association Notes* 19 (January 1917): 10.

84   Westin quoted in Innes, *Privacy, Intimacy, and Isolation*, 57; Michael G. Cooks, *Afro-American Literature in the Twentieth Century: The Achievement of Intimacy* (New Haven, Conn.: Yale University Press, 1984.

85   Quoted in Lynda Faye Dickson, "The Early Club Movement among Black Women in Denver, 1890–1925" (Ph.D. diss., University of Colorado, 1982), 155.

86   The Nineteenth Century Club of Oak Park, Illinois, still keeps all its records in the clubhouse, and the executive committee controls and supervises access to them. The same is true for the Decatur (Illinois) Art Club, the Naugatuck (Connecticut) Study Club, the New York Section of the National Council of Jewish Women, and the Woman's Club of Olympia, Washington, where I also received permission to read club materials.

87   Minutes of the Chautauqua Circle of Atlanta, August 17, 1917; Minutes of the Friday Club of Jackson, Michigan, September 20, 1889; "Biographical Sketch of Mrs. Elmina S. Taylor," *Young Woman's Journal* 2 (October 1890): 1; "Friendly Workers," *Far and Near* 3 (March 1893): 103; "Mrs. May Alden Ward," *General Federation of Women's Clubs Magazine* 17 (February 1918): 26.

88   Gilman quoted in Cunningham, *Woman's Club of El Paso*, 73; Luretta Rainey, *History of Oklahoma State Federation of Women's Clubs* (Guthrie, Okla.: Co-Operative Publishing, 1939), 224.

89   "The Small Club: Its Advantages," *Club Worker* 2 (March 1900): 1–2.

90   Edith M. Howes, [no title], *Club Worker* 5 (November 1903): 12.

91   Paul Tournier, *The Meaning of Gifts* (Richmond, Va.: John Knox, 1961), 39.

92   Minutes of the Woman's Improvement Club of Indianapolis, April 1, 1909.

93   Minutes of the Sorosis Club of New York, October 31, 1885, Papers of the Sorosis Club, Sophia Smith Collection, Smith College, Northampton, Mass.

94   Julia Ward Howe, "A Chronicle of Boston Clubs," *New England Magazine* 36 (July 1906): 613.

95   1911 Yearbook of the New York Section, 71, Papers of New York Section of the National Council of Jewish Women, privately held.

96   Frank Norris, "The 'English' Classes at the University of California" (1896), in *The Origins of Literary Studies in America: A Documentary Anthology,* ed. Gerald Graff and Michael Warner (New York: Routledge, 1989), speaks derisively about club-women consuming "cake and lemonade." Jones, "Our Browning Society," derided clubwomen who took the remainder of their funds and "bought chocolates—and more than that, devoured them." Jones goes on to suggest that the club he describes may "end as caramel devourers." Quoted in Jonathan Freedman, "Professional Amateurs: Browning Societies and the Politics of Appreciation" (Manuscript in author's possession), 27.

97   Florida Ruffin Ridley, daughter of Josephine Ruffin, the founding president of the Woman's Era Club, served as secretary in her mother's club. Claudia L. Bushman, *A Good Poor Man's Wife: Being a Chronicle of Harriet Hanson Robinson and Her Family in Nineteenth-Century New England* (Hanover, N.H.: University Press of New England, 1981), reports that Harriet Hanson Robinson, whose working-class background made her uncomfortable in the New England Women's Club, founded, along with her two daughters, the Old and New Club in Malden, Massachusetts: "On the twentieth anniversary of the founding of Old and New, in 1898, the six original members who remained (three of them Robinsons) were feted. . . . more than Mother and Daughters' gathered for this occasion, and Hattie indicated how such fellowship would strengthen them against their real difficulties: 'We will all have a good time together and forget, if we can, our trials and troubles or talk them over and help each other to bear them'" (194–95). Julia Ward Howe founded the Saturday Morning Club of Boston for her daughter Maude and her friends. Throughout the record books Julia is described as the "mother of the club." Mary Jean Houde, *Reaching Out: A Story of the General Federation of Women's Clubs* (Chicago: Mobium, 1989), writes that beginning in 1899 four generations of the Matthews family belonged to the Cosmos Club of Forrest City, Arkansas (86).

98   Carroll Smith-Rosenberg, *Disorderly Conduct: Visions of Gender in Victorian America* (New York: Alfred A. Knopf, 1985), 32. Smith-Rosenberg argues that increased opportunities for women at the turn of the century changed the mother-daughter relationship as daughters began to see mothers' lives as repressed rather than something to emulate. These changes occurred gradually, however, and the mother-daughter bond still retained its power as a model for relationships among many women through the turn of the century (32–34).

99   Mary Church Terrell, "The Fiftieth Anniversary of the National Association of Colored Women," Mary Church Terrell Papers. Note that this account leaves Josephine Ruffin out entirely, reflecting the old animosity between the two.

100   *Proceedings of the First Convention of the National Council of Jewish Women,* 64.

101   Mary Caroline Crawford, *Little Journeys in Old New England* (Boston: Houghton

Mifflin, 1909), writes, "Mrs. Hutchinson seems to have been New England's first club woman" (216); Croly, *History of the Woman's Club Movement in America,* includes an account of Hutchinson's contribution to women's clubs (679) and describes the Ossoli Circle of Knoxville (1077). Papers of Ossoli Club, Sophia Smith Collection, Smith College, Northampton, Mass., include a picture of Margaret Fuller Ossoli in its history, claiming that she "planted the woman's club idea in the hearts of American women with her meetings for literary conversations in Boston during the winter of 1840" (1). Clubs also described founding members in maternal terms, as the Cantabrigia Club did Estelle M. H. Merrill, praising her for guidance "as a mother, for her child." Croly, *History of the Woman's Club Movement in America,* 607. Similar sentiments were expressed about Kate Doggett, founding member of the Chicago Fortnightly Club. Beadle and the Centennial History Committee, *Fortnightly of Chicago,* 28.

102   Sorosis and the New England Women's Club debated fiercely about which deserved the title of "first," ironically ignoring the fact that a number of African American clubs had undoubtedly preceded both of them.

103   The Fortnightly of Chicago, founded in 1873, spawned the Young Fortnightly in 1890, a club that included "society's fairest buds, ranging in age from 18 to 25 years." Beadle and the Centennial History Committee, *Fortnightly of Chicago,* 73. Sorosis helped form a number of daughter clubs, including a collegiate chapter at the University of Michigan, and leaders of the New England Women's Club aided new clubs in Boston and throughout the country.

104   Joanne Campbell, "Controlling Voices: The Legacy of English A at Radcliffe College, 1883–1917," *College Composition and Communication* 43 (December 1992), claims that colleges did not provide women students "intimate" response to writing (473); Joan G. Zimmerman, "Daughters of Main Street: Culture and the Female Community at Grinnel, 1884–1917," in *Woman's Being, Woman's Place: Female Identity and Vocation in American History,* ed. Mary Kelley (Boston: G. K. Hall, 1979), claims that clubs at Grinnell "resembled small college classes" (162); Croly, *History of the Woman's Club Movement in America,* includes an account of the 1886 formation of Collegiate Sorosis at the University of Michigan, a daughter to the New York Sorosis (683–84).

105   "How to Be Charitable without Money," *Far and Near* 2 (November 1891): 8.

106   Romania Bunnell Pratt, "Utah Woman's Press Club: President's Farewell Address," *Woman's Exponent* 27 (November 1, 1898): 59.

107   "Mrs. May Alden Ward," *General Federation of Women's Clubs Magazine* 17 (February 1918): 26; 1918 Yearbook of the New England Women's Club, Papers of the New England Women's Club, Schlesinger Library, Radcliffe College, Cambridge, Mass., includes a seventeen-page memorial to May Alden Ward, with many feeling and personal tributes to her personality.

108   Minutes of the Friday Club of Jackson, Michigan, November 8, 1889.

109   "Club Notes," *Far and Near* 1 (November 1890): 16.

110   Mary S. Gibson, *A Record of Twenty-Five Years of the California Federation of Women's Clubs, 1900–1925* (Los Angeles: California Federation of Women's Clubs, 1927), 52.

111   Cunningham, *Woman's Club of El Paso,* 126.

112   For a fuller discussion of clubwomen's uses of print, see Anne Ruggles Gere and Sarah R. Robbins, "Literacy in Black and White: Turn-of-the-Century African-American and European-American Club Women's Printed Texts," *Signs: Journal of Women in Culture and Society* 21 (Spring 1996): 643–78.

113   Sicherman, "Sense and Sensibility," 202.

114   Solomon quoted in Golomb, "The 1893 Congress of Jewish Women," 57; Severance quoted in Ella Giles Ruddy, ed., *The Mother of Clubs: Caroline M. Seymour, an Estimate and an Appreciation* (Los Angeles: Bumgardt, 1906), 132.

115   Giddens, *Transformation of Intimacy,* 3. Later Giddens argues for a reciprocal relationship between democratized interpersonal and wider social relations (195).

116   Kathryn Kish Sklar, *Florence Kelley and the Nation's Work: The Rise of Women's Political Culture, 1830–1900* (New Haven, Conn.: Yale University Press, 1995), 16.

117   James C. Scott, *Domination and the Arts of Resistance: Hidden Transcripts* (New Haven, Conn.: Yale University Press, 1990), xii.

118   Nancy Fraser, "Rethinking the Public Sphere: A Contribution to the Critique of Actually Existing Democracy," *Social Text* 8/9, no. 3/1 (1990): 73.

119   Hester Poole, "Club Life in New York" *Arena* 6 (August 1892), writes about New York City clubs: "Prior to the bi-monthly meetings of Sorosis at Delmonico's, no woman, even in daylight, when unattended, could procure a meal at a first-class restaurant in New York; neither in the majority of cases, could she secure a room in a first-class hotel. . . . The greater liberty of action heartily and innocently enjoyed by women to-day is primarily due to women's clubs" (368).

CHAPTER 2: CONSTRUCTING AND CONTESTING AMERICANIZATION(S)

1   Josiah Strong, *Our Country* (1886; reprint, Cambridge, Mass.: Harvard University Press, 1963), 55. Jurgen Herbst, in his introduction to the 1963 edition, writes, "Its success—one hundred and seventy-five thousand copies were sold before 1916, and individual chapters were reprinted in newspapers and magazines, and published separately in pamphlet form—demonstrated the power of its message which, according to the chief librarian of Congress, compared in intensity with that of *Uncle Tom's Cabin*" (ix).

2   Strong, *Our Country,* 217.

3   John Higham, *Strangers in the Land: Patterns of American Nativism, 1860–1925* (New Brunswick, N.J.: Rutgers University Press, 1955), 246.

4   Priscilla Wald, *Constituting Americans: Cultural Anxiety and Narrative Form* (Durham,
    N.C.: Duke University Press, 1995), 246.

5   May Wright Sewall, "The General Federation of Women's Clubs," *Arena* 6 (Au-
    gust 1892): 367.

6   Benedict Anderson, *Imagined Communities: Reflections on the Origin and Spread of
    Nationalism* (London: Verso, 1983), 30.

7   Strong, *Our Country,* asserts that "the Anglo-Saxon is to exercise the commanding
    influence in the world's future" (217). Richard Hofstader, *Social Darwinism in
    American Thought* (Boston: Beacon, 1992), describes Anglo-Saxonists positing
    themselves as the superior race and advocating their domination of the country
    and, ultimately, the world (170–200).

8   Minutes of the Saturday Morning Club, November 14, 1891, Papers of the Sat-
    urday Morning Club of Boston, Schlesinger Library, Radcliffe College, Cam-
    bridge, Mass. Julia Ward Howe, an active member of the suffrage movement,
    reflected the anti-immigration stance characteristic of the later period of that
    movement. Women who sought the vote for themselves often saw a challenge in
    the "ignorant immigrant" vote and took anti-Semitic positions.

9   Emily Malbourne Morgan, "Woman's Duty to Her Country," *Far and Near* 2 (Jan-
    uary 1892): 46–47. This paper was originally given at the 1891 meeting of the
    Connecticut Association of Working Girls' Societies.

10 J. P. M. Farnsworth, "Written for the U. W.P.C.R.C.W.S.A. Reception," *Woman's
    Exponent* 21 (September 1, 1893): 30. Mormons entered the Salt Lake Valley in
    1846 and between then and 1896, when their request was finally granted, con-
    tinually petitioned for statehood. Meanwhile the United States passed the 1862
    Morrill Act, which prohibited polygamy and reaffirmed the nation's power over
    territories, and the 1870 Cullom bill, which gave federal authorities broad au-
    thority for enforcing polygamy laws. Heather Symmes Cannon, "Practical Poli-
    ticians," in *Mormon Sisters: Women in Early Utah,* ed. Claudia L. Bushman (Salt Lake
    City: Olympus, 1976), observes, "Since attacks on the Mormon theocracy focused
    on the inflammatory polygamy issues, the women's duty to defend their faith
    involved a defense of this practice" (163).

11 Strong, *Our Country,* 107, 110. Evidence for Strong's claims appears in Brigham
    Young's assertion prior to the Civil War: "For the time will come when we will
    give laws to the nations of the earth." Quoted in Cannon, "Practical Politicians,"
    161.

12 Farnsworth, "Written for the U. W.P.C.R.C.W.S.A. Reception," 30.

13 "The Difficulties of Colonization," *Woman's Era* 1 (March 24, 1894): 9; John Dav-
    id Smith, ed., *The American Colonization Society and Emigration: Solutions to "The Negro
    Problem"* (New York: Garland, 1993), xxvii. Janet Duitsman Cornelius, *When I Can
    Read My Title Clear: Literacy, Slavery, and Religion in the Antebellum South* (Columbia:
    University of South Carolina Press, 1991), explains that the American Coloni-

zation Society believed missionaries to Africa could simultaneously Christianize and "civilize" Africa, thereby increasing its capacities in business and trade (117).

14   "Difficulties of Colonization," 9.

15   Pauline Hanauer Rosenberg, "Influence of the Discovery of America on the Jews," in *Papers of the Jewish Women's Congress* (Philadelphia: Jewish Publication Society of America, 1894), 68.

16   Lauren Berlant, *The Anatomy of National Fantasy: Hawthorne, Utopia, and Everyday Life* (Chicago: University of Chicago Press, 1991), 5.

17   Strong, *Our Country*, xxvi, 172.

18   J. E. Buell, *Metropolitan Life Unveiled: Or the Mysteries and Miseries of America's Great Cities, Embracing New York, Washington City, San Francisco, Salt Lake City, and New Orleans* (St. Louis: Historical Publishing, 1882), 25.

19   Minutes of the Nineteenth Century Club, November 1899, Papers of the Nineteenth Century Club of Oak Park, Illinois, privately held.

20   "The Book Table," *Federation Bulletin* 4 (May 1906): 402. Wilbert Anderson's *Country Town* was published in 1902 by Baker and Taylor, but the 1906 edition was more commonly known.

21   The circulation of the *Federation Bulletin* for 1906 was unreported, but by 1917 this publication claimed a circulation of two million.

22   Michael Kimmel, "Men's Responses to Feminism at the Turn of the Century," *Gender and Society* 1 (September 1987): 271.

23   Michael R. Olneck, "Americanization and the Education of Immigrants, 1900–1925: An Analysis of Symbolic Action," *American Journal of Education* 97 (August 1989): 399.

24   "The Real America," *Federation Bulletin* 3 (December 1905): 102.

25   Quoted in Mary S. Gibson, *A Record of Twenty-Five Years of the California Federation of Women's Clubs, 1900–1925* (Los Angeles: California Federation of Women's Clubs, 1927), 48.

26   "Editorial: What Is the General Federation?" *General Federation of Women's Clubs Magazine* 17 (November 1918): 20; 18 (December 1919): 15.

27   Hazel MacKaye, "Americanization via Pageantry," *General Federation of Women's Clubs Magazine* 18 (June 1919): 19. Karen Blair, *The Torchbearers: Women and Their Amateur Arts Associations in America, 1890–1930* (Bloomington: Indiana University Press, 1994), details MacKaye's considerable expertise and influence in pageantry (135–42).

28   Olneck, "Americanization," 399.

29   Minutes of the Neighborhood Union, December 10, 1914, Papers of the Neighborhood Union of Atlanta, Robert W. Woodruff Library, Atlanta University, Atlanta, Ga.

30   Hope's rhetorical strategy of using a particular individual's story to illustrate a large social problem shares much with Jane Addams's technique in *Twenty Years at*

Hull-House. Sarah Robbins, "Domestic Didactics: Nineteenth-Century American Literary Pedagogy by Barbauld, Stowe and Addams" (Ph.D. diss., University of Michigan, 1993), discusses Addams's use of anecdotes (211–27).

31 Cynthia Neverdon-Morton, "The Black Woman's Struggle for Equality in the South, 1895–1925," in *The Afro-American Woman: Struggles and Images,* ed. Sharon Harley and Rosalyn Terborg-Penn (Port Washington, N.Y.: Kennikat, 1978), claims it was easier for women to assemble for meetings in urban centers (49).

32 James Grossman, *Land of Hope: Chicago, Black Southerners, and the Great Migration* (Chicago: University of Chicago Press, 1989), chronicles this migration.

33 "Boston," *Woman's Era* 1 (August 1894): 11.

34 Sarah Deutsch, "Reconceiving the City: Women, Space, and Power in Boston, 1870–1910," *Gender and History* 6 (August 1994): 202–23, makes a related point about women in Boston, but her work concentrates more directly on the city's physical environment.

35 Minutes of the Detroit Section, November 11, 1905, Papers of the Detroit Section of the National Council of Jewish Women, Reuther Collection, Detroit Public Library, Detroit, Mich.

36 Selma Berrol, "When Uptown Met Downtown: Julia Richman's Work in the Jewish Community of New York, 1880–1912," *American Jewish History* 19 (September 1980), writes that supporters of Julia Richman, an affluent do-gooder, described her as "a loyal Jewess whose every act is inspired by good motives and a desire to be helpful to the community in which she lives," but the recipients of her aid complained that she "degraded and lowered parents in the eyes of their children, took advantage of every opportunity to suggest to the children that their parents were criminals . . . [and] placed herself in an attitude of opposition to the residents" (35).

37 Susan Estabrook Kennedy, *If All We Did Was to Weep at Home: A History of White Working-Class Women in America* (Bloomington: Indiana University Press, 1979), 70–71.

38 Susan J. Kleinberg, "Technology and Women's Work: The Lives of Working-Class Women in Pittsburgh, 1870–1900," *Labor History* 16 (Winter 1976): 58–72.

39 Quoted in Joanne Reitano, "Working Girls Unite," *American Quarterly* 38 (Spring 1984): 116.

40 Ibid., 132.

41 Strong, *Our Country,* describes a woman of the city: "Here is a mother who turns her children into the street in the early evening, because she lets her room for immoral purposes until long after midnight, when the poor little wretches creep back again, if they have not found some miserable shelter elsewhere" (175). Buell, *Metropolitan Life Unveiled,* describes women as vulnerable to "the psychologizing influence of oppressive lonesomeness, the wiles of da-do young libertines, or, lastly the seductive representations of gaudily robed and matronly appearing procuresses" (29).

42 Clara Sidney Davidge, "Working-Girls' Clubs," *Scribner's Magazine* 15 (May 1894): 627.

43 Kennedy, *If All We Did,* asserts that "working-class women in the early twentieth century were more involved in the struggle to leave the working class than in the development of an awareness of themselves as part of it" (112), a position with which I differ, based on my reading of working-class clubwomen's texts.

44 Strong, *Our Country,* 140, 143, 144–45.

45 Alice Kessler-Harris, *Out to Work: A History of Wage-Earning Women in the United States* (New York: Oxford University Press, 1982), observes that "trade unionists remained locked into patriarchal attitudes that valued women's contributions to the home" (153).

46 Quoted in Davidge, "Working-Girls' Clubs," 627.

47 Richard Hofstader, *The Age of Reform* (New York: Vintage, 1955), 244. Zena Beth McGlashan, "Club 'Ladies' and Working 'Girls': Rheta Childe Dorr and the New York *Evening Post,*" *Journalism History* 8 (Spring 1981): 7–13, argues that the General Federation of Women's Clubs, particularly under the leadership of Sarah Platt Decker, also eased national acceptance of unions by uniting the upper and middle classes with the labor force in support of legislation to improve working conditions.

48 "Thoughts from Club Members," *Far and Near* 1 (July 1891): 178.

49 Clare De Graffenreid, "Trade Unions," *Far and Near* 3 (January 1893): 49.

50 Leonora O'Reilly, "Some Mistakes of Working Women: Convention Paper," *Far and Near* 4 (August 1894): 139–40.

51 Barbara Meyer Wertheimer, *We Were There: The Story of Working Women in America* (New York: Pantheon, 1977), 228. This situation changed briefly with the onset of World War I and the simultaneous migration of African Americans to urban centers. Mary E. Jackson, "The Colored Woman in Industry," *Crisis* 11 (November 1918), notes that "just as colored men are going into the Army, so colored women are being recruited into industry," and she takes pleasure in the "spectacular" changes brought about by the war (12, 14). Unfortunately, few of these changes survived into peacetime, and most African American women disappeared from factories after the war ended.

52 Booker T. Washington's *Up From Slavery* (1901; reprint, New York: Doubleday, 1963) and W. E. B. Du Bois's *Souls of Black Folk* (1903; reprint, New York: Bantam, 1989) exemplify the differences between these two leaders. Du Bois argued for a full classical education, while Washington supported the sort of industrial training that would enable blacks to take positions as unskilled laborers. While Du Bois looked to expand the horizons of the "talented tenth," Washington sought to avoid class divisions and saw an elitist education as fostering that kind of division.

53 Mrs. Arthur S. Gray, "The Negro at Atlanta Exposition," *Woman's Era* 2 (January 1896): 10, 1.

54   "Notes on Ads," *Woman's Era* 3 (July 1896): 14.

55   "A Public Calamity," *Woman's Era* 3 (January 1897): 1.

56   Joe William Trotter Jr., *Black Milwaukee: The Making of an Industrial Proletariat, 1915–45* (Urbana: University of Illinois Press, 1985), describes African Americans' efforts to create a separate institutional life when constrained by socioeconomic, political, and racial oppression (28–30).

57   Monty Ramos, "The Woman's Century Club: Municipal House-Keeping for Nearly One Hundred Years" (1985), 2, Karen Blair Class Collection, University of Washington. The 1896–97 Yearbook and 1897–98 Yearbook of the Nineteenth Century Club, Papers of the Nineteenth Century Club of Oak Park, Illinois, privately held, listed as topics "The Child-Labor Problem," "Causes of Present Discontent of Labor," and "The Labor of Women" and included a book titled *Women Wage Earners* in its bibliography. Papers delivered at the Waterville Women's Club, Papers of the Waterville Woman's Club, Manuscript Division, Colby College Library, Waterville, Maine, include Mary Harride O'Halloran's 1877 "Roots," which centered on the plight of French Canadian women who held the "lowest paying jobs" (3).

58   Minutes of the Nineteenth Century Club of Oak Park, December 6, 1920.

59   Minutes of the Friday Club, December 18, 1896, Papers of the Friday Club of Jackson, Michigan, Bentley Historical Library, University of Michigan, Ann Arbor.

60   Bessie Van Vorst and Marie Van Vorst, *The Woman Who Toils: Being the Experiences of Two Gentlewomen as Factory Girls* (New York: Doubleday, 1903), offered portraits of working women's lives for a voyeuristic audience.

61   Minutes of the New England Women's Club, January 10, 1870, Papers of the New England Women's Club, Schlesinger Library, Radcliffe College, Cambridge, Mass.

62   Claudia L. Bushman, *A Good Poor Man's Wife: Being a Chronicle of Harriet Hanson Robinson and Her Family in Nineteenth-Century New England* (Hanover, N.H.: University Press of New England, 1981), 179.

63   Minutes of the Nineteenth Century Club of Oak Park, 1897.

64   Brenda Shelton, "Organized Mother Love: The Buffalo Women's Education and Industrial Union, 1885–1915," *New York History* 67 (April 1986), observes, "It seems never to have occurred to them [middle-class clubwomen] that their own reluctance to devote their lives to domestic chores could have been shared by their 'less fortunate sisters'" (165).

65   Minutes of the Women in Council, April 25, 1911, Papers of the Women in Council of Roxbury, Manuscript Division, Boston Public Library, Boston, Mass.

66   Program of the Women's Educational and Industrial Union, 1913, 19, Papers of the Women's Educational and Industrial Union [hereafter WEIU], Manuscript Division, Boston Public Library, Boston, Mass. The WEIU's methods included

establishing a protective committee that provided free legal advice to women, an exchange for the sale of women's handwork, and an employment agency. As the WEIU grew and expanded to other cities, it offered training in dressmaking, millinery, sales, and domestic service.

67 Annual Report, 1892, WEIU, 11.

68 Annual Report, 1913, WEIU, 20.

69 Quoted in Faith Rogow, *Gone to Another Meeting: The National Council of Jewish Women, 1893–1993* (Tuscaloosa: University of Alabama Press, 1993), 134.

70 Ibid., 134, 150.

71 W. M. F. Round, "Immigration and Crime," *Forum* 8 (September 1889), associated increased crime with increased immigration, offering statistical support for his claim and claiming "a special tendency to crime among the immigrants of [certain] nationalities" (437). Ellwood P. Cubberly, *Changing Conceptions of Education* (Boston: Houghton Mifflin, 1909), states, "About 1882, the character of our immigration changed in a very remarkable manner. . . . These southern and eastern Europeans are of a very different type from the north Europeans who preceded them" (14–15).

72 Strong, *Our Country,* ix, 42, 53–54.

73 N. S. Shaler, "European Peasants as Immigrants," *Atlantic Monthly* 36 (May 1893), for example, wrote, "The peasant knows himself to be by birthright a member of an inferior class, from which there is practically no chance of escaping. He is in essentially the same state as the Southern Negro" (649).

74 Etienne Balibar, "Is There a 'Neo-Racism?'" in Etienne Balibar and Immanual Wallerstein, *Race, Nation, Class: Ambiguous Identities,* trans. Chris Turner (New York: Verso, 1991), 21.

75 Robert W. Rydell, *All the World's a Fair: Visions of Empire at American International Expositions, 1876–1916* (Chicago: University of Chicago Press, 1984), 226.

76 Higham, *Strangers in the Land,* writes, "No part of the United States was immune to the spirit of white supremacy; in all sections native-born and northern European laborers called themselves 'white men' to distinguish themselves from the southern Europeans whom they worked beside" (173). Steven Hertzberg, *Strangers within the Gate City: The Jews of Atlanta, 1845–1915* (Philadelphia: Jewish Publication Society of America, 1978), explains, "Italian tenant farmers were often ranked with nonwhite laboring groups" (196). Noel Ignatiev, *How the Irish Became White* (New York: Routledge, 1995), describes the struggles of the Irish to gain the rights of native-born whites. Albert Abernathy, *The Jew a Negro: Being a Study of Jewish Ancestry from an Impartial Standpoint* (Moravia Falls, N.C.: Dixie, 1910), argued that Jews had Negro ancestors. Mary Gay Humphreys, "The New York Working-Girl," *Scribner's Magazine* 9 (October 1896), includes this about Jews: "First one black man got in, and he brought his brother and his son. Pretty soon the room was half-filled with men in shiny clothes and big black beards who brought their relations." She insists that "born and bred American working-girls"

objected to these men because "they made the factory towel so black with their dirty hands," then "the black men seemed to choke up the room and swallow all the air," and finally the work began to disappear because "the black-bearded men were taking it home to their wives and daughters who could help them," and the factory ultimately closed (507).

77   Strong, *Our Country* , 200–202. Similarly, Madison Grant, *Passing of the Great Race or the Racial Basis of European History* (New York: Scribner's, 1918), identifies Anglo-Saxons as the "branch of the Nordic race . . . upon which the nation must chiefly depend for leadership, for courage, for loyalty, for unity and harmony of action, for self-sacrifice and devotion to an ideal" (ix).

78   David R. Roediger, *The Wages of Whiteness: Race and the Making of the American Working Class* (London: Verso, 1991), 13.

79   Evelyn Brooks Higginbotham, *Righteous Discontent: The Women's Movement in the Black Baptist Church, 1880–1920* (Cambridge, Mass.: Harvard University Press, 1993), 30, 207–29.

80   Minutes of the Saturday Morning Club, November 14, 1891; 1918 Yearbook of the Ladies' Literary Club, Papers of the Ladies' Literary Club of Salt Lake City, Special Collections, University of Utah Library, Salt Lake City. The 1898–99 Yearbook of the Women's Literary Club, Papers of the Women's Literary Club of Bradford, Pennsylvania, Manuscript Division, Boston Public Library, Boston, Mass., includes a set of papers on the topic "To One Strong Race, All Races Here Unite." The 1919–20 Yearbook of the Nineteenth Century Club of Oak Park, listed sessions titled "Americanization a Social and Civic Necessity," "The Native-born Citizen and the Foreign-born Citizen," "Process of Naturalization," and "Illiteracy in America."

81   Scrapbook of the Nineteenth Century Club of Oak Park.

82   Ernest Gellner, *Nations and Nationalism* (Ithaca, N.Y.: Cornell University Press, 1983), 7.

83   The 1898–99 Yearbook of the Women's Literary Club of Bradford, Pennsylvania, includes in its program on American history "A Forecast for Women of the Twentieth Century." This yearbook also lists a debate titled "Resolved: That Woman Suffrage Is Desirable." Similarly, the 1901–2 Yearbook and the 1902–3 Yearbook of the Monday Club, Papers of the Monday Club of Clinton, New York, Archive Division, Hamilton College Library, Clinton, N.Y., lists "Women of the Revolution," "Household Utensils," "The Life of Dolly Madison," and "The Battle Hymn of the Republic" (implying a paper on Julia Ward Howe) in its American history program. Jennie June Cunningham Croly, *The History of the Woman's Club Movement in America* (New York: Henry G. Allen, 1898), published program lists from many clubs: the program of the Denver Fortnightly Club for 1897 lists "The Middle Period of Woman's Life" (273); topics for the Decatur (Ill.) Woman's Club 1897 program include "American Pianists" and "Women in Music" (194); the Friday Morning Club of Los Angeles listed such topics as "Collegiate and Indus-

trial Education for Women," "The Health of American Women," "The Question of Woman's Rights," "The Recent Equal Rights Convention," and "Developments of Women's Work" (248). The 1897–98 Yearbook of the Olla Podrida Study Club, Papers of the Olla Podrida Study Club of Toledo, Ohio, Manuscript Division, Lucas County Library, Toledo, Ohio, includes "The Women of the White House" and "Women in the Revolution."

84 Benjamin Spencer, *The Quest for Nationality: An American Literary Campaign* (Syracuse, N.Y.: Syracuse University Press, 1957), notes, "The multiplication of fortunes after the Civil War had encouraged an acquaintance with Europe which . . . bred, especially in Eastern cities, coteries of young men who despised everything American and admired everything English" (300).

85 Sallie Southall Cotten, *History of the North Carolina Federation of Women's Clubs: 1901–1925* (Raleigh, N.C.: Edwards and Broughton, 1925), 2.

86 Minutes of the Friday Club of Jackson, Michigan, January 28, 1898.

87 Undated clipping, *Clinton Courier,* Papers of the Monday Club of Clinton, New York.

88 Guy Hubbart, "Black Mammy's Boy," *General Federation of Women's Clubs Magazine* 17 (December 1918): 4.

89 "Difficulties of Colonization," 9; Higginbotham, *Righteous Discontent,* distinguishes between poor black Baptist women and the more, in her terms, "elite" clubwomen, but I find more convincing her assertion that African American women's church and club groups intermingled in complicated ways and that both employed the politics of respectability. Kathleen Berkeley, "Colored Ladies Also Contributed: Black Women's Activities from Benevolence to Social Welfare, 1866–1896," in *The Web of Southern Social Relations: Women, Family and Education,* ed. Walter J. Fraser Jr., R. Frank Saunders Jr., and Jon L. Wakelyn (Athens: University of Georgia Press, 1985), 185; and Gerda Lerner, "Early Community Work of Black Club Women," *Journal of Negro History* 59 (April 1974): 158–67, describe African American clubwomen as aiming to help all members of the race. Lerner argues that "black club women frequently successfully bridged and concerned themselves with issues of importance to poor women, working mothers, tenant farm wives" (167).

90 Deborah Gray White, "The Cost of Club Work, the Price of Black Feminism," in *Visible Women: New Essays on American Activism,* ed. Nancy A. Hewitt and Suzanne Lebsock (Urbana: University of Illinois Press, 1993), 258.

91 Higginbotham, *Righteous Discontent,* 192.

92 Agnes Jones Adams, "Social Purity," *Woman's Era* 2 (August 1895): 24.

93 Elizabeth McHenry and Shirley Brice Heath, "The Literate and the Literary: African Americans as Writers and Readers—1830–1940," *Written Communication* 11 (October 1994): 429.

94 Vron Ware, *Beyond the Pale: White Women, Racism, and History* (London: Verso, 1992), 173.

95 Quoted in Bert James Loewenberg and Ruth Bogin, *Black Women in Nineteenth-*

Century American Life: Their Words, Their Thoughts, Their Feelings (State College: Pennsylvania State University Press, 1976), 260. Gail Bederman, *Manliness and Civilization: A Cultural History of Gender and Race in the United States, 1880–1917* (Chicago: University of Chicago, 1995), shows how Ida B. Wells used the discourse of Anglo-Saxonism against the white males who generated it (45–76).

96   Quoted in Ware, *Beyond the Pale,* 189.

97   Quoted in Charles Harris Wesley, *The History of the National Association of Colored Women's Clubs: A Legacy of Service* (Washington, D.C.: National Association of Colored Women, 1984), 9, 12.

98   Mary Church Terrell, "Why I Wrote the Phyllis Wheatley Pageant-Play," Papers of Mary Church Terrell, Moorland-Spingarn Research Center, Howard University, Washington, D.C.

99   Minutes of the Woman's Improvement Club, February 3, 1910, March 3, 1910, March 17, 1910, April 21, 1910, and May 19, 1910, Papers of the Woman's Improvement Club of Indianapolis, W. H. Smith Memorial Library, Indiana Historical Society, Indianapolis; Minutes of the Chautauqua Circle, May 15, 1914, February 19, 1915, April 20, 1917, January 17, 1919, September 23, 1919 (quote), and December 19, 1920, Papers of the Chautauqua Circle of Atlanta, Robert W. Woodruff Library, Atlanta University, Atlanta, Ga.

100   Wesley, *History of the National Association of Colored Women's Clubs,* 36.

101   Minutes of the Woman's Improvement Club of Indianapolis, January 14, 1917, include this: "Received a notice from the National Association asking us to cooperate with Frederick Douglass Day in Feb and to give a contribution toward buying his house as a memorial." Minutes of the Detroit Study Club for 1917 contain a similar notice.

102   Minutes of the Chautauqua Circle of Atlanta, January 16, 1914.

103   Laura D. Jacobson, "The Pioneers," *American Jewess* 1 (August 1895): 240.

104   "In Memoriam," n.d., Papers of Detroit Section of the National Council of Jewish Women.

105   Rosenberg, "Influence of the Discovery of America on the Jews," 68; Rudolph Glanz, *The German Woman,* vol. 2 of *The Jewish Woman in America: Two Female Immigrant Generations 1820–1929* (Washington, D.C.: KTAV Publishing and the National Council of Jewish Women, 1976), 41–42. Bernice Graziani, *Where There's a Woman: Seventy-five Years of History as Lived by the National Council of Jewish Women* (New York: McCall, 1967), explains that in 1903 the U.S. government sought the National Council's aid in greeting arrivals at the port and helping them find lodging, classes in English, training, and employment (29).

106   *Brooklyn Section History, 1900–1982* (New York: National Council of Jewish Women, 1983), 6.

107   Mrs. Percy V. [Anna] Pennybacker, "The Immigrant among Us," *Ladies' Home Journal* 32 (April 1915): 27.

108   Susan A. Glenn, *Daughters of the Shtetl: Life and Labor in the Immigrant Generation*

(Ithaca, N.Y.: Cornell University Press, 1990), 3. She distinguishes between Americanization—a wholesale acceptance of American values and institutions—and an openness to experimentation, claiming that the latter more accurately describes the perspective of Jewish women before 1930 (3).

109 Quoted in William Toll, "A Quiet Revolution: Jewish Women's Clubs and the Widening Female Sphere, 1870–1920," *American Jewish Archives* 41 (Spring/Summer 1989): 19.

110 "World Events," *Far and Near* 3 (January 1893): 53.

111 "Learning to Write English," *Far and Near* 2 (November 1891): 2–3; "Some Common Errors in English Speech," *Far and Near* 3 (April 1893): 115–16; "Some Common Errors in English Speech," *Far and Near* 3 (May 1893): 136–37; "A Talk about Letter-Writing," *Far and Near* 4 (October 1894): 171.

112 "Putting the Best Foot Forward," *Far and Near* 3 (April 1893): 113. Humphreys, "New York Working Girl," asserted that "American girls eat meat and wear bonnets" (as opposed to consuming black bread and coffee and wearing head shawls), which suggests the complex features by which "nonwhite" was constructed and the difficulties faced by immigrants who sought to become fully assimilated (503).

113 Humphreys, "New York Working Girl," 505.

114 *History of the National League of Women Workers* (New York: Pearl, 1914), 7.

115 Kessler-Harris, *Out to Work,* 93 (Dodge quotes), 94 (Kessler-Harris quote).

116 *History of the National League of Women Workers,* 10, 11, 12.

117 In a letter, "To the Editor," *Far and Near* 1 (December 1890), the United Workers of Roxbury explains a change in its bylaws to stipulate that at least half the officers be wage earners and that dues be increased from 75 cents to $2.10 per year. It also sent former subscribers a circular "stating the pleasure that the club feels that it need not call upon them for assisting in meeting the regular expenses of the coming year" (26).

118 *History of the National League of Women Workers,* 13.

119 Ibid., 9, 10. This inclusion did not extend to race.

120 Emily Solis-Cohen, "The Jewish Girl's Thoughts on Jewish Life," in *Jewish Experiences in America: Suggestions for the Study of Jewish Relations with Non-Jews,* ed. Bruno Lasker (New York: Inquiry, 1930), 102–3. This account also includes such assertions as these: "Girls do not count in Jewish life. What does it matter about us? It's the boys they educate first. . . . What's there in synagogue for us? We're girls. . . . We might as well be in the Catholic church for all the rabbis in this place care" (106).

121 Quoted in Gladys Boone, *The Women's Trade Union Leagues in Great Britain and the United States of America* (New York: Columbia University Press, 1942), 63. Addams's comment about writing a book probably refers to Van Vorst and Van Vorst's *Woman Who Toils,* in which middle-class women who worked briefly in factories claim that they "act as a mouthpiece for the woman laborer" but take a highly critical tone, claiming that most women work for pleasure (5).

122 Berlant, *Anatomy of National Fantasy,* 216–17.
123 Grace Raymond Hebard, "Americanization of the Immigrant: Americanization and Citizenship Are as Far Apart as the Poles," *General Federation of Women's Clubs Magazine* 16 (February 1917): 16–17.
124 Minutes of the Saturday Morning Club, November 14, 1891.
125 Berlant, *Anatomy of National Fantasy,* 5, 216.

CHAPTER 3: VALUING AND DEVALUING DOLLARS

1 Maury Klein, *The Flowering of the Third America: The Making of an Organizational Society, 1850–1920* (Chicago: Ivan R. Dee, 1993), 181. Susan Strasser, *Satisfaction Guaranteed: The Making of the American Mass Market* (New York: Pantheon, 1989), explains that people at the turn of the century equated an abundance of consumer goods with progress.
2 William Leach, *Land of Desire* (New York: Pantheon, 1993), 9; Elaine S. Abelson, *When Ladies Go A-Thieving: Middle-Class Shoplifters in the Victorian Department Store* (New York: Oxford University Press, 1989), explains how some middle-class women responded to department store displays by stealing and argues that such theft can be read as an "appropriate" response to the arousal of desire such displays created and that the medicalizing of theft as kleptomania blamed the women themselves, not the excesses of the institution.
3 Ann Cvetkovich, *Mixed Feelings: Feminism, Mass Culture, and Victorian Sensationalism* (New Brunswick, N.J.: Rutgers University Press, 1992), writes, "Capitalism and the body are connected in so far as stimulating the nerves is a way of stimulating exchange. The reader's body becomes a machine hooked into the circuit of production and consumption, rather than a disinterested entity floating above economic exigencies in search of aesthetic or moral truth" (21). Advertising can be described as resembling sensational novels in its ability to stimulate the nerves, and in this way the body becomes directly connected with consumerism. Jennifer Scanlon, *Inarticulate Longings: The Ladies' Home Journal, Gender, and the Promises of Consumer Culture* (New York: Routledge, 1995), describes the process by which the *Journal* encouraged readers to become consumers: "It did this by presenting fragments of opinion—in this case fiction, advertisements, and editorial matter—and then organizing those fragments into a whole which could be called the 'consensus' view" (7).
4 Martha Olney, *Buy Now Pay Later: Advertising, Credit, and Consumer Durables in the 1920s* (Chapel Hill: University of North Carolina Press, 1991), 171.
5 Christopher P. Wilson, "The Rhetoric of Consumption: Mass-market Magazines and the Demise of the Gentle Reader, 1880–1920," in *The Culture of Consumption: Critical Essays in American History, 1880–1980,* ed. Richard Wightman Fox and T. J. Jackson Lears (New York: Pantheon, 1983), explains that Curtis Publishing, which employed Edward Bok and published the *Ladies' Home Journal,* emphasized a "fam-

ily" relationship with its readers, asserting, "'The final tests of a magazine's excuse for existence are the confidence which its readers accord it, and the confidences they bring to it'" (59).

6   Quoted in Wilson, "Rhetoric of Consumption," 59, 55, 41.

7   Ibid., 41; Kathryn Shevelow, *Women and Print Culture: Constructing Femininity in the Early Periodical* (New York: Routledge, 1989), 4.

8   Daniel Miller, *Material Culture and Mass Consumption* (New York: Basil Blackwell, 1987), 189–91.

9   "Opinion about Names," *Woman's Exponent* 21 (April 15 and May 1, 1893): 153; "Club Notes," *Club Worker* 1 (December 1899): 4 (quote). The *Ladies' Home Journal*'s influence on working women extended to fiction, as Anzia Yezierska, *Hungry Hearts* (Boston: Houghton Mifflin, 1920), shows with this remark by a young immigrant woman: "Sometimes he would spend out 15 cents to buy me the *Ladies' Home Journal* to read about American life" (145).

10   Josephine Ruffin, "Editorial," *Woman's Era* 2 (April 1895): 9. The *Journal*'s racist editorial policy extended to other areas of the magazine. Advertisements included very few African Americans, and those few were always stereotypically portrayed as servants. Fiction in the *Journal* similarly ignored or deprecated black women, and Scanlon, *Inarticulate Longings,* reports that in 1911 a *Journal* marketing survey categorized all African Americans as illiterate even though their literacy rate at the time was over 77 percent (221). Susan Willis, "I Shop Therefore I Am: Is There a Place for Afro-American Culture in Commodity Culture?" in *Changing Our Own Words: Essays on Criticism, Theory, and Writing by Black Women,* ed. Cheryl A. Wall (New Brunswick, N.J.: Rutgers University Press, 1989), uses bell hooks's term *white supremacy* to describe this variation of racism, explaining that "black versions of white cultural models are of necessity secondary and devoid of cultural integrity" (184).

11   Gertrude Mossell, who published under her husband's initials N. F., wrote for a variety of publications, but unlike her more radical colleague Ida B. Wells, she maintained public modesty, adhering to what Joanne Braxton describes as "a code of race-conscious womanhood and black Christian motherhood." See Joanne Braxton, Introduction to *The Work of the Afro-American Woman,* by Mrs. N. F. [Gertrude] Mossell (1894; reprint, New York: Oxford University Press, 1988), xxix.

12   Martha E. D. White, "The Making of the Home Library," *General Federation of Women's Clubs Magazine* 16 (1917): 5

13   John Tebbel, *Between Covers: The Rise and Transformation of Book Publishing in America* (New York: Oxford University Press, 1987), describes "revival of reading" as a 1914 campaign of publishers, and the "home library" campaign followed it (176–77).

14   Mary Lynn Stevens Heninger, *At Home with a Book: Reading in America, 1840–1940* (Rochester, N.Y.: Strong Museum, 1986), 21; Medora W. Gould, "Literature Department," *Women's Era* 2 (July 1895): 19 (quote).

15   Minutes of the Indianapolis Woman's Club, November 3, 1882, Papers of the Indianapolis Woman's Club, W. H. Smith Memorial Library, Indiana Historical Society, Indianapolis; Jennie June Cunningham Croly, *The History of the Woman's Club Movement in America* (New York: Henry G. Allen, 1898), 19.

16   "The League," *Club Worker* 1 (October 1899): 1 (first quote); "Exchanges," *Club Worker* 2 (October 1900): 8 (second quote). The editor goes on to list twenty publications currently on the exchange list. These come from clubs in New York, Boston, Philadelphia, Newark, Chicago, and Montgomery, Alabama. Nearly all appear to be working women's groups, although the General Federation's *Club Woman* is on the list.

17   Quoted in David Taylor, "Ladies of the Club: An Arkansas Story," *Wilson Library Bulletin* 59 (January 1985): 325; "U.W.P.C.," *Woman's Exponent* 24 (May 15, 1896): 166. Similar distance was spanned by Boston resident Julia Ward Howe's visit to Milwaukee in 1876. According to Genevieve G. McBride, *On Wisconsin Women: Working for Their Rights from Settlement to Suffrage* (Madison: University of Wisconsin Press, 1993), Howe came at the request of a group of women who had "very few precedents in the country to guide them," and after "an inspiring talk," Howe "promised to send her club's constitution and bylaws" (138).

18   Minutes of the New England Women's Club, April 11, 1868, Papers of the New England Women's Club of Boston, Schlesinger Library, Radcliffe College, Cambridge, Mass.

19   "The Editor's Department," *Young Woman's Journal* 1 (December 1889): 96.

20   Mary I. Wood, *The History of the General Federation of Women's Clubs for the First Twenty-two Years of Its Organization* (New York: Norwood Press/General Federation of Women's Clubs, 1912), notes that the Reciprocity Committee made its report at the 1902 biennial, urging "a central bureau for the reception and distribution of papers" (151); Clara B. Adams, "Report of the Reciprocity Committee," *Federation Bulletin* 2 (October 1904): 3; "The League," *Club Worker* 1 (October 1899): 1.

21   Minutes of the Ladies' Literary Club, October 6, 1897, Papers of the Ladies' Literary Club of Ypsilanti, Michigan, Bentley Historical Library, University of Michigan, Ann Arbor.

22   Luretta Rainey, *History of Oklahoma State Federation of Women's Clubs* (Guthrie, Okla.: Co-Operative Publishing, 1939), reports, "The Bureau of Reciprocity was charged with the duty of collecting year books, programs, and meritorious papers and supplying this material to such clubs as desired them. This Bureau served a most useful purpose until the establishment of the Extension Department in our State University made its continuance unnecessary" (48). Sallie Southall Cotten, *History of the North Carolina Federation of Women's Clubs: 1901–1925* (Raleigh, N.C.: Edwards and Broughton, 1925), explains that "the Reciprocity Bureau was the forerunner of the Bureau of Information, which still follows its mission of helping women to gain knowledge. It was in the beginning an experiment but has now become a part of the Extension work of the North Carolina University" (57).

23 Igor Kopytoff, "The Cultural Biography of Things," in *The Social Life of Things: Commodities in Cultural Perspective,* ed. Arjun Appadurai (New York: Cambridge University Press, 1986), writes, "While exchanges of things usually involve commodities, a notable exception is the exchanges that mark relations of reciprocity, as these have been classically defined in anthropology. Here, gifts are given in order to evoke an obligation to give back a gift, which in turn will evoke a similar obligation—a never-ending chain of gifts and obligations. The gifts themselves may be things that are normally used as commodities (food, feasts, luxury goods, services), but each transaction is not discrete and none, in principle, is terminal" (69).

24 Marcel Mauss, *The Gift: The Form and Reason for Exchange in Archaic Societies* (New York: W. W. Norton, 1990), 73.

25 Lewis Hyde, *The Gift: Imagination and the Erotic Life of Property* (New York: Random House, 1983), 47.

26 Minutes of the Detroit Study Club, April 26, 1898, Papers of the Detroit Study Club, Bentley Collection, Detroit Public Library, Detroit, Mich., comment, "A report was also made upon cost and make-up of programmes." The April 28, 1899, minutes say, "Miss Smith reported the purchase of two quires of paper for programs at $.25 each and one yard of drawing paper at .40 returned .10 to the treasury." At this time, annual club dues were $.50 per person for the twenty members. Beginning in 1905, when dues were approximately at the same level, members voted to pay for printing programs. Minutes for November 18, 1910, state, "Miss Lewis reported that the Owl Ptg. Co. would print and furnish 100 copies of Club Constitution and by-laws for $5.00. Report was accepted." Minutes of the Detroit Section, November 18, 1910, Papers of the Detroit Section of the National Council of Jewish Women, Reuther Collection, Detroit Public Library, Detroit, Mich., report an annual budget of $299 for 1901–2, and $25.50 of this was spent on printing. Only one item—$73.00 to rent the meeting room—claimed a larger percentage of the budget.

27 Minutes of the Chautauqua Circle, November 11, 1915, Papers of the Chautauqua Circle of Atlanta, Robert W. Woodruff Library, Atlanta University, Atlanta, Ga.

28 Ibid., November 25, 1913; Minutes of the Neighborhood Union, February 11, 1910, Papers of the Neighborhood Union of Atlanta, Robert W. Woodruff Library, Atlanta University, Atlanta, Ga. Minutes of the Neighborhood Union, November 13, 1913, deal with similar issues: "The Press Committee had printed 500 placards and had also an article put in the *Independent* and is preparing to put one in the *Constitution.* The printing of the letters cost $3. $3.65 was taken up to finish paying for the placards and the pictures cost $2.50. The committee is still in need of money."

29 "Woman Journalism in Utah," *Woman's Exponent* 21 (September 1, 1893): 28; "Club Notes," *Far and Near* 1 (November 1890): 16.

30 Leach, *Land of Desire,* points out, "After 1890 the institutions of production and

consumption were, in effect taken over by corporate businesses. Business, not ordinary men and women, did most to establish the value and the cultural character of the goods,—in this case, of the new machine-made goods. At the same time merchants, brokers and manufacturers did everything they could, both ideologically and in reality to *separate* the world of production from the world of consumption" (147).

31   "The Club Worker," *Club Worker* 2 (May 1900): 6.

32   Anne Ruggles Gere and Sarah R. Robbins, "Gendered Literacy in Black and White: Turn-of-the-Century African-American and European-American Club Women's Printed Texts," *Signs: Journal of Women in Culture and Society* 21 (Spring 1996): 643–78.

33   Annette B. Weiner, *Possessions: The Paradox of Keeping-While Giving* (Berkeley: University of California Press, 1992), 7, 11.

34   Marshall Sahlins, *Culture and Practical Reason* (Chicago: University of Chicago Press, 1976), argues that "modern capitalist societies, however richly endowed, dedicate themselves to the proposition of scarcity. . . . Where production and distribution are arranged through the behavior of prices and all livelihoods depend on getting and spending, insufficiency of material means becomes the explicit, calculable starting point of all economic activity" (22–23).

35   "The Editor's Department," *Young Women's Journal* 1 (November 1889): 62.

36   "Report of the League Secretary," *Club Worker* 4 (November 1902): 41.

37   "Club Contest," *Club Worker* 5 (June 1903), published the results of one contest, listing clubs in three categories according to size, and published the name of each club and the number of subscriptions generated (144). "The Club Worker Prize," *Club Worker* 7 (May 1906), offered free trips to the Philadelphia convention as prizes (476). "An Important Suggestion to the Readers of the Club Worker from the Advertising Department," *Club Worker* 4 (January 1903): 91, urged cooperation with the ad department.

38   "Notes on Ads," *Woman's Era* 3 (July 1896), discussed the contents of advertisements and referred readers to them, closing with "see ad," much as Bok admonished his readers (14). *Federation Bulletin* and subsequent publications of the General Federation of Women's Clubs included ads and also directed readers to them. The New York Section of the National Council of Jewish Women began including advertisements in the 1918–19 edition of its yearbook, urging members to purchase such luxury items as furs, pianos, and ice cream.

39   Susan Coultrap-McQuin, *Doing Literary Business: American Women Writers in the Nineteenth Century* (Chapel Hill: University of North Carolina Press, 1990), 194.

40   Edward W. Bok, "Is Literature a Trade?" *Ladies' Home Journal* 7 (May 1890): 13.

41   Minutes of the Century Club, January 13, 1901, Papers of the Century Club of Seattle, Northwest Collection, Suzzallo Library, University of Washington, Seattle, Wash.

42   Minutes of the Ladies' Literary Club of Ypsilanti, November 12, 1898.

43   Linda E. Kauffman, *Discourses of Desire: Gender, Genre, and Epistolary Fictions* (Ithaca, N.Y.: Cornell University Press, 1986).

44   "Editorial," *Federation Bulletin* 3 (October 1905): 2.

45   To be sure, some clubs allowed individual ownership of texts. Henriette Greenebaum Frank and Amalie Hoffer Jerome, *Annals of the Chicago Woman's Club for the First Forty Years of Its Organization, 1876–1916* (Chicago: Chicago Woman's Club, 1919), include this: "On April 20, 1876, a discussion took place in regard to the retention of the essays in the archives of the Club. It was decided that those who were willing to give them to the Club should do so, but those who were not, shall make known the fact to the Secretary, who shall in that case make a clear and concise report of those essays, to be retained on the pages of the journal" (25). As this suggests, even when individuals retained their texts, the club exercised its right to the ideas contained therein.

46   Minutes of the Friday Club, May 22, 1889, Papers of the Friday Club of Jackson, Michigan, Bentley Historical Library, University of Michigan, Ann Arbor.

47   "The New Volume XXXVI," *Woman's Exponent* 36 (June 1907): 2.

48   "History of Myrtle Club," *Club Worker* 6 (April 1905): 395–97.

49   Croly, Preface, *History of the Woman's Club Movement in America,* n.p.

50   Susa Young Gates, *History of the Young Ladies' Mutual Improvement Association of the Church of Jesus Christ of Latter-day Saints from November 1869 to June 1910* (Salt Lake City: Deseret News, 1911), 121, 311.

51   Carolyn O. Poplett, *The Gentle Force: A History of the Nineteenth Century Woman's Club of Oak Park* (Broadview, Ill.: A and H Lithoprint, 1992), vii.

52   Weiner, *Possessions,* 7, 11, 33.

53   Mark Rose, *Authors and Owners: The Invention of Copyright* (Cambridge, Mass.: Harvard University Press, 1993), explains an 1890 case detailing the right to privacy that appeared in the common-law protection of an author's unpublished writings, not as a property right, but as "an instance of the more general right of the individual to be let alone" (139). The privacy necessary to the intimacy that developed among clubwomen thus connected directly with their literacy practices. Rose observes that copyright law has always mingled matters of privacy with matters of property.

54   See, for example, Grover Cleveland, "Woman's Mission and Women's Clubs," *Ladies' Home Journal* 22 (May 1905): 3–4; and Edward Bok, "My Quarrel with Women's Clubs," *Ladies' Home Journal* 27 (January 1910): 1. Cleveland and Bok typify critics who argued that women's clubs threatened the home and family except when they carried out projects of social welfare.

55   Jean Hamilton, "The Club Movement among Working Women," *Federation Bulletin* 1 (February 1904): 119.

56   Mauss, *Gift,* 68.

57   Cato Wadel, "The Hidden Work of Everyday Life," in *Social Anthropology of Work,* ed. Sandra Wallman (New York: Academic Press, 1979), 382.

58   Suzanne Lebsock, *The Free Women of Petersburg: Status and Culture in a Southern Town, 1784–1860* (New York: W. W. Norton, 1984), notes that in small local groups with little money, women sometimes exercised control over allocations, but with centralized church boards, "the women who raised the money locally lost control of it almost as fast as they made it" (222).

59   Mary Ryan, *The Empire of the Mother: American Writing about Domesticity, 1830–1860* (New York: Harrington Park, 1985), 33.

60   Lori D. Ginzberg, "Women and the Work of Benevolence: Morality and Politics in the Northeastern United States, 1820–1885" (Ph.D. diss., Yale University, 1985), 89. Ginzberg also notes that since laws forbade women to form corporations, their funds were assigned to male control (112).

61   Minutes of the Nineteenth Century Club, November 14, 1898, to January 8, 1900, Papers of the Nineteenth Century Club of Oak Park, Illinois, privately held, include continuing discussions of whether the club should join with the West End Woman's Club in supporting the West Side Workroom. Some of the hesitation stemmed from doubts about whether the contributions of the Nineteenth Century Club would be visible enough since other clubs were involved. Alternatives, such as traveling libraries and monitoring the sanitary conditions in alleys, were considered, and members decided to "drop the matter for the present" and appeal "for old clothes to send to the workroom."

62   "The Phyllis Wheatley Club," *Woman's Era* 2 (November 1895): 15.

63   Quoted in Mary S. Cunningham, *The Woman's Club of El Paso: Its First Thirty Years* (El Paso: Texas Western Press, 1978), 7.

64   Helen W. Coaley, *Statement of the Civic Achievements of the Chicago Woman's Club Prepared at the Request of the Building Committee by the President of the Club* (Chicago: Chicago Woman's Club, 1915); Frank and Jerome, *Annals of the Chicago Woman's Club*, 276.

65   Minutes of the New York Section, February 23, 1915, Papers of the New York Section of the National Council of Jewish Women, privately held.

66   Coaley, *Statement*, 1, 2.

67   Ibid., 4, 6–7, 9.

68   Scrapbook of the Nineteenth Century Club of Oak Park, clipping from December 6, 1919.

69   Georgie A. Bacon, "The Stamp Savings System," *Federation Bulletin* 2 (April 1904): 133.

70   "Methods of Selling on the Installment Plan in Boston," *Federation Bulletin* 3 (December 1904): 76.

71   "How to Be Charitable without Money," *Far and Near* 2 (November 1891): 8.

72   "Club Notes," *Club Worker* 5 (April 1904): 140.

73   "Club Notes," *Club Worker* 4 (April 1903): 126.

74   "Thoughts from Club Members," *Far and Near* 2 (December 1891): 32.

75   Minutes of the Woman's Improvement Club, September 24, 1909, Papers of the

Woman's Improvement Club, W. H. Smith Memorial Library, Indiana Historical Society, Indianapolis.

76   Quoted in Deborah Gray White, "The Cost of Club Work, the Price of Black Feminism," in *Visible Woman: New Essays on American Activism,* ed. Nancy A. Hewitt and Suzanne Lebsock (Urbana: University of Illinois, 1993), 260. Paula Giddings, *When and Where I Enter: The Impact of Black Women on Race and Sex in America* (New York: Bantam, 1984), explains the motto (97—98). "News from the Clubs," *Woman's Era* 1 (July 1894), includes a description of a fund-raising project of the Berkley, Virginia, Women's Working Club (2). "News from the Clubs," *Woman's Era* 1 (March 24, 1894), includes the Kansas City Women's League's declaration that it makes its "work largely industrial" because of the needs of members (2). Such comments, along with discussions of Sunday afternoon as the only available meeting time, point to working-class backgrounds for some groups.

77   "Work Suggested by the National Association," *Woman's Era* 3 (October/November 1896): 3.

78   "The History of the Neighborhood Union," 2, Papers of the Neighborhood Union.

79   Lugenia Hope, Diary, Papers of the Neighborhood Union.

80   Rosalyn Terborn-Penn, "Survival Strategies among African-American Women Workers: A Continuing Process," in *Women, Work and Protest: A Century of U.S. Women's Labor History,* ed. Ruth Milkman (Boston: Routledge, 1985), 142.

81   "News from the Clubs," *Woman's Era* 1 (March 24, 1894): 3.

82   Monroe Campbell and William Wirtz, *The First Fifty Years: A History of the National Council of Jewish Women, 1893—1943* (New York: National Council of Jewish Women, 1943), 33.

83   Quoted in Kathleen D. McCarthy, *Noblesse Oblige: Charity and Cultural Philanthropy in Chicago, 1849—1929* (Chicago: University of Chicago Press, 1982), 48.

84   Carrie Shevelson Benjamin, "Woman's Place in Charitable Work—What It Is and What It Should Be," in *Papers of the Jewish Woman's Congress* (Philadelphia: Jewish Publication Society of America, 1894), 146. Anne Summers, "A Home from Home: Women's Philanthropic Work in the Nineteenth Century," in *Fit Work for Women,* ed. Sandra Burman (New York: St. Martin's, 1979), writes, "Visiting the poor in their own homes could do more than demonstrate the benevolent and neighborly intentions towards them of the rich; it could also help to isolate the poor from each other" (37).

85   Quoted in Faith Rogow, *Gone to Another Meeting: The National Council of Jewish Women, 1893—1993* (Tuscaloosa: University of Alabama Press, 1993), 155.

86   "General Relief Society Conference," *Woman's Exponent* 32 (April 1, 1903), includes this: "It was a very rough country to travel over, but visited all once a year; the Indian sisters were very good, had great faith . . . they dress their children well and are fast becoming civilized" (39).

87   Cheryll Lynn May, "Charitable Sisters," in *Mormon Sisters: Women in Early Utah,* ed.

Claudia L. Bushman (Salt Lake City: Olympus, 1976), argues that while Mormon women never challenged the authority of the church, the separate physical space of the Relief Society Hall and its incorporation as the National Woman's Relief Society, which "could be independent and transact its own business in its own name with trustees and all the rights and privileges belonging to a corporate body," marked the Relief Society as different from traditional church benevolence societies (225–39).

88 "Our Little Paper," *Woman's Exponent* 32 (May 1904): 92.

89 "An Important Event," *Woman's Exponent* 33 (June 1905): 4.

90 Eliza R. Snow, "The First Relief Society," *Woman's Exponent* 32 (August 1903): 1.

91 Kathleen D. McCarthy, ed., *Lady Bountiful Revisited: Women, Philanthropy, and Power* (New Brunswick, N.J.: Rutgers University Press, 1990), writes, "Prior to the passage of married women's property acts in the mid-nineteenth century, women made their greatest contributions through fund-raising campaigns rather than individual gifts" (15). My reading of club records, however, indicates that this gendered difference in methods of raising funds still existed in women's clubs at the turn of the century.

92 "The League," *Club Worker* 2 (February 1900): 2.

93 Lebsock, *Free Women of Petersburg*, 220.

94 Louise G. Kaufman, "Women in Philanthropy," October 6, 1896, Papers of the Woman's Club of Olympia, Washington, privately held.

95 Arlene Kaplan Daniels, *Invisible Careers: Women Civic Leaders from the Volunteer World* (Chicago: University of Chicago Press, 1988), provides contemporary empirical evidence that women's volunteer work is neither casual nor sporadic, a point clubwomen made on their own behalf nearly a century ago.

96 Anne Firor Scott, "Women and Libraries," *Journal of Library History* 21 (Spring 1986): 400; Karen Blair, *The Clubwoman as Feminist: True Womanhood Redefined, 1868–1914* (New York: Holmes and Meier, 1980), 101; and Dee Garrison, *Apostles of Culture: The Public Librarian and American Society, 1876–1920* (New York: Free Press, 1979), 132, all make this claim regarding clubwomen's role in establishing libraries.

97 Mrs. Charles A. Perkins, "Library Extension Work," *Federation Bulletin* 1 (January 1904): 36.

98 "U.P.W.C. Meeting," *Woman's Exponent* 31 (September 1902): 25.

99 Rainey, *History of Oklahoma State Federation of Women's Clubs,* asserts, "A careful survey of the libraries of the state discloses that seventy-seven have been founded or materially aided by women's clubs. Besides the seventy-seven mentioned the women's Clubs of Oklahoma assisted in the establishment of libraries in many State and Federal institutions" (15). In most cases, of course, clubwomen had to create alliances with the powerful men of their community. Carnegie funding, for example, came much more readily to male applicants than to female ones. As Daniel Ring, "Carnegie Libraries as Symbols for an Age: Montana as a Test Case,"

Libraries and Culture 27 (Winter 1992), puts it, "Women's clubs articulated the need for a Carnegie library, but they would have been powerless had not the economic and political elite agreed with them" (9).

100 *Proceedings of the First Convention of the National Council of Jewish Women, New York, 1896 Nov. 15–19* (Philadelphia: Jewish Publication Society of America, 1897), 66.

101 "A Club Civic Circle," *Club Worker* 5 (November 1903): 1.

102 Gates, *History of the Young Ladies' Mutual Improvement Association,* 300.

103 Abigail A. Van Slyck, *Free to All: Carnegie Libraries and American Culture, 1890–1920* (Chicago: University of Chicago Press, 1996), offers a detailed discussion of negotiations between clubwomen and businessmen interested in Carnegie's support for library construction.

104 "Women's Educational and Industrial Union of Boston," *Federation Bulletin* 1 (May 1904): 99.

105 "Summer School for Working Girls," *Club Worker* 3 (May 1901): 2.

106 D. G. White, "The Cost of Club Work," 249.

107 "A Tabulated List of Club Classes for One Year," *Club Worker* 6 (October 1905): 374–75.

108 Elsie LaG. Cole, "The Philadelphia Trade Class," *Club Worker* 8 (December 1907): 691.

109 Minutes of the Woman's Improvement Club of Indianapolis, April–September 1909. See also Earline Rae Ferguson, "The Woman's Improvement Club of Indianapolis: Black Women Pioneers in Tuberculosis Work, 1903–1938," *Indiana Magazine of History* 84 (September 1988): 237–61.

110 Mrs. Arthur S. Gray, "The Negro at Atlanta Exposition," *Woman's Era* 2 (January 1896): 10.

111 Elizabeth E. Seittelman, "The Contributions of Jewish Women to Education in the United States," *Principal* 21 (September 1975): 1–10.

112 1914–15 Yearbook of the New York Section, 45, Papers of New York Section of the National Council of Jewish Women, privately held.

113 Alice Kessler-Harris, *Out to Work: A History of Wage-Earning Women in the United States* (New York: Oxford University Press, 1982).

114 Dee Garrison, "The Tender Technicians: The Feminization of Public Librarianship, 1876–1905," *Journal of Social History* 6 (Winter 1972–73): 131.

115 Garrison, *Apostles of Culture,* 178–79, xiii.

116 Garrison, "Tender Technicians," 132.

117 Robyn Muncy, *Creating a Female Dominion in American Reform, 1890–1935* (New York: Oxford University Press, 1991), 21.

118 Ibid., 58–61.

119 Lucy Page Stelle, "Business and Professional Opportunities for Women," *Young Woman's Journal* 2 (October 1890), reports that when Harriet Martineau visited the United States in 1840, she found only seven occupations open to women, but "today there are over three hundred different branches of industry open to the

sex whereby she can earn from three hundred to three thousand annually" (24). Mary Martha Thomas, *The New Woman in Alabama: Social Reforms and Suffrage, 1890–1920* (Tuscaloosa: University of Alabama Press, 1992), notes that members of the Alabama Federation of Women's Clubs proposed that the 1899 legislature establish an industrial school for boys. The legislature chartered the school and made this "the only one in the nation that had a board composed exclusively of women" (50). In this and similar ways clubwomen's philanthropic projects created new administrative roles and occupational opportunities for women.

120   Julia Ward Howe, *Modern Society* (Boston: Roberts Brothers, 1991), 32.

121   "Reapers' Club," *Woman's Exponent* 25 (June 1896): 1.

122   Dora Tweed, "Woman in Club Life: Her Duties and Responsibilities," Papers of Woman's Club of Olympia, privately held; Minutes of the Chautauqua Circle of Atlanta, October 19, 1917.

123   Karen J. Blair, *The Torchbearers: Women and Their Amateur Arts Associations in America, 1890–1930* (Bloomington: Indiana University Press, 1994), 124.

124   Ibid., 130, 126.

125   Mary S. Gibson, *A Record of Twenty-Five Years of the California Federation of Women's Clubs, 1900–1925* (Los Angeles: California Federation of Women's Clubs, 1927), 33.

126   Maud Nathan, *The Story of an Epoch-Making Movement* (New York: Doubleday, 1926), 59.

127   "The Woman Who Spends," *Federation Bulletin* 3 (May 1906): 393.

128   "The National Consumers' League," *Club Worker* 3 (November 1901): 29.

129   Quoted in Kathryn Kish Sklar, *Florence Kelley and the Nation's Work: The Rise of Women's Political Culture, 1830–1900* (New Haven, Conn.: Yale University Press, 1995), 375.

130   Leach, *Land of Desire,* notes that by 1915 "the clothing trade was America's third largest, outranked only by steel and oil" (93). Stanley Lebergott, *Pursuing Happiness: American Consumers in the Twentieth Century* (Princeton, N.J.: Princeton University Press, 1993), reports that women's percentage of the total amount spent for clothing in the United States increased from 38 percent in 1899 to 52 percent in 1919 (92).

131   Carolyn Kay Steedman, *Landscape for a Good Woman: A Story of Two Lives* (New Brunswick, N.J.: Rutgers University Press, 1992), writes, "Within recent history decent clothing has been a necessity for any woman or girl child who wants to enter the social world; it's her means of entry, and there are rules that say so" (89). See also Carolyn Kay Steedman, *The Tidy House: Little Girls Writing* (London: Virago, 1982), 119–28. The social world paid considerable attention to women's clothing at the turn of the century, as debates about dress reform show, and clubwomen participated in these debates. Robert Riegel, "Women's Clothes and Women's Rights," *American Quarterly* 15 (Fall 1963), explains that the New England Women's Club supported dress reform and established a store to "give advice, demonstrate various garments, provide patterns and take orders" (396). Julia Ward

Howe, a member of the New England Women's Club, published "Dress and Undress," *Forum* 3 (May 1887): 313–20.

132   Andrew R. Heinze, *Adapting to Abundance: Jewish Immigrants, Mass Consumption, and the Search for American Identity* (New York: Columbia University Press, 1990), argues that consumption was central to American acculturation of Jews: "The unusual interest of Jews in American dress, however, signaled a particularly keen awareness that items of consumption in general constituted important building blocks of American identity" (4). Barbara A. Schreier, *Becoming American Women* (Chicago: Chicago Historical Society, 1995), offers compelling illustrations of Jewish women using those building blocks. I am indebted to Diava Markelis for giving me this book.

133   Campbell and Wirtz, *First Fifty Years,* 33. The importance of clothing also appears in such fiction as Anzia Yezierska's *Hungry Hearts* (Boston: Houghton Mifflin, 1920). Perhaps the best example is when Shenah Pessah, the central character in Yezierska's short story "Wings" purchases colorful new clothing "only to be beautiful . . . for him" and receives new attentions from the scholarly young man who interests her. Later in the story she declares, "I'm through for always with old women's shawls. This is my first American dress-up," demonstrating how clothing is calibrated in Americanization (21, 25). Susan Porter Benson, *Counter Cultures: Saleswomen, Managers, and Customers in American Department Stores, 1890–1940* (Urbana: University of Illinois Press, 1986), asserts that clothing "crystallized the complicated interaction between saleswomen's roles as workers and as consumers" (235). Careful observation and imitation allowed the clerk to narrow the gap between her and her customer, it provided her the means to advance to a higher-paying position in the store, and it furnished evidence of her skill as a consumer.

134   Lillian W. Betts, *The Leaven in a Great City* (New York: Dodd, Mead, 1902), 151.

135   Bessie Van Vorst and Marie Van Vorst, *The Woman Who Toils: Being the Experiences of Two Gentlewoman as Factory Girls* (New York: Doubleday, 1903), report, "In the Parisian clothes I am accustomed to wear I present the familiar outline of any woman of the world. With the aid of coarse woolen garments, a shabby felt sailor hat, a cheap piece of fur, a knitted shawl and gloves I am transformed into a working girl of the ordinary type." Her assumption proves true immediately, as she explains, "I get no farther than the depot when I observe that I am being treated as though I were ignorant and lacking in experience" (11). Beverly Gordon, "Victorian Fancywork in the American Home: Fantasy and Accommodation," in *Making the American Home: Middle-Class Women and Domestic Material Culture, 1840–1940* (Bowling Green, Ohio: Bowling Green State University Press, 1988), describes the theme of transformation and masquerade that appeared in many needlework objects produced at the turn of the century. White silk squares were designed to look like soda crackers, matchbooks as drums, and pen wipers as parasols. Such objects were, she argues, "a symbol and a mirror of the desire for something

beyond the mundane and repetitive reality of domestic life," an escape from the confines of the home (63–64).

136 Van Vorst and Van Vorst, *Woman Who Toils,* perpetuated this claim with such statements as "The sacrifices they make for clothes are the first in importance" (92). Such comments appear throughout their account of working women: "For two nights the girls worked until twelve o'clock so that when the 'show' came they might have something new to wear that nobody had seen" (94). "What harmony can there be between the elaborate get-up of these young women and the miserable homes where they live? The idolizing of material things is a religion nurtured by this class of whom I speak" (113).

137 Elizabeth Ewen, "City Lights: Immigrant Women and the Rise of the Movies," in *Women and the American City,* ed. Catherine R. Stimpson, Elsa Dixler, Martha J. Jelson, and Kathy B. Yatrakis (Chicago: University of Chicago Press, 1981), 62.

138 "Correspondence," *Far and Near* 2 (April and May 1892): 143.

139 "Dress," *Young Woman's Journal* 1 (May 1890): 276; 1 (June 1890): 324.

140 "Thrift in the Community," *National Association Notes* 19 (January 1917): 2.

141 Elizabeth Arens, "A Word from Experience," *Club Worker* 8 (February 1907): 571.

142 Rozsika Parker, *The Subversive Stitch: Embroidery and the Making of the Feminine* (London: Woman's Press, 1984), 75.

143 Linda Faye Dickson, "The Early Club Movement among Black Women in Denver, 1890–1925" (Ph.D. diss., University of Colorado, 1982), 153.

144 Minutes of the Women in Council, December 30, 1892, Papers of the Women in Council of Roxbury, Manuscript Division, Boston Public Library, Boston, Mass.

145 Parker, *Subversive Stitch,* 179.

146 Quoted in Cunningham, *Woman's Club of El Paso,* 29.

147 "Old Colony Trust Company," *Federation Bulletin* 2 (June 1904): 190.

148 Minutes of the New England Women's Club, February 25, 1868.

149 See, for example, *Godey's,* May 1868, January 1869, August 1874, and January 1878.

150 Joan Shelley Rubin, "Self, Culture, and Self-Culture in Modern America: The Early History of the Book-of-the-Month Club," *Journal of American History* 71 (March 1985), observes that women, of course, borrowed the term *club* from men (795), but Anne Firor Scott, *Natural Allies: Women's Associations in American History* (Urbana: University of Illinois Press, 1991), notes that clubs occupied a much more central place in the lives of women than in men's (177).

151 A column titled "Clubwomen and Clubwork" began appearing in *Harper's* in 1891 and continued until 1899, when it was replaced by a column titled "Club News." Edited by Margaret Hamilton Welsh, it featured news and notes from (white middle-class) clubs throughout the country.

152 Leigh North, "A Girls' Literary Club," *Ladies' Home Journal* 9 (January 1892): 16; Marion Harland, "Reading Clubs in the Country," *Ladies' Home Journal* 7 (June

1890): 12; M. Louise Thomas, "Presiding over a Woman's Club," *Ladies' Home Journal* 9 (December 1892): 12; Louise Stockton "Organizing a Literary Club," *Ladies' Home Journal* 11 (March 1894): 17.

153   See, for example, "What Women's Clubs Are Doing," *Ladies' Home Journal* 30 (February 1913), 20; and "The Woman's Club This Autumn," *Ladies' Home Journal* 31 (October 1914): 2.

154   Caroline French Benton, *The Complete Club Book for Women* (Boston: Page, 1915). Others included Catherine Benedict Burrell, *Woman's Club Work and Programs* (Boston: D. Estes, 1913); Alice Hazen Cass, *Practical Programs for Women's Clubs: A Compilation of Study Subjects for the Use of Women's Clubs and Similar Organizations* (Chicago: A. C. McClurg, 1915); Augusta Harriet Leypoldt, *List of Books for Girls and Women and Their Clubs* (Boston: American Library Association, 1895); Olive Thorne Miller, *The Woman's Club: A Practical Guide and Hand-book* (New York: U.S. Book Company, 1891); and Kate Louise Roberts, *The Club Woman's Handybook of Programs and Club Management* (New York: Funk and Wagnalls, 1914).

155   Jeff Nunokawa, *The Afterlife of Property: Domestic Security and the Victorian Novel* (Princeton, N.J.: Princeton University Press, 1994), makes this argument.

CHAPTER 4: FASHIONING AMERICAN WOMANHOOD(S)

1   Frances Ellen Watkins Harper, "Woman's Political Future," in *The World's Congress of Representative Women* (Chicago: Rand McNally, 1894), 433–34. Members of the Chicago Woman's Club, particularly Bertha Palmer, led in creating a female presence at the exposition. In the face of continuing opposition, they constructed the Woman's Building to display women's accomplishments. (An 1889 petition to Congress to include women on the exposition's governing board had been rejected, and the Board of Lady Managers, chaired by Palmer, was established instead.) Most of the board was composed of white clubwomen, and they steadily opposed including any African American women, despite numerous requests. Six African American women—nearly all of them clubwomen—were eventually invited to speak at the congress, among them Frances Harper. In addition to white middle-class Protestant and African American groups, Jewish, Mormon, and working-class clubwomen were represented. The National Council of Jewish Women was formed here, and national publications of all clubwomen include numerous references to the Congress of Women.

2   Josiah Strong, *Our Country* (1886; reprint, Cambridge, Mass.: Harvard University Press, 1963), 218.

3   Gerda Lerner, *The Majority Finds Its Past: Placing Women in History* (New York: Oxford University Press, 1979), 20.

4   Nancy Cott, *The Bonds of Women: "Woman's Sphere" in New England, 1780–1835* (New Haven, Conn.: Yale University Press, 1977), 199.

5   Although his essay on race suicide appeared in 1907 (see below), Roosevelt used
     race suicide in a prefactory letter for Bessie Van Vorst and Marie Van Vorst's *Woman
     Who Toils: Being the Experiences of Two Gentlewomen as Factory Girls* (New York: Dou-
     bleday, 1902). Written in response to the serialized magazine version of the book
     and included at the Van Vorsts' request, the letter shares the book's condemna-
     tion of working women as self-indulgent. Roosevelt identifies race suicide as
     "more important than any other question in this country," criticizes the desire to
     be "independent," and charges those who choose not to have children as being
     "criminal against the race" (vii–viii). For the more widely published version, see
     Theodore Roosevelt, "A Letter from President Roosevelt on Race Suicide," *Re-
     view of Reviews* 57 (May 1907): 35.
6   Eric Hobsbawn and Terrence Ranger, *The Invention of Tradition* (London: Cambridge
     University Press, 1983).
7   Quoted in Jane M. Hatch, *The American Book of Days* (New York: H. W. Wilson,
     1978), 440.
8   Hobsbawn and Ranger, *Invention of Tradition,* 4.
9   Quoted in Thomas Woody, *A History of Women's Education in the United States* (New
     York: Science, 1929), 423.
10   "Jewish Women," *Woman's Journal* 6 (October 1875), included this: "The position
     of women in the Hebrew Church has been, and still is one of more marked sub-
     jection and inferiority than in any other church, except perhaps the Mormon. In
     the Hebrew Church women have always sat apart in the gallery, old ladies roil-
     ing up the stairs, while their vigorous sons sat with all other men in the body of
     the house below" (244).
11   Edward H. Clarke, *Sex in Education: A Fair Chance for Girls* (Boston: Osgood, 1873),
     18, 40, 41.
12   Joan Burstyn, *Victorian Education and the Ideal of Womanhood* (London: Croon Helm,
     1980), writes, "Medicine was the first occupation to be assailed by women in their
     drive to enter the professions, and it was medical practitioners who made the
     strongest attack against higher education for women. Specialists in gynecology
     and obstetrics, who were the first to feel competition from women doctors, were
     prominent in the attack, claiming that the dangers of mental fatigue lay in its ef-
     fects on women's reproductive system" (85). Some clubwomen who were Clarke's
     contemporaries recognized his design. Julia Ward Howe, *Sex in Education: A Reply
     to Dr. Clarke's Sex in Education* (Boston:Roberts, 1874), charged that Clarke pre-
     dicted diseases for women simply because "some of them wish to enter Harvard
     College and some of them have already passed through other colleges" (37).
13   E. S. Martin, "Mothers and Daughters," *Good Housekeeping* 64 (May 1917): 27;
     Ouida, "The New Woman," *North American Review* 272 (September 1887): 612.
     Cynthia Eagle Russett, *Sexual Science: The Victorian Construction of Womanhood* (Cam-
     bridge, Mass.: Harvard University Press, 1989), argues that late nineteenth-cen-

tury scientists helped maintain middle-class dominance and men's peace of mind by deprecating women and portraying them as arrested/underdeveloped males. "Women and savages, together with idiots, criminals, and pathological monstrosities, were a constant source of anxiety to intellectuals in the late nineteenth century" (63), Russett states.

14   Quoted in Arthur M. Schlesinger and Dixon Fox, eds., *The Rise of the City, 1878–1898,* vol. 10 of *A History of American Life* (New York: Macmillan, 1933), 61.

15   Sarah Grand, "The New Aspect of the Woman Question," *North American Review* 158 (March 1894), is frequently credited with coining the term *new woman* (271). Author of several novels, Grand was best known for *The Heavenly Twins,* a text familiar to most clubwomen. As originally articulated, *new woman* referred to the career-oriented, middle-class woman active in urban reform, but after 1920 the term included women who challenged ideas of female restraint and asexuality. As used here, *new woman* refers only to the former.

16   Ruth M. Winton, "Literature via the Woman's Club," *Critic* 23 (January 1904): 35; Nancy A. Hewitt, *Woman's Activism and Social Change: Rochester, New York, 1822–1872* (Ithaca, N.Y.: Cornell University Press, 1984). Elizabeth Ammons, *Conflicting Stories: American Women Writers at the Turn into the Twentieth Century* (New York: Oxford University Press, 1991), shows that women writers of the period, including Willa Cather (*The Song of the Lark*), Mary Austin (*A Woman of Genius*), Jessie Fauset (*The Sleeper Wakes*), Angelina Grimke (*Rachel*), Edith Wharton (*House of Mirth* and *Summer*), and Sui Sin Far (*Mrs. Spring Fragrance*), all provided nuanced and thoughtful explorations of the debates surrounding the "new woman."

17   Margaret Deland, "The Change in the Feminine Ideal," *Atlantic Monthly* 105 (March 1910): 289.

18   Alice Kessler-Harris, *Out to Work: A History of Wage-Earning Women in the United States* (New York: Oxford University Press, 1982), 97.

19   Glenna Matthews, *The Rise of Public Woman* (New York: Oxford University Press, 1992), cites statistics on the enormous increase in the number of working women living alone between 1880 and 1930 (152).

20   Kessler-Harris, *Out to Work,* 152.

21   The 1862 Morrill Act prohibited polygamy, and the 1870 Cullom bill gave federal agents broad authority to enforce antipolygamy laws in the territories (as opposed to states). Utah sought statehood between 1846 and 1896, when it was finally granted. Rudolph Glanz, *The German Woman,* vol. 2 of *The Jewish Woman in America: Two Female Immigrant Generations, 1820–1929* (Washington, D.C.: KTAV Publishing and the National Council of Jewish Women, 1976), quotes cynical observers of Mormon politics: "We are told that, in private Brigham Young expresses the most unqualified opposition to woman's political equality. However this may be, both parties have appealed to the women for help, which is a new proof that 'when rogues fall out honest women get their due'" (142).

22 Giles Jackson, *The Industrial History of the Negro Race* (Richmond, Va.: Negro Education Association, 1919), writes, "The race needs wives who stay at home, being supported by their husbands, and then they can spend time in the training of their children" (341).

23 Martha Banta, *Imaging American Women: Ideas and Ideals in Cultural History* (New York: Columbia University Press, 1987), 45–92.

24 Quoted in Helen Damon-Moore, *Magazines for the Millions: Gender and Commerce in the Ladies' Home Journal and the Saturday Evening Post, 1880–1910* (Albany, N.Y.: SUNY Press, 1994), 159.

25 Ella R. Bartlett, "The New Woman," *American Jewess* 1 (April 1894): 169–70.

26 Kessler-Harris, *Out to Work*, 98–99.

27 Elsie Ada Faust, "The New Woman," *Woman's Exponent* 25 (December 15, 1896): 111; "Reapers' Club," *Woman's Exponent* 25 (June 1896): 1.

28 *Young Woman's Journal* 1–8 (1889–96); Homespun, "Whatsoever Man Soweth," *Young Woman's Journal* 1 (October 1889): 1–9, 45–50; Genie, "Polished Stones" *Young Woman's Journal* 1 (March 1890): 193–209.

29 M. A. V. Greenhalgh, "Woman's Progress," *Young Woman's Journal* 2 (September 1891): 552; Claudia L. Bushman, ed., *Mormon Sisters: Women in Early Utah* (Salt Lake City: Olympus, 1976), xix (quote on effects of polygamy).

30 "Our Girls," *Young Woman's Journal* 1 (April 1890): 225.

31 Aria Macdonald, "The New Woman and the New Man," May 28, 1896, Papers of the Olympia Woman's Club of Olympia, Washington, privately held.

32 Quoted in Mary S. Gibson, *A Record of Twenty-Five Years of the California Federation of Women's Clubs, 1900–1925* (Los Angeles: California Federation of Women's Clubs, 1927), 109.

33 Minutes of the Chautauqua Circle, October 13, 1913, Papers of the Chautauqua Circle of Atlanta, Robert W. Woodruff Library, Atlanta University, Atlanta, Ga.

34 Mary Church Terrell, "What the National Association Has Meant to Colored Women," Mary Church Terrell Papers, Moorland-Spingarn Research Center, Howard University, Washington, D.C.

35 "Pleasantries and Parallels of Earlier Days," Papers of the Naugatuck Study Club of Naugatuck, Connecticut, privately held, indicates that the debate "Resolved that Equal Suffrage Should Prevail" was introduced in 1910, with club members taking both sides. Subsequently, the club invited an antisuffrage speaker and included this in introducing her: "In no sense was Study Club committed to one side or the other of this problem." The next year the club heard a lecturer who favored woman's suffrage, and when it was later approached by the State Committee for Woman's Suffrage, the club issued this statement: "As a club we do not care to do anything in connection with the suffrage movement, but individuals would be glad to attend the upcoming mass meeting at Columbus Hall."

36   Minutes of the Hillsdale Women's Club, 1894–95, Papers of the Women's Club of Hillsdale, Michigan, Bentley Historical Library, University of Michigan, Ann Arbor; Minutes of the Inman Park Study Club, 1910–13, Papers of the Inman Park Study Club of Atlanta, State Historical Society, Atlanta, Ga.; Minutes of the Olympia Woman's Club, 1897, Papers of the Olympia Woman's Club of Olympia, Washington.

37   1891 Yearbook of the Detroit Section, 1, 4, 8, 11, Papers of the Detroit Section of the National Council of Jewish Women, Reuther Collection, Detroit Public Library, Detroit, Mich.

38   "About Women," *Far and Near* 3 (March 1893): 99; "Women in Business," *Far and Near* 3 (June 1893): 159; "About Women," *Far and Near* 3 (July 1893): 186.

39   Leonora O'Reilly, "Some Mistakes of Working Women," *Far and Near* 4 (August 1894): 139–40.

40   *History of the National League of Women Workers* (New York: Pearl, 1914): 5.

41   "The Real America," *Federation Bulletin* 3 (December 1905): 102, 103–4.

42   Eva Cherniavsky, *That Pale Mother Rising: Sentimental Discourses and the Imitation of Motherhood in Nineteenth-Century America* (Bloomington: Indiana University Press, 1995), x.

43   "Motherhood of State," *General Federation of Women's Clubs Magazine* 16 (February 1917): 17; Henry F. Sherwood, "Better Films for Children," *General Federation of Women's Clubs Magazine* 16 (March 1917): 20; "The Problems of Maternity," *General Federation of Women's Clubs Magazine* 17 (December 1918): 19.

44   "Editorial," *Federation Bulletin* 3 (December 1905): 99.

45   "Editorial," *Federation Bulletin* 5 (October 1907): 1. This quotation appears in a three-page response to the article that appeared in the September 1907 *Atlantic Monthly* criticizing women's increased education, which the *Bulletin* described as "one of the most bitter attacks upon the women of our country which has ever appeared in any responsible or thoughtful publication" (1).

46   Annette M. Meakin, *Woman in Transition* (London: Methuen, 1907), 38.

47   Minutes of the Friday Club, May 13, 1890, Papers of the Friday Club of Jackson, Michigan, Bentley Historical Library, University of Michigan, Ann Arbor.

48   Susan K. Harris, *Nineteenth-Century American Women's Novels: Interpretive Strategies* (New York: Cambridge University Press, 1990).

49   Minutes of the Women in Council, November 24, 1914, Papers of the Women in Council of Roxbury, Manuscript Division, Boston Public Library, Boston, Mass. It is worth noting that the "slaughter of potential life" represented a new turn in the ideology of motherhood—*potential* motherhood was introduced as a concept when it became clear that few working women were actually mothers.

50   Ibid., December 8, 1914.

51   Ibid., February 15, 1915.

52   Ibid., November 12, 1916. As club records from other states indicate, voting for

the school board was indeed a privilege. Sallie Southall Cotten, *History of the North Carolina Federation of Women's Clubs: 1901–1925* (Raleigh, N.C.: Edwards and Broughton, 1925), points out that the North Carolina Federation encountered a wall of opposition when it first proposed that women vote for school boards. When clubwomen created an alliance with the Teachers' Assembly, the legislature finally passed a "statue permitting women to serve on the school boards of the State" (51). This legislation did not pass easily, however. After failing twice, it passed because the president of the North Carolina Federation urged clubwomen to bombard "the legislators with letters and telegrams while the bill was being discussed so that no one could fail to understand the wish of the women. The vote was 39 to 39, but the Speaker broke the tie by voting for it" (61–62).

53 Lynn Weiner, *From Working Girl to Working Mother: The Female Labor Force in the United States, 1820–1980* (Chapel Hill: University of North Carolina Press), 44–46.

54 Quoted in Kessler-Harris, *Out to Work,* 154.

55 Cherniavsky, *That Pale Mother Rising,* xi.

56 Fannie Barrier Williams, "The Club Movement among the Colored Women," *Voice of the Negro* 1 (March 1904): 101.

57 Julia Ward Howe, "Woman's Great Work for Peace," *Federation Bulletin* 2 (November 1904): 36. Hatch, *American Book of Days,* reports that Howe suggested renaming July 4 Mother's Day and urged that "the occasion be used for promoting peace" (239). Harriet Hyman Alonso, *Peace as a Women's Issue: A History of the U.S. Movement for World Peace and Women's Rights* (Syracuse, N.Y.: Syracuse University Press, 1993), writes: "As late as 1909, thirty-six years after its founding and a year before Howe's death, members of the Peace Society were still sponsoring the Mother's Day for Peace activities every June 2" (46–47).

58 Howe, "Woman's Great Work," 37.

59 "Mrs. Henrotin's Letter," *Woman's Exponent* 26 (March 15 and April 1, 1898): 275.

60 Quoted in Gibson, *Record of Twenty-Five Years of the California Federation of Women's Clubs,* 94–98.

61 Bernice Graziani, *Where There's a Woman: Seventy-five Years of History as Lived by the National Council of Jewish Women* (New York: McCall, 1967), 26, 32, 34.

62 "We and the War," *Club Worker* 9 (June 1914): 8; "Ellen Key on Antimilitarism," *Club Worker* 9 (November 1914): 2–3.

63 Eileen Boris, "The Power of Motherhood: Black and White Activist Women Redefine the 'Political,'" in *Mothers of a New World: Maternalist Politics and the Origins of Welfare States,* ed. Seth Koven and Sonya Michel (New York: Routledge, 1993), 233.

64 "The Peace Conference," *Woman's Exponent* 25 (June 1896): 5 (first quote); "Peace Meeting" *Woman's Exponent* 28 (June 15, 1899): 6 (second quote); "Working for Peace" *Woman's Exponent* 30 (May 1902): 100.

65 "Anchorage Woman's Club," *Daily Times,* May 24, 1920, reports that "all ordinary

work of the club was laid aside and made secondary to the demands of the Red Cross and other patriotic work" (3). Annual Report of the Women in Council of Roxbury, 1918, reports that "a beautiful silk flag was purchased at the beginning of the year through individual subscriptions, and it is our custom to open each meeting with the salute to the flag" and that "the meeting closed with all joining in singing the Star Spangled Banner." The 1918 report recounts women's actions: "Mrs. Chase Morgan was scheduled to give a demonstration on conservation, Mrs. Morgan changed her subject and told how Americans had helped to feed Belgium and France and the wonderful result which the women had accomplished in conservation" (February 11); "Mrs. Brigadier Sheppard of the Salvation Army told of her experiences under fire helping troops in France" (February 25). Muriel Beadle and the Centennial History Committee, *The Fortnightly of Chicago: The City and Its Women, 1873–1973* (Chicago: Henry Regnery, 1973), reports this from Fortnightly records: "It seems only right that we should become the loyal possessors of our flag" and give club rooms to the "great and noble present need." As one member put it, the club became a "patriotic society" between 1917 and 1919 (136).

66 See, for example, Jill Conway, "The Woman's Peace Party and the First World War," in *War and Society in North America*, ed. J. L. Grantstein and R. D. Cuff (Toronto: Thomas Nelson, 1971); and Susan Zieger, "Finding a Cure for War: Women's Politics and the Peace Movement in the 1920s," *Journal of Social History* 24 (Fall 1990): 69–86. I am grateful to Rashela DuPuis for making me aware of this interpretation of the peace movement. William L. O'Neill, *Everyone Was Brave: The Rise and Fall of Feminism in America* (Chicago: Quadrangle, 1969), takes a much more pejorative view, arguing that clubwomen's complicated responses to the war indicated "confusion" (217).

67 Quoted in Cotten, *History of the North Carolina Federation,* 100. In supporting the war effort, some clubwomen also managed to assert a feminist perspective. Luretta Rainey, *History of Oklahoma State Federation of Women's Clubs* (Guthrie, Okla.: Co-Operative Publishing, 1939), notes that the Oklahoma Federation of Women's Clubs established the War Victory Commission and that "the principal duty assigned that committee was raising funds to defray expenses of young women sent over-seas" (18).

68 "Belgium Relief," *Club Worker* 10 (December 1915): 7.

69 "Colored American Women in War Work," Papers of the Neighborhood Union of Atlanta, Robert W. Woodruff Library, Atlanta University, Atlanta, Ga.

70 Lugenia Hope, "Report on Camp Upton," Papers of the Neighborhood Union of Atlanta.

71 Ann Massa, "Black Women in the 'White City,'" *Journal of American Studies* 8 (December 1974): 320. Jeanne Madeline Weimann, *The Fair Women* (Chicago: Academy, 1981), reproduced one typical reaction to the congressional designation: "There has been a great deal of unfavorable comment on the ridiculous title 'Lady

Managers' . . . and the criticism is just, but the fault . . . is not with the women. The title congress gave us conveys the impression that we are a useless ornament—; idle women of fashion; whereas our board comprises as many workers, as much representation of the active industries of the country, as if it were composed of men" (36).

72 Quoted in Virginia Grant Darney, "Women and World's Fairs: American International Expositions, 1876–1904" (Ph.D. diss., Emory University, 1982), 108.

73 Darney, "Women and World's Fairs," reports that a bazaar sponsored by the Friday Club of Chicago netted $35,000, which paid for the construction of the Woman's Building. This building, the only one at the exposition designed by a woman—Sarah Hayden of Boston—demonstrated women's accomplishments with both its exhibits and its method of construction. The board had originally wanted to integrate women's contributions into every exhibit instead of segregating them into the one Women's Building, but male exhibitors rejected this idea (85–90).

74 Donald Miller, "The White City," *American Heritage* 44 (July 1993): 71, 85.

75. Robert W. Rydell, *All the World's a Fair: Visions of Empire at American International Expositions, 1876–1916* (Chicago: University of Chicago Press, 1984), 60. "A Glimpse of a Great Exposition" *Club Worker* 5 (June/July 1904), includes a description of the 1904 St. Louis Exposition that confirms Rydell's claims by emphasizing the exotic villages "inhabited by Filipinos, Hawaiians and other representatives from beyond the seas" (176).

76 Quoted in Massa, "Black Women in the 'White City,'" 322.

77 Darney, "Women and World's Fairs," 113.

78 Massa, "Black Women in the 'White City,'" 327.

79 Miller, "The White City," 85.

80 Quoted in Massa, "Black Women in the 'White City,'" 335.

81 Linda Gordon Kuzmack, *Woman's Cause: The Jewish Woman's Movement in England and the United States, 1881–1933* (Columbus: Ohio State University, 1990), writes, "Women's clubs shared racial and economic biases, rather than the religious exclusivity of men's clubs, so they were content to admit middle- and upper-class Jewish women" (31).

82 Program, 1891, Inaugural Meeting of the Woman's Club of Temple Beth El, Papers of the Detroit Section of the National Council of Jewish Women.

83 "Correspondence Column," *Far and Near* 3 (September 1893): 132–33; Isabel Bates Winslow, "Some Curious People," *Far and Near* 4 (November 1893): 9 (first quote); Dora M. Morrell, "About Going to the Fair," *Far and Near* 3 (May 1893): 137 (second quote); Irene Pratt, "Woman's Work at the World's Fair," *Far and Near* 3 (December 1893): 27 (third quote).

84 *Bulletin of the New York Association of Working Girls' Societies* (1893): 2.

85 Quoted in Weimann, *Fair Women*, 250.

86 "Woman's Part in the Exposition," *Woman's Exponent* 21 (January 15, 1893): 110.

87 Graziani, *Where There's a Woman,* reports that Hannah Solomon attended the 1904 International Congress of Women in Berlin with Susan B. Anthony and, because of her fluency in German and French, acted as Anthony's interpreter (26). A "Welcome Reception Program" was held on August 10, 1904, when Terrell returned from this congress. "Welcome Reception Program," August 10, 1904, Mary Church Terrell Papers. Theodora Penny Martin, *The Sound of Our Own Voices* (Boston: Beacon, 1987), includes an 1895 photograph of three clubwomen departing "on their own" for Europe (146). Jennie June Cunningham Croly, *The History of the Woman's Club Movement in America* (New York: Henry G. Allen, 1898), reports on several successful clubwomen's trips to Mexico and the Holy Land led by the Tourist Club of Grand Forks, North Dakota (324).

88 Schlesinger and Fox, *The Rise of the City,* report that in 1825 a trans-Atlantic trip cost $100, and in 1896 it cost $26 because of the shift from sail to steam ships (174). *Far and Near* included among its regular columns "Letters about . . . ," which provided travelogues featuring such places as Egypt, Jerusalem, and Dresden written by clubwomen. A series of articles titled "Some Fugitive Experiences in Europe" also provided a continuing account of European travel. Individual clubs also sponsored imaginary travel experiences, where clubwomen would look at slides, read books, and write in their diaries about itineraries. "The World as Seen through a Woman's Eyes," *Young Woman's Journal* 2 (September 1891), indicates how broadly accounts of clubwomen's travel circulated: "Mrs. Potter Palmer is now in Europe in the interest of the World's Fair. She has recently had an audience with the wife of the President of the French Republic" (555). Although few Mormon clubwomen knew Palmer personally, their common identity as clubwomen lent significance to her travels.

89 Croly, *History of the Woman's Club Movement in America,* 291, 313, 448, 458, 467, 561, 601, 705, 1002.

90 "Club Gossip, *Woman's Era* 1 (March 24, 1894): 15. W. E. B. Du Bois, *The Souls of Black Folk* (1903; reprint, New York: Bantam, 1989), describes African Americans as "ever feeling their twoness—an American, a Negro; two souls, two thoughts, two unreconciled strivings; two warring ideals in one dark body" (3).

91 Hannah G. Solomon, "Report of the National Council of Jewish Women," *American Jewess* 1 (April 1894): 31.

92 "The World's Events," *Far and Near* 3 (December 1892): 29; "The World's Events," *Far and Near* 3 (January 1893): 53.

93 "The World as Seen through a Woman's Eyes," 359, 408, 457, 553.

94 Minutes of the Friday Club of Jackson, Michigan, March 25, 1898, include the topic "Has Spain Any Right to International Existence?" Both the topic and the timing (right after the U.S. battleship *Maine* had been sunk in the Havana harbor and just before the April declaration of war against Spain) demonstrate that clubwomen read and wrote about the changing relationships between the United States and other countries. Mary Anne Bourne, *The Ladies of Castine: From the Min-*

utes of the Castine, Maine, Woman's Club (New York: Arbor House, 1986), reports a 1915 lecture on relations with Mexico given by Professor Tubbs of Bates College that pointed to the role of business in U.S. imperialism (49). Minutes of the Chautauqua Circle of Atlanta, 1914 to 1916, include papers club members wrote on the Mexican Revolution, conditions in South Africa, the opening of the Panama Canal, Negro missionaries to Africa, and relations between the United States and Japan. See also Christine Green, "Is Japan a Menace to the U.S.?" Program of Annual Convention of State Federation of Colored Women's Clubs of Colorado and Jurisdiction, 1920, Papers of the Colorado State Association of Colored Women's Clubs, Western History Department, Denver Public Library.

95 1906 Clipping, Papers of the Sorosis Club of New York, Sophia Smith Collection, Smith College, Northampton, Mass.

96 A. H. H. Stuart, "What Education Has Done for the Negro," February 6, 1900, Papers of the Olympia Women's Club, Olympia, Washington.

97 Quoted in Lynda Faye Dickson, "The Early Club Movement among Black Women in Denver, 1908–1925" (Ph.D. diss., University of Colorado, 1982), 141.

98 Quoted in "Mrs. Booker T. Washington Lectures to Large Audience at Shorter A.M.E. Church," *Colorado Statesman* 17 (January 1, 1906): 3.

99 Gloria Wade-Gayles, "The Truths of Our Mothers' Lives: Mother-Daughter Relationships in Black Women's Fiction," *Sage* 1 (September 1984): 12; Stephanie J. Shaw, *What a Woman Ought to Be and Do: Black Professional Women Workers during the Jim Crow Era* (Chicago: University of Chicago Press, 1996), does not focus on the impact of clubs, but she includes a number of clubwomen in her study of "a construction of gender that was deliberately designed to enable women to transcend what has often been perceived by scholars as the multiple disabling factors (for black working women) of race, class and sex" (10).

100 Quoted from "Greetings from the National Association of Colored Women to the National Congress of Mothers" (1899), in Boris, "Power of Motherhood," 223. Boris makes a similar point about how Terrell used the language of motherhood.

101 Ida B. Wells, *U.S. Atrocities* (London: Lux, 1892), 11.

102 "Editorial," *Woman's Era* 2 (April 1895): 9.

103 Quoted in Charles Harris Wesley, *The History of the National Association of Colored Women's Clubs: A Legacy of Service* (Washington, D.C.: National Association of Colored Women, 1984), 34.

104 Minutes of the Women in Council of Roxbury, January 1, 1918.

105 Ibid., March 26, 1918.

106 Darlene Clark Hine, "Rape and the Inner Lives of Black Women in the Middle West: Preliminary Thoughts on the Culture of Dissemblance," *Signs: Journal of Women and Culture* 14 (Summer 1989): 912–20.

107 Gloria T. Hull, ed., *Give Us Each Day: The Diary of Alice Dunbar-Nelson* (New York: W. W. Norton, 1984), 174–75.

108 Eleanor Tayleur, "The Negro Woman: Social and Moral Decadence," *Outlook* 76

(January 30, 1904): 267, 269, 270; "Editorial," *Woman's Era* 2 (February 1896): 10.

109   Quoted in Wesley, *History of the National Association of Colored Women's Clubs,* 58.

110   Louise Venable Kennedy, *The Negro Peasant Turns Cityward: Effects of Recent Migration to Northern Centers* (College Park, Md.: McGrath, 1969), 30, 32.

111   1915–16 Yearbook of the Monday Club, Papers of the Monday Club of Clinton, New York, Archive Division, Hamilton College Library, Clinton, N.Y. Croly, *History of the Woman's Club Movement in America,* lists "The Race Problem" as a topic for the Hypatia Club of Wichita, Kansas, in 1897 (493). The 1901–2 Yearbook of the Nineteenth Century Club, Papers of the Nineteenth Century Club of Oak Park, Illinois, privately held, lists "Industrial Conditions among the Negroes of the South" among its topics.

112   "Minstrel Show of the Fall River Club," *Club Worker* 5 (May 1904), describes the Fall River Club's production and encourages other clubs to borrow this "idea for our successful minstrel show" (154); Robert Toll, *On with the Show: The First Century of Show Business in America* (New York: Oxford University Press, 1976), 111. I am indebted to William Cook for calling Toll's work to my attention. Eric Lott, *Love and Theft: Blackface Minstrelsy and the American Working Class* (New York: Oxford University Press, 1993), makes a similar point about blackface serving as a working-class strategy for dealing with an eroding economic position.

113   Minutes of the New England Women's Club, January 3, 1901, Papers of the New England Women's Club, Schlesinger Library, Radcliffe College, Cambridge, Mass.

114   Ibid., February 4, 1901.

115   John William Gibson, *Progress of a Race: Or the Remarkable Advancement of the American Negro* (Washington, D.C.: Austin Jenkins, 1920), writes that the California State Federation had a "courteous but strenuous" discussion of admitting colored clubs to the General Federation and "finally arrived at a point where it seemed wise to allow the California delegates to go the Sixth Biennial [of the General Federation] uninstructed" on the issue (21).

116   "The Chicago Woman's Club Reject Mrs. Williams," *Woman's Era* 1 (December 1894): 20. Anna Cooper, *A Voice from the South* (1893; reprint, New York: Oxford University Press, 1988), makes a similar point as she recounts a black woman's being rejected for membership in the white Wimodaughsis Club (80–84). In addition to being outspoken about the racism of the club, Cooper offers what Hazel Carby, *Reconstructing Womanhood: The Emergence of the Afro-American Woman Novelist* (New York: Oxford University Press, 1987), describes as "a unique perspective on racist and sexist oppression, a perspective which gave insight into the plight of all oppressed peoples" (103), once again implying agency rather than victimization.

117   "Address of Josephine St. P. Ruffin, President of the Conference," *Woman's Era* 2 (August 1895): 14.

118   Quoted in "New York Letter," *Woman's Era* 1 (March 24, 1894): 2.

119   Medora W. Gould, "Literature Notes," *Woman's Era* 1 (December 1894): 19.

120   Sara N. Johnson, "Report of Work among Colored People," *National Association Notes* 4 (February 1901): 1.

121   Mary Church Terrell, "What the National Association Has Meant to Colored Women."

122   Ellen Carol DuBois, "Harriot Stanton Blatch and the Transformation of Class Relations among Woman Suffragists," in *Gender, Class, Race, and Reform in the Progressive Era,* ed. Noralee Frankel and Nancy S. Dye (Lexington: University Press of Kentucky, 1991), 164.

CHAPTER 5: (RE)CALIBRATING CULTURE

1   George Santayana, "The Genteel Tradition in American Philosophy," in *Winds of Doctrine: Studies in Contemporary Opinion,* ed. George Santayana (New York: Scribner's, 1913), 185–215.

2   John Tomsich, *A Genteel Endeavor: American Culture and Politics in the Guilded Age* (Stanford, Calif.: Stanford University Press, 1971), asserts, "Whatever its reputation may have been, however, genteel culture did exert a significant and pervasive influence in America from the Civil War until about 1910" (4).

3   Lawrence Levine, *Highbrow/Lowbrow: The Emergence of Cultural Hierarchy in America* (Cambridge, Mass.: Harvard University Press, 1988), 229.

4   T. J. Jackson Lears, *No Place of Grace: Antimodernism and the Transformation of American Culture, 1880–1920* (New York: Pantheon, 1981), 72.

5   Tomsich, *Genteel Endeavor,* 5.

6   Quoted in Joan Shelley Rubin, "Between Culture and Consumption: The Mediations of the Middlebrow," in *The Power of Culture: Critical Essays in American History,* ed. Richard Wightman Fox and T. J. Jackson Lears (Chicago: University of Chicago Press, 1993), 169.

7   Raymond Williams, *Culture and Society, 1780–1950* (1958; reprint, New York: Columbia University Press, 1983), 233.

8   Christopher Herbert, *Culture and Anomie: Ethnographic Imagination in the Nineteenth Century* (Chicago: University of Chicago Press, 1991), 23.

9   Joan Shelley Rubin, *The Making of Middlebrow Culture* (Chapel Hill: University of North Carolina Press, 1992), cites concert halls, theaters, higher education, publishers, and public lectures as instruments of diffusion (and subversion) of culture (17–22). Karen Blair, *The Torchbearers: Women and Their Amateur Arts Associations in America, 1890–1930* (Bloomington: Indiana University Press, 1994), provides the first comprehensive examination of clubwomen's contributions to art, music, pageantry, theater, and architecture. Blair emphasizes the relationship between women's art and political interests, but I am more concerned here with the ways

women's clubs contributed to the changing definitions of culture at the turn of the century.

10 Earl Barnes, *Woman in Modern Society* (New York: B. W. Huebsch, 1912), 85.

11 Ibid., 93–94, 103.

12 Andreas Huyssen, "Mass Culture as Woman: Modernism's Other," in *Studies in Entertainment: Critical Approaches to Mass Culture,* ed. Tania Modleski (Bloomington: Indiana University Press, 1986), 191, 205–6.

13 Richard Butsch, "Bowery B'hoys and Matinee Ladies: The Re-Gendering of the Nineteenth-Century American Theater Audiences," *American Quarterly* 46 (September 1994): 396–97. Linda Dowling, "The Decadent and the New Woman in the 1890's," *Nineteenth-Century Fiction* 33 (March 1979), makes a similar point about women posing a threat to "established culture" (435).

14 "Reapers' Club," *Woman's Exponent* 25 (June 1896): 1; Mary S. Cunningham, *The Woman's Club of El Paso: Its First Thirty Years* (El Paso: Texas Western Press, 1978), 7; Laura D. Jacobson, "The Pioneers," *American Jewess* 1 (October 1895): 241; Mary Kupiec Cayton, "The Making of an American Prophet: Emerson, His Audiences, and the Rise of the Culture Industry in Nineteenth-Century America," *American History Review* 91 (June 1987): 606.

15 "Washington Letter," *Woman's Era* 1 (March 24, 1894): 2; "Club Notes," *Far and Near* 1 (June 1891): 145.

16 "The Twentieth Century Club Woman," *Federation Bulletin* 5 (January 1907): 149.

17 Sadie American, "Organization," in *Papers of the Jewish Women's Congress* (Philadelphia: Jewish Publication Society, 1894), 259, 261.

18 "Editorial," *Woman's Era* 1 (March 24, 1894): 8.

19 Fannie Barrier Williams, "Shall We Have a Convention of the Colored Women's Clubs Leagues and Societies," *Woman's Era* 1 (June 1, 1894): 5.

20 Quoted in Josephine Silome Yates, "Missouri," *Woman's Era* 1 (December 1894): 13.

21 Mary Van Kleeck, *Working Girls in Evening Schools* (New York: Survey Associates, 1914), 27.

22 Barnes, *Woman in Modern Society,* 90.

23 Edward Bok, "My Quarrel with Women's Clubs," *Ladies' Home Journal* 27 (January 1910): 1.

24 Augusta H. Leypoldt and George Iles, *A List of Books for Girls and Women and Their Clubs with Descriptive and Critical Notes and a List of Periodicals and Hints for Girls' and Women's Clubs* (Boston: American Library Association, 1895), v. This book also contains a chapter titled "Hints for a Girls' Club," and its longest section deals with forming a club library.

25 See David Halle, *Inside Culture: Art and Class in the American Home* (Chicago: University of Chicago Press, 1993), 195.

26 Jane Addams, "The Hull House Woman's Club," *Club Worker* 3 (November 1901): 1.

27   Helen Lefkowitz Horowitz, *Culture and the City: Cultural Philanthropy in Chicago from the 1880s to 1917* (Chicago: University of Chicago Press, 1976), has observed that Addams's experiences at Hull-House led her to abandon traditional ideas about high culture in favor of valuing the worker's "understanding of the long established occupations and thoughts of men, of the arts with which they have solaced their toil" (136).

28   "Lucy Larcom: Biographical Sketch," *Far and Near* 1 (November 1890): 10–11.

29   Ibid. Another edition of *Far and Near* published Larcom's poem "The Work of the World," with a headnote indicating that it had been composed for the April reunion of the Boston Association and was sung to the tune of "The Watch on the Rhine." In publishing this poem, which affirms and invites a vocal performance focused on the value of work, the editor appropriates a culturally approved genre to portray work as a cause of celebration rather than as a grim necessity.

30   Harriet Robinson, "The Early Mill-Girls of Lowell," *Far and Near* 1 (February 1891): 51.

31   "Home Culture Clubs," *Far and Near* 1 (May 1891): 124.

32   "Self-Culture," *Far and Near* 3 (August 1893): 196.

33   Lucy Warner, "Why Do People Look Down on Working Girls," *Far and Near* 1 (January 1891): 37.

34   Edith Howes, "How Can a Working Girl Best Improve and Elevate Herself?" *Far and Near* 1 (September 1891): 200.

35   "Some Aspects of Literature," *Far and Near* 1 (April 1891): 93.

36   J. W. Porcher, "Correspondence Column," *Far and Near* 2 (June 1892): 165.

37   "Clubs and Reporters," *Far and Near* 2 (September 1892): 215.

38   Lucia B. Tunis, "The Literary Circle of the Walworth Club," *Club Worker* 2 (June 1900): 4.

39   "Club Notes," *Far and Near* 1 (January 1891): 48.

40   Paul Dimaggio, "Cultural Entrepreneurship in Nineteenth-Century Boston: The Creation of an Organizational Base for High Culture in America," *Media, Culture and Society* 4 (January 1982): 33–50.

41   Harriet Clisby, "A History of the Women's Educational and Industrial Union," Papers of the Women's Educational and Industrial Union, Schlesinger Library, Radcliffe College, Cambridge, Mass.; "Survey by the President," Annual Report, 1914, 20, Papers of the Women's Educational and Industrial Union [hereafter WEIU], Manuscript Division, Boston Public Library, Boston, Mass.

42   Annual Report, 1884–85, WEIU, 7.

43   Laura Jacobson, "The Pioneers," *American Jewess* 1 (August 1895): 242.

44   Eve L. Stern, "Culture," *American Jewess* 4 (January 1897): 157, 158, 159.

45   Quoted in Jack Nusan Porter, "Rosa Sonneschein and *The American Jewess:* The First Independent English Language Jewish Women's Journal in the United States," *American Jewish History* 68 (September 1978): 62.

46   Evelyn Bodek, "'Making Do': Jewish Women and Philanthropy," in *Jewish Life in*

Philadelphia, 1830–1940, ed. Murray Friedman (Philadelphia: American Jewish Committee, 1983), 160.

47 1904–5 Yearbook of the Detroit Section, n.p., Papers of the Detroit Section of the National Council of Jewish Women, Reuther Collection, Detroit Public Library, Detroit, Mich.

48 "The Revival of Judaism" (Paper delivered at New York Section, May 9, 1893), n.p., Papers of the New York Section of the National Council of Jewish Women, privately held.

49 Quoted in Faith Rogow, *Gone to Another Meeting: The National Council of Jewish Women, 1893–1993* (Tuscaloosa: University of Alabama Press, 1993), 14.

50 Quoted in ibid., 39.

51 Quoted in ibid., 104.

52 Quoted in Amy Ginsburg, "From Club Women to Progressive Philanthropists: The New York Section of the NCJW, 1894–1918" (B.A. thesis, Harvard University, 1982), 16–17.

53 Quoted in ibid., 52.

54 Quoted in "Council of Jewish Women," *American Hebrew,* December 4, 1908, 54.

55 Sadie American, "Organization," in *Papers of the Jewish Women's Congress* (Philadelphia: Jewish Publication Society, 1894), 232, 227.

56 Quoted in Deborah Gray White, "The Cost of Club Work, the Price of Black Feminism," in *Visible Women: New Essays on American Activism,* ed. Nancy A. Hewitt and Suzanne Lebsock (Urbana: University of Illinois Press, 1993), 261.

57 Ibid.

58 Fannie Barrier Williams, "Illinois," *Woman's Era* 2 (June 1895): 4.

59 "Literature," *Woman's Era* 3 (June 1896): 9.

60 "Literature Department," *Woman's Era* 3 (October/November 1896): 7.

61 Medora Gould, "Literature," *Woman's Era* 1 (March 24, 1894): 10 (first quote); 1 (May 1, 1894): 10 (second quote); 1 (June 1, 1894): 11 (third and fourth quotes); 1 (August 1894): 14 (fifth quote); 1 (December 1894): 19 (sixth quote).

62 Clubwoman Nannie Helen Burroughs, founder of the National Training School for Women and Girls, had as her motto "We specialize in the wholly impossible," a saying used as the title of Darlene Clark Hine's recent book, *We Specialize in the Wholly Impossible: A Reader in Black Women's History* (Brooklyn: Carlson, 1995).

63 Fiftieth Anniversary History, Chautauqua Circle, Papers of the Chautauqua Circle of Atlanta, Robert W. Woodruff Library, Atlanta University, Atlanta, Ga.

64 Minutes of the Chautauqua Circle, December 31, 1913, Papers of the Chautauqua Circle of Atlanta.

65 Medora Gould, "Literature Department," *Woman's Era* 1 (September 1894): 10.

66 Medora Gould, "Literature," *Woman's Era* 1 (June 1, 1894): 11.

67 N. N. Nelson, "Shakespeare," *Young Woman's Journal* 1 (June 1890): 295, 297.

68 "Current Literature," *Woman's Exponent* 22 (June 15, 1894): 149.

69 "A Few Thoughts: How Far Should Home Talent Be Cultivated and to What Extent Should Outside Talent Be Introduced in Woman's Clubs," *Woman's Exponent* 22 (May 15, 1894): 133.

70 "About Art," *Woman's Exponent* 30 (July 1901): 12.

71 "Our Girls," *Young Woman's Journal* 1 (April 1890): 237.

72 Homespun, "Whatsoever a Man Soweth," *Young Woman's Journal* 1 (October 1889): 1.

73 "The Editor's Department," *Young Woman's Journal* 1 (1889): 160.

74 J.S., "Social Advantages in Salt Lake," *Young Woman's Journal* 1 (April 1890): 209.

75 "Utah Women in Chicago," *Woman's Exponent* 21 (June 15, 1893): 179.

76 "U.W.P.C.," *Woman's Exponent* 29 (March 1901): 72.

77 *Bay View Reading Circle Information Circular,* November 1893, Bentley Historical Library, University of Michigan, Ann Arbor, Mich. Bay View, a Michigan adaptation of Chautauqua, spread, like Chautauqua itself, throughout the country. Luretta Rainey, *History of Oklahoma State Federation of Women's Clubs* (Guthrie, Okla.: Co-Operative Publishing, 1939), includes several clubs that describe themselves as following the Bay View course of study (212, 216).

78 *Bay View Magazine* 1 (November 1893), for example, asserts, "The Reading Course is a substitute for the aimless and haphazard reading of many, and the unprofitable literary selection of others. It is a four years' course, each year a separate and complete year that may be taken with or without the others. Instead of reading a variety of unrelated subjects, each year attention will be largely concentrated on a few subjects, in order that more thorough and satisfactory work may be done" (3).

79 "What Is a Program?" *General Federation of Women's Clubs Magazine* 18 (July 1919): 3.

80 Kate S. M. Rotan, "Of What Use Is a Federation Organ?" *Federation Bulletin* 2 (March 1905): 193. Joan Shelley Rubin, "Self, Culture, and Self-Culture in Modern America: The Early History of the Book-of-the-Month Club," *Journal of American History* 71 (March 1985), describes how ads for the Book-of-the-Month Club constructed the reading public as intellectually chaotic and powerless in conflict—qualities that putting oneself in the hands of the club could alleviate (790–91).

81 "Children and Reading: Reading Is a Form of Living:—Let Us Choose Books for Our Children That Inculcate the Virtues We Desire for Them," *General Federation of Women's Clubs Magazine* 16 (April 1917): 19.

82 Mary B. Poppenheim, "Is the Club a Place for Serious Study or for General Culture?" *Federation Bulletin* 4 (October 1906): 7.

83 "Editorial," *Far and Near* 1 (December 1890): 17. With the formation of the National League of Women Workers in 1899 (from 1897–99 the group was called the National League of Associations of Working Women's Clubs) and the establishment of the *Club Worker* in 1899, the patronizing tone was considerably reduced.

84   Warren Susman, "'Personality' and the Making of Twentieth-Century Culture," in *New Directions in American Intellectual History,* ed. John Higham and Paul K. Conkin (Baltimore: Johns Hopkins University Press, 1984), describes the shift from a culture of character to a culture of personality (212–26).

85   Julia Ward Howe, "Modern Society," in her *Modern Society* (Boston: Roberts Brothers, 1881); Ella R. Start, "Whatever Influences Character," October 5, 1897, Papers of the Olympia Woman's Club of Olympia, Washington, privately held; Mrs. John H. Witemore, "Personality," April 30, 1907, Papers of the Naugatuck Study Club of Naugatuck, Connecticut, privately held.

86   Quoted in Levine, *Highbrow/Lowbrow,* 164.

87   Ibid., 173.

88   Howes, "How Can a Working Girl Best Improve and Elevate Herself?" 200.

89   Katherine Fullerton Gerould, "The Extirpation of Culture," *Atlantic Monthly* 116 (October 1915), offers an excellent example of this position by insisting that culture bears no relation to democracy, describing as "misguided" settlement workers who brought Dante and Shakespeare to slum dwellers, and dismissing most educators as illiterate (445–55).

90   Blair, *Torchbearers,* 5.

91   Mrs. William R. Thayer [Charlotte Emerson] Brown, "The Study of Literature," *Federation Bulletin* 4 (October 1906), asserted that the genesis of clubs lay in self-cultivation and argued that this "preparation and study" must precede practical work (15).

92   Gaye Tuchman, "Women and the Creation of Culture," in *Another Voice: Feminist Perspectives on Social Life and Social Science,* ed. Marcia Millman and Rosabeth Moss Kanter (New York: Anchor, 1975), 171.

93   Hazel Carby, *Reconstructing Womanhood: The Emergence of the Afro-American Woman Novelist* (New York: Oxford University Press, 1987), 120. Carby goes on to observe, "The movement of black women was able to give birth to and support the particular practices of individual women, and the individual practices in turn shaped and transformed the movement" (120).

94   Helen Winslow, "Literature via the Woman's Club," *Critic* 44 (January–June 1904): 244.

95   Minutes of the Naugatuck Study Club, 1891, Papers of the Naugatuck Study Club.

96   Mark A. Schneider, *Culture and Enchantment* (Chicago: University of Chicago Press, 1993), 10.

CHAPTER 6: (UN)PROFESSIONAL READING AND WRITING

1   Thomas W. Higginson, "Women and Men: A Typical Club," *Harper's Bazaar* 22 (March 30, 1880): 826–27.

2   Quoted in Tilden G. Edelstein, *Strange Enthusiasm: A Life of Thomas Wentworth Hig-*

ginson (New Haven, Conn.: Yale University Press, 1968), 344. Edelstein reports that Higginson read Dickinson's poetry to a Boston women's club (without her permission) because it was, in Higginson's words, "weird and strange" (quoted on 344). He offered no encouragement for her to publish, although he was in a position to do so and later condemned her for remaining so private (349). His ruthless editing of her poetry after her death distorted the meaning of many of her verses (345–52).

3   Ibid., 373.

4   Higginson, "Women and Men," 826–27.

5   Jennie June Cunningham Croly, *The History of the Woman's Club Movement in America* (New York: Henry G. Allen, 1898), 597.

6   Gerald Graff, *Professing Literature: An Institutional History* (Chicago: University of Chicago Press, 1987), 38.

7   Graff, *Professing Literature,* maintains the battle between scholars and critics began in 1915, but I argue that the roots of this conflict were laid during the 1875–1915 period because the generalists, represented by such figures as Higginson, Corson, and Rolfe, evolved into the critics of the later period. In addition, the ideology of research based on the model of the German university, which undergirded the work of scholars, also emerged late in the nineteenth century.

8   Henry Austin Clapp Freeport, *Reminiscences of a Dramatic Critic* (1902; reprint, New York: Books for Libraries Press, 1970).

9   Francis A. March, "Recollections of Language Teaching" (1893), in *The Origins of Literary Studies in America: A Documentary Anthology,* ed. Gerald Graff and Michael Warner (New York: Routledge, 1989), 27.

10   William Riley Parker, "The Beginning, Development, and Impact of the MLA as a Learned Society, 1883–1954," Part 2, *PMLA* 68 (March 1953): 26–27. Even pedagogical issues became less and less prominent until 1903, when the Pedagogical Section disappeared entirely.

11   H. C. G. Brandt, "How Far Should Our Teaching and Text-books Have a Scientific Basis?" (1884), in *Origins of Literary Studies,* ed. Graff and Warner, 32. Brandt, whose wife long served as president of the Monday Club of Clinton, New York, must have had some firsthand knowledge of the work of women's clubs, but this apparently did not modify his gendered perspective on the professionalization of English.

12   Burton J. Bledstein, *The Culture of Professionalism: The Middle Class and the Development of Higher Education in America* (New York: W. W. Norton, 1976); Magali Sarfatti Larson, *The Rise of Professionalism: A Sociological Analysis* (Berkeley: University of California Press, 1977).

13   Alisa Klaus, "Women's Organizations and the Infant Health Movement in France and the United States," in *Lady Bountiful Revisited: Women, Philanthropy, and Power,* ed. Kathleen D. McCarthy (New Brunswick, N.J.: Rutgers University Press,

1990), 157. Barbara Ehrenreich and Deirdre English, *For Her Own Good: 150 Years of the Experts' Advice to Women* (Garden City, N.Y.: Anchor, 1978), makes a related point about males' asserting professional authority in (reproductive) medicine.

14 Frank Norris, "The 'English' Classes of the University of California" (1896), in *Origins of Literary Studies in America,* ed. Graff and Warner, 134.

15 Christopher Wilson, *The Labor of Words: Literary Professionalism in the Progressive Era* (Athens: University of Georgia Press, 1985), argues that literature itself changed as a masculinized professionalism infused American culture, becoming "more scientific, more vigorously realistic, more political, more masculine" (1). Writers, formerly positioned as aristocratic or inspired, took on qualities of professional expertise. They no longer waited for the muse but emphasized "ritualized routines, careful soundings of the market, and hard work" (3).

16 Helen Winslow, "Literature via the Woman's Club," *Critic* 44 (January 1904): 242. "The National Council of Jewish Women," *Charities and Commons* 15 (January 6, 1906), offers a similar account in listing the council's philanthropic projects. The author observes, "No mention need be made here of the lectures and study circles" that lay behind the development of playgrounds, kindergartens, rescue work, free loans, and probation work (426). Mary S. Gibson, *A Record of Twenty-Five Years of the California Federation of Women's Clubs, 1900–1925* (Los Angeles: California Federation of Women's Clubs, 1927), reports that the California Federation decided to eliminate its literature department in the early 1900s because clubs did not need its help: "It is true that more than one-half of our federated clubs are literary clubs, but nearly all of them are following lines of study that they have found acceptable and desirable" (52).

17 Mrs. William Thayer [Charlotte Emerson] Brown, "The Study of Literature," *Federation Bulletin* 4 (October 1906): 15.

18 Albert S. Cook, "English at Yale University," in *English in American Universities by Professors in the English Departments of Twenty Representative Institutions,* ed. William Morton Payne (1894; reprint, Boston: D. C. Heath, 1895), 34.

19 Cook's peers shared his views. Theodore W. Hunt, "The Place of English in the College Curriculum" (1884) in *Origins of Literary Studies in America,* ed. Graff and Warner, laments the "current errors that English literature is a subject for the desultory reader in his leisure hours rather than an intellectual study for serious workers; that it ranks as an accomplishment only, and that the terms literary and philosophic are mutually exclusive, are errors that have been strengthened by the superficial methods on which the subject has been taught" (44). Martin Wright Sampson, "English at the University of Indiana" (1895), in ibid., insists that "instructors must draw the line once for all between the liking for reading and the understanding of literature. . . . It is only by recognizing this difference that we professors of English cease to make ourselves ridiculous in the eyes of those who

see into the heart of things, that we can at all successfully disprove Freeman's remark—caustic and four-fifths true—'English literature is only chatter about Shelley'" (54).

20 Graff, *Professing Literature,* devotes several pages to the activities of men's literary societies, arguing that they helped break down genteel moral opposition to secular literature (44–46). Arthur N. Applebee, *Tradition and Reform in the Teaching of English: A History* (Urbana, Ill.: National Council of Teachers of English, 1974), identifies literary societies as one of the three forces that contributed to the emergence of English studies (40). Jonathan Freedman, "Professional Amateurs: Browning Societies and the Politics of Appreciation" (Manuscript in possession of author), argues that these societies contributed to the professionalizing process even though they have been largely ignored in the discourses of professionalism. Freedman's point that Browning societies rather than the academy are responsible for Browning's emergence as a canonical author is reinforced by Julia Sprague's *History of the New England Women's Club* (Boston: Lee and Shepard, 1894), which recounts "the gifted Sarah Starr's essay in 1875 on Robert Browning's poems: 'a loving, appreciative tribute to the poet's genius, but the discussion languished from want of interest in the poet's works.' *Now* Browning Clubs are flourishing" (27–28).

21 Karen Blair, "The Limits of Sisterhood: The Woman's Building in Seattle, 1908–1921," *Frontiers* 8, no. 1 (1984), explains how clubwomen attempted to help female students at the University of Washington develop confidence in their own abilities by providing a woman's building. Functioning autonomously instead of seeking university assistance and working with a dean of women, who was active in club life, they established the building, but without university support they were unable to sustain it (46–47, 49).

22 Paul Lauter, "Race and Gender in the Shaping of the American Literary Canon: A Case Study from the Twenties," in *Feminist Criticism and Social Change,* ed. Judith Newton and Deborah Rosenfelt (New York: Methuen, 1985), writes that "influence over reading shifted before the 1930s from women who were not academic professionals to academics, the great majority of whom were white and male" (24). My thanks to Martha Vicinus for reminding me of this essay and to Anne Berggren for providing it.

23 Samuel Weber, "The Limits of Professionalism," *Oxford Literary Review* 5, no. 1/2 (1982): 70.

24 1899 Yearbook of the Decatur Art Club, Papers of the Decatur Art Club of Decatur, Illinois, privately held; 1910 Yearbook of the Agnes Morris Shakespeare Class, n.p., Papers of the Agnes Morris Shakespeare Class of Toledo, Manuscript Division, Lucas County Library, Toledo, Ohio; Minutes of the Hillsdale Women's Club, October 28, 1896, Papers of the Women's Club of Hillsdale, Michigan, Bentley Historical Library, University of Michigan, Ann Arbor.

25   David R. Shumway, *Creating American Civilization: A Genealogy of American Literature as an Academic Discipline* (Minneapolis: University of Minnesota Press, 1994),
explains that literature did not stand in for the Bible as transmitter of explicitly
moral truths, but it "came to represent imagination, creativity, and spirituality"
(40).

26   N. N. Nelson, "Shakespeare," *Young Woman's Journal* 1 (July 1890): 295. Gladys
Woodmansee, "Chaucer," *Woman's Exponent* 23 (December 1894): 211.

27   Brown, "The Study of Literature," 16.

28   "National Council of Jewish Women," *American Jewess* 1 (July 1894): 189.

29   "The Earnest Workers," *Club Worker* 2 (March 1900): 1.

30   Medora Gould, "Literature," *Woman's Era* 1 (May 1, 1894): 10; 1 (September 1894):
11. The 1904 Yearbook of the Detroit Study Club, Papers of the Detroit Study
Club, Manuscript Division, Detroit Public Library, Detroit, Mich., features a
drawing of a well, with this written below: "Geoffrey Chaucer: The Well of English Undefiled," n.p. Many meetings of this club included laudatory "poetical
estimates" of canonical writers.

31   Kermit Vanderbilt, *American Literature and the Academy: The Roots, Growth, and Ma-
turity of a Profession* (Philadelphia: University of Pennsylvania Press, 1986), writes
that at the turn of the century the "highbrows isolated themselves from the writings of living authors," making "American professors quite peculiarly academic"
(199).

32   Jean Madeline Weimann, *The Fair Women* (Chicago: Academy, 1981), 355, 392.

33   Elaine Showalter, ed., *Daughters of Decadence: Women Writers of the Fin de Siècle* (London: Virago, 1993), describes Gilman and several of her peers as "New Women
writers" (x).

34   Medora Gould, "Literature," *Woman's Era* 1 (September 1894), writes about the
"high purpose" of *The Heavenly Twins* (11); "Current Literature," *Woman's Exponent*
22 (June 15, 1894): 149, describes Grand's book as "one of the most talked of
and widely read books of the present time"; and "The Practical Results of Wom-
en's Clubs," *American Jewess* 1 (July 1894), claims that *The Heavenly Twins* "are more
in demand than *The Woman Who Did*" (192). This assertion, part of a paper read at
the Illinois Federation of Women's Clubs, indicates that the audience was also familiar with Grand's work.

35   Sarah Grand, "The New Aspect of the Woman Question," *North American Review*
158 (March 1894): 270–76.

36   Quoted in Croly, *History of the Woman's Club Movement in America,* 15.

37   Elizabeth Ammons, *Conflicting Stories: American Women Writers at the Turn into the
Twentieth Century* (New York: Oxford University Press, 1991), writes that for
Harper "action and art were totally inseparable" (26), and as evidence she points
to the fact that "Iola was the penname that Ida B. Wells used in her political jour-

nalism" (29). Harper, who was sixty-seven when she published *Iola Leroy,* had a long history of writing and activism on behalf of her race.

38   Claudia Tate, *Domestic Allegories of Political Desire: The Black Heroine's Text at the Turn of the Century* (New York: Oxford University Press, 1992), writes, "Without a doubt the vigorous activity among black women's clubs during the decade of the 1890s made this proliferation of novels possible, by stimulating their production and by creating an audience for them" (4).

39   "Quincy Section," *American Jewess* 2 (February 1896): 186.

40   *Proceedings of the First Convention of the National Council of Jewish Women, New York, 1896 Nov. 15–19* (Philadelphia: Jewish Publication Society of America, 1897), 85.

41   Abram S. Isaacs, "The Jewess in Authorship," *Ladies' Home Journal* 9 (October 1892): 17.

42   "Book Brieflets," *American Jewess* 4 (February 1897): 236; 1906–7 Yearbook of the New York Section, 39–40, Papers of the New York Section of the National Council of Jewish Women, privately held.

43   John Willinsky, "Matthew Arnold's Legacy: The Powers of Literature," *Research in the Teaching of English* 24 (December 1990), argues that Arnold deliberately withheld, under the phrase "force until right is ready," criticism from pedagogy. Although students might draw on literature to "form the soul and character," the "criticism of life" was reserved for the critic (357). See also John Willinsky, *The Triumph of Literature / The Fate of Literacy: English in the Secondary School Curriculum* (New York: Teachers' College Press, 1991).

44   "Books Old and New," *Far and Near* 1 (April 1891): 105.

45   Richard Brodhead, *Cultures of Letters: Scenes of Reading and Writing in Nineteenth-Century America* (Chicago: University of Chicago Press, 1993), underscores the class-based definitions of literature by considering Dorothy Richard's account, *The Longest Day: The Story of a New York Working Girl as Told by Herself* (New York: Century, 1906), of working women who have no knowledge of "the simple, every-day classics that the school-boy and -girl are supposed to have read" (these classics include *David Copperfield, Gulliver's Travels, The Vicar of Wakefield, Robinson Crusoe, Little Women, The Cloister and the Hearth,* and *Les Miserables*) and who in turn express amazement at the narrator's ignorance of such titles as *Little Rosebud's Lovers; Daphne Vernon or a Coronet of Shame; and Doris or the Pride of Pemberton.* Brodhead comments, "In this astonishing passage, social divisions focused through different reading habits have become an unbridgeable gap. Two literary cultures stare at each other in mutual incomprehension, with what passes for literacy in each signifying illiteracy in the eyes of the other" (105–6).

46   "Utah's Literary Fame," *Woman's Exponent* 36 (February 1908): 27; Annie Wells Cannon, "Pioneer Literature and Writers," *Woman's Exponent* 37 (November 1908): 25 (final quote).

47 Quoted in Mary Jean Houde, *Reaching Out: A Story of the General Federation of Women's Clubs* (Chicago: Mobium, 1989), 68. Howe included this statement in her address to the 1894 biennial of the General Federation of Women's Clubs in Philadelphia.

48 Susan K. Harris, *Nineteenth-Century American Women's Novels: Interpretative Strategies* (New York: Cambridge University Press, 1990), 19.

49 Minutes of the Chautauqua Circle, 1913–19, Papers of the Chautauqua Circle of Atlanta, Robert W. Woodruff Library, Atlanta University, Atlanta, Ga.

50 Minutes of the Woman's Improvement Club, February 3, 1910–June 23, 1910, Papers of the Woman's Improvement Club of Indianapolis, W. H. Smith Memorial Library, Indiana Historical Society, Indianapolis; Minutes of the Detroit Study Club, October 11, 1899, and November 25, 1899, Papers of the Detroit Study Club.

51 S. Elizabeth Frazier, "Victoria Earle," *Woman's Era* 1 (May 1, 1894): 1.

52 Victoria Earle Matthews, "The Value of Race Literature" (1895), in *With Pen and Voice: A Critical Anthology of Nineteenth-Century African-American Women,* ed. Shirley Wilson Logan (Carbondale: Southern Illinois University Press, 1995), 129, 130, 136, 144–46.

53 Tate, *Domestic Allegories of Political Desire,* 7.

54 Mrs. N. F. [Gertrude] Mossell, *The Work of the Afro-American Woman* (1894; reprint, New York: Oxford University Press, 1988), 61. Medora Gould, "Literature Notes," *Woman's Era* 1 (December 1894), reviewed this book (19).

55 Janet Duitsman Cornelius, *When I Can Read My Title Clear: Literacy, Slavery, and Religion in the Antebellum South* (Columbia: University of South Carolina Press, 1991), claims that for African Americans "the ability to read was both spiritual and utilitarian" (92). Hazel Carby, *Reconstructing Womanhood: The Emergence of the Afro-American Woman Novelist* (New York: Oxford University Press, 1987), claims that Frances Harper wrote *Iola Leroy* "in an attempt to morally rearm the black intellectual and to contest the terrain of racist retrenchment. . . . Harper intended to hand her readership a political weapon" (94).

56 Michael Denning, *Mechanic Accents: Dime Novels and Working-Class Culture in America* (New York: Verso, 1987), shows that romantic stories appeared frequently among working women's reading materials (185–200). Discussions of romantic stories do not appear in the club records I examined, and it may be that women who read them preferred to protect their interest in such texts from the gaze of middle-class women who participated in their clubs.

57 "Suggested Reading on the Problems of the Day," *Club Worker* 8 (May 1907): 817. The list included *Democracy and Social Ethics* by Jane Addams, *The Woman Who Spends* by Bertha Richardson, *The Long Day* by Dorothy Richardson, *The Good Neighbor* by Mary E. Richmond, *The Genesis of the Social Conscience* by Henry T. Nash, *The Leaven in a Great City* by Lillian W. Betts, *Some Ethical Gains through Legislation* by

Florence Kelley, *The Employment of Women in the Clothing Trade* by Mabel Hurd Willett, *Employment of Women in Industry* by S. P. Breckenridge and Edith Abbott, *Women's Work and Wages* by E. Cadbury, M. C. Matherson, and G. Scharm, and *The Russian Jew in the United States* by Charles S. Bernheimer.

58 "Current Literature," *Woman's Exponent* 22 (May 15, 1894): 149.

59 Quoted in William Toll, "A Quiet Revolution: Jewish Women's Clubs and the Widening Female Sphere, 1870–1920," *American Jewish Archives* 41 (Spring/Summer 1989): 17.

60 1904–50 Yearbook of the Detroit Section, n.p., Papers of the Detroit Section of the National Council of Jewish Women, Reuther Collection, Detroit Public Library, Detroit, Mich.

61 Minutes of the Friday Club, January 22, 1897, Papers of the Friday Club of Jackson, Michigan, Bentley Historical Library, University of Michigan, Ann Arbor.

62 Ibid., March 28, 1890. Mary Kupiec Cayton, "The Making of an American Prophet: Emerson, His Audiences, and the Rise of the Culture Industry in Nineteenth-Century America," *American Historical Review* 91 (June 1987), reports that early critical reviews of Emerson's essays characterized them as "tough, distorted, inharmonious, opaque, ponderous, and labored" (602).

63 Brown, "The Study of Literature," 15.

64 "The Woman's Era Literature Department," *Woman's Era* 2 (June 1896): 2.

65 Matthews, "The Value of Race Literature," 132.

66 *Proceedings of the First Convention of the National Council of Jewish Women,* 92. The Atlanta Section makes this claim: "The study of the Bible and kindred subjects has been our principal work. The Bible is studied at home, and papers prepared upon the chapters read by members in turn, and these papers are read and discussed in the circle. Other readings are done by members at the circle meetings" (69).

67 "Current Literature," *Woman's Exponent* 22 (June 15, 1894): 149.

68 Nelson, "Shakespeare," 353.

69 Theodore W. Hunt, "The Place of English in the College Curriculum" (1884), in *Origins of Literary Studies in America,* ed. Graff and Warner, 44.

70 Minutes of the Friday Club of Jackson, Michigan, August 9, 1889.

71 J. MacDonald Oxley, "Literary Improvement Clubs," *Ladies' Home Journal* 11 (January 1894): 16.

72 Winslow, "Literature via the Woman's Club," 244.

73 Muriel Beadle and the Centennial Committee, *The Fortnightly of Chicago: The City and Its Women, 1873–1973* (Chicago: Henry Regnery, 1973), 46.

74 Houde, *Reaching Out,* describes a club critic (55).

75 Mary Church Terrell, "Washington," *Woman's Era* 1 (December 1894): 7.

76 Bledstein, *Culture of Professionalism,* 267.

77 "The Earnest Workers," 1.

78 Barbara Sicherman, "Sense and Sensibility: A Case Study of Women's Reading in Late-Victorian America," in *Reading in America: Literature and Social History,* ed. Cathy N. Davidson (Baltimore: Johns Hopkins University Press, 1989), 215.

79 David Bartine, *Reading, Criticism, and Culture: Theory and Teaching in the United States and England, 1820–1950* (Columbia: University of South Carolina Press, 1992), describes a pragmatic theory that owes much to the nineteenth-century language theorist Benjamin Humphrey Smart (57–85).

80 "U. W. P. Club," *Woman's Exponent* 21 (September 15, 1893): 35.

81 "Charleston, W. VA. Club Notes," *National Association Notes* 3 (April 1900): 3.

82 Luretta Rainey, *History of Oklahoma State Federation of Women's Clubs* (Guthrie, Okla.: Co-Operative Publishing, 1939), includes this report from the Lindsay Literary Club: "Shakespeare was a subject of study for a number of years, during which time the club creditably produced four of the plays" (289). Croly, *History of the Woman's Club Movement in America,* lists nearly twenty Shakespeare clubs, most of which included some performance.

83 "Plays for the Asking," *Club Worker* 1 (October 1899): 4.

84 "Council of Jewish Women," *American Jewess* 7 (April 1898): 39.

85 "Press Club Entertainment," *Woman's Exponent* 27 (December 15, 1898): 1.

86 Hiram Corson, *The Aims of Literary Study* (New York: Macmillan, 1901), did, of course, emphasize this sort of performance, but he represented a minority position.

87 Houde, *Reaching Out,* reassures readers that clubwomen were not "bluestockings" with "unkempt hair and ill-fitting dresses" but wore "elegant spring suits, dainty blouses, well fitting gloves, and boots and trains a la mode" (6). The 1873 Annual Report of the New England Women's Club, Papers of the New England Women's Club, Schlesinger Library, Radcliffe College, Cambridge, Mass., includes this description of Elizabeth Stuart Phelps's paper on dress reform: "listened to by an audience by no means limited to the size of our rooms: it overflowed all bounds. The paper has since been printed in 'The Independent,' and is now about to appear in pamphlet; so all our members may read it for themselves. An animated discussion followed the reading of the paper" (14).

88 Papers of the Saturday Morning Club of Boston, Schlesinger Library, Radcliffe College, Cambridge, Mass., include newspaper clippings that indicate the social censure aroused by the club's restricting this 1893 performance to women only.

89 "Correspondence Column," *Far and Near* 2 (November 1891): 15.

90 Marjorie Garber, *Vested Interests: Cross-Dressing and Cultural Anxiety* (New York: Harper, 1992), 11.

91 Miriam Brody, *Manly Writing: Gender, Rhetoric, and the Rise of Composition* (Carbondale: Southern Illinois University Press, 1993). Daniel Kilham Dodge, "English at the University of Illinois," in *English in American Universities,* ed. Payne writes, "Much freedom is left to the students in the choice of subjects, and satisfactory

articles in the college paper and the various college societies are accepted as equivalents for regular class themes" (73). Giving credit for the writing done in student literary societies and the college newspaper, Dodge and his colleagues incorporated elements of amateur culture into academic English studies, but such moves remained the exception.

92 *Report of the Twenty-First Anniversary of Sorosis Celebrated by a Convention of Clubs Held in New York City, March, 1889* (New York: Styles and Cash, 1889), includes a report from the Woman's Club of San Francisco that lists these paper topics: "The Position of Women in Ancient Rome," "Arguments for and against Suffrage," "Physical Culture," "Legal Status of Women in California," "Representative Women's Clubs of the East," and "Dress and Dress Reform" (149).

93 "Philadelphia Section," *American Jewess* 1 (July 1895), includes this list of paper topics: "What Has Judaism Done for Women, Ancient and Modern?" "Our Sabbath Schools," and "What Was and Is the Messianic Idea among Jews?" (191).

94 Judith R. Baskin, "Women of the Word: An Introduction," in *Women of the Word: Jewish Women and Jewish Writing,* ed. Judith R. Baskin (Detroit: Wayne State University Press, 1994), observes that "to become a Jewish woman writer was to become a cultural anomaly; often the price of such achievement was equivocal exile" (18). Mary Martha Thomas, *The New Woman in Alabama: Social Reform and Suffrage, 1890–1920* (Tuscaloosa: University of Alabama Press, 1992), reports that Julia Stutweiler wrote a paper titled "The Technical Education of Women," which a man read for her before Alabama officials because "at that time it was not viewed as proper for a woman to speak in public" (61).

95 "A Study of Middlemarch," *Club Worker* 6 (March 1905): 288.

96 Minutes of the Friday Club of Jackson, Michigan, March 20, 1891. Minutes of the Friday Club of Jackson, Michigan, July 24, 1898, show that writing club minutes could become a competitive activity: "As I recall the minutes of the last four weeks, I am brought to a standstill in consideration of the comparison that must follow upon this that possess not the strength of wisdom or the sparkle or wit, neither the charm of rhyme or the art of quotation."

97 1911 Yearbook of the New York Section, 73–78, Papers of the New York Section of the National Council of Jewish Women. Clubwomen also composed poems that could be set to music and become the club song. See, for example, Sallie Southall Cotten, *History of the North Carolina Federation of Women's Clubs: 1901–1925* (Raleigh, N.C.: Edwards and Broughton, 1925): "The song written by Mrs. Cotten was selected and music for it written by Mrs. Duncan. This song was first sung at the Henderson Convention. . . . A motion was carried that it should be sung at all succeeding conventions of the clubs" (36).

98 "The Enthusiastic Club Member," *Far and Near* 1 (June 1891): 141–42.

99 "Immigration Script," 1911, Papers of the Detroit Section of the National Council of Jewish Women, was written by club members and featured characters in the

lounge of an ocean steamer who are greeted by Miss Levy, a member of the National Council.

100 Sixtieth Anniversary Celebration, Papers of the Chautauqua Circle of Atlanta, include a play recounting the founding of the club. "Masque of the Green Trunk, Papers of the Saturday Morning Club," celebrated the fiftieth anniversary of the club and featured the club archive as its central figure.

101 Paulina Brandeth, "The Pageant of the New York Association of Working Girls' Societies," *Club Worker* 15 (March 1914): 11, 13, 14.

102 Mary Church Terrell, "Phyllis Wheatley," Papers of Mary Church Terrell, Moorland-Spingarn Research Center, Howard University, Washington, D.C.

103 Thomas Strychacz, *Modernism, Mass Culture, and Professionalism* (New York: Cambridge University Press, 1993), 28.

104 "Paper by Mrs. Arthur Gilman," in History of Cambridge Mother's Club (1904), 5, Papers of the Cambridge Mother's Club, Schlesinger Library, Radcliffe College, Cambridge, Mass.

105 Minutes of the Naugatuck Study Club, October 11, 1896, Papers of the Naugatuck Study Club of Naugatuck, Connecticut, privately held, typify the resistance to writing: "Mrs. W. T. Rodenbach announced that there were several musical ladies who would like to join us, and would contribute of their musical talent as opportunity offered, but wished to be relieved from writing papers." This resistance was met with the assertion that "it would be pleasant to have these ladies join us, but it would not be wise to depart from writing a paper."

106 Rainey, *History of Oklahoma State Federation,* 158.

107 Lucy Ann Warner, "From a Letter to the Editor," *Far and Near* 1 (February 1891): 56.

108 Minutes of the Friday Club of Jackson, Michigan, November 11, 1896, indicate that these audiences included future generations: "If the history of the Friday Club is ever written for the benefit of future generations our 'little books' of autobiography will serve to furnish materials for such an important work. We may smile at such an idea but more improbable things have happened and may again."

109 "Advice for Young Writers," *Young Woman's Journal* 1 (March 1890): 191.

110 "The Prize Article for October," *Far and Near* 2 (October 1892): 246.

111 L. A. Warner, "From a Letter to the Editor," 56.

112 Cotten, *History of the North Carolina Federation,* 37, 43, 82.

113 Kate Flint, *The Woman Reader, 1837–1914* (Oxford: Oxford University Press, 1993), observes that in the sixteenth century women were warned to beware of books "like as of serpents and snakes" and women's reading continued to be a site of contest through the nineteenth century, when it became hotly debated (22).

114 James L. Machor, "Historical Hermeneutics and Antebellum Fiction: Gender, Response Theory, and Interpretive Contexts," in *Readers in History: Nineteenth-Century American Literature and the Contexts of Response,* ed. James L. Machor (Bal-

timore: Johns Hopkins University Press, 1993), writes, "Ironically, therefore, the strategies of response promoted by periodicals may have empowered women to approach reading as an intellectual, emotional, and critical activity for controlling the very discourse of public interpretation that sought to control them" (79). Although Machor's comments address an earlier period, attempts to contain women's literacy practices and women's responding subversions of them continued throughout the nineteenth century.

115 Pierre Bourdieu, "Cultural Reproduction and Social Reproduction," in *Knowledge, Education and Cultural Change: Papers in the Sociology of Education,* ed. Richard Brown (New York: Harper and Row, 1973), 71–112.

116 Denning, *Mechanic Accents,* makes a similar point about the establishment of public libraries, claiming that the "desire to reform and direct working-class reading is a main thread in the discussions of public libraries" (48). Denning also quotes Jennie June Cunningham Croly, founding member of Sorosis and the General Federation of Women's Clubs: "'Such girls do not care much about sitting down to read. If they have had a day of spare time they want to get out of doors, they want air . . . as for reading, they want something very different from what they have in their daily lives, and so they run to the story papers that contain flashy stories. . . . They are crazy for something that is outside of themselves, and which will make them forget the hard facts of their daily lives'" (33). The certainty with which Croly reports (to the Senate Committee on Education and Labor in 1883) on the desires and practices of women whose experiences differ significantly from her own is typical of middle-class clubwomen.

117 Frances J. Dyer, "How to Read the Newspapers," *Far and Near* 1 (March 1891): 77; "Books Old and New," *Far and Near* 2 (January 1892): 58 (final quote).

118 "Books Old and New," *Far and Near* 3 (January 1892): 59. In addition to expressing surprise at the intelligence and (self-)education of working-class women, middle-class clubwomen often saw that intelligence as an indication that working-class females were moving into the middle class, becoming "sweet beautiful girls" like themselves.

119 "Mary's Room," *Far and Near* 2 (August 1891): 180.

120 Cotten, *History of the North Carolina Federation,* 32.

121 Michael Warner, "Professionalization and the Rewards of Literature: 1875–1900," *Criticism* 27 (Winter 1985): 11. I am greatly indebted to Jonathan Freedman for calling this article to my attention, for several very helpful conversations about interpretation, and for sharing with me his unpublished manuscript "Professional Amateurs: Browning Societies and the Politics of Appreciation."

122 M. Warner, "Professionalization and the Reward of Literature," 6. "The Cleofan," *Woman's Exponent* 26 (March 15 and April 1, 1898): 259, reports that this Mormon club did, in fact, have a discussion of *The Faerie Queene,* proving women's clubs did sit around wondering what it meant. In addition, the central character in

Elizabeth Stuart Phelps's *Story of Avis* (1877; reprint, Rutgers University Press, 1985) belongs to a club that considers this poem, and this fictional representation gives further currency to the idea that the interpretive impulse might emerge outside as well as within the academy.

123 Friday Club record book for March 26, 1897, Papers of the Friday Club of Jackson, Michigan, Bentley Historical Library, University of Michigan, Ann Arbor.

124 Minutes of the Saturday Morning Club of Boston, February 27, 1892.

125 Minutes of the Naugatuck Study Club, October 16, 1894.

126 James Berlin, *Rhetoric and Reality: Writing Instruction in American Colleges, 1900–1985* (Carbondale: Southern Illinois University Press, 1987); James Berlin, *Writing Instruction in Nineteenth-Century American Colleges* (Carbondale: Southern Illinois University Press, 1984); Susan Miller, *Textual Carnivals: The Politics of Composition* (Carbondale: Southern Illinois University Press, 1991); John C. Brereton, ed., *The Origins of Composition Studies in the American College, 1875–1925* (Pittsburgh: University of Pittsburgh, 1995). Donald Stewart, "Harvard's Influence on English Studies: Perceptions from Three Universities in the Early Twentieth Century," *College Composition and Communication* 43 (December 1992): 455–71, shows how Harvard's composition program influenced many others in the nation.

127 Lucy Page Stelle, "Helps for Young Writers," *Young Woman's Journal* 3 (May 1891), outlines rhetoric's relation to grammar and logic and details strategies for invention, which she terms "the most important division of rhetoric," and she urges her readers to undertake this "special study" to find "materials for writing" (266–68).

128 The Harvard reports, issued in the 1890s, had a particularly reductive effect on college writing instruction. Written by overseers with backgrounds in business and finance, they emphasized surface correctness at the expense of larger rhetorical issues, such as questions of audience and purpose in writing. This so-called Harvardization of composition studies shaped the field nationally, as Stewart, "Harvard's Influence on English Studies," has observed.

129 Robin Muncy, *Creating a Female Dominion in American Reform, 1890–1935* (New York: Oxford University Press, 1991).

130 Although Sarah Robbins, "Domestic Didactics: Nineteenth-Century American Literary Pedagogy by Barbauld, Stowe and Addams" (Ph.D. diss., University of Michigan, 1993), draws on different contexts (individual women constructing themselves in pedagogical terms as opposed to clubwomen), she uses the term *domestic didactics* to describe the home-based practices that provided collaborative, conversational, and sociomoral education under the guidance of a maternal figure.

131 Mary Lee (no date) and Annie Winsor (March 9, 1887), both quoted in Joanne Campbell, "Controlling Voices: The Legacy of English A at Radcliffe College,

1883–1917," *Journal of the Conference on College Composition and Communication* 43 (December 1992), wrote that female students could not "get from all their instructors sympathy and help . . . many think conducting recitations and listening to the students the stupidest and most inessential part of their lives" (477).

132 Bruce Robbins, *Secular Vocations: Intellectuals, Professionalism, Culture* (New York: Verso, 1993), 223, 222, 224.

133 Bruce A. Kimball, *The "True Professional Ideal" in America* (Cambridge, Mass.: Blackwell, 1992), traces the changing meanings assigned to the term *professional*.

134 Michael Bérubé, *Public Access: Literary Theory and American Cultural Politics* (New York: Verso, 1994), 244.

135 William Cain, "Notes toward a History of Anti-Criticism," *New Literary History* 20 (Autumn 1988): 33–48. My thanks to Michael Bérubé for calling this article to my attention and for several helpful exchanges about professionalism.

136 "The Book Table," *Federation Bulletin* 2 (October 1904): 93.

137 Gerald Graff, "Feminist Criticism in the University: An Interview with Sandra M. Gilbert," in *Criticism in the University,* ed. Gerald Graff and Reginald Gibbons (Evanston, Ill.: Northwestern University Press, 1985), 112–13.

138 bell hooks, *Black Looks: Race and Representation* (Boston: South End Press, 1992); Ann Snitow, "Pages from a Gender Diary: Basic Divisions in Feminism," *Dissent* 36 (Spring 1989): 205–24; Jane Tompkins, "Me and My Shadow," *New Literary History* 19 (Autumn 1987): 169–78; Patricia J. Williams, *The Alchemy of Race and Rights: Diary of a Law Professor* (Cambridge, Mass.: Harvard University Press, 1991).

139 Henry Louis Gates, "Niggaz with Latitude," *New Yorker* 70 (March 21, 1994): 143–48; Michael Bérubé, "Life as We Know It," *Harper's* 289 (December 1994): 41–43; Louis Menand, "What Are Universities For," in *Falling into Theory: Conflicting Views on Reading Literature,* ed. David Richter (Boston: Bedford, 1994): 88–99; Morris Dickstein, "Damaged Literacy: The Decay of Reading," in *Profession 93,* ed. Phyllis Franklin (New York: Modern Language Association, 1993), 36.

CHAPTER 7: IMAGES AND PUBLIC MEMORY

1 Martha E. D. White, "The Work of the Woman's Club," *Atlantic Monthly* 93 (May 1904): 623.

2 Mrs. J. H. Young, "Among the Women's Clubs," *National Association Notes* 3 (August 1899): 3; "History of the U.W. Press Club," *Woman's Exponent* 36 (September 1907): 31; 1904 Yearbook, Detroit Section, n.p., Papers of the Detroit Section of the National Council of Jewish Women, Reuther Collection, Detroit Public Library, Detroit, Mich.; Sarah S. Platt Decker, "The Meaning of the Woman's Club Movement," *Annals of the American Academy of Political and Social Sciences*

28 (September 1906): 6; Edith Howes, "The Club Spirit," *Club Worker* 8 (November 1906): 558; Emma Fox, *Parliamentary Usage for Women's Clubs* (New York: Baker and Taylor, 1902).

3 Karen J. Blair, *The Torchbearers: Women and Their Amateur Arts Associations in America, 1890–1930* (Bloomington: Indiana University Press, 1994), 200. William O'Neill, *Everyone Was Brave: The Rise and Fall of Feminism in America* (Chicago: Quadrangle, 1969), reports that when Mrs. Thomas Winter became president of the General Federation of Women's Clubs in 1920, "she found the federation at its lowest point in memory" (258).

4 Faith Rogow, *Gone to Another Meeting: The National Council of Jewish Women, 1893–1993* (Tuscaloosa: University of Alabama Press, 1993), 170; Paula Giddings, *When and Where I Enter: The Impact of Black Women on Race and Sex in America* (New York: Bantam, 1984), 203.

5 Giddings, *Where and When I Enter,* 203.

6 Nancy F. Cott, "Across the Great Divide: Women in Politics before and after 1920," in *Women, Politics, and Change,* ed. Louise A. Tilly and Patricia Gurin (New York: Russell Sage Foundation, 1990), 165.

7 Rogow, *Gone to Another Meeting,* 173.

8 Nancy Tate Dredge, "Victim of the Conflict," in *Mormon Sisters: Women in Early Utah,* ed. Claudia L. Bushman (Salt Lake City: Olympus, 1976), 150.

9 Alice Kessler-Harris, *Out to Work: A History of Wage-Earning Women in the United States* (New York: Oxford University Press, 1982), 229.

10 Blair, *Torchbearers,* 201.

11 Carroll Smith-Rosenberg, *Disorderly Conduct: Visions of Gender in Victorian America* (New York: Alfred A. Knopf, 1985), 66.

12 Estelle Freedman, "Separatism as Strategy: Female Institution Building and American Feminism, 1870–1930," *Feminist Studies* 5 (Fall 1979): 514.

13 Nancy F. Cott, *The Grounding of Modern Feminism* (New Haven, Conn.: Yale University Press, 1987), 263.

14 Cott, "Across the Great Divide," argues for the continuity of women's voluntarist lobbying efforts before and after the Nineteenth Amendment: "Where one large or vital pre-1920 women's organization declined or ended, more than one other arose to take its space, if not its exact task" (162). If the National League of Women Workers disappeared, its role in protecting wage-earning women was assumed by the Women's Bureau in the Department of Labor and its social associations by the YWCA's industrial clubs. Similarly, the General Federation of Women's Clubs might have lost members after 1920, but the Parent-Teacher Association, which grew to over 1.5 million by 1931, took up its tasks of establishing playgrounds, libraries, and health clinics as well as lobbying for film standards and international peace. Cott's awareness of the accomplishments of women's clubs remains, however, unusual.

15   Alice Yaeger Kaplan, *Reproductions of Banality: Fascism, Literature, and French Intellectual Life* (Minneapolis: University of Minnesota Press, 1986), 168–69. I am grateful to Margaret Willard for calling Kaplan's work to my attention.

16   Michael Kammen, *Mystic Chords of Memory: The Transformation of Tradition in American Culture* (New York: Alfred A. Knopf, 1991), 100, 136, 13.

17   Chris Browne, "Hagar the Horrible," *Seattle Times,* July 7, 1995. I am grateful to Maxine Brengan for giving me this cartoon.

18   "Modern Menads," *New York World,* March 27, 1868, 5.

19   Quoted in "The Book Table," *Federation Bulletin* 2 (May 1904): 143.

20   George Rugg, *The New Woman: A Farcical Sketch,* in *English and American Drama of the Nineteenth Century* (Boston: W. H. Baker, 1896), 1–2.

21   Charles G. Bush, "Sorosis 1869," reprinted in Monika Franzen and Nancy Ethiet, *Make Way! 200 Years of American Women in Cartoons* (Chicago: Review Press, 1988), 18–19.

22   "The Wedding Ring as Sorosis Would Like to See It Worn" (1893), reprinted in Franzen and Ethiet, *Make Way,* 61; "The Lady Managers Passing through the Midway Plaisance with Their Husbands" (1893), reprinted in Jeanne Madeline Weimann, *The Fair Women* (Chicago: Academy, 1981), 269.

23   "Old Gent . . . Young Gent" (1869), reprinted in Anne L. Macdonald, *No Idle Hands: The Social History of American Knitting* (New York: Ballantine Books, 1988), 147.

24   Quoted in Fannie Barrier Williams, "Some Perils of Women's Clubs," *New York Age,* December 28, 1905, 3.

25   "Sorosis," *New York World,* May 5, 1868, 4.

26   "This Gathering" (1873), reprinted in Franzen and Ethiet, *Make Way,* 95.

27   Kammen, *Mystic Chords of Memory,* describes the effort of Hester Richardson, organizer of the Jamestown Tercentennial Exhibition in 1907, to display "the original signatures of great numbers of Colonial women to show that women could write and were educated in those days," an effort that an official of the Carnegie Institute in Washington "managed to squelch" (267).

28   Edward Bok, "In an Editorial Way," *Ladies' Home Journal* 25 (March 1908): 5.

29   Henry James, "The Speech of American Women" (1906), in *The Speech and Manners of American Women,* ed. E. S. Riggs (Lancaster, Pa.: Lancaster House, 1973), 25.

30   Edith Wharton, "Xingu," in *Roman Fever and Other Stories* (New York: Scribner's, 1911), 31–32, 36.

31   "Sorosis Opens the Winter Season," *New York World,* n.d., Folder 41, Box 8, Sophia Smith Collection, Smith College, Northampton, Mass.

32   Helen Hokinson, *The Hokinson Festival* (New York: Dutton, 1956), n.p. Hokinson drew her cartoons to illustrate captions written by James Reid Parker.

33   Harry Romaine, "Correcting a Popular Prejudice," *Life* 25 (February 9, 1895): 85.

34   Quoted in Miriam Anne Bourne, *The Ladies of Castine: From the Minutes of the Castine, Maine, Woman's Club* (New York: Arbor House, 1986), 30.

35   Edward Beer, *The Mauve Decade: American Life at the End of the Nineteenth Century* (London: Alfred A. Knopf, 1926), 35–36, 40.

36   Ibid., 61.

37   John Erskine, *The Influence of Women and Its Cure* (New York: Bobbs Merrill, 1936), 11. It is worth noting Erskine's dedication for his book, "To the Men of America (Those Who Remain)," which restates the trope of the world turned upside down by women taking a role in public life.

38   Ann Douglas, *Terrible Honesty: Mongrel Manhattan in the 1920s* (New York: Farrar, Strauss and Giroux, 1995), 252–53. Douglas also notes that Beer's choice of the term *Titaness* "was telling" because it signified "a race not of mortals but of gods" (241). Glenna Matthews, *The Rise of Public Woman* (New York: Oxford University Press, 1992), makes a related point by attributing the erosion of women's culture to changing demographics as well as "respect for the expert, for value-free social science, for tough-mindedness as a virtue" (171).

39   Robert Rydell, *All the World's a Fair: Visions of Empire at American International Expositions, 1876–1916* (Chicago: University of Chicago Press, 1984), 227.

40   Robert Sklar, *Movie-Made America: A Cultural History of American Movies* (New York: Random House, 1975), claims that the "directors and players he [Griffith] trained, and the techniques and styles he had developed . . . served to carry on the Griffith influence as Hollywood became a source of entertainment, mores, and culture throughout the world" (64).

41   Emily Conant, Annual Report, Social Economic Department, 1900, Records of the Nineteenth Century Club, Oak Park, Illinois, privately held.

42   An American Citizen, "Are Women's Clubs 'Used' by Bolshevists?" *Dearborn Independent,* March 15, 1924, 2, 12.

43   "Mr. Cleveland and Club Women," *Federation Bulletin* 2 (May 1905): 251. See also "Editorial" and "Men's Views of Women's Clubs," *Federation Bulletin* 2 (June 1905): 289–96.

44   Minutes of the Naugatuck Study Club, December 11, 1894, Papers of the Naugatuck Study Club of Naugatuck, Connecticut, privately held.

45   Regina Barreca, *They Used to Call Me Snow White . . . But I Drifted: Women's Strategic Use of Humor* (New York: Penguin, 1991), 11.

46   "Council of Jewish Women: Savannah, GA.," *American Hebrew,* May 6, 1898, 43.

47   Eliza S. Turner, "The Uses of Guilds," *Far and Near* 4 (August 1894): 138.

48   Beer, *Mauve Decade,* 55.

49   Cadija quoted in Williams, "Some Perils of Women's Clubs," 3.

50   Langston Hughes, "The Negro Artist and the Racial Mountain," *Nation* 122 (June 23, 1926): 692.

51   "The Book Table," *Federation Bulletin* 1 (May 1904): 143.

52   Sallie Southall Cotten, *History of the North Carolina Federation of Women's Clubs: 1901–
      1925* (Raleigh, N.C.: Edwards and Broughton, 1925), 3.
53   1918 Yearbook of the New England Women's Club, 28–29, Papers of the New
      England Women's Club, Schlesinger Library, Radcliffe College, Cambridge, Mass.
54   Philip Fisher, *Hard Facts: Setting and Form in the American Novel* (New York: Oxford
      University Press, 1985), 4.

Index

ANNE RUGGLES GERE is a professor of English and a professor of education at the University of Michigan. Her publications include *Roots in the Sawdust: Writing to Learn across the Disciples; Writing Groups: History, Theory, and Implications;* and *Into the Field: Sites of Composition Studies.*